BALTI BRITAIN

Also by Ziauddin Sardar

Desperately Seeking Paradise: Journeys of a Sceptical Muslim

What Do Muslims Believe?

The A to Z of Postmodern Life

The Consumption of Kuala Lumpur

Orientalism

Postmodernism and the Other

Explorations in Islamic Science

Islamic Futures: The Shape of Ideas to Come

The Future of Muslim Civilization

The Touch of Midas: Science, Values and the Environment in Islam and the West

The Revenge of Athena: Science, Exploitation and the Third World

Islam, Postmodernism and Other Futures: A Ziauddin Sardar Reader

How Do You Know?: Reading Ziauddin Sardar on Islam, Science and Cultural Relations

with Merryl Wyn Davies

Why Do People Hate America?

American Dream, Global Nightmare

Barbaric Others: A Manifesto on Western Racism

Distorted Imagination: Lessons from the Rushdie Affair

BALTI BRITAIN

A Journey through the

British Asian Experience

ZIAUDDIN SARDAR

GRANTA

Granta Publications, 12 Addison Avenue, London W11 4QR

First published in Great Britain by Granta Books 2008

A CIP catalogue record for this book is available
from the British Library.

1 3 5 7 9 10 8 6 4 2

ISBN 978 1 86207 911 1

Typeset by M Rules

Printed and bound in Great Britain by
MPG Books Ltd, Bodmin, Cornwall

For Saliha

Contents

Introduction

'WELCOME TO LEICESTER'

Kashmir Singh thought my accent was funny. 'Your Punjabi sounds like the gurgling of a *gora*,' he chuckled.

'The *goras* – white folk – think my English accent is just as odd,' I replied. I was in Leicester, and we were driving towards Belgrave Road, an area renowned for its Asian shops. Kashmir, an impressive man with a full, long, salt 'n' pepper beard divided and curled into two distinct strands, and wearing a blue turban, had been a taxi driver most of his life. He came to Britain in 1972, he said in his pukka Punjabi. I decided to fall back on my mellifluous Urdu, my mother tongue. Punjabi and Urdu are distinct languages – as is Hindi – but they are spoken by people who have lived, mixed and interacted with each other for centuries. Multilingual conversation is a 'no brainer' for Asians; and when filaments of English are added to the mix, you get the typical facility for polylogue, multi-language communication characteristic of the British Asian community.

'What was Leicester like then?' I asked, confident of being understood.

'Oh, it was a very racist place,' Kashmir said in a matter-of-fact way. The National Front was active, racial tension was high and

Asians were looked upon with suspicion. Kashmir recalled reading an advertisement in a local paper. 'It was from the City Council. It said, "Do not come to Leicester in your own interest and those of your family".' But all that was history: Leicester was now 'a very welcoming place'.

I noticed a placard inside the taxi that announced: 'I am proud to be a Sikh.' I asked, 'Are you also proud to be British?'

Kashmir turned to look at me; then switched to English. 'As proud as any *gora*,' he said.

Most Asians in Leicester express similar sentiments. Somehow, Leicester invokes a fierce loyalty from its Asian inhabitants, who constitute over a third of the city's population, making it one of the most ethnically diverse cities in Britain. Not too long ago, Leicester was known for its university and traditional manufacturing industries. Its main claim to fame was as the birthplace of the travel agency founded by Thomas Cook, who took the first group of tourists from Leicester to Loughborough in 1841. It was also the birthplace of the Attenborough brothers (Richard and David) and the footballer Gary Lineker. But Leicester's recent history has been shaped by Asians. The bulk of the Asian migrants to the city arrived during the 1970s. Most were Punjabi Sikhs and, like Kashmir, had a history of outward migration that stretched back to the nineteenth century. They played a central role in the British Indian Army and were often stationed overseas. As ex-British Army soldiers, coming to Britain was a natural thing to do. Indians and Pakistanis moved to properties in the Spinney Hill and Belgrave areas of Leicester, where affordable private housing was available. By 1974, when BBC Radio Leicester, at the time the only local station in the country, started a weekly programme for the city's Asians, the community was well established.

In Leicester one is never too far from a Hindu temple, a Sikh *gurdwara* or a Muslim mosque. The city is dotted with educational, social and leisure services that cater for Asians, with names such as

Shama Women's Centre and Leicester Asian Youth Association. The city that considers itself to be the birthplace of the English language now welcomes visitors – as the sign above a coffee kiosk at Leicester railway station demonstrates – in four Asian languages: Punjabi, Gujarati, Hindi and Urdu. City Council documents, and most displays in banks and businesses, provide information in all these languages. The entire city dresses up as gaudily as an Asian bride for the festivals of Diwali, Eid and Vaisakhi, attracting visitors from all over the Midlands. In Evington, where one of the city's biggest mosques is located, one can even find young men playing hockey and *kabaddi*, the ancient Indian form of wrestling with teams of seven players. The city has two local Asian stations (BBC Asian Network and Sabras), a television station that claims to be the first Asian terrestrial channel (Midland Asian TV) and three cinemas devoted exclusively to Bollywood films. Ethnic diversity appears to be the corner-stone of Leicester's prosperity and harmony, which means it is now seen as an ideal multicultural city, an example of how diversity works in the age of globalization. As the City Council boasts, Leicester has the 'potential to become the UK role model for cultural diversity and inclusion'. Just as well, for by 2011, Leicester's Asian population is predicted to expand to fifty per cent, making it the first city in Britain with a non-*gora* majority.

Leicester personifies the vibrancy and mind-boggling diversity of the British Asian experience. The fusion of so many different Asian cultures and experiences is a wondrous sight to behold. But British Asian identity is shaped not just by the coming together of so many diverse and complex groups with different roots and backgrounds. The attitudes of white Britons towards them have also played an important part. No city in Britain is without racial tensions, and Leicester has had its fair share of racist incidents. But its success as a multicultural city is largely due to the business skills of its Asian community, and the fact that they eagerly represent themselves in all walks of life – including local politics. In 1979, two per cent of City Council employees were from the ethnic minorities. By 2006, the figure had risen to twenty-two per cent, and around a third of the city's councillors came from ethnic backgrounds.

Kashmir introduced me to Councillor Culdipp Singh Bhatti, a former Lord Mayor who was first elected to the City Council on the Labour Party ticket for the Rushey Mean ward in 1983. Councillor Bhatti, an imposing man in his mid-seventies, spoke English with a distinctive Punjabi accent. Unlike Kashmir, he was clean shaven, with short hair and glasses. He noticed that I was surprised by the absence of the usual Sikh trademarks (turban and long beard).

'I am a socialist Sikh,' he said by way of introduction. 'Not all of us come in ready-made apparels.' He was born in Lyallpur, a part of India that later became Pakistan. After Partition, he migrated to India, then migrated again in 1959 – this time to England. He studied and worked in London before moving to Leicester in 1977 to teach mathematics at a comprehensive school.

'What is the secret of Leicester's success?' I asked.

'Dialogue,' Councillor Bhatti replied without a moment's hesitation. 'We changed Leicester by creating an atmosphere of dialogue. We fostered inclusiveness by encouraging all the different communities in the city, including the whites, to talk to each other, to participate in civic activities, get involved in local politics and stand for council elections.' This is why, Councillor Bhatti said proudly, Leicester produced the first Asian MP in Britain, has more Asian councillors than any other city, and can boast two former Asian Lord Mayors. Leicester also created Britain's first race relations committee, which played a part in every aspect of council policy. 'We took an active lead in fighting racism and promoted Leicester as a welcoming city for everyone,' he continued. One of the council's main policies was to actively encourage Asian businesses in the city by providing incentives. The council also worked hard, he added, to develop a harmonious relationship between Muslims and Hindus. Most Hindus in Leicester are East African; Muslims are mainly from India. But there is no distrust between the two communities – and both participate eagerly in each other's festivals.

But I wondered whether Councillor Bhatti was painting too rosy a picture. Surely multiculturalism, one of the most used and abused terms in modern Britain, requires much more than festivals and race relations committees. 'More than anything else it requires civic engagement,' Councillor Bhatti said. 'That's where we have excelled.' He admitted that there are always undercurrents of discord. Take the Sikhs, for example. Leicester has five *gurdwaras* – two are pro-India, two pro-Khalistan (an independent Sikh homeland) and one neutral. However, subcontinental politics, he noted, seldom interfered with community relations. 'We tend to find ways of smoothing over the differences and to focus on common ground.'

Councillor Bhatti's wife, Bhupinder Kler, came to Britain from India in 1961 to marry her husband. A graceful woman in her early sixties, she was particularly interested in women's issues and was involved in helping young Asian women afflicted by domestic abuse or forced marriage.

'Did you have an arranged marriage yourself?' I asked.

'Yes, I did,' she replied. 'I liked what I saw and got my parents to arrange it.' She laughed. Bhupinder came from a prestigious army family, she told me. Her father, Captain Chhajja Singh Kler, was a decorated officer in the British Indian Army. Not to be outdone by his wife, Councillor Bhatti intervened to tell me that his father, Gurdial Singh Bhatti, had also joined the British Army. He had fought on behalf of the British in the Burma campaign.

Most Punjabis in Leicester, I discovered, had some link with the British Army. A very important part of the city's history is bound up with the Leicestershire Regiment, which served in pre-Partition India from 1804 to 1947. Known as the Tigers, the regiment served alongside Indian regiments with names such as the Baluch (which still serves within the Pakistani Army), the Gurkhas, the Sikhs and the Punjabis. By the 1930s, the Tigers also had its own Indian platoon. Many of its soldiers are buried in the war cemeteries in Karachi and Rawalpindi. When Leicester's City Museum Service wanted to add a new regimental wing to Newarke House, its museum of social history, it appealed to the Asian community for help. It was inundated with stories, letters, photographs, press cuttings and other souvenirs from Asians who had encountered the regiment in the Punjab. The refurbished Newarke House, complete with a new wing for the Royal Leicestershire Regiment, opened with much fanfare in June 2007. The British Army, and its exploits on the subcontinent, is just one among many areas in which the histories of Britain and British Asians are deeply entangled.

'Where do you think you belong?' I asked Bhupinder. 'In Britain or in Punjab?'

She thought for a moment. 'Punjab was my *jenam bhumi* – my birthplace. Britain is my *karam bhumi* – the place where I have made my life. I am attached to both places. But I feel I have always belonged here.' Then, she turned the question around. 'What about you? Do you feel you belong here?'

The question of belonging was not new in my experience. But in the wake of terrorist attacks in London – the horrors of 7 July 2005 – it has acquired renewed urgency for everyone. It is the question of the moment, and inescapable. It has confronted us remorselessly on television, in the papers and on the streets, as well as in the intimate confines of our own minds. It has become a national preoccupation of intense anxiety, the sum of all fears refined to a single pertinent enquiry. Not all Asians feel like Bhupinder and Culdipp Singh Bhatti, even if Britain is their *jenam bhumi*. Not all British cities can claim to be an ideal model of multiculturalism. Yet even Leicester has had its brush with terrorism. The city's Asians robustly explain that the only radicals in their midst allegedly implicated in terrorist-related offences have been people of North African origin who brought the foreign-incubated infection with them on their recent arrival. However, it demonstrates that even the most 'integrated' communities cannot escape the issues of terrorism.

My visit to Leicester began my exploration of the British Asian experience for this book; an experience that in its complexity, diversity and entangled history helps set the harrowing events of 7/7 in context. And in this undertaking I am no neutral *rapporteur*, no mere channel for the thoughts and feelings of others, but a fully participant observer. I am an integral part, an agent in that which I seek to describe. The question on everyone's lips interrogates my own identity, life and history. My report could not be an objective exercise; it had to encompass a personal reflection on all that I am, and how I came to be here and now in Britain.

Migration is a disruptive process. It scoops up lives, traditions and histories, and deposits them somewhere else. But how can you ever be severed from that place you first called home? The wreckage of your former life is always somehow present, a vital element of personal and collective history. The life before, the former lives in distant places that shaped you, remain a sensibility, a style, an influence on the life begun anew in a new place. Who were our forefathers? How did they live? What did they teach us? What was left behind in the subcontinent is just as much a part of the British Asians' experience as how they live and who they are in Britain.

Belonging is not just about where you end up; it is also about remembering the trailing connections carried along in the voyage from there to here. The quest for identity is a journey that unravels relationships spun in the web of history. It is not possible to know me, or the Asian community, without grasping the quality of the relationships in which we exist. Discussion of these relationships, and how they shape our lives, are often absent in all the talk of British Asians. Without them I am diminished, Asian communities are reduced. We become a series of 'problems', an agenda of issues of exclusion and inclusion, tradition versus modernity, of 'why don't they change?' or 'when will they change?' dilemmas. In all its facets, good and bad, the British Asian experience is a product of real lives lived by real people. These lives are lived as a chain of connections, in extended families and communities that can be traced all the way to the subcontinent and back into its history. To understand British Asians one must see them as they see themselves: as part of networks of relationships and connections, not as isolated individuals.

Belonging is a two-way process. The British Asian experience is not solely about what people from the Indian subcontinent brought with them. It is also about what they found, what they made of themselves and for themselves, as well as what Britain made of them. Identity is formed in the matrix of multiple connections and influences in which Britain plays a role of immense significance. But Britain, it seems to me, still fears difference. It is not possible to belong to a nation that sees itself in terms of a narrow and exclusive identity, or feels uncomfortable with the idea of multiple identities. To belong, you must be included; to feel included, you must be accepted with all your differences and multiple identities. I have struggled throughout my life to belong, and encountered many barriers en route. This is the story of that struggle, the hurdles I faced, the people I met in my journeys, and the discoveries I made about my family and friends.

There was no quick and easy answer to Bhupinder Bhatti's question about belonging, or to this same question when posed by British society. As I chatted with Councillor Bhatti and his wife, it occurred to me that the kind of answer, even the meaning of the question, was not necessarily the same for them as for British society in general. They saw themselves as an integral part of

Britain and its history. Britain may accept them, sometimes grudgingly, but it has never acknowledged that their history is also the history of Britain. There can be no clear and settled answer to the questions of identity and belonging when they exist in a swirl of different assumptions, different expectations, different meanings and perhaps even different intentions. My own identity and belonging have been shaped within these differences and diverse assumptions. I am a product not just of my life here in Britain but also of the life I left behind on the subcontinent. What the British did in India, where I began, has a direct bearing on my existence here and now, where I live. What Britain makes and thinks of me is as important as what I think of Britain. Resolving how I feel about my identity and belonging, finding an answer to satisfy all concerned – Bhupinder Bhatti and British society at large – requires making all these connections. In conclusion and by way of introduction, I realized that finding an answer that identifies my belonging, as well as that of people like me, must begin by addressing the question: what makes a British Asian British?

Chapter 1

EATING BALTI

On the morning of Thursday 28 July 2005, the city of Birmingham, West Midlands, was struck by a tornado. It was a category four tornado – just above 'severe' and just below 'incredible' – technically it was 'devastating'. A tornado is a whirling wind, a violently spinning column of air with slow progressive motion. In this instance, winds of over 250 mph were generated within the vortex. It was, by all accounts, the worst natural disaster in living memory. The progress of the tornado was marked by a trail of debris deposited higgledy-piggledy in its wake. Devastation often uncovers hidden truths. In Birmingham roofs peeled away like orange skins, automobile-sized missiles flew through the air, trees were debarked. The tornado chose the southern district of Sparkbrook for its particular fury. What was exposed in this predominantly immigrant area was much more than the privacy of people's homes. It focused attention on the fact that poverty, degradation and unemployment were thinly concealed features of an already blighted landscape.

Sparkbrook is not unlike many of the areas in Britain where migrants from the Indian subcontinent have made their homes. The dilapidation tells the familiar story of migrant groups down the centuries: they find the niche everyone else is ready to vacate and start their lives again from there. Immigration itself is a kind of tornado, dissembling people and communities and placing them elsewhere. And like a tornado, the slow progressive motion of migration starts far away from where it touches ground. Looking at the wreckage, I wondered where and when we should begin the story of British Asians, and how far away and long ago the whirling wind began disordering lives and rearranging hopes before depositing the detritus of new identities. I hoped Sparkbrook would answer some of these questions.

As I walked along Highgate Road, a few months after the tornado, it was easy to feel at home. I have walked many such streets with their pervasive aura of neglect and unavoidable stench of decay. From the grey facade of Karachi Fried Chicken on one side and a dilapidated garage ('Cars Wanted for Cash') on the other, I could distinguish the smell of rusting iron and the rotting leftovers of yesterday's chicken and chips. I trudged on through the all-too-familiar landscape of council flats; row upon row, street after street of uniform terraced houses with 2.5 bedrooms, a living room that allows no space for living and an impossibly small kitchen. Not exactly the usual idea of a place for a 'city break'.

But something happened as I turned into Ladypool Road. Visually there was no discernible change, but my nose began to twitch. Some atmospheric alteration had occurred. My step quickened, taking me deeper into the miasma laden with its plethora of aromas. I was drawn by something more tantalizing and distinctive, a pungent anomaly nestling within the down-at-heel, struggling to survive the ambience of an immigrant area. To begin with, it smelled like curry, that unmistakable odour of Indian restaurants. Heavy and overbearing, it is a smell I associate with colonialism, with the British Raj, with the stench of what the British did in and to India. But I was not granted capacious nasal passages to linger on the surface of smells. I breathed deep and detected beneath the familiar, dominating scent a number of more inviting evocative bouquets. I tried to distinguish the different fragrances, to savour the associations stirred by each particular spice, vegetable or sweetmeat I could isolate as I wandered through this olfactory playground. There was the invigorating smell of fresh coriander, which is guaranteed to drive me wild. Then I detected the warm musky scent of turmeric, which always evokes deep memories of my childhood in Pakistan. The aromas of cardamom, clove, nutmeg and camphor wafted by – these I always sense collectively because they are the ingredients of *paan*, the kingly assemblage of condiments that comes wrapped in betel leaf. *Paan* is usually taken after a meal to stimulate saliva and gastric flow; it is also an auspicious symbol of hospitality and nourishment. Often it is proffered as a moral commitment to bring people closer together, to bind friendships, to demonstrate family bonds. It always reminds me of my infant days with my grandfather. Then, my eyes became moist: the strong, hot and strangely sweet smell of *hari mirch*, the slim, long green chilli, which my mother used to cook as a vegetable and affects not just the nose but the eyes. It never fails to rekindle the bitter-sweet memories of my youthful days in East London. Finally, my mouth began to water. First I picked out the whiff of *biryani*, the standard fare of all Asian weddings. It reminds me of my own wedding and summons images of all future weddings, those of my nephews and nieces, my daughter and sons. Next, I feel – yes, *feel* – the unmistakable bitter stink of bitter gourd (surely the ugliest vegetable in the world), which invokes a whole range of complex emotions, of racism and multiculturalism, loss and exile, home and belonging. Underneath it all, the rich, sweet, delicious aroma of *barfi*, the fudgy sweet made from milk, which I always associate with my crazy, madcap uncle, Waheed.

You can't have this experience just anywhere in Britain. The presence of the ubiquitous Indian restaurant on an average high street is no guarantee of such aromatic delights. Sparkbrook is different: even before it was hit by a category four tornado, it was blown over by a category six – technically 'inconceivable' – whirlwind, the twister of 'Balti'. Tourists from all over Britain, indeed the world, make for this ramshackle, crumbling neighbourhood for 'the hottest weekend breaks in Britain'. Special guided tours are taken to revel in the culinary pleasures of what has come to be known as the 'Balti experience'. Ladypool Road meets Highgate Road perpendicularly; Highgate Road sprouts Stoney Lane. And these three define the 'Balti Triangle', an area that boasts over fifty Balti restaurants, the highest concentration in Britain. Why had so many Balti restaurants sprung up in a single location, and what did it tell us about British Asians? This was the phenomenon I wanted to investigate.

In Urdu, the word *balti* means bucket – a receptacle, a pitcher, a vessel, a pail of the kind once lugged up a hill by Jack and Jill to fetch some water. In the Indian subcontinent a *balti* is put to numerous uses. It can carry water for washing or taking a bath, and may even be used to flush the old-fashioned squatting lavatory. The roles and uses of the *balti* are numerous and as diverse as Indian civilization itself. Yet one thing the *balti* has never been known for is as a receptacle in which to cook food. This may be because it is too deep, too wide, too rough and too primitive for the preparation of such varied and sophisticated cuisines as those of the subcontinent. I remember the first time my father heard of Balti he shook his head in disbelief: 'What nonsense! Are British Asians mad enough to cook in a bucket?' he enquired rhetorically with an uncomprehending air. It was a good question. What exactly is a Balti dish? How does it differ from conventional, if there could be such a thing, Indian cooking? How can you tell an 'authentic Balti' from an unauthentic, ersatz one? Where does it come from anyway? And what does it say about multicultural Britain? I was in Birmingham to seek answers to these questions.

Ahmed Estates is located at the bottom of Clifton Road, where it meets Stoney Lane. I knew instinctively that there was more to this 'estate and letting agents' than met the eye. The 786 written in Urdu numerals just above the shopfront caught my attention. It is a declaration that you are entering a Muslim enclave: 786 is the numerical shorthand for 'In the name of God, the Beneficent, the Merciful', the phrase that precedes each chapter of the Qur'an and has become the most idiomatic utterance in Muslim parlance, employed at each and every kind of opening or beginning. Inside, a number of bearded men attended to various clients. At the rear, a narrow flight of stairs led to the first floor and the office of the Asian Balti Restaurant Association (ABRA): a small room, with a large desk on which stood a computer, and a long plastic sofa.

Behind the desk sat a beaming young man in his early twenties. 'My name is Tabriz Hussain,' he said in a strong Brummie accent, extending his hand. Tabriz, a management graduate, had cropped his hair so short he almost looked bald. He had a round, jolly face, deep-set brown eyes and a complete complement of brilliant white teeth. There were a few minor cuts on his forehead.

'What happened?' I asked.

'Oh,' he replied, 'I was in a chip shop, a tree came down and I was hit by flying glass – thanks to the tornado.'

'And you're not an avid consumer of Balti dishes?' I asked.

He looked puzzled.

'Otherwise your teeth would not be so bright and white.'

He laughed. 'The Asians are more sceptical of bowel-ty cuisine than anyone else.'

I liked the way he pronounced *bowel-ty*; it was almost as though he was conjuring the word from deep within his intestines. A nightmare vision of my worst fantasies of the uses and abuses of a *balti* flashed on my inward eye. I resisted the impulse to elaborate the picture and confined myself to a simple statement of doubt: 'I don't believe anyone would cook in a *balti*.'

'Before we go anywhere,' Tabriz replied, 'let me tell you that bowel-ty is now an established English word. It's pukka, man! It's in the dictionary.' And he handed me a hefty volume of the *Oxford English Reference Dictionary*.

I turned the pages and found the entry for 'Balti'. I read aloud: 'A type of Pakistani cuisine in which the food is cooked in a small bowl-shaped frying pan. 20thc. orig. uncert.'

'So the first thing you need to appreciate about bowel-ty is that it's Pakistani cuisine, brother. Not Indian, but Pakistani, and Kashmiri. The second thing is that true Balti restaurants are halal – they are not licensed and do not serve alcohol.' Halal, the most basic category of all things permissible to the Muslim – buckets included, booze not.

'OK,' I replied in a matter-of-fact way. 'But where does it come from? No one in Pakistan cooks in a balti'.

Tabriz rummaged through his desk, found a booklet, and handed it to me. I read the title – *Essential Guide: The Balti Triangle, Birmingham*.

'Turn to page six, the story of bowel-ty,' Tabriz told me.

On said page, I read:

Balti owes its introduction to Birmingham's large Pakistani and Kashmiri communities, who brought it to Birmingham in the mid-1970s through cafe-style restaurants – the traditional glass-topped tables beloved by Balti purists are still in evidence in some of the area's Balti houses ... Legend surrounds the origin of Balti. It is thought to have been a convenient method of cooking for mountain tribesmen. There is even a place called Baltistan inhabited by an ancient tribe called the Baltis. Did they invent the Balti? Did they wear Balti bowls instead of helmets when at war? It doesn't really matter because Balti has well and truly arrived in Britain, and Birmingham is where it all began ...

I couldn't believe what I was reading: a tribe called Balti who lived in Baltistan? It reminded me of the fairy stories I used to read as a young boy in Pakistan about jinns – spirit people – who lived in Jinnistan.

'There are three restaurants that claim to have invented the bowel-ty,' Tabriz explained. 'Do you want to visit all three?' I nodded earnestly. 'Let's go and eat some bowel-ty, then,' he said. We walked out of Ahmed Estates onto Stoney Lane and made our way to the first restaurant luxuriating in the cachet of being the birthplace of Balti.

In no time we entered Adil Restaurant, owned and managed by Rashid Mahmud, also its main chef. A shy, self-effacing man in his early forties, Mahmud described himself as a 'pioneer of Balti cuisine'. The tornado had taken away the signboard and a little bit of the roof, so from the outside it was difficult to grasp the true nature of the enterprise. But walking into the restaurant was like slipping into a time warp. The tables had 'authentic' glass tops, with menus underneath; there was the old trademark flock wallpaper (blue, green and white stripes) and a string of neatly framed paintings (drawings of pots and black-and-white portraits of Hollywood stars). Before we tackled the birth of Balti I wanted to know something about this pioneer. I needed to locate him in the progressive movement of the whirling wind of migration. For in carving its path there are ages and stages, each of which leaves its distinctive imprint on successive generations of those people generically identified as British Asians. If you are such a person, enquiries about your family are the most natural precursor to conversation, the locating device for honing in on whom one is talking to, and for catching the proper idiom for comfortable communication.

Without hesitation Mahmud retraced the great trek that had begun when his grandfather, Abdul Latif, came to Britain, along with his three brothers, from Azad Kashmir in the early 1950s. They settled in Bradford. Other relatives from Mirpur, across the frontier in northern Pakistan, joined them. His father, Mohammad Arif, a factory worker and taxi driver, moved to Birmingham and opened the Dream House Cafe. 'It served rough-and-ready food largely to a male immigrant clientele,' Mahmud told me. A few years later, when he had made enough money, his father bought a larger café. Mahmud was born in Birmingham. At the age of twelve he returned to Pakistan, but came back four years later to help his father manage the business. Adil's became a fully fledged restaurant in 1977. When Mahmud took over from his father he introduced two innovations. 'My father's generation did not have a surname. Well, people in Pakistan don't, do they?' So Mahmud was established as the family name. The restaurant catered largely to 'cynical goras' who 'looked down on us'.

'When I first started in the restaurant business,' Mahmud said, 'everything was curry. And all restaurants serving food from the Indian subcontinent were Indian restaurants. "Eating Indian" meant eating curry no matter whether the cuisine was from India, Pakistan, Bangladesh or Sri Lanka; Punjabi, Mughal or South Indian; vegetarian or non-vegetarian. Everything was "Indian", and everything was a "curry". We used to have herds of young lads who came in after the pubs closed; they gobbled up everything put in front of them, insulted the waiters and vomited their intoxication all over the restaurant.' He paused for a moment. 'I wasn't going to put up with what my father put up with.'

He wanted to move the restaurant upmarket, to draw in a more refined clientele, and to establish a Pakistani identity for both the cuisine and the restaurant. Hence the second innovation: Balti.

'When did you first come up with the term "Balti"?' I asked.

'Around 1981,' came the reply.

Initial sightings of the term indeed date from around that period. My research indicated that the first use of Balti occurred in the Winter 1984 issue of *Curry Magazine*. However, a local community newspaper, the *Balsall Heathan*, claims the term was in use even earlier. The July 1982 edition of the *Heathan* carried an advertisement for Ambala Restaurant and Sweet Centre: 'Specialists in Kebab, Tikah, Balti Meats, Tandoori Chicken and all kinds of curry'.

'How did you go about inventing the dish?' I asked without even a hint of sauciness.

'Well,' Mahmud replied reflectively, 'you've got to be honest to your tradition but you also have to move on.'

'You mean one has to reinvent tradition?'

'Precisely,' replied Mahmud. 'I wanted to do something traditional but also something new. So I thought, what if one cooked the food in a small *balti* and served it in the same *balti*?'

'You mean a small *karahi*. No one in their right mind would cook in a *balti*.' My insouciance lurked beneath a veneer that was wearing dangerously thin. But this was, of course, the crucial question. A *karahi* is a round-bottomed metal pan, not unlike a Chinese wok, well known and widely used in subcontinental cooking. So when is a *balti* not a *karai*? What alchemy transmuted the usual fare prepared in a *karahi* to genuine Balti?

'You see,' Mahmud leaned forward to explain, 'when a *karahi* is treated in a specific way it becomes a Balti. Let me show you.'

He took me to the kitchen. It was small and crowded, with a rectangular cooker marooned in the middle, a conventional *tandoor* at one end and a special steel *tandoor* at the opposite end.

'A good chef can prepare an excellent Balti in just three minutes,' Mahmud said as he poured some oil in a wok-like object of as yet unstated provenance, added tomatoes and onions and started stirring. 'At this moment I am cooking in a *karahi*. But as I cook it is being transformed into a Balti.'

While I concentrated, determined to catch the very moment of transmutation in the deft actions he was performing, Mahmud startled me by switching the subject to football. It turned out he was a passionate Liverpool supporter. Then it further transpired that he had an arranged marriage with his cousin a couple of years earlier and now had an infant son. 'I want my son to become a footballer,' he said, as he added some meat, which had already been cooked, to the wok currently serving as a *karahi* and soon to be a fully fledged Balti. Flames leapt from the wok as fenugreek leaves, garlic and green chilli were added. 'Now, for the final transformation,' Mahmud said, as he added a 'special sauce' to the infusion. 'When it reaches the table, in the same pot in which it has been cooked, it is a Balti,' he declared triumphantly with proprietorial pride.

Feeling like a bemused observer of a conjuring trick, I accepted that something had happened but what – or indeed how or why – still escaped me. 'You can't eat that with rice,' I said with the pedantry of the true epicurean.

'No,' replied Mahmud. 'It is best eaten with a *naan*. And we are going to serve it with a table *naan*.'

An assistant chef had already kneaded some dough. He flattened it into a rectangular shape, placed it on a large pillow-shaped cloth, and carefully lowered it into the special steel *tandoor*. 'You can't cook a *naan* that size in a conventional *tandoor*. But this one is specially designed for *naans* this size.'

When the *naan* was eventually plucked from the special *tandoor*, it was two feet long and a foot wide. I had never seen a *naan* that size. The sizzling Balti and the hot large *naan*, which covered most of the table, were placed before us. 'This is an authentic traditional Balti,' Mahmud said. There was a definitive tone in his voice. 'Enjoy your Balti experience.'

The Balti had a quite distinct flavour, rather different from anything else of subcontinental origins I had eaten. Through the overarching taste of garlic, onions and tomatoes, I savoured a profusion of spices. The meat almost melted in my mouth. The gravy was smooth, not too hot, a bit buttery, almost good enough to drink.

The menu at Adil's was full of Balti dishes: chicken Balti, meat

Balti, mince Balti, prawn Balti, *rogan josh* Balti, *korma* Balti and so on. But there was one Balti that I could not fathom: *maliah* Balti. Now *maliah* is what you get when you boil milk: it is the thickened, scalded skin that forms at the top of the liquid. How in God's name, I wondered, could one turn that into a Balti?

'That is one of my most recent innovations,' Mahmud explained. 'Since the introduction of the Balti our customers have become highly educated. Most of them are *goras* who are really into good food and appreciate their Balti. Look around you: the customers in here are pukka Balti purists.'

I looked around and confirmed his thesis. Most people eating in the restaurant had burn marks on their wrists, a clear indication that they had spent a lifetime dipping their *naans* into a burning hot Balti and catching their wrists in the process.

'But occasionally,' Mahmud continued, 'we do get an odd member of the chicken *tikka masala* brigade.'

Chicken *tikka masala* is the dish purported to be Britain's favourite meal. According to the late Robin Cook, one of the most memorable foreign secretaries of recent times and an intellectual of some standing, chicken *tikka masala* is 'a perfect illustration of the way Britain absorbs and adopts external influences'. At the time he made this statement I remember being struck by what a fine piece of nonsense this was. Surely, I reasoned, the boot was on the other foot. It was not Britain that had adapted to chicken *tikka masala* but countless Indian restaurants that had manipulated their cultural repertoire with ingenuity to find a niche in British life. The popularity of this made-in-Britain dish arose from the willingness of Indian restaurants to be open all hours, serve the drunken dregs as they left the pubs, be abused for the service they provided, and all at prices well within reach of the pocket of ordinary working folk.

But what exactly is chicken *tikka masala*?

'It is nothing more,' Mahmud explained, 'than *garam masala* [a standard mixture of black pepper, cinnamon and cloves] and chilli powder with lashings of cream. It is a concoction Indian restaurants of Bangladeshi persuasion designed for the undiscerning palates of curry munchers.' He paused for breath. 'As I was saying, the *maliah* Balti is enriched with added cream which makes it more suitable for the chicken *tikka masala* brigade who do not like many and varied spices in their food.' The perfect solution for those who preferred their curry with its essence excluded.

The following day Tabriz was busy so I went on my own to Al-Faisal's, a few doors from Adil's on Stoney Lane, which also claimed to be the original source of Balti. The contrast could not be greater. The black art deco, tinted-glass exterior, with its revolving sign (reminiscent of the famous icon in front of Scotland Yard, featured in endless British detective films), announced an altogether classier, upmarket joint. Clearly, I was about to enter another era of the British Asian experience. Inside, Al-Faisal's had a corporate feel: black leather and steel chairs, chic brown tables, brilliant white walls adorned by portraits of cricketing stars in action and a signed cricket bat that was ostentatiously framed. A separate smoking area had cushy leather sofas and a glass table with a couple of *huqqas* (Pakistani water pipes), overshadowed by a huge, decorative Arab coffee pot. The cooking area at the back of the restaurant was open to and visible from the dining area, not just providing the assurance of freshly cooked food but also restating the direct and tactile relationship between the hand that cooks and the hand that eats. The menu looked like an art book.

Al-Faisal's is owned by Chaudhry Ajaib, a flamboyant businessman. Dressed in an elegant black suit and red tie, he was making deals on his mobile phone while engaged in face-to-face negotiation for the purchase of something important with an Englishman, who repeatedly lavished praise on the restaurant. When I had the chance I took the necessary reading of his history. Mr Chaudhry had migrated to Birmingham from Mirpur in 1957 with his father and uncles. His brothers and sister followed a few years later; a few years after that they were joined by other relatives and neighbours from his village, Karak. They all settled around Sparkbrook and everyone worked in the local factories. Family business remains the communal connective tissue. Mr Chaudhry's three sons hovered around him, showing respectful deference. It was obvious he was the boss, and they did what they were told. The eldest, Adil, had a law degree but worked for the family business. He had recently married his cousin. Umar dropped out of architecture school but ended up designing the restaurant. The youngest, Al-Faisal, studied accountancy.

We sat on the sofa in the smoking area drinking '*dasi* tea'. Mr Chaudhry told me he first opened a restaurant in 1976; it was named Adil's, after his eldest son. Soon afterwards he sold it to Mohammad Arif, the father of Rashid Mahmud. The following year he opened Al-Faisal's. 'It was during a visit to Pakistan in 1976 that I first came up with the idea of Balti,' Mr Chaudhry said. 'While travelling in the northwestern provinces, further north from Peshawar, I came across tribal people who cooked meat in a rough-and-ready way. These people are known as Baltis and their province is called Baltistan.'

I looked him in the eye disbelievingly. Mr Chaudhry looked directly at me: 'It's in the dictionary.'

To my utter surprise, it is. Just underneath its account of 'Balti', the *Oxford English Reference Dictionary* contains an entry for 'Baltistan': '(also called *Little Tibet*) a region of the Karakoram range of the Himalayas, to the south of K2'.

'So your Balti is actually cooked in a *balti*?'

'No,' Mr Chaudhry replied. 'Who would want to be so uncouth? Actually, Balti people do not cook in a *balti* either. They just call the *karahi* a *balti*.'

'Urdu not being their strong point,' I felt impelled to add.

'Balti has more power, it's a brand name that attracts people. But the food, whether it is called Balti or *karahi*, is the same.' He got up as though impatient with me. 'Try some.'

I sat alone by the kitchen. *Bhuna ghost* – fried meat – Balti was served on a white, elegant square dish. It had a thick sauce, overwhelmed with yoghurt, which made its varied ingredients difficult to distinguish. The meat was tough and almost tasteless. Overall, it was spicy but bland. I ate it with a small *naan*, and washed it all down with carrot juice. Dessert was *rasmalai*, flattened patties made of curdled milk floating in thickened sweet milk, which tasted rather like rubber. As I ate I noticed most of the other customers in the restaurant were of Pakistani origin.

Mr Chaudhry returned. The restaurant had been 'totally redesigned about a year ago', he told me.

'How has this affected the kind of customers you get?' I asked.

'Before the new look,' he replied, 'most of our customers were *goras*. Now over ninety per cent are Asian.'

While the white folks look for 'authenticity' and 'tradition', I mused to myself, British Pakistanis want flamboyance and modernity, even if it results in banality.

The final port of call on my Balti tour was Imran's Restaurant and Sweethouse on Ladypool Road. I arrived at around four o'clock in the afternoon when the restaurant was largely empty. Tabriz joined me; he had brought a gift. 'With ABRA's best wishes,' he said. It was an elegant yellow box. Inside was a wok (or was it a *balti*?), a copy of *Essential Guide to the Balti Triangle* and a packet each of ground cumin, garlic powder, ground turmeric, garam masala and chilli powder. 'Just in case you want to cook a Balti at home,' Tabriz added with a grin. I accepted the gift graciously.

Imran's was divided into two sections. The front one had a serving area, where the waiters prepared drinks and bills, and several neatly arranged rows of tables. The back section was all tables, and led to the kitchen, accessed by two doors, one for entering and one for exiting. The tables had standard 'authentic' glass tops, with menus underneath, and certain walls had the same flock wallpaper that I had seen at Adil's. Even the framed paintings (bottles, pots and portraits in the style of Mughal miniatures) seemed rather familiar. The restaurant was being extended and modernized; the extension was almost complete but it needed painting and fittings. The place had a certain earthy self-confidence that playfully mixed tradition and modernity. We sat at the back, and were joined by Afzal Butt, the owner and founder of the restaurant, and another of the main claimants to the invention of Balti.

Afzal Butt was a large, unassuming man in his early sixties. His face, with its thick lips, and general demeanour suggested experience and wisdom. He talked softly and slowly, paused frequently to think, and when he spoke it was with confident authority. He came to Britain in 1969 and joined his elder brother in the restaurant business. In 1979, he opened his own restaurant, named after his son who was born in the same year. The restaurant was now managed by his three sons, all born and brought up in Birmingham. They gathered around us, one by one. Imran, the eldest, was in his early thirties; like his father he was gentle and well mannered. He had just finished an estate agent's course and had opened up a practice next to the restaurant. Osman was a giant of a man: in his mid-twenties, he was six feet four inches tall. A graduate of Birmingham College of Food, he was the main chef of the restaurant. He talked animatedly and punctuated his conversation with Punjabi swearwords. The youngest, Irfan, was still in his teens, and a duplicate of his brother Osman. Jovial and boisterous, he liked to tease his father and brothers. The relationship between father and sons radiated a radically different feel from the one I noted at Al-Faisal's. Here was warm respect, a product of love; there was reverence but also challenge and argument. I went straight to the point. 'Afzal Sahib, this Balti business: have you too journeyed among the Baltis of Baltistan to bring back a distinctive cuisine?'

'*Sab bakwas hai!*' ('It's all nonsense'!), he pronounced, breaking the pattern of our conversation, in which he spoke Punjabi while I replied in Urdu. I watched the glinting smile in his eyes and saw it hovering playfully around his lips. Suddenly I relaxed, felt more at ease with myself, my project and the entire universe of Balti. We had established a mutual recognition and understanding that freed my imagination and cleared the way for comfortable, homely conversation.

'Have your ever eaten a Balti in Pakistan?' he asked.

'No,' I replied.

'There you have it,' Afzal Sahib said with refreshing honesty. 'It's a joke. It all started as a joke. Hundred per cent joke. It was an invention for the *goras*.' He paused, and thought for a while. 'Balti is like curry. It exists and doesn't exist. Do you know what curry is?'

'No,' I replied. 'I don't.'

'Neither do I,' he declared, beaming. 'In fact, I have never had curry in my life!'

Our attention was distracted by a commotion in the front of the restaurant. A short, hefty white man had come running in. He grabbed the nearest table and ordered a mutton Balti. 'As fast as possible.' He had come from Birmingham International Airport, he announced, and had left his taxi, with meter in full swing, outside the restaurant. He was on his way to Dubai, had checked in, got his boarding pass, and wanted dinner before getting on his flight. 'The food at the airport is awful,' he said. 'Besides, I can't leave without having a Balti.' Everyone rushed to serve him.

I used this interlude to reflect on Afzal Sahib's words. I knew what he meant. Since the 1960s Britain has grown ever more in love with curry. It has become the most convenient choice of millions, readily available not just in Indian restaurants but also in any supermarket. It made its first ready-meal appearance as Vesta curries, Britain's original flirtation with ready-prepared exotic cuisine. Heavily advertised on television, Vesta meals popularized new food sensations. What people actually got was a box containing two packets. The curry packet was the one which, so I have been informed, contained wizened bits. This collection of deformed, desiccated Smarties was deposited in a pan and reconstituted with boiling water. The second packet contained the rice. My fellow countrymen and women really did consume such amazing concoctions, allegedly with relish. Thankfully for all concerned things moved on rapidly, as tinned, freeze-dried, frozen, vacuum-packed or ready-to-heat takeaways joined the repertoire on supermarket shelves. Gradually, the land was covered with Indian restaurants which also delivered to your door locally adapted curry dishes, with chips, to domesticate what might otherwise be too alien. There was not a cookery programme on television or celebrity food guru who did not offer the flavours of the East in authentic or fusion mode among their repertoire. Curry is king!

But what is curry? There is an invariant association between India and curry, yet the term is never heard in some rather significant locations: the South Asian households of Britain and on the Indian subcontinent itself. So far as I am aware, my mother, affectionately known as Mumsey, has never cooked a curry in her life. Now Mumsey is nothing if not a superb cook. I salivate at the thought of her *salens* and *shurbahs*, the variety of meat and vegetable dishes that were the daily delights of my upbringing.

Curry is a generic term. A grand abolition of all distinctions, a piling on a plate of everything until what results is merely a grand mess. It is the *reductio ad absurdum* of the immense variety, delicacy and sophistication of the innumerable cuisines of the subcontinent. Mind you, the last time I was in India they seemed to be doing a rather good line in digestive reduction themselves. Whenever I travelled by Air India, or on any of the domestic airlines, a smiling stewardess would confront me with the basic bifurcation of culinary choice, 'Veg/non-veg?' – vegetarian being the proper choice for Hindus, Jains and Buddhists, while the polite periphrasis for the meat option was designed to accommodate Muslims, Sikhs and all stripes of foreigners. I once answered distractedly, 'Whatever,' causing immense philosophic confusion. Perhaps I was merely confirming my own identity crisis – the existential condition of the diasporic exile. Nowadays in India, it seems one can be only veg or non-veg; it is not a matter of inference, never one of indifference, but a badge of belonging. It is the ultimate category test in a nation where dietary affiliation is a political statement intent on generating ever-increasing separation through ritualized difference. If I happened to be a strict Hindu, and was served non-vegetarian food, it could become an 'incident'. To my 'Whatever,' the air hostess retorted: 'Coffee, tea or pee?' The philosophical confusion had been thrown back at me. Was she being flippant? Or was this a genuine choice – given the fact that a prime minister of India, Maraji Desai, who succeeded Indira Gandhi, drank his own pee and advocated that all India should follow his example?

A casual look at the menus of Al-Faisal's and Imran's, or indeed most Indian restaurants, will reveal them to be formulaic: *korma, bhuna, dopiazza, dhansak, jalfrazi, tikka* and *tandoori, karahi, Balti*, each grouping available in chicken, lamb, occasionally beef, and always prawn variants. These are words with which we could play mind games with history. Indeed, they are words which could be used to imagine history differently. But how many people discount the formula and opt for the quick ready-reckoning provided either by the number of chillies depicted beside each entry or the generic ranking of mild, medium and hot, the gradations of curry? Are we interested that most of the offerings in restaurants are categorized as Mughal, Punjabi or Kashmiri? Do we ever stop to consider that most 'Indian' restaurants are in fact anything but, being as they are, and always have been, run predominantly by people we now generically term Bangladeshi or Pakistani? We have every encouragement to know there are more things in curry than we think. But Britons remain content to opt for an 'Indian', to go out for or order in a 'curry'.

It would be wrong to suggest Britain's increasing engagement with curry has not developed. Just as Asian restaurants have introduced new variants, such as *karahi* and Balti, the clientele have also moved on from a curry after a skinful of beer on a Friday night. Both restaurants and clientele have grown more adventurous over the years, more prepared to become sophisticated. But change has failed to dethrone the generic classification and therefore the assumption that it means something relevant. The meaning is assumed to contain an explanation of history. It is a statement about how the specifics of the historic relations of Britain and India came into existence and operated. 'Curry' is a word derived from India and the taste for the generalized variety of food encompassed by that word came about as a consequence of Britain's part in the discovery of India.

Consult any reference work and you will learn that India and its myriad languages have been ransacked in search of the apocryphal homonym of curry. The consensus of opinion has come to rest on the Tamil word *kari* or even *karil*, which once possibly referred to a spiced stew. Now, even the estimable Bible of Anglo-Indian terminology, *Hobson-Jobson*, which describes itself as 'a glossary of colloquial Anglo-Indian words and phrases, and of kindred terms, etymological, historical, geographical and discursive' (by Henry Yule and A. C. Burnell, 1903), suggests this is a somewhat tenuous resolution. As it points out, there is no linguistic history of the generic term 'curry' in Indian languages. The one instance of someone trying to find this putative ancestral term relied on the mistranslation of the Sanskrit word *supa*.

The enigma of curry is twofold: the origin of the word, since it has hardly been settled to the satisfaction of *Hobson-Jobson*; and its meaning. As *Hob-Job* puts it, curry refers to a spiced stew. It then proceeds to remark, with appropriate historical references, that there was nothing special, or indeed new, to the European mind or taste buds about spiced stews. The word 'curry' is applied to the spiced sauce in which meat or vegetables may be cooked and that is eaten as an accompaniment to bread (north India) or rice (both north and south India). *Roti* (bread) or *chawwal* (rice) is another of those basic bifurcations the Asian restaurant offers only for British tastes to dismiss. Europeans tend to regard both as obligatory accompaniments to an 'Indian'. South Asians see them as distinct: this dish accompanies bread of various weights and consistencies, while rice is more appropriate with other dishes of different kinds. And when it comes to rice, the Indians have discovered almost infinite things to do with it. Punctilious as they are with the basis of a meal, would South Asians be content merely with generic curry as the accompanying dish that lifts and gives variety and life to the cereal staple? Doubts about that Tamil word *kari* grow with deeper thought.

What does this portend for the origin of the term 'curry'? Everybody everywhere has some candidate for spiced stew, in which case the entire world belongs to curry! And what is more, spiced stew acquired its ubiquity long, long ago. As *Hob-Job* notes, the ancient Persians, Greeks and Romans all spiced their stews, and the high tables of medieval Europe positively groaned with spiced foods of several kinds. Why did the first European arrivals find something so novel and surprising in the fact that Indians also ate spiced stew that they needed a generic name to distinguish the culinary predilections of the subcontinent?

The common ingredients, the things that make curry what we think it is, are the spices. Everyone may have spiced stew but spices do not occur just anywhere, and certainly not everywhere. To create one's stew the constituent spices have to be acquired.

Those necessary to make the stews generically termed curry are principally pepper, ginger, garlic, turmeric, nutmeg, clove, mace, galangal, cinnamon – and, of course, chilli. There are a goodly number of others from asafoetida to fenugreek, onion seeds, poppy seeds and amchor – a ground powder made from the stones of mangoes – but these seldom detain the consciousness of Europeans. The question is from where did this rich profusion of condiments hail? The answer – with the signal exception of chilli – is Asia. Spices came to the West via Egypt. It is recorded that two peppercorns were discovered lodged in the nasal passages of the mummy of Ramses II, the narcissistic monumentalist Egyptian Pharaoh who died in 1224 BC. We do not know how the skilled embalmers of ancient Egypt came by these peppercorns or indeed the other spices found in their kitboxes, some dating as far back as the 1400s BC, and came to use them as part of the complex ritual that prepared Egyptians for the long ages of the afterlife. Archaeology and ancient history are unclear on the mechanics. All we can be sure of is that we have contact. Contact with far distant places where spices grow. Furthermore, this contact long predates anything Europe looks upon as its history and ancestry. What Ramses' peppercorns show is that the widespread exchange of spices was part of the most ancient of worlds, beyond and before Europe.

The story of spices begins where spices are native species. It starts with the inhabitants of Asian regions who gathered the roots, leaves, fruits and kernels of local plants, discovered their properties, then cultivated them and refined their multiple applications. Long-lasting and easy to transport, spices with their myriad uses were natural candidates for creating a chain of connection between one place and another. And wherever spices went they made the ubiquitous spiced stew possible. There can be little doubt they travelled along the network of trading sites that, from prehistoric times, linked Asia to the Fertile Crescent, the region where what we call civilization began. We can even speculate that the spices of life quickened the pace of civilization, for down the millennia ideas have travelled as the ballast of trade. What we do know is that the chain of connections long precedes the Eurocentric perspective.

The cultural repertoire of their uses first developed in the native home of spices. They were used in food, but it is extremely unlikely these foods would have been thought of as curry, a generic spiced stew. They were also known for their medicinal properties, which covered the whole gamut of human ailments and included assistance with various aspects of sexual performance and dysfunction in their role as the Viagra of the ancient world. Common knowledge of the medicinal properties of spices became systematized, developed and enhanced with the growth of Ayurvedic medicine, the ancient Indian system of thought in which food was part of a holistic life balance. You are what you eat, so therefore what you eat should promote the health of the body as well as pleasing the taste buds – a dictum intrinsic to the worldview of Indian philosophy. Spices were used in cosmetics, for ritual purposes in life and death, to purify as well as to sanctify the air. The history of ancient worlds placed the Indian subcontinent as a hub from which the rich panoply of spices emerged as ingredients of knowledge and ways of doing.

Not all the spices known and used in ancient times on the subcontinent are native. Cloves, nutmeg and mace, some of the most prized flavours in the spice world, originate in the easternmost islands far beyond Java of the Southeast Asian archipelago, the only place they were cultivated until after the coming of Europeans. Knowledge of these spices and trade in them connected the Indian subcontinent to the Malay world and is traced through the history of what are termed the Indianized states of Southeast Asia. So whether one looked westwards from India, overland through Afghanistan and Persia to the Middle East, or eastwards across land and sea, there never was an insular subcontinent waiting to be discovered and unlocked by Europe. India is only far beyond the hearth of civilization, or anything else for that matter, if one looks at history from the vantage point of Europe and the ignorance of life in the East that framed the development of the West.

The history of European food has been shaped by influence from and contact with the East. This influence can be read in the cookbooks of the medieval period. Among them was a work containing 196 recipes produced by the 200 cooks in the employ of King Richard II of England entitled *The Forme of Cury*, written in the year 1390. Yes, *cury*, we find, is an Old English word derived from the French *cuire* – to cook – from which also comes the word 'cuisine'. By Richard II's time, pepper, once a rare and costly ingredient, was not quite the thing so far as the upper classes were concerned. It had become sufficiently available to be considered 'bourgeois'. Now ginger, cinnamon, nutmeg, cloves, galangale, coriander, cumin, cardamom and aniseed were in regular use to satisfy the superior palates of the nobility. The spices were used to make piquant sauces. The word '*cury*' or '*curies*' was a part of the English language and food writing long before the supposed first direct European encounter with 'Indian' food.

Throughout history the tastes of the wealthy, their need to demonstrate and display their riches and hence their power, required spices. For medieval Europe, spices, along with other exotic produce of the East, were increasingly a drain on European currencies. They had to be paid for in ready silver money, and that was in short supply. So Europeans began to seek a route to the East in search of something more than just spices. The momentous breakthrough occurred when Vasco da Gama, piloted across the Indian Ocean by a Muslim navigator he encountered in the port of Malindi on the coast of East Africa, made landfall in Calicut on the west coast of India. He was met on the dock by two Tunisian merchants, who addressed him in impeccable Spanish. Why, they wondered, had he bothered to come all the way to India when the spice routes were so well known and so reliable? The Portuguese adventurer set about monopolizing the trade after his less than ground-breaking arrival. Domination and monopoly are what Europe went east to obtain, a prize even more precious than spices. When in 1612, the English made a determined effort to break the Portuguese monopoly of the spice lands they sought exclusive trading rights in India from the Mughal Emperor Jahangir. The emperor was about as impressed as the Tunisian merchants had been. He kept the envoys of the East India Company cooling their heels at his court for months – more than enough time for them to record that a 'dumpukht fowl stewed in butter with spices, almonds and raisins' they were served was very similar to an English chicken pie. The spiced cuisine of India, far from being strange, turned out to be sufficiently familiar to their own tastes for the English to realize they already had a word to describe it. And by creating the generic description 'curry' for all the teeming vitality that was India, the British created a literal nonsense.

There is another common fallacy about curry: it must be 'hot'. Ask any frequenter of an Indian restaurant for the quintessential ingredient of curry and without doubt the answer will be 'chilli powder'. Chillies are the ready-reckoning visual aid on many Indian restaurant menus. Yet the chilli is not native to Asia. The pungent fruit was made known to Europe in 'the Indies'. Its original cultivation was the work of people known to history as 'Indians' – but the kind of Indians who, like the hottest chillies, are Red. Chilli was introduced to India by the Portuguese, who brought it with them to the headquarters of their Empire of the Indies, established in Goa. How the chilli was integrated into India's cuisines, how it became the staple ingredient of what it pleased the British to describe as curry, is not a matter of historic interest to Europe. Nor do the annals of colonial history record the gradual domestication of chilli. This was the work of Indians, and it occurred beyond the European obsession with their own affairs. Today, no modern travel guide to India is complete without a picture of fields of red chillies quietly drying in the sun – a 'typical' tourist photo op. Most of the world's ground chilli powder is currently produced in India.

The dish most closely associated with chilli is *vindaloo*, so much a part of British consciousness that it has become a folk idiom for 'hot stuff' worked into the chants of football fans – a fact I became aware of only when it was used as the refrain for an inescapable advertising campaign by a leading supermarket chain during the 2006 World Cup. On Imran's menu, it was listed under 'Classic Curries' and described as a 'highly flavoured dish consisting of lemons, crushed chillies and hot spices'. But *vindaloo* is not an Indian word. In fact, it is a corruption of the Portuguese term '*vindalho*', literally meaning wine and garlic, and indicates a recipe (dare I mention a spiced stew?) where vinegar, wine or blood is used for cooking, and pork is the main ingredient. The Portuguese introduced it to Goa, and from there it was diffused and transformed across south India, before being picked up by the British. Its association with chilli was acquired along the way. The Portuguese, as the first European arrivals in India, began the great global exchange of foodstuffs and culinary practices – chillies and pineapple were rerouted from Columbus's imagined Indies in South America to da Gama's real India. So, it turns out that *vindaloo*, chilli and curry are as Indian as they are European – or indeed British!

When the Dubai-bound Balti fanatic had been served at Afzal's restaurant, everyone returned to the table and recalled me from my musings on literal nonsense. Afzal Sahib resumed his explanation of the history of Balti. 'We tried to civilize the natives by introducing different kinds of cuisine,' he said. 'We tried to emphasize different kinds of subcontinental cuisine. In particular, we introduced the *tandoor* and *karahi* dishes.' It seemed to me Afzal Sahib was recounting a way of reacting to the colonial connotations and generic imperialism of curry. The *tandoor* – the clay oven used for making *naan* and *roti* – was dragged from the subcontinent and proudly deployed in the high streets of Britain to indicate that real 'Indian' restaurants did not just serve curry. The *karahi*, the Urdu/Hindi word for a wok and one of the most common ways of cooking on the sub-continent, was a symbol of authenticity – a way of reclaiming not just food but the very tradition and identity of people like me and Afzal Sahib.

'We soon discovered,' Afzal Sahib continued, 'that the *goras* had problems pronouncing the word *karahi*. So as a joke we said why not call it Balti. It will make the life of *goras* so much easier! A Balti is something far more sophisticated than a curry but not too far removed from a *karahi*.'

'Of course,' Osman the chef intervened, 'it has evolved. *Karahi* is cooked in a large cast-iron wok. It usually contains a number of mixed ingredients that are left to simmer for some time. It has thick gravy and is dry. Balti is cooked in a small iron wok and is usually served in the same wok. It contains more onions and fewer tomatoes. It also contains a number of spices and the dish is fast cooked over a high flame so you can taste the spices individually.' At Imran's, Osman explained, food is cooked not just in a *karahi* or a *balti* but also in a *handi* – a clay pot. Each utensil gives its own unique flavour to the cooking, which can easily be discerned by the *cognoscenti*. Osman ushered me into the kitchen to demonstrate by cooking a Balti chicken.

The kitchen was huge, neatly arranged and divided into sections for different kinds of cooking. An assistant chef was making *naans* in a *tandoor*. Another sat in front of a cooker with two rows of burners and numerous grills, peeling vegetables. Osman threw some chicken he had already marinated – 'according to my special recipe' – into a frying pan and it began to sizzle. After a few minutes, he sprinkled various spices into the pan and mixed them with the chicken. Suddenly, the frying pan caught fire, and flames shot up several feet in the air. Osman continued to mix and stir. When the flames died down, he sprinkled in some fresh coriander. The Balti was ready. It was a virtuoso performance.

The invention of the Balti too has been quite a performance. By attaching a different label to what is basically the same food and creating a myth around it, the Indian restaurant reframed its image. It lifted itself from the bog-standard confines of curry and *vindaloo* and acquired a more fashionable and upmarket persona. The Balti has performed a genuinely authentic miracle. It suggests that the British Asian community has the ability to reinvent itself, repackage tradition and reposition itself in relation to British society. British Asians can be authentic and true to themselves, and reclaim their history, in any number of different and innovative ways they choose. The Balti has also been instrumental in educating British society. By teaching the British how to eat Indian, even such a fabricated dish as Balti, Asians have broadened the cultural horizons and experience of a rather parochial people. The Balti has not only changed British Asians – it has transformed the cultural landscape of Britain. It expresses the confidence of having arrived.

Chapter 2

BEING ASIAN

It has always fascinated me that in the process of migration those who previously were Indians became Asians. In its slow progressive motion the body of assumptions bound up in Indian identity became disarticulated. On making landfall in Britain, its fragmented particles required a new kind of description. The British bit of British Asian does give a sense of belonging in Britain. But why Asian? What significance is gained and what is lost in the translation from Indian to Asian? Why the shift from sub- to full continental badge of identity? People living in Asia do not see themselves as Asians. Their identities are linked to their nationalities: Chinese, Malaysian and Afghani, for example. Or, more commonly, they see themselves in terms of their ethnicities: Hui, Malay or Pashto. My father, and the immigrants of his generation who made their home in Britain, never saw themselves as Asians.

Despite the common currency of the term, the one thing you will not find in Birmingham, or any other British city with a migrant population, is 'the Asian community'. Walk for miles in areas such as Sparkbrook and you see mostly 'Asian' faces. However, the majority of migrants from the Indian subcontinent are, according to the standard classification drawn up by Europe, Caucasians.

Like the British themselves and all Europeans, they are from what is called Indo-European stock, with variable degrees of suntan. Like all the descriptive categories thrust upon me, this too has an indeterminacy that defies consistency or logic. White Britain seems content that it knows what it means by 'Asians', and tells us that. Birmingham supports one of the largest concentrations of 'Asians' in Britain. But search for this 'Asian community' and you discover an elaborate variety of communities: Kashmiri Pakistanis in Sparkbrook, Bengalis in Perry Barr, Hindus in Sutton Coldfield. The label simply does not fit these people's sense of who they are. It does not define the various strands of belonging they consider significant. 'Asian' is a catch-all term indifferent to their conception of themselves as distinct peoples, with different cultures, speaking different languages, with different histories and different outlooks. Asians, like curry and chilli, exist and do not exist.

According to the 2001 census published on 13 February 2003, there are around 2.2 million Asians living in Britain. This is just over 3.5 per cent of the total UK population. Of these, around a million are British-Indians, 675,000 are British-Pakistani and 257,000 are British-Bangladeshi. There are a further 242,000 people who are said to be from 'varying Asian backgrounds' – people from places such as Sri Lanka and Afghanistan, and Indians and Pakistanis who came to Britain via East Africa. Around half of all Asians were actually born and bred in Britain. The majority describe their identity as British or English, Scottish or Welsh: 78 per cent of Sikhs, 70 per cent of Muslims and 69 per cent of Hindus gave one of these British identities in the 2001 census. The overwhelming majority of Asians born in Britain see themselves as British (Sikhs, 93 per cent; Muslims, 91 per cent; and Hindus, 89 per cent). The statistics hide as much as they reveal. What they don't tell us is whether Asians actually *feel* British, whether they are at ease with their British selves; nor can they indicate how they reconcile their Asian cultural heritage with their British identity.

On one of my numerous visits to Birmingham, I met Tahir Abbas. A youthful, joyous man in his late thirties, Abbas constantly brushes his crop of neatly cut and styled hair with his left hand. For some years he has taught sociology at Birmingham University, and he is the director of the University's Centre for the Study of Ethnicity and Culture. His specialist subject has been the ethnic diversity of Birmingham, and he spoke of his work with considerable enthusiasm and authority. 'The generic Asian,' he said, 'exists only in the mind of Anglo-Saxon folk.' To understand who Asians really are and how they see themselves one has to develop a differentiated gaze, to learn to distinguish between the plethora of different so-called Asians. The distinctions did not begin here in Britain. Their journey of migration includes their place in the political economy of what once was British India. Indians with varied experiences in education and industry were differently fitted to make a place for themselves in Britain. Their condition on arrival affected how they adapted to the pattern common to migrants of all nationalities and backgrounds who have come to this country down the ages. The professionals found their niche, the artists and writers could mingle in the mainstream or not, the tradesmen and salesmen could walk the streets from door to door offering their goods and services, and all the rest simply hoped for a job and found themselves on a factory floor, on the buses and trains, or labouring away in a sweatshop. Of course, as time went on they sought to provide themselves with their own familiar accoutrements of living, from foods to pots and pans and clothing – making new economic niches for themselves.

Birmingham's migrant population, Abbas told me, had its own pecking order, one that has developed and changed over time. This change is visible in the areas where various Asian communities live. First, the English sold their houses to Indians who were relatively wealthy and came from urban backgrounds. When the Indians moved out, the Pakistanis, who came mainly from rural areas, moved in. Then the Pakistanis sold their houses to the Bengalis, the poorest of all Asian ethnic minorities. The cycle has been played out for decades. During the 1990s, the new breed of upwardly mobile Asians, mainly Hindu millionaires, took over the leafy suburbs of Solihull. They are generically Asians, but they are miles away from the Pakistanis and Bangladeshis.

There are also variations from city to city. The distribution of 'Indian restaurants', which tend not to be Indian, is a good way to appreciate this. London has more Bangladeshi restaurants than Pakistani ones. Go north and the number of Pakistani restaurants increases. Birmingham has more Pakistani restaurants than Bangladeshi. By the time you reach Bradford and Manchester, the restaurateurs are almost entirely Pakistani, Kashmiri in particular. By Glasgow, the concentration is exclusively Pakistani and Punjabi. There are also variations in the nature of Asian businesses: 'ranging from individuals desperately struggling to survive through to highly successful fast-growing businesses with seven-figure annual turnovers. In between the two extremes, we find the takeaways that tick over reasonably satisfactorily but seldom grow,' Abbas said.

The first Indian restaurant in Britain served Bengali dishes. It was opened by Sake Dean Mohamet (or Mohomad). He had served in the Bengal Army, the military force that made the fortune of the East India Company. When, in 1784, his commanding officer returned from India with his newly acquired personal fortune to set up house in Ireland, Dean Mohamet accompanied him. They settled in Cork, another outpost of colonial society, whose landed ruling class had multiple and growing connections with the subcontinent. It is evident from another of Dean Mohamet's claims to fame – that of being the first Indian to write a book in English – that his patron ensured he acquired a proper gentleman's education, which at that time included learning Latin and mastering Greek mythology. Through his patron's connections Dean Mohamet became familiar with the elite circles of Anglo-Irish society. His exact status within this circle, or indeed the nature of his connection with the household of his patron, is unclear. But it seems to have provided sufficient protection for him to elope with and marry the daughter of a well-known Protestant family. The couple resumed their life in Cork, where Dean Mohamet's book of *Travels* was published. Following the death of his patron, there must have been some rupture with the family. Dean Mohamet next appears in London, and for the rest of his life makes no further mention of his time in Ireland.

In London, Dean Mohamet opened the Hindustani Coffee House at 34 George Street, Portman Square, a fashionable part of town, in 1809. The coffee house was furnished with bamboo chairs and sofas and, according to press reports, its walls were decorated with 'Chinese pictures and other Asiatic embellishments'. It promised 'Indian dishes, in the highest perfection, and allowed by epicures to be unequalled to any curries ever made in England'. For this was not the first establishment in London to offer curry on its menu. A coffee house at Norris Street on the Haymarket had achieved that milestone in 1773. A few years later the grand tradition of generalizing led to the commercial production of curry powder, the pre-packaged melange that permitted one spoonful to transform a dish into a curry instantly without the trouble of balancing, or experimenting with, a blend of varied spices. Where medieval recipes had specified each spice, the more England knew of India the more generic things became. Calling a restaurant a 'coffee house' was a standard marketing ploy that carried allusions of Eastern promise. Coffee was first introduced from the Middle East and was firmly associated in the British mind with the Ottoman Empire. The first coffee house in London opened in 1652 at Cornhill in the City, the hub of London's financial and trading businesses. The East was seen as a cornucopia of novelties disgorged by Europe's expansion and the opening up of world trade. Ottoman Turkey as the gateway to the East left an indelible impression on English sensibilities. So when the domestic fowl we know as turkey was introduced, that's how it acquired its name, on the general assumption that it came from Ottoman lands rather than its native North America. The Turks themselves had their own take on the origin of the fowl, calling it *hindi* – a product of 'the Indies' – which at the time at least inferred some reference to the Americas.

The environs of Portman Square housed many rich nabobs. These nouveau-riche residents, English returnees from India, were wealthy enough to maintain their own cooks, from the subcontinent or not, to prepare their taste of the Orient at home. So after an initial burst of success, the Hindustani Coffee House ran into trouble. By 1812 Dean Mohamet had to sell up, though the coffee house, recapitalized and under English management, continued in existence till 1833. The Mohamets – Dean and his indomitable wife, Jane – moved to Brighton. There they began a third career, again offering the English a novelty with all the allure of the East. One of the great selling points of spices down the ages was their reputed health benefits. Eastern medicinal wisdom still had market value among the English public. Dean Mohamet exploited this old association for all it was worth, and Brighton offered just the right opportunity as a fashionable place specializing in the medicinal benefits of the new craze for sea bathing. He adapted the newfangled equipment for a vapour bath, invented by an Englishman, but retained allusions to the already known Turkish bath. To this he added not only Indian oils but an ancient Indian technique. Shampooing, from *champi*, is the procedure we would identify as massage. In any Indian household massage is an everyday courtesy and comfort, the warm ease of domestic bliss extended from tip to toe, the soothing application of pressure on stressed, tense and aching muscles, joints and limbs. Shampooing did not acquire the meaning of washing the hair until much later in the nineteenth century. In its original incarnation as massage it took

Brighton by storm. Clients were put in a flannel tent and massaged by someone who poked their arms through slits in the flannel walls. In a local paper, Dean Mohamet described the process as 'the Indian medicated vapour bath' that could cure a number of diseases, including rheumatism, gout, stiff joints, and general aches and pains. He was so successful that he became 'shampooing surgeon' by appointment to both George IV and William IV. The elegant purpose-built premises he eventually owned, with separate floors for the treatment of men and women, were decorated with murals in which Indian scenes were graced by Greek goddesses.

Dean and Jane Mohamet worked hard throughout their lives. They lived through periods of feast and famine, reinventing themselves and their fortunes by using and adapting aspects of Indian culture to fit the fads and fancies of the English market. Once settled in Brighton, the more Sake Dean Mohamet learnt of the appalling state of health and medicine in England the more interested he became in the medicinal aspects of the treatments he offered. He read the current literature and contributed to it too. After his death his sons continued in what was gradually becoming the medical profession. In many parts of Britain people's first experience of Asian migration, long before places beyond the main cities acquired 'Indian' restaurants, was the arrival of an 'Indian' doctor as a local GP or in an NHS hospital. I like the thought that this association of Asians with Britain's health service is what might be termed foundational.

Dean Mohamet was a Bihari: he was born in Patna, Bihar, to a Muslim family related to the Nawabs of Murshidabad. Like Dean Mohamet, the Biharis were originally 'Indian'. After the Partition of India in 1947, the Biharis, who are mainly Muslim, migrated from Bihar, Orissa and West Bengal to East Bengal, which was allotted to East Pakistan, and Biharis became Pakistani. After the creation of Bangladesh in 1971, the Biharis, who are Urdu speakers, opted for Pakistan rather than Bangladesh. But Pakistan didn't want them. So Biharis, who are Bengalis but speak Urdu, see themselves as Pakistanis, even though they actually live in Bangladesh. They provide a good illustration of just how complicated 'Asian' ethnic identity has become.

I asked Abbas, rather provocatively, if he thought of himself as Asian. He looked at me incredulously. 'Asia is a continent,' he shot back, 'not an identity. You can fit several Europes into Asia.' Asia and Asian have become a new kind of 'Indies', meaning whatever a Western observer chooses. It is all a matter of context. In America, Asians are Chinese, Koreans and Filipinos; and an Indian is, of course, a Native American. In Holland, Asians are Indonesians and people from Surinam, which is not even in Asia. In Germany, Asians are Turks. 'Such generic descriptions are designed to hide diversity and paint people with the same – often tarnished – brush.' Abbas thought for a moment. 'All Asians,' he said, 'have compound identities. To understand Asians in Britain, we have to understand the nature of these compound identities and appreciate how they come together as a composite whole.'

'OK,' I said in an effort to test this hypothesis. 'British Asians have come to Britain from India, Pakistan, Bangladesh and Sri Lanka. So we have four national identities to begin with.'

'This is largely correct but not as clear cut,' replied Abbas. 'In as far as these "nations" are imaginary constructions, they also serve as overlapping identities. Most Pakistanis migrated from India in the great upheaval of Partition. So many older Pakistanis also see themselves as Indian: they lay claim not to "India" the nation state but "India" the civilization that existed over millennia, of which the distinct variety of "Indian Islam" is an integral part. Punjabis, who come from the province of Punjab, can be either Indians or Pakistanis. And so on.'

'So within the national identities you have a host of Asian ethnic identities?'

'Punjabis, Kashmiris, Gujeratis, Sindhis, Bengalis, Biharis, Tamil, Singhalese, and it goes on. Each ethnicity is a universe in its own right, with its own language, customs, traditions and histories. Often these ethnicities were in conflict back in the subcontinent; and they bring their conflicts here.' Abbas paused. 'We haven't even mentioned religion yet,' he continued, with a long sigh. 'Hinduism, Jainism, Sikhism, Buddhism, Christianity and numerous varieties of Islam. Each adds a different and distinctive layer of identity.'

'What about those who are born and bred in Britain?' I asked. 'Surely, they don't subscribe to subcontinental regional and ethnic identities.'

'British Asians, whether born in Britain or not,' Abbas said emphatically, 'have a sense of belonging, involvement and empathy beyond British borders. Those who are born here may grow up speaking English, but they still grow up as Bengalis or Punjabis, as Muslims or Hindus. Moreover, Asians exist not as individual isolated units of nuclear families but as communities of extended families. Every Asian family in Britain has large numbers of relatives on the subcontinent. So family bestrides Britain and the subcontinent; visits are frequent, family responsibilities are fulfilled no matter where family members physically live; and what happens on the subcontinent has a direct bearing on what happens on the streets of Birmingham or Manchester. To understand British Asians, we have to understand how they lived in South Asia – to understand the future to which they aspire, we need to comprehend the past they carry with them.'

The enigma of Asianness is its immense variety, and it is not resolved by replacing one generic term with another: Indians for Asians. Geographically, India is so huge that we refer to it as a subcontinent. However, it is not one place but many. There is no single all-embracing concept, but numerous ideas of India. There is no single 'Indian culture' – there are countless Indian cultures. India does not have one religion; it is home to Hinduism,

Islam, Jainism, Sikhism, Buddhism, Christianity and even had an ancient and once-thriving Jewish community. As a nation, India has twenty-three different official languages, including English. But there are also 800 unofficial languages, each spoken by up to a million people, and 2,000 dialects, most of which are mutually unintelligible. Pakistan has nine languages, including English. Only Bangladesh, 98 per cent speak Bengali, has apparent homogeneity, but with complications as we have noted. Sri Lanka has the vexed division between the Buddhist Singhalese majority and the Tamil Hindu minority, but that again skates over the surface of a diversity of minorities, such as the Muslim community and legions of the Christianized, or not, da Silva brigades redolent of the island's long history of openness to and involvement with the wider world. So India is not just a multicultural society – it is multi everything.

India has always been a land of multiple civilizations, each as different as the fundamental tenents of Hinduism and Islam. But these different civilizations were not discrete wholes, bounded and exclusive. The great accomplishment of India was the way ideas flowed across permeable boundaries. What India achieved was not merely the means of tense coexistence (and at times open antagonism) but, alongside this, the interpenetration of different ways of thinking and living. For each of its ways of thinking and living interacted, influenced and affected all the rest. Consequently, India does not have one voice – the voice of English-speaking liberal secularists, or of Hindu fundamentalists, for example – but countless voices. And it does not have a single history but multiple histories with multiple perspectives. It is not surprising that Ramila Thaper, the doyenne of Indian history, subtitled her seminal book on the alleged ransacking of the Hindu temple in Somanatha by the Muslim Sultan Mahmud of Ghazni in 1026 – one of the founding myths of modern Hindu nationalism – *The Many Voices of History*.

'Asians' brought these multiple histories and numerous voices with them to Britain. Religion and culture, ethnicity and language, customs and beliefs, as well as numerous traditions and histories, all add to the multi-layering of identity for those uniformly designated 'Indians' or 'Asians' in Britain. And being in Britain adds its own layers. What results is a legacy of complex diversity through which one's sense of self and belonging is shaped. Your home is in Britain, your household follows its own variety of the workings of culture, religion, language and custom filtered and refined by history and family experience. Each of these connective links was formed by the personal choices and predilections of ancestors and parents, each is a product of how they lived their past to create the opportunities of your future. You are loyal to Britain, but you are always concerned with the fate of the land where your father or grandfather was born, and where a large segment of your extended family lives. You see British history as your history; but then you wonder why the history that has shaped you, the history of British colonialism, the history of the Empire and what the Empire did to you and yours, is so absent from and silent in that history. To be a 'British Asian' is to constantly encounter questions about colonialism and to be imbued with the legacy of Partition. It is to share in a distinctive way with people around the globe the knowledge that colonialism was a very bad thing. But it does not follow that one looks at Pakistan, or Bangladesh, or Sri Lanka or India as an answer, certainly not *the* answer to the problems created by Empire. Being British provides Asians with an objective distance for a more dispassionate view of the subcontinent. But being British does not mean you are going to ditch your heritage, abandon your family or jettison your memories. Untangling this nexus, reordering the fragments jumbled higgledy-piggledy by migration, is no straight-forward matter. It is as complex, convoluted, multiple and compound as the nature of Britishness itself.

Even Britain allows its ancestry to be more complex than the choices it offers British Asians. Think of the official designations to be found on the census form. If you are white British you can choose to compound your identity by designating yourself English, Scots, Welsh, Irish or European Other. These are complex identities, trailing history. They remain vexed contemporary political and cultural issues, as arcane and yet as vital as the West Lothian question. British Asians merely get to be Indian, Pakistani or Bangladeshi, new historical entities that, as labels, do not reach the parts of affective bonding embraced by being Scots, Welsh, Irish or English. And no one seems to think their experience in Britain might also provide Asians with connections to the cultural conundrums of English, Scots, Welsh or Irish identities. The more British Asians I meet, the more I am constantly amazed by the new and diverse layers of compound identities I discover. There is an old Urdu proverb, *giragh talay undehra*; it points to the shadows of darkness that surround a burning candle. Ignorance, the maxim tells us, is a constant companion of knowledge. It is folly to assume each and every British Asian understands and is in sympathy or of a piece with all other Asians. My own ignorance of certain things Asian, I readily admit, is legion.

How British Asians live in Britain, the kind of life they have created for themselves, depends to a large extent on what they brought with them from the subcontinent. They have tended to recreate the life they left behind. Along with culture and tradition, they also brought certain perceptions. How they perceive Britain itself, for example, depends on the region they came from and how traditional their own communities were in the subcontinent. Those who hailed from rural areas, where traditional bonds were strong and deep and modernity was viewed with suspicion, saw twentieth-century Britain as hostile. Urban and middle-class immigrants, on the other hand, adjusted to their new homes with relative ease – though here too, tradition had a direct bearing on their conception of life in Britain. But even this distinction is too simplistic. I came from a mixed-up background: my parents belonged to an urban middle class in India but joined the ranks of the rural working classes when they migrated to Pakistan in 1947. As Muslims, they were deeply traditional, but as Pakistanis they aspired to modernity.

My own identity is a complex amalgam of different bits of my history. In Pakistan, I was a particular kind of Asian. I was born with a new identity, Pakistani, formed out of the multiple layers of Indian history and tradition. I was born at a time when the essence of Indian history was being unravelled and reforged into new nationalities. It was being changed by the assertion of new nationalism. My parents were caught up in all the connotations of these connections. They were Indians before migration took them to Pakistan, and then brought them to Britain, where they became British Asians. A number of different histories merge to produce a single label behind which stands the story of my life.

I know I was born three weeks prematurely. 'You have no patience,' my mother frequently intones, 'not even the minutest quantity.' She is, of course, best placed to know what others merely suspect to be my original condition. The question of when I was born is not straightforward because it was caught up in the complexities surrounding where I made my precocious appearance. I was born in a small village on the Pakistani side of the India–Pakistan border. Dipalpur was in disputed territory. Just four years after Partition the two countries were exchanging hostilities, debating exactly where the line of demarcation should stand. My parents decided to let things settle down before registering the birth. A few years passed. My parents became more established in their new life and the fact that we were indeed in Pakistan was confirmed. My mother packed my father off to the local district council in Okara to have the birth of their son registered, a tiring train journey from where we lived. It took my father over a day to find the relevant place, by which time he had forgotten my date of birth. He could not remember whether it was the 3rd, 13th, 23rd, 30th or 31st of October. He settled on the last number in the sequence for his first-born son. But worse followed:

he was vague on whether this momentous event, to which I rushed with such dispatch, occurred in 1951 or 1952. He opted for 1951, thinking, as he later told me, 'It is better for you to be older than younger.' On his return journey, however, my father was caught in one of those seasonal rainstorms that turn everything into a large paddy-field. He arrived home drenched, heavily decorated with mud, but proudly clutching my birth certificate. When my mother examined it she was aghast. She gave a loud, high-pitched, shrill scream – the sort she still utters when confronted by incomprehensible horror. The birth certificate, written in Indian ink, had been washed clean by the perfidious rain. But it had been written with a hard, wooden pen which had left indentations on the thick paper. By manipulating the certificate carefully in a good light, and after painstaking scrutiny, my mother could just about make out my name and a 3 where the date was supposed to be.

Imagine what havoc not knowing your exact date of birth plays with your astrology. Am I a balanced Libra or a sting-in-the-tail Scorpio? Should I 'take destiny in my own hands' or 'defer all important decisions' because of the full moon? Infancy, mercifully, is free of such momentous quandaries. The necessary decisions are taken for you.

Soon after the debacle we moved to Bhawalnagar, where I spent most of my childhood. Our household was filled with relatives – all variety of aunts and cousins, and grandparents – mostly women and children, as the men, including my father, were spread the length and breadth of Pakistan looking for employment. Our extensive family was dominated by the towering presence of Abdul Razziq Khan, a *hakim* (traditional Islamic doctor) who hated the Raj and the British in equal measure. He was affectionately known as Hakim Sahib, and I called him Nana. But he was not, as this word should signify, my mother's father, but his younger brother. In fact, I have no personal memory of my real Nana, Said Ahmad Khan. He died when I was around six years of age. All I remember is that he suffered from TB and was hospitalized in Lahore for a long time. One day my mother received a letter from Lahore. She opened it but did not read it. The corner of the letter had been torn – a traditional indicator that it contained bad news. Hakim Abdul Razziq Khan thus became what I had always assumed he was: not just mine, but everyone's Nana.

Hakim Sahib was a tall, well-built, handsome man, with a long, wispy white beard. He wore thick-rimmed glasses and always carried a towel-like cloth draped around his shoulders, which he used to dry his sweat. He looked quite different from his elder brother who, in pictures I have seen, had a short, neat beard and always wore a fez. Hakim Sahib had an infectious sense of fun and often played with children. Frequently, I would sit on his lap, twiddling his beard. As a child, I hated being kissed. He was the exception; only him would I willingly allow the distinction of kissing me. Sometimes, he would take me with him to his surgery in the middle of Railway Bazaar.

As a *hakim*, Nana was not just an expert in Islamic, traditional medicine. He was also a psychologist, a councillor and a marriage-broker. He was widely regarded as the wisest man in Bhawalnagar. As he was the only affordable doctor in town, his surgery was always crowded. As I remember it, he seldom gave medicine to anyone – he seemed to heal with his words. Everyone received his undivided attention – even while I sat on his lap, pulling his beard and occasionally throwing whatever I could lay my hands on at an unsuspecting patient. Nana had a special knack for listening. 'Half of medicine,' he used to say to one of my uncles, who he was training to be a *hakim*, 'consists of listening. A sympathetic ear can cure so many diseases in our society.'

One day, Hakim Sahib said in exasperation, after I had wandered off as I was prone to do, 'It seems no one can keep an eye on you. From now on you will come with me to the surgery every day.' It was all I ever wanted. And that's what happened: I spent the most memorable, most beautiful part of my childhood with my Nana at his surgery. Holding his index finger, I would walk with him to work, where I played with the empty bottles in one corner. In between seeing patients, when he had time to spare, Nana would read me stories and I would listen with absolute attention. Those I remember best were about a man called Abu Zayd. He was a rascal, prone to wandering, and, like me, frequently got lost. Each story began with Abu Zayd giving an eloquent sermon in the bazaar, which Nana always enacted with great gusto. 'How long will you persist with your folly?' he asked the people in the bazaar who gathered around him. 'How long will you cheat, steal, and do and eat all those things that God has forbidden? How long will you be greedy and chase material goods? How long will you hide from yourself?' The bazaar crowds were very impressed, both by his message and his oratory. When he finished, the gathered audience gave him money and thanked him. Soon we discover Abu Zayd lived a life of luxury in a cave where he greedily consumed forbidden things and did exactly what he had denounced in the bazaar. Years later, I realized Hakim Sahib was actually recounting the stories of *The Assemblies of al-Hariri*, the twelfth-century Arabic masterpiece. There are fifty encounters or tales in the *Assemblies* – and Nana told them all.

After each story, Hakim Sahib would draw some moral which he would explain with great affection. 'Why does Abu Zayd keep getting lost?' I asked one day.

'Ah,' replied Nana, 'like you, he is looking for himself.'

'But I am here, I am not lost.'

'We are all lost,' Nana said, 'till we find ourselves.'

Later, I realized that migration had a profound impact on Nana. He was at home in Pakistan, but he also felt displaced. For Pakistan was only a partial home – he belonged to India as a whole and the whole of India belonged to him. The tales of Abu Zayd were all about the experience of moving away from home. In the end,

Abu Zayd settles down to a life of simplicity, devotion and contemplation. I, said Nana, would find myself through books.

It was Hakim Sahib who inspired in me the love of books. He read constantly and he read everything: religious texts, philosophy, history, high literature, poetry, pulp fiction, comics and, of course, the great books of *tibb*, or Islamic medicine. I never saw him without a book in his hand. It was not unusual to see him lying on his *charpai* – a rough-and-ready bed with a wooden frame, its mattress a lattice of knotted jute – on the veranda, reading by paraffin lamp late into the night. He set aside a corner of his surgery for me to make a library. I soon filled it with comics, volumes of children's poetry, and special exercise books that helped you write Urdu properly, as calligraphic works of art. When my collection grew larger, I was given an old cupboard in the house. I remember decorating it with paper cut-outs and placing a large notice – which Nana had written in Urdu on my behalf – on one of its doors: 'Zia's Library. No Admission Without Permission.'

Nana had a reverential attitude towards books. You were not allowed to drop them on the floor or leave them lying around. 'When reading,' he would say, 'do not place a book on the ground. Place it on a book rack or some such thing.' He used a pillow. 'Handle the book with grace, show dignity to its author.' Every new volume had to be covered; usually he would take a newspaper, cut it to the right size and turn it into a dust jacket. 'When you borrow a book from the library or from someone, always, always return it.' 'Do not fold the pages of books, use a book marker.' 'Do not write in the margins of books you have borrowed.' But he allowed you to write in the margins of your own books, provided 'you do not disfigure the book, and write with elegant strokes'. You could never use ink – it might get smudged and ruin the page – only pencil.

Hakim Sahib himself used ink: he wrote copious notes in the margins of his medical books in red ink. The surgery was full of texts on Islamic medicine – all neatly protected with newspaper jackets –

carefully arranged in subject order. A text he consulted frequently was al-Biruni's *Materia Medica*, a list of over 600 medicinal plants. There were several volumes published by the Hamdard Foundation, which pioneered the revival of Islamic medicine in Pakistan, as well as rows and rows of the foundation's journal, *Hamdard Medicus*. Hamdard also supplied most of his medicines, though he made some of his own. His surgery consisted of two sections. The front was like a large, open shop. Hakim Sahib sat there on the floor leaning on a large cushion, behind a low table. The walls of the front room had shelves right up to the ceiling crammed full of medicines. Patients would simply walk in and take a seat wherever they could on the carpet. When their turn came for consultation, they would move to sit next to Nana. Hakim Sahib would lean towards them and listen attentively. Sometimes he took their pulse or measured their blood pressure. Occasionally, he would take them to another corner of the surgery, secluded by a thick curtain, for closer examination. The second section of the surgery was a much smaller room, filled with equipment. The two rooms were not connected by a door, but a small opening in the wall, over which hung a carpet. This is where Hakim Sahib made his medicine.

One particular drug Hakim Sahib made was known as *Khamira Gawzaban*. Consisting of numerous herbs, whose names I still cannot pronounce, it was a thick, brown paste in which the small, white seeds of some fruit or vegetable were clearly visible. It tasted absolutely delicious. I thought it was a cure for constipation as it provided a good bowel movement in the morning. It turns out its essential functions are to strengthen the brain, relieve stress, banish melancholia and open the mind to hitherto unimagined possibilities. I ate the stuff as if it were chocolate, whenever Hakim Sahib was not looking.

Islamic medicine is a sophisticated enterprise; it was the dominant medicine of the world up to the eighteenth century. When the British first took control of the Punjab they were forced to admit, as the reports of early observers indicate, that the cities possessed 'sophisticated' medical techniques and contained large numbers of men trained in medicine. The *hakims* were able to treat successfully most of the common maladies of the area and commanded high respect from the indigenous population. As the Punjab Civil Secretariat's Proceedings in the General Department recorded in October 1856, they came from respectable families in the community, they were careful as to their behaviour and 'above all their systems of practice are carefully adapted to the prejudices and practices of their patients'. Even though British administrators identified Islamic medicine as a clear threat to Western medicine, initially there was an alliance of convenience. Thus, in a number of emergencies during the middle of the nineteenth century, *hakims* were used by British administrators to assist in the treatment of disease. For example, in a programme proposed by the District Commissioner of Sialkot, Lieutenant Colonel T. W. Mercer, *hakims* were employed in a district-wide scheme to treat diseases, distribute simple medicines (primarily quinine), to act as sanitary inspectors and as registrars of vital statistics, and to aid in the provincial vaccination programme. The collaboration was based on the assumption that they were socially acceptable to the local population (which had already rejected Indian doctors trained in Western medicine and shown indifference to British doctors); that they knew the minds of their patients and, in time, would come to appreciate the superiority of Western, allopathic medicine. Mercer was not concerned with the merits of Islamic medicine; he was seeking the most expedient solution to the health problems in the area under his supervision. His declared intention was 'the gradual substitution of English medicine for useless native drugs, the attendance of the sick of all classes, to afford prompt medical relief, and ultimately, the subversion of the system of medicine as practised by the natives'.

The programme involved the selection of one *hakim*, nominated by the local population, to oversee a circuit consisting of thirty-seven villages. A central village was selected as his residence. The circles were organized in a district that was administered by a graduate of the government's allopathic medical school in Lahore. The chosen individual was given the title of Hakim Ali. They proved more resilient and adaptable than Mercer could imagine. He was astounded by the success and popularity of his programme and believed it was due to the involvement of local people. This success led Mercer to start a training programme designed to instruct the sons of *hakims* in Western medicine. Indeed, in 1870 Lahore Medical College started classes for the relatives of *hakims*. These lessons emphasized anatomy and surgery – two areas where Islamic medicine lagged behind. Eventually, the college developed a programme for training in the English system and awarded 'Titles of Oriental Medicine' to candidates proficient in Western medicine in addition to *Yunan-I tibb*. No formal teaching was conducted in *Yunan-I tibb* but the candidates were required to produce a certificate of their competence from a recognized authority.

However, the initiative at Lahore Medical College was not allowed to mature. Right from the beginning the college faced opposition from British doctors. In 1882, when the government of India proposed to set up a register of medical practitioners, this opposition reached its apex. In the years since Sake Dean Mohamet's arrival in Brighton, where he caused a medical sensation, much had changed. Then, by virtue of the activities of the East India Company, Britain had only a tenuous hold on the province of Bengal. By 1882, it was an imperial power whose writ ran across the whole of India. The dominance of British ideas, attitudes and relationships expanded as rapidly and extensively as control over the land and its teeming populace. Everything was changed. Distances became immense, marking off huge differences. The British no longer delighted in ideas from the East. The scientific advance of British medicine, now a fully fledged science and profession, was just one among so many proofs of Britain's dominance and hence fitness to rule over its colonial preserve. The proposed bill would confer certain rights on medical practitioners: the right to sue for fees, the right to sign government certificates and the right to be called a registered practitioner. Under the system, both *hakims* and doctors trained in Western medicine were to have equal status. But the British medical establishment in the Punjab would not tolerate this.

British doctors opposed Islamic medicine for two reasons. On the one hand, they considered Western medicine to be superior and more scientific than *tibb*. Promoting *tibb* meant promoting 'reactionary elements' and regressive tendencies in Indian society – all of which were seen to oppose British rule in India. On the other hand, they saw *tibb* as a professional and economic threat; *hakims* clearly commanded respect and trust from the local population and tended to undermine the sole authority and control of the medical establishment. Not surprisingly, they wanted a complete ban on indigenous medicine.

Not content with simply raising their voices against Islamic medicine, British doctors began an active campaign to discredit it, magnify its shortcomings and neutralize praise for the successes of its practitioners. Their major weapon was the pages of the *Punjab Dispensary Report*, an annual document submitted via the Governor-General of India to the Secretary of State for India in London. The barrage of complaints against *hakims* used in the campaign did not initially succeed. In 1869, the Punjab government replied to critics of Islamic medicine by pointing out, 'the most opposite of opinions have been expressed to its utility; by some, the benefits are said to be "immense" while others declare it to be "worse" than useless; the fact probably being . . . that its success or failure mainly depends on the amount of encouragement and co-operation it receives from the District Officer and Civil Surgeon . . . So far as the Lt. Governor can judge the establishment of *Hakim* arrangements has in many cases led to a large increase of subscriptions from the native community, and insofar as it has been voluntary, this forms an additional recommendation of the measure.'

But this declaration did not deter British doctors or Punjabis trained in Western medicine from attacking practitioners of Islamic medicine. In 1876, the government of Punjab made its last stand. It declared that while Islamic medicine was in many ways inferior to Western medicine, medical science was nevertheless empirical and there was no doubt *hakims* did some good as 'there is no reason to doubt that the native treatment of many diseases is to some extent effective and highly appreciated by patients'. But the following year all courses for the training of *hakims* were abandoned. This exclusion from the government medical services effectively banned them as legitimate doctors.

Hakim Sahib loathed the British for what they had done to his profession. He was an extremely generous and polite person who never uttered a bad word against anyone. Even when he was angry, he expressed his anger with humour and wit. But he made an exception in the case of the British. The British were *farangi* – ignorant, arrogant foreigners – an Urdu term that had wide currency during the Raj. He used a single expletive to describe them: *haram zaday* – bastards. '*Haram zaday farangi*,' he would say, 'they took the very idea of medicine and hospitals from us, and they have the audacity to say we know nothing of medicine.' '*Haram zaday farangi*, the very surgical instruments they use were designed by us and they have the insolence to tell us we do not know how to perform surgery.' '*Haram zaday farangi*, we cured polio, typhoid, smallpox, scarlet fever, measles, diphtheria, tuberculosis, pneumonia and the diseases of the digestive system before they had an inkling of what constitutes a disease, and they have the impudence to say we do not understand diseases.'

But Hakim Sahib was wise enough to appreciate the limits of Islamic medicine. 'We *hakims*,' he would say, 'cannot treat the diseases of modernity or Western affluence. Only modern medicine can do that. Each to his own. There's more than one way of knowing.' This last sentence was his *takiya kalam* – literally 'words he spoke on his pillow' – his signature and often-repeated motto. Hardly a day would pass without his declaration that there was more than one way of knowing. Of course, when I was a child the sentence meant nothing to me. Later, during my adolescence, I thought he meant there was more than one way of learning. Only after I graduated did I discover the true import of Nana's wisdom. He considered Islamic and Western medicines as two different ways of knowing, with their distinctive methods, both equally rational and equally valid. He could not understand why the *farangi* could not practise the philosophical and methodological egalitarianism that defined his life and which he sought to teach everyone around him.

This is the legacy I brought with me to Britain. Hakim Sahib inculcated in me a distaste for colonialism and what the British did in and to India. For me, this is not about some dead and distant past. This history lives with me, and shapes the way I see Britain. I can detect its influence on how Britain, for example, formulates its foreign policy, behaves towards new immigrants and refugees, and glorifies colonialism in its honours system and the popular history one encounters on television. I imbibe his love of tradition, and feel that tradition is important not just for British Asians but for Britain itself. But, like him, I am also keenly aware of the limitations of tradition. I know, indeed I have seen, just how oppressive tradition can become among Asians. And like him, sometimes I too feel lost and want to find myself. This is the kind of Asian I am.

Chapter 3

WHAT'S IN A NAME?

My friend AbdoolKarim Vakil is the most unusual Asian I know. At first glance he looks like an ordinary 'Asian', but this is merely the illusory surface of the particular kind of 'Asian' he is. Thin to the point of emaciation, he is tall, tawny-brown skinned, with an uncontrollable mop of curly black hair and an unkempt beard. He has the scruffy aura of the distracted academic. His bohemian attire and his tendency to laugh frequently and nervously belie a razor-sharp mind. He can analyse arguments in immaculate detail, his pleasure in the cut-and-thrust of dissecting a contention all too evident on his face. His tendency to give detailed attention to everything – except his physical self – begins with his name.

Asian names reveal a lot about their bearers; indeed, the first step to understanding Asians is to understand their names. Asian names have enormous significance; they are complex representations that describe a person's identity with implications for their lives and behaviour. If you are a Kapoor, a Lal, a Sherma or a Ravi, then you are Hindu. If you are a Singh, a Kaur or even a Sardar, then you are a Sikh. If you are a Jain or a Kalraiya, then you are a Jain – someone who rejects the authority of the Vedas and Upanishads – and thus distinct from a Hindu, and by definition someone who is non-violent. A Muhammad, Rashid or Saddiq is a Muslim. A Khan or a Chaudhry is most likely Pakistani; the former a person of Pathan lineage, the later a Punjabi. Conventionally, on the Indian subcontinent names were not divided into first, or given name, and surname. The 'family name' tended to describe one's profession or association with a region or tribe. Asian families also employ nicknames, most frequently for their children, used only at home. Bengalis have a 'good name' that serves both as a nickname and a reflection of the parents' ambition for their child and is usually given several years after birth.

The Vakil (literally, barrister) in AbdoolKarim Vakil told me he came from a family of barristers. But it was AbdoolKarim, written as a single word, that intrigued me. Most Muslims would write Abdul Karim as two distinct words. But this is open to cultural misunderstanding. It is common enough for Abdul to be regarded as the first or given name, while its companion definer, in this case Karim, would be disregarded. Since Abdul literally means 'slave of' this misunderstanding could have serious consequences. The full name, Abdul Karim, means slave or servant of the Generous One. Karim is one of the ninety-nine names of God in Islamic tradition; Muslims often select names that combine Abdul with one of the names of God. By turning AbdulKarim into a single word, the finicky academic was making sure no misunderstanding could possibly arise. But why spell Abdul as Abdool? It suggests a Euro-Asian connection. The name spelt phonetically was how the English – or other Europeans – would (mis)pronounce Abdul. In British-Indian transliteration, as the Anglo-Indian Bible *Hobson-Jobson* confirms, 'u' is often rendered as 'oo'.

'My family name emerged at the time of my grandfather, who was a judge,' AbdoolKarim explained one day. Most of the male members of his family were called Abdul Something; he was always called Abdool Karim at home to distinguish him from his father. 'This is one reason I never became accustomed to accepting plain

Abdul. Later, as I grew up and became more conscious of the Islamic meaning of the name, I fiercely rejected being called Abdul without Karim, which I took to be offensive.' Interestingly, it was England that provided him with the unexpected opportunity to express this personal predilection. On entering university and opening a bank account he had written AbdoolKarim in his preferred manner, joined as one name. 'In a country without identity cards, and because I took to this practice at the exact moment I was acquiring an official and legal identity, each new registration looked to the last for validation; and AbdoolKarim stuck.'

AbdoolKarim is also rare in being both a Muslim and a fanatic vegan. Muslims, unlike most Hindus, are big on meat. Muslim vegetarians are uncommon; Muslim vegans are exceptional. I had known the vegan AbdoolKarim for years. We met because his father, a respected leader of the Muslim community in Portugal, had a habit of inviting me to conferences – invitations I declined with regularity, citing other commitments. It then fell to AbdoolKarim, an academic at a London university, to chase me until eventually I agreed out of sheer exhaustion. Once, while attending one of his father's conferences in Lisbon, I met his mother. I watched her as she bustled about overseeing the proceedings of the house with a keen, stern eye; she struck me as a typical Asian mother. She spoke to me in Urdu; or rather, she spoke a kind of Urdu I could not pin down. AbdoolKarim explained she was speaking a mixture of Urdu and Gujerati, or rather an Urdu version of Katchi-Memni – the language of the Memon community, Gujerati Muslims noted for a keen sense of business who became a significant presence in East Africa. Yet, equally, it was evident AbdoolKarim's mother was anything but a typical Asian mum. She was, to use her own word, a *gora* – a white woman. I found there were just too many layers of identity, community, cultures, Indian-ness, Asian-ness, African-ness and European-ness at play in his family for me to fathom. In the end, my perplexity led to one of the long, discursive explanations that are an AbdoolKarim speciality.

His maternal grandfather was from Andalusia and born in Seville, but of Catalan parents who had migrated south, for reasons that remained a family mystery but were serious enough to prevent him from returning to Spain for many years. This grandfather moved to Portugal and settled in a small town on the periphery of Lisbon, where AbdoolKarim's mother was born. On his father's side, his paternal grandparents were from Gujerat. The family house was in Vanthali, in Junagadh state, which is also where his paternal grandmother was born. Many Gujeratis from Vanthali, Porbandar and other places migrated to East Africa. His grandfather's older brother made the move first, arriving in Mozambique in the 1890s, where AbdoolKarim's grandfather joined him a few years later. The brothers set up a shop; it became a prestigious department store, the first in Lourenço Marques to have a lift. Although AbdoolKarim's father and his two uncles were born in Mozambique, the family was living in Vanthali in India at the time of Partition. They were forced to flee to Pakistan, where they and most of the extended family settled in Karachi. When, many years later, his grandmother 'returned' home to visit the family, she went back not to Vanthali but to Karachi. Indeed, the family returned to Vanthali for the first time only in 2005.

Nevertheless, AbdoolKarim's father grew up in Mozambique, raised mainly by his mother, his father having died when he was fourteen. This grandmother must have been a very determined and singular woman, for she encouraged her three sons, contrary to the practice of the Memon community at the time and even against family advice, to pursue their schooling. As a colony of backward Salazarist Portugal, Mozambique offered little in the way of higher education, which had to be pursued in the metropolis. So Abdool Magid took the extremely unusual step of going to Portugal to study at the Higher Institute of Economics and Finance. It was there he met his future wife, a fellow student. News of a serious courtship prompted the family matriarch's immediate, unhesitating decision to move to Portugal with her other two sons. Thus, the first Muslim family household was established in Lisbon in the 1960s – the home where Eid (the festival that marks the end of Ramadan) was celebrated by the handful of bachelor students from the colonies living in rooms rented out by widowed ladies, from which they were generally barred access during the day. Lisbon had neither mosque nor imam then, so AbdoolKarim's parents were married in Paris, where his mother became a Muslim. Later the couple returned to Mozambique, where AbdoolKarim was born and partly grew up.

I wondered, did AbdoolKarim think of himself as an Asian? Indian or Pakistani? Portuguese or African or British? 'The only time I've thought of myself as "Asian",' AbdoolKarim told me, 'is when presented with questionnaires that require one to tick ethnicity – though I usually tick both Asian and European. I see myself as beyond and above both, as a new kind of fusion. When I moved from Portugal to Britain in 1979, in the design and technology class of my local comprehensive, taught by the headmaster and attended by most of the school's National Front skinheads, I discovered to my surprise I was a "Paki". My grandmother was a Pakistani-passport holder, something I wasn't even aware of at the time; she herself always, proudly and to me very confusingly, referred to herself as "British India" [sic].'

'The whole of the Raj?'

'Yes, every bit of it! I certainly had no identification of any sort with Pakistan, but in the National Front/Jews/Blacks/Pakis/Indians (the plain natives didn't figure much!) matrix of classroom and playground I soon learnt my place. I never thought of my parents as anything but Portuguese, though, through my father, I also thought of myself as "Indian" and Memon. In the years my grandmother lived with us I had been brought up speaking what I knew only as *pangi-gal* (appropriately enough, literally, 'our language'), my grandparents' Katchi-Memni. Arriving in Portugal in the summer of 1974, following the Revolution in April of that year, I was called a *retornado* [literally, "returnee": strictly speaking the name given to the white settlers from the metropolis and their descendants returning "home", but extended to all those who left the ex-colonies for Portugal in the lead up to decolonization]. During my school days in Britain, I referred to myself as Portuguese; during my university year abroad in California, my accent, to my great surprise and not a little delight, made me "English".'

'OK,' I said. 'You are Asian under duress. But what about Indian? Do you feel and think of yourself as Indian?'

'Of course,' AbdoolKarim replied, throwing his hands in the air. 'We all feel emotionally attached to India – whether we are Pakistani or Bangladeshi, Muslim or not. Before Partition we were all Indians. But I have a problem with being described as Indian.'

I share his problem. In many ways I am deeply Indian. I look like most Indians, speak the language, have a distinguished Indian accent, love Bollywood films, and on occasion think and behave like the characters lampooned in *Goodness Gracious Me*. Indeed, my genealogy is Indian, the culture and civilization I identify with is rooted in India, and, sometimes on weekends, I even dress as an Indian. But I do not see myself as an Indian in the sense of belonging to the nation state called 'India'. India has become one of those generic terms, much like 'curry' or 'Asian' or 'Indian restaurants' – something monolithic and meaningless. It's a label that hides more than it reveals.

We were in agreement: for both of us India is inescapable. Yet it is no simple matter of switching label, from Asian to Indian. No, for us India begs a whole set of questions about meaning. What is India? Whose India are we talking about? When and where is the

India we take as our point of reference? As we talked we began to find multiple overlapping layers in our problems with and answers to India. The India we were searching for, the one we belonged to and could never deny, existed beyond the categories and labels, the twists and turns of historic discourse. It was out there and we had to clamber over all the accumulated rubble of other people's imposed, gerrymandered and reconstructed ideas to find her: our Mother India.

AbdoolKarim was quick to observe that India as a unified, monolithic nation was a British invention. Indeed, the whole concept of Indian nationalism is a legacy of the Raj. The British presence provided the unitary focus around which the conception of India as a nation coalesced. India, having acquired the nationalist itch from its colonial master, could then be denounced for upstart effrontery in pursuing independence. I reminded AbdoolKarim about Fielding, the school principal in E. M. Forster's novel *A Passage to India*. '"She [meaning India],"' Fielding declares, '"whose only peer was the Holy Roman Empire, she shall rank with Guatemala and Belgium perhaps! What an apotheosis!"'

'Yes, exactly the get-out clause Independence provided. The newly independent India immediately became responsible for its own condition, a byword for poverty, as if that had no connection with its colonial past. It was a perfect opportunity for another of the regular and recurrent seismic shifts typical of British attitudes to India,' AbdoolKarim said.

Eventually, we settled on the conclusion that for both us – as for many Pakistanis, Bangladeshis, Sri Lankans and African-Asians – India symbolizes the antithesis of the nation state of India. Our idea of India includes the idea of Pakistan, the notion of Bangladesh, the assumption of Sri Lanka and the sentiments of Nepal and Bhutan. It is not possible to talk about 'India' without reference to the other countries in the region. India cannot even conceive of itself, or even develop a self-definition, without reference to Pakistan – even though that reference is often to an imaginary, fantasized Pakistan. Pakistan returns the courtesy. And Bangladesh and Sri Lanka have to incorporate India and Pakistan, as constructed images or concrete realities, in their own self-definition. The plain fact is that the myths and histories, cultures and traditions, visions and aspirations of these countries are so tied together that it is meaningless not just to talk about one without reference to the others, but even to imagine them as distinctively different nation states.

'Would it not be better,' AbdoolKarim wanted to know, 'if we referred to the region as South Asia and ourselves as South Asians?'

I saw that as an abstruse academic exercise. A new name does not resolve the problem. I hold to the idea of India as a civilization; India in its broadest sense. The problem with all the labels is that they describe closed units, things entire unto themselves and different from all others. The India I identify with as an inescapable part of my belonging is not merely an India of many parts, many differences and many voices. The voices speak to each other; it is a conversation, or some complex orchestral work of themes and sub-themes interwoven into a great idea. My India has porous boundaries, indeed defies our modern conceptions of bounded anything. Its authenticities are multiple and represent numerous multiple selves. This is, after all, how we think of Europe; indeed, it is why so many Europeans deny the possibility, as well as the political project, of creating a single, super-state, federal European Union. 'India' was and is a great deal more varied in its makeup than the diverse national cultures of France and Germany or the English, Greeks and Poles. It is home to such radically different people as Punjabis and Bengalis, Tamils and Rajput.

The best way to understand India is to see it in its glorious, unabashed – often mind-boggling – plurality. It is one of the things I loved about the Indian movies I grew up watching here in Britain, the films of the great era of Indian popular cinema. They eulogize village India, but what they represent as village India is a plurality where difference made no difference. Or perhaps what I mean is that difference was not seen as any kind of impediment – it was part of the landscape, a common feature of coexistence. When thought of, understood and accepted in that way India becomes something infinitely more than a nation state. 'It's exactly what Britain needs to make sense of us as British Asians, a recovery of what we have all lost of our Indian-ness,' AbdoolKarim said.

But our Indian-ness has not been entirely lost. It has been partially transformed and lovingly layered on the landscape of Britain. When those Asians whose multiple identities were rooted in the civilization that was India came to Britain, they found the mother country of the Raj was not quite the place they had been taught to expect. They came to a nation termed the United Kingdom. They dispersed across a realm composed of nations – England, Scotland, Wales and Ireland – each with its own distinctive history and culture. They settled in various parts of a country with strong regional traditions, cross-cut by the complicating factor of class with all that meant for ways of living, expectations of life and even how people spoke the English language. However different 'this earth, this majesty' turned out to be from the image deployed across the Empire, for Asians its real diversity had a homely familiarity. They began their lives anew in many and varied little enclaves and responded to their environment with all the reflexes and instincts of their Indian heritage. Before multiculturalism was devised to accommodate British Asians, they had already incorporated multi-Britain into their multiple layered identities.

This was the theme of a fascinating novel I discovered a few years ago called *Psychoraag*, by Suhayl Saadi. The author's surname, Saadi, paid homage to the pen name of a celebrated thirteenth century Sufi Persian poet. The title *Psychoraag*, a made-up hybrid term, could translate as 'a symphony of the mind' or 'the *raga* of madness'. I took the ambiguity to be deliberate, and a few pages into the novel found my suspicions confirmed. The plot describes the adventures of D. J. Zaf, a presenter at a Scottish Asian radio station. The narrative whirled me through an exploration of identity, history, culture, songs and how they interact in various ways to produce fusion and synthesis. I especially enjoyed the gusto with which the novel used language; it combined standard English with urban Scots patois and Urdu words. It had the feel of the multi-levelled poeticism of Arabic, Farsi and Urdu texts, where a single word can imply twelve different meanings and suggest links with a host of ideas elsewhere in the text. I could detect references to anecdotes from *Gulistan* (*The Rose Garden*) and *Bustan* (*The Fruit Garden*), collections of epigrams by the Persian poet Saadi Shirazi. And in keeping with this Sufi inspiration, the style of the novel sought to propel the reader to a state of *rasa*, the ecstatic experience in which Sufis seek to attain a higher state of knowledge. The reader becomes a *rasiq*, the lover, of the Sufi parlance. And for me, *Psychoraag* opened up new ideas of what it means to be a British Asian. It was not about 'the Scottish Asian experience', as if that were some exotic theme park one could visit.

The book raised a couple of questions in my mind. Was the Scottish Asian experience different from the English Asian experience? And did this lead to a distinct and unique Scottish Asian identity? There was only one way to find out: I had to visit Suhayl Saadi.

An occasion soon presented itself. I was invited to show my BBC film *Battle for Islam* at the first ever festival of Pakistani film, media and arts to be organized outside Pakistan. 'It's all about building links between film-makers in Pakistan and Scotland, and allowing the Pakistani Scots community to see some of the challenging films and documentaries being made in Pakistan,' festival director Alina Mirza told me. Armed with this invitation I sought Suhayl's telephone number through the offices of his publishers and rang him. 'I am coming to Glasgow and would like to meet you,' I said. In reply a rather soft, hesitant voice mumbled. I carried on: 'There's this Pakistani film festival I've been invited to attend . . .'

'Yes, yes,' came the reply. 'I know. My wife is organizing it. I'm the one who's bringing you to Glasgow!' So our connection had been formed before our acquaintance had been made.

Suhayl and Alina were waiting to collect me when I arrived at Glasgow airport. He was suave, slim, clean shaven, sporting a Bruce Willis hairstyle, and looked rather serious. She was petite, wore glasses and bubbled with enthusiasm, an extrovert who talked incessantly. Suhayl tended to the introvert; he paused frequently to think before answering a question. I talked in English to Suhayl and in Urdu to Alina. Soon we were joking, reciting Urdu poetry, enacting scenes from our favourite Pakistani films and discussing our favourite novelists, as if we were long lost friends.

They took me on a circuitous drive around Glasgow to introduce me to the city's Asian communities. Suhayl slipped a CD into the stereo system and the car filled with the sound of the *Enigma Variations*. We drove around Pollokshields, a suburb on the south side of the River Clyde, about two miles from the city centre. It was bustling with halal butchers, women's clothes shops, sweetmeat shops, specialist immigration and asylum lawyers, community centres, Asian jewellers, music and video stores. The names of the shops suggested the area was overwhelmingly Pakistani.

'It's not quite like the ghettos that exist in some cities in England,' I said. 'It looks rather . . .'

'There are many white people living here. Lots of tenements and lots of big, detached mansions. Asians and whites live in both so it's multi-*multi*-cultural,' Alina intervened.

This was the perfect opening to pop my question. 'Is there really such a thing as Scottish Asian-ness?' I enquired casually.

'Yes,' Suhayl replied emphatically. 'There is a distinct Scots Asian identity.'

'What are its main features?'

'Well, for one thing,' Suhayl explained, 'it is a product of the long-standing, unresolved metaphysical relationship of Scotland to colonialism.' Scots have been agents of Empire but they also perceive themselves as oppressed by Empire – which helps leaven imperial triumphalism but contributes to a lack of confidence. Scots also incorporate different ethnicities in their outlook. The west of Scotland has a huge Irish (Catholic and Protestant) influence, and in spite of sectarianism, Suhayl saw this Irish–Scots dynamic as mostly a force for great good. Then there was the strong left-wing tradition in Scotland based on a deep-rooted liberal, dissenting tradition. So dissent and difference are not so unusual in Scotland.

'In most circles of "Middle Scotland" you can openly denigrate the monarchy or throw scorn at such sacred notions as freedom of expression. Try doing that in Middle England!' Suhayl offered by way of example.

'It's very easy to become Scots,' Alina said as Suhayl paused to think again. You only have to wear a kilt, play the bagpipes, join in the Hogmanay celebrations and occasionally have a haggis or two. 'Did you know that Pakistan is one of the biggest manufacturers of bagpipes in the world?' I did not.

'The symbols of Scottish identity are simple and can be inclusive,' Suhayl continued his wife's thought. In contrast, he suggested, Englishness was more diffuse and associated with the privileges of the House of Lords, foxhunting and the exclusiveness of class. 'It's why Asians down south tend to have a problem with seeing themselves as English.' Class is a very different and equivocal thing for Scotland. Communities remember the Highland Clearances and incoming English landowners buying up everything, marginalizing the Scots in their own land. Industrialization built a strong working-class culture. This relationship to England gave rise to different resonances, more potential ways of thinking about migrants, their background and experience, and created more space for Asians to make a place for themselves in Scotland. And anyway, did not the national poet, Robbie Burns, say it all – 'We are bought and sold for English gold' – as well as setting the strongest humanist benchmark for Scots sensibilities: 'A man's a man for a' that'?

From Pollokshields we made our way to Govanhill, which looked even more cosmopolitan, with the visible presence of Africans and other minorities. The atmosphere in Govanhill and Pollokshields seemed not unlike that of Asian areas in London such as Green Street and Kingsbury. All the things that are associated with serving the basic material and celebratory-spiritual needs of the Asian community were there: fruit and veg shops with unruly pavement displays of colourful produce, whiffy halal butchers, fragrant sweetmeat shops, cloth emporiums with ostentatious displays of the latest designs of *shalwar khammez*, spicy takeaways and restaurants, including halal fried-chicken establishments, and the odd shop selling Islamic stuff such as prayer mats and books.

The enigma and variation of our journey was accompanied by the commentary of my guides, explaining the themes, the characters that passed the car windows and their significance. Suhayl wanted me to understand how the relatively small size of the Asian community – there are some 30,000 Asians in Glasgow – while adversely affecting community confidence, had to some extent been a positive factor. In a seaport with such wide-ranging connections as Glasgow, Asians found themselves among a diversity of migrant communities. Over the years, they had had to get on, to help one another out. Early on, many Asians were helped by Jewish people and Irish Catholics – both groups perceiving themselves as underdogs at that time. As a result, inter-communal relations between Muslims, Sikhs and Hindus, as well as Jews and the Irish, were good.

We were entering the Cessnock/Kinning Park area, a poorer and shabbier part of the Southside. It was closer than Pollokshields to the city centre. 'This area is much more solidly Pakistani than Pollokshields,' Alina pointed out. But there seemed to be a cut-off point between Cessnock, with its mixed population, and Ibrox, the home of Rangers football stadium, which was almost entirely white. We passed a gas cooler; Alina pointed towards a police station. 'It's the infamous state-of-the-art station where "terrorist suspects" were held following 9/11,' she said. We drove through Brand Street. 'This is where "failed asylum-seeking families" are taken at the crack of dawn before being deported by way of those dreadful detention centres in Scotland and England. There's been lots of demos at the gates of the Brand Street place,' she said.

Suhayl was still intent on answering my question about the uniqueness of Asian Scots identity. He felt the long-term Labour hegemony in Scottish local government was relevant. This had not always produced benefit. Like any entrenched establishment, it brought the usual problems with corruption and cronyism, but in general over the past four decades, Scotland's electoral politics had moved in marked contrast to England's. It might not be correct to say it had moved to the left, but it was certainly accurate to say the right became increasingly irrelevant. The emergence of the Scottish National Party as a force also changed the political landscape. It was more welcoming of newcomers and its immigration policies provided a better milieu for Asians to feel at home in Scotland. That's why Glasgow has had Asian councillors for decades and also provided the first MP of Pakistani origin – Mohammad Sarwar, elected in 1995 for the constituency of Glasgow Central.

Suhayl and Alina seemed to sense a smirk on my face. 'We are not trying to paint some "How Green is Our Glen" picture of Scotland.' They were offering not an idyll but a portrait fraught with enormous problems. Both were agreed on the source of these problems. 'It's socio-economic in origin,' they said simultaneously. In economic terms, the Asians in Glasgow are at the bottom of the heap. They drive buses and work mostly in the health sector; they suffer from high levels of unemployment and poverty. Racial harassment and violence in the working-class area tends to be related to such issues as housing and council funding. The situation was aggravated further, Alina pointed out, when groups of asylum seekers were simply dumped in tower blocks on estates already housing the most economically deprived members of the most blighted and neglected pre-existing population. In some (white) areas of Glasgow, life expectancy was the same as in war-torn Iraq. The British economic system has been waging war against these Glaswegians for centuries, and then it pits them against another desperate and deprived incoming group and is surprised when a fight develops.

Then, there is the problem of gangs. Asian gangs in Glasgow came to prominence in the early 1990s. It was a response, Suhayl said, to deprivation and racism, a strategy to defend themselves against marauding white racists who arrived from Paisley Road West, tooled up and looking for a fight. The anger of the Asian gangs was directed as much at the white and black gangs as at the police. The high police presence in Shawlands and Pollokshields at weekends, they claimed, resulted in harassment rather than protection. The response of community leaders also came in for strong criticism from Asian youth, who felt no one was listening to them. Many community leaders were too busy with long, protracted fights in Glasgow City Council to pay attention to the needs of the community. As a result spending cuts decimated community amenities, leaving no real facilities for young people and few initiatives to find areas of common interest between white and Asian youth. 'There are also problems within the Asian communities,' Alina suggested. Generational differences led to conflicts between parents and children, and the covering up of abuses such as forced marriage and religious bigotry that forces women, particularly the older generation, to work from home. 'On top of all this,' Suhayl added, 'there's institutional racism and clever, bourgeois racist exclusion, and these are actually very hard to deal with.'

Despite these problems, they insisted, different communities were much more closely knit in Scotland than elsewhere in Britain. 'Communities came together to show their strength. As they did when an Asian woman was raped and murdered by a white youth,' said Alina.

Suhayl added: 'When a white boy was horribly murdered by an Asian youth, the leader of the BNP rushed up to Glasgow to try to stir things up. The murdered boy's mother immediately made a public statement to the effect that her son's death should not be used as a political tool by the far right and the BNP had no place here – an incredibly powerful thing for her to do.'

We drove towards Glasgow University and the affluent West End. The adjacent area of Woodlands seemed very cosmopolitan: the whites and Asians looked comfortably rich. For the first time, I noticed Chinese, Arab and Latin American shops, and a string of rather self-conscious mixed-race couples. As they've become more affluent, Alina and Suhayl explained, some Pakistanis and Indians have moved out to leafy suburbs such as Newton Mearns, Giffnock, Milngavie, often congregating in pockets. This replicates the pattern set by East European Jewish people some decades earlier. Pakistanis account for over fifty per cent of the total minority ethnic population of Scotland (and this includes white minority ethnic groups). Most of those in Glasgow originate from villages around Faisalabad and from villages in Kashmir. Hindus are mostly found in the northern green suburbs of Milngavie and tend to be from more affluent socio-economic groups than Pakistanis or Sikhs. Most Sikhs in Glasgow come from the villages of East Punjab. Despite good community relations there is some subtle but effective exclusion. There is the perception, said Suhayl, that 'power groups' of Indians and patriarchal cliques among all Asian communities discriminate against less powerful South Asians and that 'white people prefer secularized Indians to religiously inclined Pakistanis.'

The particular history and context of Scotland meant many Asians, and the young in particular, feel distinctively Scots. They seem to have more in common, in terms of language, accent, behaviour and outlook, with fellow Scots of the same age and social class than with, say, South Asians living in London. As the generations go on, this effect will probably intensify. 'As a writer,' Suhayl said, 'I've certainly not felt excluded within Scottish literary circles and the Scottish media – quite the opposite, in fact – but by contrast I feel very excluded from the mainstream England-based literary world and the Oxbridge–London nexus at the heart of that world. Many English Asians don't even know there's an Asian Scottish community! It took a white English director, Ken Loach, to gain any exposure in England for the Asian Scots community through his film *Ae Fond Kiss*. To me, at times the border feels like an iron curtain.'

The tour over, my guides took me to their home in Hillhead. 'It was originally owned by the council,' Suhayl explained, 'rented out to senior cops, then sold to a housing association. It slowly fell apart before being bought by builders who did a rather splendid job of renovating it. We bought it from the builders.' I noticed their neighbours came in all the colours of the rainbow. 'This is a cosmopolitan neighbourhood. Our neighbours are German-Polish, Pakistani Christian, Polish-Scots-Vietnamese, as well as white Scots,' Alina clarified.

I made myself comfortable in Suhayl's study. 'Do you,' I asked him, 'think of yourself as Asian?'

'I do not accept the division of the geographical continent of Eurasia into "Europe" and "Asia",' Suhayl shot back. Like most people, he said, his consciousness comprised a swirling mass of inchoate energy, with elements of Asian-ness, European-ness, British-ness, Scottish-ness, Muslim-ness, Pakistani-ness, Afghan-ness, Indian-ness, middle-class-ness, left-wing-ness, artist-ness, physician-ness, twenty-first-century-ness and maleness. 'This is neither evasion nor confusion,' he said. For many people, he thought, this state – he called it 'existential heteroglossia' – was closer to the truth than wrapping a particular flag around one's midriff as though it were a shroud. At its extreme, he argued, there existed the danger that if one relentlessly attempted to pin people down to a single national, ethnic, political or religious identity to the exclusion of all the others, the end product was a golem, a dangerous, dehumanized construct such as Josef Stalin or Osama Bin Laden.

'Where does Afghan-ness feature in your mental makeup?' I couldn't help asking.

'I'm Afghan on my mother's side,' Suhayl replied, and without pausing launched into an explanation of his family history.

His father was a surgeon based in Karachi. Before the partition of India and Pakistan, his father was studying medicine in Lahore. At the time of Partition, he was on a visit to his family in Agra. He became stranded in India, cut off from the rest of the family. He travelled by train amid the blood and slaughter, posing as a Christian named 'John' to evade death and then, injured, walked across the desert into Pakistan, where he completed his course and qualified as a doctor. Most of his family also migrated from Agra to Karachi. His father worked in the refugee camps in Lahore, where he met Suhayl's mother, Afza Sultana, who had also volunteered to help. She was from an aristocratic Afghan background ('Farsi- and not Dari- or Pashto-speaking,' said Suhayl). She was part of the family of the deposed Afghan king who had sought political refuge and was granted land in India in the early nineteenth century in one of the episodes between the

British and Russian empires. His parents' was a love marriage, Suhayl added, supported by all their parents.

Then he said something that totally astonished me; it brought me face to face with my own family history. 'It was the first time anyone in my mother's family had married outside the Afghan Sadozai Durrani clan to which they belonged, the first time anyone had married an Indian. It's all very epic.'

I jolted upright but words failed me. Suhayl did not notice and continued the story. He told me about his maternal grandfather, born in 1900, who was a career soldier: a major and adjutant in the British Indian Army and then in the Pakistani Army. He fought on the Burma Front in the Second World War on behalf of the British. Despite being a soldier, said Suhayl, he was a mild-mannered gentleman who had the title of 'Shahzada' (Prince) and was rich. His real name was Sharyar, but no one except his wife called him that. Everyone else in the family (those younger than him, at any rate) called him 'Agha Jaan'. He died in 1979. There were hints that he was into hermeneutic Sufism in some way and used to perform spiritual experiments of some sort. 'One of my cousins claims he still occasionally talks to Agha Jaan – not in a dream, but when he's wide awake – and he attributes this to spiritualism.'

The more I heard of Suhayl's family history the more astonished I became; there was a remarkable parallel between his and my family background. But I was prepared to hear his full account, less narrated than acted out in appropriate characters as dramatic monologue, before turning the conversation to what had piqued my interest.

Suhayl's drama moved on to his parents. 'They came to the UK on a Peninsular and Oriental cruise liner in 1955 to enable my father to gain postgraduate qualifications.' A neat parallel to all those voyages that took colonial administrators and eager husband-seeking young ladies to India, I thought. His parents lived in Hull for about ten years before moving to Beverly in Yorkshire where

Suhayl was born. 'Of all people, Philip Larkin's home town! I love to say that – I hope the old bugger's spinning in his grave at the thought.' They moved to rainy Glasgow in 1965, following his father's work as a surgeon. Like most Pakistanis of their generation his parents fully intended to return to Pakistan, but ended up not even visiting the country more than twice in thirty years. Pakistan did not turn out, politically or socio-economically, the way so many immigrants had hoped in the 1950s and 60s. 'Gradually my parents let the dream of return slip away.' By 1971, when East Pakistan split from West Pakistan after bloody civil war and became Bangladesh, the dream 'was totally dead.'

They became deeply attached to Scotland even though they were never able truly to straddle both societies. The difficulties in those days must have been enormous. 'My mother was white – as many Afghans and northern Pakistanis are – and dressed in both Asian [saris until the 1971 India–Pakistan War] and Western clothes. In Western clothes she was usually mistaken for continental European.' But Dr Ahmed was darker and so, when they were together, people assumed they were a 'mixed' marriage – which, of course, they were, but not in the way white people thought. 'They got the full gamut of abuse stemming from that. But they protected us from all that, as much as they could, and unlike me, they were never bitter.' Suhayl's mother died in 1999. 'My father,' Suhayl said after a melancholy pause, 'is in happy retirement in suburbia and loves working in the garden . . .'

'And why do you call yourself Saadi?' I asked.

'My mother's family's sub-sub-clan is Sadozai, which is part of the general clan of Durrani. My father's actual tribal name is Saadi. His father, my paternal grandfather, dropped the Saadi bit of the name and kept the bit which was Ahmed. My father doesn't know why. Some of his cousins and their children are still called Saadi. Anyway, I was Ahmed till the mid-1990s. When I started writing I wanted a distinction between my working life as a physician and my persona as a writer. I liked the sound of the name Saadi. Also, there are obvious resonances with Sheikh Saadi of Shiraz, the great medieval Persian poet. Suhayl Saadi is alliterative and mellifluous, much more poetic than Sohail Ahmed, that's much more the name of an Asian doctor.'

'I'll let you in on a little secret,' I said, at last unleashing the information I had been stifling through most of Suhayl's epic. 'I am a Durrani too. What's more, my grandfather was also a career soldier, a lieutenant in the British Indian Army.'

'You don't say!' Suhayl exclaimed. 'We may be related.'

'Steady on!' I replied with a grin.

Like most people, I continued, I have two grandfathers: in Asian parlance a Nana and a Dada, the father of my father. During my childhood in Pakistan, I knew nothing of my Dada. He had died decades before I was born. Moreover, no one ever talked about him. His conspicuous absence from family history was to become as enigmatic as the label Asian; and in the end turned out to be as significant as the lessons I learnt from Nana in shaping my notions of belonging.

'My great, great, great grandfather,' I told Suhayl, 'was an Afghan of the Durrani clan who migrated to India. All of my father's family use the surname Durrani to this day. But my grandfather dropped Durrani in favour of Khan, since we are also Pathans, and part of my family comes from the North West Frontier of Pakistan. My father also added Sardar for reasons that require some explaining.'

'Explain, explain!' Suhayl shouted.

'My grandfather was called Ahmad Ullah Khan,' I began as Suhayl settled back in his chair. Dada died in March 1934, long before my day, in fact when even my father, Salahuddin Khan Sardar, was a mere child. So while he occupied his authentic and proper place in my lineage, Dada was not a presence in my life. My Dada was only a faded image in a tattered old photograph my father brought with him from Pakistan. There, in the photo, he stood tall and proud, gazing confidently at the camera in his full regalia: turban, sword in his left hand and a string of medals on his chest. Dada looked every inch a military man.

My father seldom spoke of his father. It was a silence I hardly noticed for much of my life. As a child in Pakistan I was surrounded by relatives, each with their own character and stories to divert attention from the things I did not know, and about which I felt no need to enquire. With Asian families you know exactly where you stand, each relative has a designation that defines how they relate to you, a father's sister or a mother's brother, and so on. But this punctiliousness does not preclude flexibility. Nana was not my actual Nana, and Dada was not around to be Dada. But in extended families there are always people to take up the slack and fill in for absences. Families are webs of connection, extended families even more so. Extended families are ever present, they envelop you in the busy daily round of constant activity. My father did mention his father was a medical doctor. But the incongruity with the image in the photograph never occurred to me. It never prompted me to ask for clarification.

All I gleaned from the chattering of my ever-present relatives was that Dada had two marriages and seven children. Silence reigned about the three children – two daughters and one son – produced by the first marriage, although they are still around. My father was the eldest of Dada's four children – two sons and two daughters – with his second wife, my Dadi or grandmother, Ahamedi Begum, who was an unmistakable presence in my childhood. A woman of commanding presence and by nature prone to declaiming and pronouncing, Dadi was not the kind to indulge in personal gossip with a mere child. I suppose this must be the reason I can neither remember her telling stories of her husband nor me asking for such stories. I did know Dadi was already a widow when she married Dada, for she had two sons from her previous marriage: Bashir

Ahmad Khan and Sultan Zafar, who is now over ninety years old. My father would have been seven when Dada died. His sisters and brother were even younger. If I ever did stop to think about it, it seemed logical that none of them would really remember much about their father. The only relative who had personal memories of Dada was my *taya*, the elder stepbrother of my father, Sultan Zafar Durrani, a celebrated surgeon, who has never been keen to talk about him.

So my Dada is something of an enigma. The first inkling to his history came in 1970, the year I was naturalized, along with the rest of my family, under the British Nationality Act of 1948 (as amended by section 12 (2) of the 1962 Commonwealth Immigration Act) and 'confirmed' and 'registered' as 'a citizen of the United Kingdom and Colonies'. When the certificates arrived, my father gathered everyone around him and proudly announced that we were now 'genuinely British'. Everyone got to hold and read their certificate, before my father sealed them in an envelope and placed them in 'a very safe place'. (I always assumed this was under his pillow.) I noticed that on my father's certificate he had added a few initials after his own father's name: Ahmad Ullah Khan K.B., S.B., O.B.I., I.O.M. What did these initials mean?

I now know that the initials relate to the institution that was the backbone of British India: the Indian Army. KB stood for Khan Bahadur, a title that went with the award of OBI, the Order of British India. SB signified Sardar Bahadur and was the honorific of a recipient of an IOM, the Indian Order of Merit, a decoration older than the Victoria Cross and awarded in various classes – first, second and third – for valour. It all sounds very *Boys' Own* and, had I thought about it, I might have been stirred to interest in tales of derring-do on faraway battlefields. In fact, I was more fascinated to have resolved how we came to have the family name Sardar, rather than Khan or Durrani like most of our relatives. I was at a seminal moment in the acquisition of identity. Acts of Parliament in the Mother of Parliaments had conferred on me a new status. I had never been troubled by whom or what I was. Now, unlike most people, I had identity officially thrust upon me. At this stage, my surname, the identity marker that Britain so cherishes, was most important for me. It unmistakably represented, as I now appreciated, patrilineal connections of significance. But a settled surname did not remove all ambiguities of identity confronting me. My new nationality came replete with descriptive epithets whose content and meaning was yet to be determined. A neat parallel exists between the flexibility and individual choice Asians apply to their names and the flexible nature of the range of categories on offer for a 'genuinely British' person of my ilk: Paki; Pakistani British; British Pakistani; Muslim Briton; British Muslim; Asian; black.

Amid all the ambiguities to which I was heir the one option I overlooked was the gambit of 'genuine Britishness'. What my father spelt out in the enigmatic initials he wrote on his naturalization certificate was the encrypted key to the code of that most British reflex: deference to hierarchy and status. No institution is more hierarchical than an army. The Indian Army and its predilections created British India – the Raj. Rank, order and precedence were the watchwords by which the British enveloped India ever more firmly in its grasp. And somehow my identity and history had been forged within this web. Ahmad Ullah Khan, my Dada, was given a title of honour in a system of honours, Khan Bahadur. And the system was applicable not just to the army. It spread its silken web across the whole of Indian society to produce grades and ranks of rajas and princes, defined by the decorations and honours showered upon them and the order of precedence in which they were presented at durbars to viceroys and emperors. So compelling was this distracting obsession with rank and precedence that in the scramble for titles and honours the elites of India lost sight of the fact that they had lost power over their own land, lives and destiny.

How wonderfully paradoxical and appropriate that having

constructed an entire world out of rank and precedence over which they ruled mercilessly, the British should blame the stultification and stuffiness of this obsession with hierarchy on the victims, those they had required to abide by such strictures. When the East India Company agents investigated the social system of India their reports made hardly any mention of caste. Historians, in India and the West, now argue that, before British rule, caste was only one among many markers of identity and organizing principles in Indian society. In India's history caste was not fixed but flexible, a variable system of rise and fall according to diverse socio-economic and political shifts. Caste became the pernicious institution we know when it became the central metaphor for all British understanding of India. Indians were given the itch and indulged, beguiled, bought and paid for, and reconstructed by Orientalist scholarship until they could be demonstrated to be backward and unfitted for modernity because of their addiction to caste hierarchy.

'Among the numerous titles my grandfather received was Sardar Bahadur [Brave Leader]. My father adapted the title to name us Sardar, both to honour his father's memory and in deference to British . . .'

'Authority and superiority,' Suhayl noticed my hesitation and completed the sentence.

'Let a polite veil be drawn over the fact that Sardar signified a military commander and in civil terms was applied to a junior class of raja,' I said.

'Only the British could invent and find a role for "a junior class of raja", Suhayl commented shaking his head. 'So how did you feel when you discovered that your surname is a reverential nod to the Empire?'

'There is no need to rub it in, Suhayl,' I said, pointing a finger at him. 'By the time the authorities got round to issuing the piece of paper that confirmed me as "genuinely British" I'd been in Britain long enough to become a child of the times,' I continued.

'The 1960s made it seem as if an age of the world had passed away, that all the class and precedence stuff was old hat, long ago, bygone and best forgotten. So under the pillow went the piece of paper with all those colonial titles. It would be a closed book to me.'

'Except it kept nagging you,' Suhayl shot back

'The question of Dada's identity rested under my pillow for almost two decades. Whenever I tried to engage my father in conversations about Dada, he would change the subject. Then, in the winter of 1991, I bought a copy of *Record Your Own Family History* as a present for him.'

It seemed like a timely present to have selected. The intervening decades had effected a sea change. In youth both as an individual and as regards the Asian community in Britain – the rush had been to get on, to just belong. It was less important to question exactly what you were belonging to than to assert you had an identity and it was British. The intervening years had shown there was nothing straightforward or self-explanatory about the label 'British'. What transpired was a lesson in how tricky a thing is identity. With the passage of time we began to discover the British addiction to hierarchy and class was not a thing of the past. More people of working-class origins were upwardly mobile and had gone to university, for example, but this was a function of the baby boom. The overall structure of society and social class – the proportions – remained stubbornly consistent. The focus on wealth was creating an underclass, or rather pockets of under-classes among which Asian migrants, Pakistanis and especially Bangladeshis, featured as enduringly disadvantaged. Classlessness was becoming a cruel joke visited on the poorest and weakest whose ladder of upward mobility was disappearing as the safety net of social provision was being withdrawn. And Britain just kept coming up with more and more tests about what it meant to be British for people like me to answer.

If the 1960s had been about wiping away the impediments of the past, by the 1990s genealogy had become a popular growth industry. It seemed everyone wanted to know about their ancestors. How else would a book marketed specifically for the purpose of recording family history ever have come into my possession? It was all terribly postmodern – the philosophy of the time. And it was also the entire antithesis of postmodernism. It had a lot to do with history and, especially, the revolution in how history was being taught in schools, I suspect. History from below, the history of the common man, and the fascination with oral history placed a premium on remembrance, on filling in the gaps. It was a product of deconstruction, the process of felling the great narratives that previously explained everything, and it worked by capturing the contingency of millions of individual lives. But the predilections of postmodernism also opened whole new areas of ambiguity. Tracing one's ancestry, for most people, was about placing themselves more firmly in time, standing against all the eclecticism and free-floating happenstance going on around them.

The instinct was to define the lingering call of ancestry, patrimony, heritage and cultural identity. I was British, there was the piece of paper under the pillow. But I was also Muslim and a writer anxious to reinvigorate the meaning and operation of that inescapable identity the better to define the nature of my Britishness. The great lacuna, it transpired, was my Asian-ness, my links with the land where my ancestors were and all that derived and infused my consciousness as a result. It was not idle curiosity that made me choose the present I gave my father. I needed him to remember his father so that I could know myself. By now I, too, was a father. I had to live out complex questions of identity, transmission, heritage and continuity not in myself but for and through what I would pass on to my children. I could not pass on irrevocable silence. If I did not ask the vital questions while I had the chance, while those who were the living links in the chain of my ancestry were still around, would there be any way back for my children? Even if they would inherit a different set of ambiguities and enigmas, I believed they had a right, indeed a positive need, to be connected to a past that, so far as I could see, would always be inherent in their questions of identity.

As we, the Asian community, became more British, more rooted in time and place, here and now in Britain, we also needed to build more barricades against losing touch with where our parents came from. We needed barricades to protect us from the increasing sense of rejection by British society. We needed the bulwark of greater remembrance of origins beyond Britain to explain and understand why the routine patterns of our lives had and should maintain distinct tempos and customs particular to ourselves. And we faced increasingly complex choices about the kind of barricades we erected and what they could or should mean. We wanted to be different, but not to the exclusion of being British. We wanted to be Asian in all the diverse cultural variety that signified. But did we want to be Asian in exclusive compartments and categories? Did we want pure, refined heritages formed of fundamental certainties? What kind of history and attachment to history did we want? We wanted respect for our cultures and religions and space for them to breathe. But part of the recovery process is explaining to our children the expectations of lives that went before them, the ways of life that constructed the customs we want to pass on to them. Without that vital link with real lives, custom has no meaning and therefore no reason to be observed and respected. If we know too little to respect our own culture it becomes impossible to secure the respect we desire from the rest of British society. There are hosts of questions about how to handle our status as migrants. But there is one certainty. If there are no answers about family history there can only be imaginative leaps, and no hope of reforging a connection of any kind for future generations. So my father, whom I called Bawaji (an Urdu honorific for father), simply had to be made to fill in some of the gaps.

What I learnt from Bawaji, I told Suhayl as we turned in for the night, was that my own past was an enigma. I had to resolve it to be true to myself and to discover why I ended up in Britain. But first, I must turn to how I came to be here and my early experiences of life in Britain.

Chapter 4

A HACKNEY ADOLESCENCE

There are as many reasons why Asians are in Britain as there are Asian communities. Each community has its own narrative of migration, its own particular reasons for leaving the subcontinent and making a new home in Britain. Some came to improve their economic lot, some to find better educational opportunities for their children, some to escape persecution; others came to pursue higher education and decided not to return. Beyond communities, individuals too have their own particular reasons for coming to and putting down roots in Britain.

I once asked my life-long friend Rasheed Araeen why he came to Britain. Rasheed is a well-known artist, noted for his pioneering 1989 exhibition at the Hayward Gallery in London, entitled 'The Other Story: Afro-Asian Artists in Post-War Britain'. We were sitting in the office of *Third Text*, a journal of 'Critical Perspectives on Contemporary Art and Culture'. I had been sharing editing duties on the journal with Rasheed for some years. The 'office' was a large room in his house in London's West Hampstead. He had lived in Britain for over forty years; but every Christmas, like clockwork, he went back to Pakistan for a month or two.

Rasheed took off his glasses, pushed the manuscript he was

editing aside, and breathed an inordinately long sigh. 'I came to discover modernity,' he finally answered.

The subcontinent was the home of tradition. The Asians who came to Britain in the 1950s and 60s looked up to Britain as the source of modern culture and education. Doctors and other professionals came to acquire higher qualifications that would be internationally recognized. Those seeking academic careers came to obtain their doctorates. Artists came to these shores to become part of the modern movement and to make a reputation. 'I needed a challenging modern metropolis that would fire my imagination and push it to its full potential,' Rasheed said. In London he found the challenge he needed.

But Rasheed did not discover the kind of modernity he had hoped and longed for. The subcontinent was not entirely devoid of modernity, and had played its part in shaping what we understand as modern culture. In Britain, he was looking for an inclusive idea of modernity, one that includes the art and cultures of Asia and recognizes different beginnings, with a few located in the subcontinent. His life has been one long struggle to redefine an all-encompassing modernity that recognizes black and Asian artists' contribution to modern art. What sustained him in his struggle was the unswerving belief that the significance of one's work in modernism depended on the freedom of one's own imagination rather than on specific cultural roots. Asian artists should not be required, as is often demanded by various arts councils and cultural bodies, to demonstrate their ethnic roots. Ethnicity should not be used to locate them outside modernism.

Others have been more fortunate. Abdus Salam, Pakistan's only Nobel laureate, came to Britain to discover physics and found it. He was born in 1926 in the Punjab village of Jhang; he spoke an earthy rural Punjabi I found hard to decode. He first arrived in Britain to study at Cambridge, then returned to Pakistan to serve as a professor at Punjab University. But Pakistan could not provide an appropriate environment for his intellectual energies. There was no official support, no tradition of postgraduate work, no body of colleagues to consult with, no journals, and no funds to attend conferences. The nearest physicist was in Bombay – by then a city in another country.

During the 1970s and 80s, I got to know Salam well. 'What brought you back to Britain?' I asked him once at his office in Imperial College, where he was appointed professor of theoretical physics in 1957 and where he remained until his death in 1996.

The question brought tears to his eyes, which rolled down his full-bearded face. 'I was totally isolated in Pakistan,' he said, drying his eyes. 'The head of my institution told me to forget about physics. He offered me a choice of three jobs: bursar, warden of a hall of residence or president of the football club.' Later, he wrote movingly of the tragic dilemma he faced: physics or Pakistan. Britain gave him the opportunity to pursue physics, and he went on to make an outstanding contribution to his discipline.

I came to Britain for more humble reasons: I simply accompanied my parents. My father decided to abandon his financial struggle to survive in Pakistan and migrate. By that time we had moved from Bhawalnagar to Sahiwal, known then as Montgomery. The decision was part of a pact with his brother, Rashid Muslaheed Ahmed Khan. I knew this relative only by his nickname, Chunak; to me he was Chunak Chacha, Uncle Chunak. The *chacha* signified he was not just any uncle but the younger brother of my father. Neither brother was doing very well in Pakistan. My father worked as an engineer in a biscuit factory, and things were not nearly as nice as the Nice Biscuits he helped to manufacture. He was a union leader and always getting into some sort of trouble with the management. Chunak Chacha was an unemployed communist who dreamed of proletarian revolution. He was the first to migrate; he chose to go to the United States.

I remember it rained heavily on the day of his departure; it was decided that only my father should accompany his brother to the airport. A taxi arrived. Chunak Chacha hugged every member of the family one by one, and drove off. We never saw him again.

I remember we returned to Sahiwal, and my father announced his decision to leave for England. Why England and not the United States, he did not say. The problems at the biscuit factory had multiplied. He was leading a strike that had been underway for several months. During this time Martial Law had been declared; Field Marshal Ayyub Khan proclaimed himself Chief Martial Law Administrator and President of Pakistan. The army, now in effect the government, had ordered my father to call off the strike or face the consequences. Instead, he chose to buy a one-way ticket to London. It was 1959.

I remember my father wrote weekly letters, though they said very little about London. Occasionally, he would talk about the fog, the double-decker red buses, the wonderful policemen who were always ready to help, and the poor quality of food. Sometimes he would write in glowing terms about the job he was going to get and how good life would then be. He was, during those initial days, always hopeful: the streets of London might not be paved with gold but England would serve him well, the Empire always looked after its sons, particularly those who came to Mother England. Gradually, his letters became gloomier and gloomier: the policemen turned out to be 'quite biased', the job he was going to get never materialized. His qualifications as a mechanical engineer were dismissed as worthless. The letters dried up; they were replaced with parcels.

I remember the excitement I felt when the first parcel arrived. It contained three books, all bearing the legend 'The Great Books of Mankind'. Bawaji enclosed a short note: 'Dear son, I know you will find it difficult to read these books, but do try your best. When you come to London, you will meet my friend Lady Birdwood.' The parcels of books arrived regularly, each with one or two books, each containing a note that outlined the virtues of Lady Birdwood. Who was Lady Birdwood, I wondered? My mother wrote on my behalf to ask. My father would only say: wait till you come to England and meet her. I did learn she had a dog; I took this to be a very good sign. Soon I had an enviable library of books in English: *Black Beauty, Treasure Island, The Secret Garden, The Lost World, Oliver Twist, The Concise Oxford Dictionary* and all sorts of fairy tales. I struggled with them as best I could. Whenever I felt myself floundering, there was always an auntie around to read aloud to me.

I remember my aunt Aisha Puppu, my father's younger (*choti*) sister, trying to read *Pride and Prejudice* to me. The book had an introduction to Jane Austen which she found fascinating. She became absorbed in the details of (dear Aunt Jane) Austen's life, and even more absorbed in comparisons with her own life. 'How wonderful,' she said, 'that the writer's sister, Cassandra, loved her so much – not like *my* sister who dislikes everything I do.'

'So why did she destroy all her letters?' I asked.

'Shut up,' said Choti Puppu, 'and listen.

'How wonderful that she wrote in semi-seclusion and ended up as a timid spinster fearing the ridicule of her family. *I* know *I* too will end up as a spinster living a semi-secluded life.' (Which she did.). Eventually, she got to the novel itself. '"It is a truth universally acknowledged,"' she read, '"that a single man in possession of a good fortune, must be in want of a wife." What *bakwas*!' Choti Puppu exclaimed. 'How can such a wonderful spinster woman write such rubbish? Even in England is there nothing for women to do but become wives? Do we need an English woman to tell us this? Aren't there enough men possessing good fortune running around Pakistan shouting, "I need a wife, I need a wife"?' She chucked the book on the floor. That's about as far as I got with *Pride and Prejudice*.

One day, in the spring of 1960, we learnt it was time for us to join Bawaji. A few months later, we set off from Karachi with a great deal of pride. We arrived in a dark, cold and frosty London, my mother shepherding her three children to a new life in which prejudice was to play a major part. When Asians first arrived in the migratory waves of the 1950s and early 60s, their initial experience was of racism. It amounted to a double whammy. First, we had to contend with the disorientation and displacement of migration. Then, we had to put up with discrimination and bigotry. We arrived here full of love for the home of Empire to face rejection and discover that we were less-than-equal citizens. That experience left an indelible mark on my parents' generation and my own. It is an integral part of our British identity.

My first experience of London, or perhaps the first experience I remember, was looking at snowfall through a window. The winter of 1960–1 was severe. We all lived in a single large room in Evering Road, Clapton. I was entranced by the pure whiteness of snow. How, I wondered as I admired the crystals drifting lazily through the air, could such beauty make landfall as such freezing cold? I had never experienced this kind of cold before: it penetrated my body, clutching for my bones. All we ever needed in Pakistan was a few blankets; during the winter I seldom wore anything more than a *kurta*, the traditional long overshirt. In London I had to wear sweaters, coats, scarves, gloves and a woollen hat. Yet I still shivered. Our small paraffin heater singularly failed to keep us warm enough. I remember my mother's constant worry about the paraffin running out before the weekly arrival of the Esso van. 'Bum, bum, bum, Esso Blue,' I would respond with the catchy refrain from the advertisement.

We didn't have a television, but a Sikh family who lived a few houses down the road did. We would often go to their house in the evening to watch television. The 1960 8th Winter Olympic Games was being held in Squaw Valley, California; we watched the ski-jumping, figure-skating and speed-skiing events in utter amazement. Evidently, for some, winter could be fun; but for me, indeed for the whole family, it was thoroughly miserable. What I missed most was the freedom to run around with nothing on except my *chaadi*. I longed for the smell of the forest, the hustle and bustle of the bazaar, the ability to walk out of the house and lose myself in familiarity. And nothing was more oppressive, more depressing than the darkness, which arrived early in the afternoon and stayed till late in the morning.

Our landlady, a huge, boisterous, Afro-Caribbean woman, was wonderful. She constantly worried about us. She called me 'love'. 'Love,' she would say, 'you could catch your death going out like that.' I was intrigued. How could I be 'love'? And how could one 'catch death'? Initially, I believed her manner of speaking meant I was special to her. But when I noticed she called everyone 'love', the thought disappeared. She knew her room was inadequate for our needs and tried to help my father find more appropriate accommodation.

There was no lack of 'To Let' signs on Evering Road and nearby Kenninghall Road, but they all had an addendum: 'No Coloured Need Apply'. I remember asking my father: 'What is coloured?'

'You need not concern yourself with such matters,' Bawaji replied.

It was our landlady who explained: 'It's us, you and me. We're coloured.'

'But what does it mean – coloured?' I asked.

'Love,' she replied, 'we are not white. White people don't like people like us, from the colonies. They think we smell or something. They're prejudiced against us.'

I still didn't really understand. But I began to notice how, when we encountered white people on the street on our way to visit the Sikh family, they would cross the road. Whenever I went to a local shop to buy something, I was served quickly, ushered out, and told not to come again. Slowly, I began to accumulate the experience that explained what prejudice was. Bawaji kept looking for other accommodation and even went to see some rooms. As soon as he arrived at the doorstep he was told the rooms had already been let. Eventually, after six months of effort, he managed to secure an unfurnished flat at 9 Hillsea Street near Clapton Pond.

It was directly opposite Millfields Primary School. It had two bedrooms, a living room which merged with a tiny kitchen, and an outside toilet. There was also a very small garden. The flat was owned by an elderly Jewish man, who was a philatelist. He managed a minuscule stamp shop on Lower Clapton Road. My parents occupied the front room; my sister, my brother and I slept in the larger back room. At about this time, my father finally gave up his ambition of finding a job as an engineer and started work at the Ford factory in Dagenham. He worked fifty to sixty hours a week; leaving the house early in the morning, at around 6.30, he would return at about eight in the evening. The commuting and hard labour took its toll. He was constantly tired, and we were constantly short of money. His wages just about paid the rent, with little left for basic necessities. So my mother too started work in the Corgi factory, located in the nearby Lea Valley, making match-box cars. She complained continually about how her male colleagues treated her in a degrading manner. But, with the extra income, we were able to buy some furniture, and our own window on the world of Britain – a television.

My mother enrolled her three children into Millfields. However, I don't remember ever actually attending primary school. I developed a strange stomachache. My mother thought it a convenient excuse, a timely device to skip school or indeed evade going outside. The pain persisted. Finally, my father realized something really was wrong. Late one night, as I lay crying in unbearable pain, he went to the local telephone booth and called an ambulance. The hospital informed him my appendix was about to burst. They managed to get me to the operating theatre just in time.

Ten days later, I was back home. This time, minus both appendix and excuse, I would have to cross that road and attend school. Fortunately, though, I was saved. The summer holiday intervened.

The winter of 1962–3 ushered in the Great Freeze. Clapton Pond froze and became a popular venue for ice-skating. Our garden was buried under a foot of snow. Wherever I looked there was ice, frost and snow. Still, I resisted wearing anything other than a light shirt and trousers. Then I noticed I had difficulty walking; like some inept snowman unseasonably caught in a thaw, I felt as though my bones were melting, crumbling under the pressure of my weight. The doctor was called. He diagnosed rheumatic fever and transferred me to Hackney Hospital, then a convalescent home in Broadstairs, Kent.

I returned to London from my convalescence just in time to enrol in a secondary school. Up to now, my life in London had been largely hassle-free, if eventful. I was hardly aware of racism, but, although they seldom talked about it, I could detect that my parents encountered prejudice. Perhaps their silence was a strategy to protect their children. Like so many Asians of my generation I discovered what racism was all about at school. Neither of my parents was able to get time off work to enrol me into a local school. 'Tomorrow,' Bawaji would say. So I took matters into my own hands. There were two options: Hackney Downs School and Brooke House Secondary School. Hackney Downs was a grammar school. I calculated my chance of obtaining admission there was slim to none. So I made my way to Brooke House, explained my desire to become a pupil and asked to see the headmaster.

His name was Mr Harris. He emerged from his office wearing a black gown over his brown suit and tie and holding a large cane. He examined me from head to toe. 'Where are your parents, laddie?' he asked.

'At work,' I replied. 'They can't get time off.'

'So you want to join the school?'

'Yes, sir.'

He gave me a form. 'Get your dad to fill it in,' he said. 'But we don't have to wait for the paperwork. Let's get you started.' Mr Harris explained Brooke House was streamed. Each year had six forms: the most intelligent boys were in the top form, the least intelligent in the bottom form. 'Let's see where you fit in.'

I was given a short 'intelligence test'. I could read and speak English reasonably well, but I couldn't write more than a sentence or so. I found it difficult to answer all the questions. Mr Harris marked my test and announced: 'It's 1.6 for you, laddie.' My heart sank; my face must have expressed the anguish I felt. 'Don't worry,' the headmaster said, 'you will improve.' Then he told me the school had four houses, named after famous British scientists; I was going to join Newton House. My house master was going to be Mr Hobson. Mr Harris checked the timetable: 1.6 was taking maths. 'Today we will let you in as you are,' he said, 'from tomorrow you wear the school uniform.' He asked a prefect to escort me to Mr Pallister's maths class.

I sat at the back of the classroom. Mr Pallister, a large jovial man, was teaching elementary algebra. There was an equation on the board. 'Does anyone know how to solve it?' he asked. A few boys put their hands up, but no one could get it right. Then he asked me. I may not have been able to write English, but I knew my maths. I solved the equation without much problem. Mr Pallister rubbed the blackboard clean; he wrote another more difficult equation. This time I did not wait to be asked. He wrote an even harder equation. The same result. 'See me after the class,' he said.

Mr Pallister was an attentive teacher who cared about his pupils. He adopted me as his 'cause'. 'You're an intelligent chap,' he said, 'and shouldn't be in this form. To move up you'll have to do something about your English.' He handed me a copy of the Bible: 'best book in the English language'. I was set a problem: 'Find the shortest sentence for me.' But I had another problem that required more urgent attention.

The school had a hard core of troublemakers, regular recipients of Mr Harris's cane. The usual suspects inside the school became altogether more sinister outside the school gates. They called themselves 'Black Shirts' and belonged to the Union Movement of Oswald Mosley, modelled on the Italian *Fasci di combattimento*. Of course, I knew nothing of Mosley, the Union Movement or Italian fascists. What I did know was that the walk from school to home resembled a war zone: it was like crossing no-man's-land under a heavy barrage with all incoming firepower aimed directly at me.

I encountered the Black Shirts the moment I left school. They would be standing outside, mainly young men in their twenties, distributing leaflets calling for 'an end to immigration'. They would be joined by boys from the school. Together, they would pick on every black and Asian boy they could lay hands on. It would begin with shouts of 'We don't want you darkies here,' 'Go back where you belong' and 'We don't want your filth here'. Then they would start pushing and shoving. Finally, it would degenerate into punching and kicking. My strategy was simply to run like mad the moment I was outside the school gate. Usually, I managed to escape. But occasionally I was caught and given a good going over. It was not unusual for me to arrive home battered and bruised. I fought back by individually picking out boys from my school. When they were massed in a gang there was little I could do but run, but when I recognized them in the school grounds or the classroom, it was another story. I would simply wait for an opportunity and then attack them. Many of these attacks took place in Mr Pallister's class; his only response was to give 'six of the best' to both boys.

The short daily journey to and from school was even more painful than Mr Pallister's 'bend down and touch your toes' routine. Since I lived only a ten-minute walk from school, I also went home for lunch. With mathematical certainty my encounters with racists doubled. By the time I got to my fourth year, by which time I had made the top form – 4.1 – the Black Shirts had disappeared. Their place was taken by the 'skinheads'. These ultra-nationalists, with cropped hair and army boots, patrolled the length and breadth of Lower Clapton Road, randomly picking on blacks, Jews and Asians. They were not teenagers but young men between twenty and thirty. No matter who they picked on, who they beat up, their game was generically termed 'Paki-bashing'. Their most repeated slogan was 'Pakis out' and 'Deport the Paki bastards'.

In face of this onslaught black and Asian youths joined forces, with the help of a group from *Socialist Worker*, to fight back. There were regular punch-ups around Clapton Pond. The police were frequently called, but I never noticed anyone being arrested or anything actually being done about it. Sometimes I would join in with others of my kind and throw stones at the police in frustration at their inaction. One day I was chased by a group of skinheads and cornered near the shop of our landlord, the Jewish philatelist. I decided to come out fighting. I threw a punch at the first skinhead who approached me. The others set about me, pinning me to the ground, sitting on me, pummelling my stomach and face. One landed a punch of such ferocity he broke my nose. Blood spattered profusely. I was rescued by the timely arrival of the police, who had been called by the elderly Jew. He came out of the shop, wiped my face with his handkerchief, and tried to calm me. The officers simply escorted me back to the house, where my mother washed the wound and put a Band-Aid on my nose. 'The price of being an immigrant,' she said, and left it at that. I still sport the wreckage of my once noble nose.

There was even bigger trouble in the classroom. It came from Mr Brilliant (his real name), the history teacher. He was a big, flamboyant man with hair like Einstein. He thought highly of himself and modelled himself on his idol, the great discoverer of the theory of relativity. But he wasn't very clever; almost every other teacher beat him at chess. Mr Brilliant started by teaching us about the Crusades and regaled us with the adventures of Richard the Lionheart. I had problems with Mr Brilliant's description of 'Saladin'. I pointed out there was no such man; the man he was referring to was actually called Salahuddin Ayubbi, the Muslim general who recaptured (or in my view liberated) Jerusalem, an immensely magnanimous and cultured man, and decidedly someone who deserved detailed attention, not mere dismissal. But Mr Brilliant would have none of it. He told me to stop interrupting. When I refused to stop, I was asked to go and stand outside.

A few weeks later, Mr Brilliant introduced the topic of the 'Indian Mutiny'. This was a subject I knew a great deal about. I protested immediately. 'That was no mutiny,' I shouted, 'it was a struggle for freedom from British domination.' As usual, Mr Brilliant ignored me. He opened the lesson with the European 'discovery' of India and went on to the formation of the East India Company. I started throwing bits of paper at the blackboard. He shouted: 'Behave yourself or it's six of the best for you.' The lesson continued, and Mr Brilliant went on to describe how the Company brought civilization to India. I could not take it any more. I got up, turned my table upside down and threw my texts and exercise books on the floor.

Every child of my generation grew up with the story of the Raj. Our parents and grandparents had lived under colonialism; we learnt about the East India Company sitting on their laps, and it bears little resemblance to the standard version found in British textbooks. I learnt about the Raj through poetry in the company of my grandfather. I was just seven.

Hakim Sahib was passionate about poetry; it was a 'drug' in his medicine cupboard. He would often change the mood of his patients by reciting selected verses from great Urdu poets. He knew whole anthologies of most of the prominent poets by heart. And almost every patient received a parting gift: a couplet specifically selected for them to give hope, make them smile, or force them to think about their lifestyle or face their problems. When we walked to or from the surgery, his index finger firmly in my grip, he would softly sing a poem to himself.

His favourite poet was Bahadur Shah Zafar, the last in the lineage of the Mughal kings of India. Zafar was born in Delhi in 1775, the son of Akbar Shah and his Hindu wife Lalbai. By the time he ascended the throne, in 1837, political power in India was firmly in the hands of the East India Company. Zafar was king in name only; he had little interest in, or indeed ability for, administration. His real passion was poetry. This was the era when Urdu poetry reached its zenith; Zafar patronized and rubbed shoulders with such titans as Mirza Ghalib, Zauk, Momin and Daagh. Urdu is a relatively young language; it first emerged around the fifteenth and sixteenth centuries – about the time English was coalescing as the language of Shakespeare and the King James Bible. It is a fusion of a number of different languages, including Turkish, Arabic, Persian, Hindi and Sanskrit, a product of the eclectic synthesis of Muslim and Hindu cultures. During the Mughal Empire, it was used by courts and courtiers, Sufis and saints, scholars and writers, as well as the common people. By the end of the eighteenth century it had been perfected as the medium of poetry by scores of masters. Surprisingly free from religious dogma, the poetry's deep humanism reflects the contemplative and transcendental mood of the South Asian mind. Early Urdu poetry of the sixteenth and seventeenth centuries found expression in the *ghazal*, love poems usually consisting of seven couplets. Urdu poetry always works on a number of different levels, open to numerous interpretations and a whole range of meanings. Behind the veiled romantic metaphors and the conventions and connotations of *ghazals* there is a deeper philosophical, mystical or political meaning. At the time of Zafar, Urdu poetry was for the first time permeated with patriotic and nationalistic sentiments. British colonialism had spread from Bengal to Oudh and Delhi. A decisive battle was on the horizon.

One day, walking back from the surgery to our house, I heard
Hakim Sahib humming a couplet:

O gazelle, you are witness to the death of Majnoon,
The madman is no more, what now will be the fate of the desert?

'What does it mean?' I asked Nana.

'It is a poem,' he explained, 'about the Battle of Plassey.'

'What was the battle about?'

'It was a battle between the *farangi* and Indian patriots. The
Majnoon, the madman, of the poem is Siraj-ud-Daula, the Nawab
of Bengal. The desert is the country ruined by alien rule.' *Farangi*
is a Persian/Urdu word for 'foreigner', but it is largely used in the
subcontinent, particularly among the elder generations who
remember the Raj, as a general label for the British.

When we got back home, Nana settled in his *charpai*. 'The
farangi came to Hindustan,' he began to explain, 'in the guise of
businessmen. But they were fraudulent and deceitful businessmen.
Their East India Company obtained permission from the Mughal
emperor Jahangir to establish a factory at Surat. Slowly they spread
to Calcutta, Bombay and Madras. They even managed to get the
Emperor to exempt them from paying tax. When Siraj-ud-Daula
became Nawab of Bengal, at the youthful age of twenty-seven, he
decided to contain the influence of the *farangi*. He demanded the
farangi destroy their forts in Calcutta, which were designed to be
used against him. His demand was not heeded so he occupied
Calcutta and Fort William.' When Nana stopped to dry his sweat
with the towel he always carried with him, I noticed all the
youngsters of the family, and a few from the neighbourhood, had
gathered around us. This was a story Nana retold frequently.

'Now the *farangi*,' Nana resumed, 'you must all always
remember, are very deceitful. They lie without compulsion. They
say one thing and do another. Their Company claimed that, after

he occupied Fort William, Siraj-ud-Daula threw 146 of their compatriots into a dungeon where 123 suffocated to death. This they described as the "Black Hole" of Calcutta.' Nana paused and laughed. 'Anyone who has been to Fort William,' he continued, 'knows the dungeon there can hardly hold 50 people, let alone 146. It is probably just a story circulated by the *farangi* to make the Hindustani look cruel and cowardly. And even if it happened, Siraj-ud-Daula had nothing to do with it.'

'What happened next?' asked one of my cousins.

'The forces of Siraj-ud-Daula and the Company confronted each other on 23 June 1757 at Plassey. It is a small village and mango grove between Calcutta and Murshidabad. I visited it during my youth. Siraj-ud-Daula had a considerable force on his side and he should have won the battle. Except the battle was lost even before it started. The Company forces were led by a man called Robert Clive, an incredibly duplicitous and deceitful fellow. He had bribed Mir Jafar, who wanted to become the Nawab himself, and most of Siraj-ud-Daula's soldiers. And the remaining loyal soldiers were unlucky. During the battle a monsoon storm started. When the Indians fired they discovered their gunpowder was wet. But when they charged the *farangi* forces, they were repulsed by heavy fire. The *farangi* had managed to protect their gunpowder. Mir Jafar deserted and joined the Company's forces. Most of Siraj-ud-Daula's soldiers threw away their arms and surrendered prematurely; some even turned their arms on their fellow patriots. The whole battle was finished in a few hours.'

'What happened to Siraj-ud-Daula?'

'He fled but was captured near Bihar, and brutally murdered by Mir Jafar's son Miran.' Nana paused to survey his audience. We were mesmerized. He continued: 'The Battle of Plassey marks the darkest hour of our history. It led to the final collapse of the Mughal Empire. And it gave us the most treacherous name in our history: Mir Jafar. Our beloved poet Allama Mohammad Iqbal has said that

Mir Jafar, along with the traitor Sadiq, who betrayed Tipu Sultan, will be rejected even by hell.'

Nana paused to recite a few verses:

The dwelling-place of spirits excluded from resurrection,
Which even hell disdained to burn,
Wherein reside two ancient demons
Who to save their skin slew the soul of a people.
Jafar of Bengal and Sadiq of Deccan,
A shame to humankind, to religion and to the fatherland.

'What happened next?'

'By winning the Battle of Plassey, Robert Clive gained the title of Lord Clive of Plassey and became the king of Bengal in all but name. Clive had been a thug even from childhood. As a small boy, he ran a protection racket in his village in England. He led a gang of youths who terrorized local shopkeepers into giving them money to prevent them breaking their windows. He continued in the same vein after taking over Bengal, and plundered a rich province, leaving it in a state of utter destitution. He took everything he could from Murshidabad, and in 1765 robbed the *Dewan* (public treasury) of Bengal. During that time Murshidabad was twenty times as rich as London: it took 181 carts for Clive to transport the contents of the looted treasury. Bengal was equal in size to France, and the richest province of the Mughal Empire. All this led to the famous 1769–70 famine in which one third of the province's population perished. The Company imposed heavy taxes on the people. If a peasant could not pay his taxes, or defaulted, his land was possessed by the Company. You can imagine what it did to Bengal.'

'What happened to Clive?' someone asked.

'Clive became a very rich man. None of the traitors of Bengal received what they were promised. But all the wealth Clive accumulated from our country did not bring him satisfaction or happiness. He became an opium addict. His debauched lifestyle led him to contract a horrible disease call syphilis. He died back in England at the age of forty-nine in his toilet. Unable to bear the pain of the disease, he stabbed himself with his own penknife.'

Nana paused. 'What do we learn from this?' he asked the gathering. Without waiting he supplied the answer. '*Haram ki kamaii* [ill-gotten wealth] seldom produces genuine prosperity or makes you happy. It does not have *barakat* [blessings]. And you should never forget that the wealth of England is built on our wealth. They are rich now because they drained us of all our wealth and made us miserably poor.'

Nana sighed. 'Clive was by no means unusual. Most of the Company men were freebooters like him. The War of Independence against British rule started during the time of Bahadur Shah Zafar, in 1857. The British call it the "sepoy mutiny". But a mutiny is a revolt against legitimate rule. The British were always alien oppressors – you can't revolt against dacoits and pirates. Bahadur Shah Zafar became the symbol of resistance to the British and the freedom fighters nominated him their commander-in-chief. Initially, the freedom fighters were quite successful. But Zafar was a poet, not a warrior. Treason and well-organized British forces eventually defeated the freedom fighters. Zafar was arrested at Emperor Humayun's tomb, in Delhi, where he was hiding with his three sons and a grandson. A man called Captain Hodson killed his sons and grandson, and their severed heads were brought before him. For standing up to marauding invaders, the emperor himself was tried for treachery! He was exiled to Rangoon in Burma in 1858 where he lived his last five years. It is in Rangoon that Zafar wrote these immortal lines.' Nana paused for a deep breath, and with tears welling visibly in his eyes, sang:

Hai Kitna Bad Naseeb Zafar Dafn Ke Liye
Do Ghaz Zameen Bhee Na Milee Koo-E-Yaar Mein.
(How unfortunate is Zafar, as he did not even get
two yards for burial, in his homeland.)

One of my more mature cousins joined in:

Na kisii kii aanNkh kaa nuur huu
na kisii ke dil kaa qaraar huu.
Jo kisii ke kaam na aa sakaa
main vo ek musht-e-Gubaar huu.
(I am neither the light of someone's eye
nor the anxiety of someone's heart.
I am like a particle of dust that is of no use to anyone.)

The gathering suddenly transformed. Elders were drawn to join us. And everyone started to recite verses from their favourite poets. Poetry was being used to preserve and refresh memory, as well as being used to show off one's knowledge of Urdu literature. One of my younger aunts began with a celebrated poem by Mirza Ghalib, 'the father of Urdu poetry', who witnessed the 1857 defeats:

Surely today every English Tommy considers himself God.
Everyone going from his house to the bazaar is struck with panic.
The market place looks like a slaughterhouse,
And the houses look like prisons.
As if every particle of dust in Delhi
Thirsts for the blood of the Muslims.

The events of 1857 were as deeply etched on the minds of Nana's many relatives as they were on the Delhi poets who witnessed them first hand. Almost every major poet wrote about the fall of Delhi, the forced exile of Bahadur Shah Zafar to

Rangoon, the spirit of the freedom fighter and the general behaviour of the British troops. A disciple of Ghalib, Tafazzul Hussain Khan Kaukab, compiled an anthology of twenty-seven such poems – *The Lamentations of Delhi*. Nana kept a copy by his pillow; and many of the women in the household had memorized, and frequently recited, the anthology in total. But to quote an all-too-familiar verse was unimpressive in what had swiftly become an open competition. To impress, one had to stick to the theme but quote poets from beyond the Delhi circle.

An elder aunt came in with a *Qatah*, a poem composed of four short lines. It was Iqbal's comment on the 1919 massacre of the Jallianwala Bagh in Amritsar:

> *To every visitor, the dust-particle of this garden declares:*
> *Beware of the treachery of the times*
> *The seed (of freedom) here was sown with martyr's blood*
> *Which you must now nurture with your tears.*

Nana immediately picked up the reference and provided the historic detail. 'You should know, children, that the massacre at Amritsar happened a few days after the end of the First World War. A *farangi* woman, who had come to India to spread Christianity, claimed she was molested by an Indian. The local Company commander, Brigadier General Reginald Dyer, issued an order: as a punishment for this insult to the *farangi* woman, all Indian residents of the city were required to crawl the length and breadth of the street where the alleged incident had happened. Moreover, any Indian who came within a few feet of a British policeman was to be whipped in public. Not surprisingly, the native people of Amritsar protested about these absurd and barbaric measures. It was the day of Baisakhi – 13 April. On this day, the Sikhs celebrate the birthday of Guru Gobind Singh, the tenth in the line of Sikh Gurus, who founded the Sikh brotherhood in 1699. In the city's

Jallianwala Bagh, which was more like a public square than a garden, a crowd of about 10,000 men, women and children was listening peacefully to speeches and testimonies when Dyer appeared leading a contingent of British troops. He ordered fifty soldiers to fire into the unsuspecting gathering. The shooting continued for over fifteen minutes; in all some 1,650 rounds of ammunition were fired into an innocent, peaceful, unarmed civilian crowd, who ran screaming in all directions. The British killed 379 people, and wounded over 1,000. So much for Western civilization.'

The poetry contest continued for quite some time. Slowly the younger members of the household fell asleep where they were sitting. One by one, they were picked up and placed in their proper beds. But the elder members of the family continued. The gathering dispersed only when Nani – sitting diametrically opposite Nana, on her own *charpai* – recited the concluding verse. It was from a poem by Josh Malihabadi (1898–1982), written when independence was not too far off:

The prison is under attack and the shouts of victory rent the sky
The prisoners at last have risen in revolt and are shattering the
   chains.

I knew most of these poems by heart. Perhaps it has something to do with the fact that Urdu poetry is specifically written to be recited aloud and easily memorized. These history lessons in verse remained deeply etched in my mind. There was no way I would put up with Mr Brilliant's version of history.

Indeed, I had had enough – both of being a regular punch-bag for racist bullies and thugs and of Mr Brilliant and his 'history'. For his next lesson, I came prepared. He continued with the theme of the 'British Empire' – 'half the map of the world was once coloured red', he proudly told his class. He described the achievements of Clive and went on to compare them with the 'savage behaviour' of 'Indian leaders such as Tipu Sultan'. I immediately shouted, 'Clive was a scoundrel, a duplicitous and deceitful fellow; if there's a barbarian, it is him,' echoing the words of Hakim Sahib. Mr Brilliant jumped up. 'Right,' he said, 'you are out of the class, but first you need a jolly good thrashing.' Before he could lay hold of me I grabbed as many textbooks as I could, piled them on my desk, calmly took a match from my pocket, and ignited a funeral pyre on the table. Mr Brilliant went berserk. Other teachers came running to the class. Soon, the headmaster arrived. 'This is criminal behaviour,' Mr Brilliant told Mr Harris. 'Police have to be called in.'

Mr Harris took me to his office. As soon as I entered, I unbuckled my trousers and touched my toes. 'No need for that,' he said to my surprise. He sat on his chair, rubbing his face with his palms, deep in thought, while I stood in front of him. Eventually, he said: 'What's the problem, laddie?'

For the first time it dawned on me that it hurt Mr Harris to cane his pupils. Despite his tough exterior and his frequent resort to the cane, he was a decent, gentle man. He might have been a bit old fashioned, but he cared about his school, of which he was very proud, and loved his pupils. The realization prompted an explanation: Mr Brilliant, I contended, was teaching a nonsensical distortion of history. And I began to pour out the rest of my troubles: almost every day I was attacked by racist thugs on my journey home. He listened patiently, although I am not sure he understood all I had to say. He was well aware of the skinhead problem, he said, and would try harder to do something about it. As for the problem of history, he decided to resolve it by absenting me from Mr Brilliant's clutches; I would be switched to geography.

Mr Harris lived up to his promise. Now I had time to devote to other things. In the fourth form I had made two very good friends: Abe Jacobs, a liberal Jew distinguished by his curly hair and suave style; and tall and round Anthony Smith, an Anglican with 'brainy' spectacles. We were the 'Chemistry-Physics-and-Maths' brigade.

Among ourselves we formed a more extensive Judeo-Christian-Islamic alliance. What cemented our friendship was more than science, swottery or trendy stylistic embellishments. We shared a common passion, the temper of our times. We were unhappy about the state of society, dissenting and dissatisfied. In particular, all three of us were concerned about racial prejudice, about what Smith called 'the exploitation of the working classes', and the war in Vietnam. We were a band of brothers, true to the inheritance of the place where we lived, the latest incarnation of the spirit of the East End, the latest in the long line of fusion and synthesis by which, down the centuries, new immigrants had mixed with earlier waves of newcomers and locals and found common cause in the shared hardships of their lives and in dreams of bettering their fate. Even the racial prejudice we so objected to had serially been targeted at each new group as it arrived. The East End had always been a school of hard knocks where the struggle to thrive had nurtured radical outlooks, fiery orators passionate in the causes of political reform and social change. The detail of such history was absent from Mr Brilliant's educational repertoire. I was unaware of the Indians or Asians or even 'Pakis' who had pioneered this course before my time; that would come later. My participation in our common cause was taught by and learnt from the fabric of our lives, acquired across the differences of our origins and backgrounds; it was the education of the place that was our home.

About this time, my family found itself caught up in a new whirl of migration. We were relocated from Hillsea Street to our first council flat on the nineteenth floor of Seaton Point. It was one of six new tower blocks specially built as part of the regeneration of the old East End. By now we were sufficiently seasoned migrants not to expect the rosy glow of high hopes to deliver all their promise. Our new Elysium had two particular problems. The lifts were frequently out of order; we often had to climb endless flights of stairs to get to our flat. And the tower blocks were built without any consideration for aerodynamics: they generated their own distinctive whirling wind, frequently hitting hurricane level. Young, fit and able, I could cope with the buffeting. But for many pensioners, relocated from the familiar – if dilapidated – street-level living, it was nothing short of a nightmare. Climbing those stairs if you were over seventy? Forget it! It was not uncommon to find an old person immobilized with terror before an inoperative lift, or stationary by the main entrance, hopeless and defeated in a way no Blitz had ever made them, pondering just how they might make the few yards to the main road without being blown away. Many old people simply refused to leave their flats. A group of younger Seaton Point residents took it upon themselves to shop on behalf of elderly neighbours. I was entrusted with a more delicate task. It became my duty to check whether any of the elderly residents had lost any of their laundry, which had a habit of detaching itself from clothes-lines and taking flight at the behest of passing gusts of wind. Retrieving the clothes deposited higgledy-piggledy when they fell to earth was the easy bit; ascertaining their rightful owner was a diplomatic minefield.

I was acquiring a community as I was securing friends. One elderly gentleman reminded me of my grandfather. He had fought in two world wars and I often spent Sunday evenings listening to his stories, just as I had listened to Hakim Sahib. Normality, as I had known it, was reasserting itself. Soon, I acquired a whole extended family by adopting whoever happened to be resident where I lived. There ought to be old people to populate one's environment, they ought to be respected and assisted. How could they be abandoned to their fate? How could their stories be forgotten, their need for ease and comfort be so thoughtlessly neglected? It was an affront to my Asian values. But I discovered one did not need to be Asian to be angry. I was not alone. The plight of the elderly in Seaton Point prompted the establishment of Hackney Citizens' Rights. I campaigned with them for the rights of the old age pensioners, and I was occasionally required to manage a stall in Ridley Road market, where we distributed leaflets and got passers-by to sign petitions.

The Judeo-Christian-Islamic Alliance found many good reasons to rage against society, but we had no idea how to channel our rage. We wanted to build an alternative society. It was a natural, organic response for us to latch onto the 'alternative movement', the beat generation, the marchers to Aldermaston, who supplanted the Teddy boys. I remember our excitement when Smith (somehow we never called him Anthony, certainly not Tony) secured a copy of *Playboy* (September 1966), which contained an interview with Timothy Leary, the guru of the alternative movement. 'When this man "turns on",' we read, 'he sees the horror of his mind reflected in his surroundings. If he "tunes in" he begins to change his movements and his surroundings so that they become more in harmony with his internal beauty. If everyone in London were to "turn on" and "tune in" grass would grow on the Strand and tieless, shoeless divinities would dance down the car-less streets. This will happen within twenty-five years. Deer will graze down Charing Cross Road.' All three of us identified with this vision, although none was too keen on Leary's suggestion that the only way to 'tune in' was to experiment with LSD.

However, there were other elements of 'tuning in' that appealed to us. We learnt about these from a variety of alternative magazines then widely available: *IT* (allegedly it stood for 'International Times'), which promoted an anarchist version of liberal socialism and was edited by the anarchist Mick Farren; *The Red Mole*, edited by the rising Trotskyite star Tariq Ali, an unabashed revolutionary; and *Oz*, which encouraged sexual anarchy and was edited by the Australian radical Richard Neville. *Oz* was actually published from Kingsland Road, not too far from our school. We elicited three propositions from the alternative movement. First, property had no exclusive ownership. Everything belongs to everyone and is there to be shared. We believed in this, and would have shared everything with each other if we actually had anything to share. Second, work *per se* was not necessarily a good thing. It is not work, in and of itself, that is important, but rather achieving personal fulfilment, which can be done in many ways. We were heavily into fulfilment – our dilemma was an inability to find any means to fulfil ourselves. Third, sex in all shapes and forms is good. It should be based on the spontaneous and sincere impulses and mutual consent of two people – third parties ought not to be offended or suffer damage. Unfortunately, there was not much sex to be had at Brooke House. The only girls we knew were from Our Lady's Convent and they were not at all forthcoming. Indeed, all they wanted to do was to beat us at almost everything. With sex and sharing compromised, the only alternative the alternative movement left us with was finding fulfilment. We found it on the cricket pitch and in the debating chamber. The three of us became the school debating team and travelled all over London, in the company of Mr Pallister, debating with other schools, and went on to bring a few trophies for the school. When we were not debating, we were playing cricket, for the school, for Hackney – and here too we scored a few successes.

Our quest for alternative fulfilment, our obsession with debating and cricket, had a serious effect on our studies. Our academic achievements were not as stunning as they could be. Nevertheless, they were sufficient to allow us to join what seemed like the swelling ranks of working class students taking up places at university. Abe Jacobs went to the University of Kent in Canterbury to study mathematics. Anthony Smith went to a university in the north of England to pursue a degree in chemistry. Mr Clarke, my physics teacher, persuaded me to read physics – 'If you can do physics, you can do anything, Zardar,' he said. Family finances limited my choice, so I went to the nearby City University.

Soon afterwards, Mr Harris retired. A few years later, Brooke House School, where over half the pupils were eligible for free school meals and half did not have English as their first language, was declared the worst school in England and closed. The building became the Community College of Hackney, a general further education college; that too closed after failing several inspections. In September 2002, Brooke House Sixth Form College was opened on the site. Brooke House could be closed, reinvented, redeveloped and serially condemned as a failure, yet that tells you nothing of what it meant to those it educated. Was it the school that failed? Or was it a convenient scapegoat for a society that failed to resolve how it wanted to deal with, or what it wanted to make of, people like me? Mr Brilliant was at the incendiary heart of my problem with education, and the problem was not mine alone. But neither the teacher nor the school were the source of the problem, and it could not be solved by redefining or sweeping away Brooke House. In the same way, the school did not create the Black Shirts or skinheads who bedevilled the lives of so many of its students – those who did the beating as much as those who received it.

Brooke House opened me to all life had to offer. It was the portal through which I entered upon my life as a British Asian. I owe an immense debt to the essential humane goodness and professional dedication of so many of those who taught there. Yet it is not sufficient to say: 'If it was good enough for me, it'll do for everyone.' Education is not solely a matter of what you are taught; it is about what you learn and how what you learn prepares you to cope with life, the life that will come after schooling. I learnt, or, rather, became aware of, two things by the time I left Brooke House. First, things must change. Forget tilting at windmills of the Brooke House kind. The real challenge was identifying what had to change and how such change could be effected. Second, I had at least two different selves: one that lived in and was shaped by Britain, and the one I had brought with me from Pakistan. Were they destined to live in two distinct worlds? Could they be synthesized? Learning to cope with multiple selves became the quest of my adult life, as it is for many other British Asians.

Chapter 5

HOME AND AWAY

The British Asian experience has always had two basic components. The British component is rooted firmly in the United Kingdom; the Asian component always harks back to the subcontinent. Even Asians born here have deep connections with the subcontinent: family ties, emotional pull, a genealogy that cannot be ignored and a heritage they often return to unearth. For a majority, as for my family, a return to the subcontinent became obligatory once a home away from home had been created in Britain.

We lived in Britain, but our address changed regularly. Our family moved along to accommodate the consequences of migration, buffeted by change in our struggle to thrive. My sister, brother and I grew up. We were not the people we would have been had we remained in Pakistan. But Pakistan was recreated in our home. Our home was a haven of familiarity shaped by all that my parents considered valuable and enduring. Our shelves were crowded with books in Urdu: novels, poetry and works on Islam. Every other Saturday, we held a *mushaira* – a poetry recital. Friends of my father would gather to read their latest compositions and participate in poetry contests, reminiscent of the poetry gatherings I witnessed in Hakim Sahib's house in Bhawalnagar.

Virtually everything we wore inside the house was sewn by my mother. Almost every month, a door-to-door salesman would arrive loaded with colourful fabrics. My mother would spend hours sifting through them, selecting those she wanted to buy, and then negotiating the price. She made *shalwar kameez* for herself and my sister, and *kurta pajama* for the male members of the household. Most of these were simple everyday wear, but sometimes she would make elaborate dresses, lavishly embroidered, for special occasions.

In time, each of us found interests beyond the confines of our home. My father became active in a Muslim welfare organization; my mother was addicted to her weekly excursions to the cinema. There she would meet her female friends, all kinds of Indians who like her were in search of the familiar. The comfort of a weekly gossip provided their relief and cohesion. Then they would give themselves over to the heaving seas of emotion that are Hindi/Urdu movies, cry buckets and emerge invigorated. Mumsey would return home with songs and poetic images alive in her head to be shared with her household – whether they were receptive or not. I did not receive my education only at Brooke House School. I did not become myself only through what I learnt outside of each address we called home. As people we were always more than Britain made of us, not least because no matter where we moved the letters from Pakistan would always find us.

Whatever we became in our lives in Britain it was never just a little nuclear family, isolated in a myriad of other nuclear units. Our family extended. There were the relatives who also migrated and came to rest in Manchester. There were the friends and acquaintances who became honorary family members, because that is the instinctive metaphor on which Asian existence is founded. And by means of those letters we maintained our connection to the lives of those we left behind in Pakistan. News of their doings, the children born, the marriages made, the exams passed and jobs secured came closely compressed via airmail. Much of the news from abroad became a blur of household background noise to us growing adolescents. We were preoccupied with discovering the limits beyond which no family tentacle could reach. But to my parents the letters were a lifeline, as vital a part of their continued existence as securing a copy of the weekly *Mushriq*, the Urdu-language newspaper they devoured from cover to cover. The letters and newspaper and all the other familiarities they could acquire in Britain made up for their absence from the lives they had lived in the place that in its emotional pull was still their real home.

Meanwhile, India, Pakistan and later Bangladesh were being recreated in Britain itself. In London, Southall became a little Sikh Punjabi village before my eyes. Tower Hamlets acquired the basic characteristics of a Bangladeshi town. While these 'ethnic' urban landscapes provided homely comforts for Asians, they also generated fear and apprehension in the population at large. Without doubt, it was Bradford that came to personify the sum of all fears, source of all stereotypes, location of all anguish, and hotbed of all problems. Yet, as a British Asian myself I know virtually nothing of Bradford – and so say many of us. Growing up in Hackney meant that I too was a product of that quintessential British phenomenon: the North–South divide. What discussion of British life, from house prices to historic voting patterns, is not constructed along this seminal bifurcation? Except of course, discussions of anything to do with British Asians; where all else is at least bifurcated, we are uniform.

My ignorance of Bradford became all too evident when I met Javed Bashir, a man who not only grew up in Bradford but, for me at least, personified the city itself. He was a well-built, elegantly dressed man approaching forty, with a round face, a neatly trimmed beard, and deep-set, soulful eyes. The beard told me a great deal about him. It was not a regulation 'Islamic beard', which requires the absence of a moustache. Javed had a neat, trimmed moustache that effortlessly followed the contours of his upper lip and joined his beard, like two tributaries merging into an ocean. Here was a man, I thought, religiously pious but also worldly wise, one who liked to follow tradition but was not tied obsessively to custom. He described himself as an 'Achievement Coordinator' working for Bradford Education. Recently, he had been appointed a visiting fellow of the University of Bradford; and he had stood for election to the council in Keighley, a neighbouring town within the conurbation covered by the Bradford Metropolitan Council. When he invited me to Bradford, I jumped at the opportunity.

Bradford is home to around 85,000 British Asians; there are 5,000 Hindus, and as many Sikhs, but the bulk of Asians, 75,000, are of Pakistani origins. The most interesting thing about Bradford is that its British Pakistani population comes predominantly from a single area in Azad Kashmir: Mirpur. The district of Mirpur, which is divided into three subdivisions – Mirpur, Chaksawariand and Dadiyal – is so small that it is hard to find on most atlases. It has a total area of under 400 square miles, with a population estimated in 1999 to be less than half a million.

Javed took me to Keighley, home to around 10,000 Pakistanis. We drove around the town and it became obvious the community was congregated in a couple of well-defined areas. Row upon row of terraced houses, some recently sand blasted, conjured a bleak atmosphere. Boys played football in the street; old men chatted on street corners; women fully covered in variations of traditional dress walked hurriedly to their destinations. *Coronation Street*-style back-to-backs were joined together by washing lines, recently laundered garments billowing gently in the breeze. I got out of the car to explore the area on foot. Within minutes, all eyes were focused on me. I could sense an air of resentment and hostility at my presence. A boy came running. 'What are you doing here?' he demanded. 'Get lost!' Javed explained that almost everyone in Keighley belongs to the same *biradari*, or clan. 'They're not just from Mirpur, but all from villages within three miles of each other.' And they don't like strangers.

Most of the Mirpuris in Bradford arrived in the 1960s. There was one major reason for their migration: the Mangla Dam. The twelfth largest dam in the world, it was constructed in 1967 across the Jhelum River, about 60 miles southeast of Islamabad, the capital of Pakistan. As a result, the whole of the ancient historical town of Mirpur and over 400 surrounding villages were submerged. Many of those displaced ended up in Bradford, where a process of chain migration had been in place for over a decade. The early migrants, explained Javed, were mostly males who worked long hours on night shifts and sacrificed all comforts, even neglecting their health, with the aim of building a house in Mirpur and returning one day to their families. The dam drowned the dream. So they brought to Bradford not just their families but also displaced members of their clan and villages. Now one of the largest Kashmiri communities outside Kashmir lives in Bradford.

The Mirpuris were forced to abandon the idea of eventually returning to Pakistan because what they had left behind had disappeared. So they tried to recreate the spirit of their villages in Bradford. The initial flow of immigration had consisted primarily of single men. Their common experiences of displacement and at work meant that distinctions of region and sect, which cross-cut even the small area of Pakistan they came from, were less important than mutual support and collective survival. The mosques they initially established in Bradford, for example, tended to cater for all Muslim sects. Soon, an infrastructure of local shops and restaurants developed to look after other community needs such as halal meat, traditional garments and textiles, Indian films and music and Mirpuri cuisine. A small network of *hakims* and *pirs* (spiritual guides) also emerged to help with the health needs of the community and to provide non-Western therapies. These first Kashmiri migrants came to be known as 'pioneers', and initiated the subsequent chain migration from Azad Kashmir. (The word 'Azad' means free and is used by Pakistan to described the region of Kashmir it administers; India, with its own interpretation of history, sees the region as 'Pakistan-occupied Kashmir'.) When, over time, these single men were joined first by members of their immediate families, then by their extended families and villages, internal religious and ethnic boundaries came to the fore. The arrival of immigrants from other parts of Pakistan, from the Punjab and North West Frontier, further strengthened sectarian divisions. Mosques changed their ecumenical character and became sect-based. Contemporary Bradford is thus home to distinctive Pakistani communities located in specific areas across the city. The best indicator of this variation is language: in different parts of the city, one can hear Mirpuri, Punjabi, Pothwaari and Pushto. Bradford has also acquired the architectural iconography of Islam. A string of mosques, all built in the traditional style, criss-crosses the entire city.

The Mirpuris could not return to what they had left behind. But for other Asians, the option of returning to the subcontinent was real. The generation who came to Britain between 1950 and 1970 as economic migrants always intended to go back. It was all part of the tradition, of considerable historic ancestry in parts of the subcontinent, of sending one family member away, elsewhere across India or even abroad, to find work to supplement the income of the extended family. As Muhammad Anwar outlined in his seminal 1979 book *The Myth of Return: Pakistanis in Britain*, they saw their stay in Britain as transient rather than permanent. Migration was to be an interlude, a stage they would survive sustained by the promise of return. In the long term, one day, it would be possible. In the meantime there were better things to spend their hard-earned resources on, such as ensuring the best possible start in life for their children, and saving to build a property in the subcontinent. Indeed, some actually returned – only to turn back again. Those who returned found it difficult to adjust to the life of the subcontinent and made a beeline back to Britain. The more life was lived in Britain, the more ties to and engagement with Britain – despite the caveats – bound them to it. Gradually, it dawned on the majority of British Asians that the dream of return was a myth. We were here to stay.

The tradition of regular visits to the subcontinent, begun in the mid-1970s, has continued ever since. Asians on the whole do not go 'on holiday': they go 'back' for 'a visit' almost every year. And they go for a number of reasons: to check on their extended families, to find spouses for their children, to emphasize their cultural roots to the new generations. What they find when they return, and what they often bring back with them, depends on their particular cultural roots and family backgrounds. The Bradford Mirpuris, for example, visit Pakistan regularly to enhance their links to their clans (*biradari*), and bring a fortified version of the norms and values of their *biradari* back to Bradford.

Both caste and *biradari* have been embedded in Indian society for thousands of years. The word 'caste', however, is not indigenous to India; it derives from the Portuguese word '*casta*', which means race, breed or lineage. It was one of the central enigmas Europe wrestled with in trying to make sense of India. The East India Company, as a commercial concern, needed to understand the law to work out how to get the best rate of return from the lands they ruled. It was fascinated with the complex profusion that was and is India. The British turned to old texts to unlock India's secrets. In the code of Manu, regarded by early Orientalist scholars as the most authoritative ancient legal code, they found the Hindu concept of four *varnas*. *Varna* is not quite the equivalent of caste, as it signifies 'kind'. To English minds it seemed like an ideal, simple structure into which to fit all the unwieldy impossibilities they described as caste. The four *varnas* are *Brahmin, kshariya, vaishya* and *shudra*, with *dalits* variously being seen either as the lowest group of *shudra* or completely outside the caste system altogether. *Varna* is infused with notions of purity – a highly complex and multifaceted religious concept – and also associated with social roles and occupations. So *Brahmins* are priests and academics; *kshatriya* rulers and military; *vaishya* farmers, landlords, merchants and artisans; *shudra* labourers, peasants, servants and workers in 'non-polluting' occupations; while *dalits* are those whose occupations are 'polluting'.

In a way, the idea of caste appealed to the Victorian mind. Some who studied village India idealized it, and the place of caste within it, because it chimed with their worldview: everyone in their place and a place for everyone, all overlaid with a sense of deference analogous to British class and aristocratic reflexes. The concept's appeal was malleable: it could even be eulogized as a kind of idyllic village soviet. Ideally, caste is an endogamous group: one marries within the caste one is born into; it ascribes one's profession in life, which is fixed and given. It also operates as a system of social distance, reflecting ideas of purity, which finds expression in groups that do or do not eat together. Caste was implicated in British minds as a central cause of the great trauma, the Indian Mutiny of 1857. And it was also the bête noire of Christian missionaries, who were convinced it was the great impediment to conversion and consequently loathed it. So, on the one hand, it was too sensitive and impossible a political reality to tamper with, and on the other, it was an immovable sign of the stultification and arrested development that explained the backwardness of India.

The trouble was, however, that the profusion of what the British identified as caste did not easily or neatly fit into this structure. There were thousands of what came to be termed subcastes with regional and occupational distinctions often jostling and disputing their place in what the British were certain was a fixed, ossified hierarchy. The more British scholarship and administration became fixated on caste, the more Indians came to know themselves through the prism of Orientalism and the usages constructed by colonialism. A whole diversity of Indian responses to and understandings of caste developed; a for and against that ranged from defence of pure tradition which must be retained at all costs through to rejection of the abuses, oppression and misconstructions that made caste what it was not and should never have been: absolute and fixed. After Independence, in 1949, India outlawed discrimination on the basis of caste. It introduced affirmative action based on quotas to ensure educational and employment opportunity for caste groups historically seen as disadvantaged. But caste, in good and bad aspects, remains a fact of life in India.

Even though Islam rejects the concept of caste and insists everyone is born equal, many Muslims in India, particularly the descendants of converts from Hinduism, retained some notions of the caste system. It is one of the ways Indian Islam demonstrates its connection to the subcontinent, and it transcends the national divisions of India, Pakistan and Bangladesh.

Biradari is an amalgam of the idea of caste and the clan or tribe. It defines people as members of a group, usually genealogically connected with strong blood ties, that originates from a specific area. Where caste is concerned about purity of blood, *biradari* operates on the basis of an honour code: maintaining the honour of the *biradari* is paramount. In this it is just like the system that operated in Mediterranean societies, and indeed still seems to linger in places such as Sicily. Honour translates into a code of practice based on retribution: an eye for an eye, a tooth for a tooth, a rape for a rape, a murder for a murder. Women, in the *biradari* system, are cherished property; they represent the epitome of honour. By standing against the *biradari*, breaking its rules or leaving it altogether, a woman dishonours the *biradari*. Women have to be guarded at all times if their honour is not to be compromised. As the embodiment of the group's honour, women become the medium of compensation for crimes against another *biradari*. The exchange of women in marriage becomes the means of settling disputes that otherwise would become ongoing blood feuds.

As Javed explained the background, I noted he could not hide the repulsion he felt at the *biradari* system. In Pakistan, he said, bowing his head as though carrying the shame of the entire country, *biradari* customs force parents of girls as young as five or six to offer them as compensation for a relative's crimes, such as murder. The girls are given to assuage the anger of the injured parties under a package deal known as *vani* or *swara*. While the formal laws in Pakistan do not condone these practices, the courts do little to address the problem. He cited the famous case of June 2002 when six girls from a Punjab village, all below the age of puberty, were given in marriage to another clan. Their 'wedding' was performed instantly and 'verbally' by the local mullah. The girls' mother appealed successfully to President Pervez Musharraf and the Chief Justice of Pakistan to have her daughters freed from *vani*. Javed also described the even more notorious case of Mukhtaran Mai.

Mukhtaran belonged to the Tatla clan. Her brother was accused of raping a girl from the rival Mastoi clan. The accusation was later proved to be false, but this did not stop the Mastoi clan from abducting and brutally sodomizing him. Their honour was still not satisfied and Mukhtaran's family proposed to settle the matter: her brother would be married to the girl he had allegedly raped, Mukhtaran herself would be married to one of the Mastoi men, and, if her brother was found guilty, they would also give some land in compensation. The Mostoi rejected this proposal. Instead, they demanded rape for rape as the only means of restoring honour. Mukhtaran was kidnapped by Mastoi men and gang raped. Mukhtaran's family were reluctant to file charges but were eventually persuaded to do so. The story became headline news in Pakistan and attracted much international attention. Eventually, the six guilty men were tried and sentenced. Mukhtaran became a symbol of women's rights in Pakistan and received a financial settlement from the government with which she built two schools in her village. *Time* magazine included her in its 2006 'most influential people in the world' list.

All this happened in the remote, dark corners of Pakistan. Surely this sort of thing does not happen in Bradford? 'In Bradford,' Javed said, 'the *biradari* system is not visible in normal life. But it is in evidence when it comes to choosing a marriage partner, providing a helping hand at functions such as weddings, death, supporting other *biradari* members at times of crisis or family feuds, and rallying support during elections for the council, community centres and places of worship.' During elections people feel obliged to vote for someone within their own *biradari*. Ability, policies or party affiliation are irrelevant; what matters is the *biradari* the candidate represents. All members of the *biradari* vote for him; and if their numbers are large enough, they carry the election. This is how 'Asian votes' are delivered in bulk during general elections.

Another product of the *biradari* system is honour killings. Central to the notion of honour killing, Javed explained, is the idea that only death can clean a stain and recover the lost or compromised honour of the *biradari*. He cited the 1998 case of Rukhsana Naz. She had been forcibly married to a relative in Pakistan and had two children from this marriage. She left her husband in Pakistan and returned to the Midlands, where she reconnected with an old boyfriend. She was seven months pregnant when she was brutally murdered by her mother and her brother. While the mother held her down, her brother wrapped a plastic flex around her neck and strangled her. When her younger brother tried to intervene, the mother told him: 'Be strong, son.' The family dumped her body a hundred miles from their home. 'Honour killings,' Javed said with a deep sigh, 'do occur with regularity.'

Like the Mirpuris in Bradford, the bulk of the people who came to the Midlands and the towns across the north of England from Pakistan during the 1950s and 60s came through the *biradari* system. 'It was the bond of the *biradari* that determined who the early immigrants invited to join them. They helped them to find employment and accommodation, and provided financial assistance as well as assistance with social and welfare problems,' Javed explained. The end result was that certain *biradaris* became predominant in certain localities. When textbooks speak of chain migration, the link in the chain was *biradari*. *Biradari* provided its own social security network for the first generation to arrive in Britain, the support system that eased their transition into the very different circumstances of British life. Thus the positive aspects of the *biradari* retained real meaning in radically new circumstances for this older generation. It bound them more firmly to tradition, rather than lessening its hold. This tradition clearly comes with consequences. It is not only the charitable solidarity that was revitalized in different circumstances, but the pernicious and inhumane aspects too.

Thankfully, tradition does not exist in splendid isolation and change is afoot. It is frequently challenged by modern practices, a challenge that often leads to creative synthesis in Britain as well as on the subcontinent. Young British Asians are always reinventing tradition, infusing it with modern spirit, developing an amalgam that tries to incorporate the best of both worlds. When they succeed, they manage to change things while remaining true to the positive spirit of tradition. The whole issue of arranged marriages has itself been slowly transformed as a result of the never-ending tension between tradition and modernity.

When I met Javed again, on one of my numerous visits to Bradford, he invited me to join him for a gathering of Pakistani families. 'Meet me at the Banquet Hall of the Bradford Hilton, at six,' he said. 'We're expecting a large crowd.' I arrived exactly on time to find I was the only person in the hotel lobby: no crowd, no crush of bodies jostling for the best seats. Eventually, Javed turned up. 'Asian time,' he said.

Slowly, the crowd materialized, and the long, undistinguished, rectangular banquet hall began to fill. Ostentatiously dressed women – gold jewellery in full display – led their children, three or four boys and girls per gaggle, young men and women all resplendently turned out. Dilatory fathers straggled behind acknowledging acquaintances, making brief side excursions to talk before being recalled to the business of settling the family group in pride of place. Wherever Asian families gather – in each other's homes, in mosques and temples, at the numerous *melas* (the word literally means 'getting together', but in the British context has come to mean a celebratory festival incorporating subcontinental and British Asian music, food and fashion) that have become a regular feature of most cities in Britain, the topic of marriage is ever present. Mothers – the all-seeing, all-dominating 'Maa' of Bollywood movies – keenly eye potential brides and grooms for their children, and the children themselves cleverly manipulate their parents in the direction of their desires. Young men, in total violation of tradition, were eagerly – but respectfully – eyeing young girls; young girls were openly gawking and laughing at young men. 'Look around the hall,' Javed said, 'and you will quickly establish one thing.' I surveyed the hall. It seemed evident to me the girls were not only better dressed than the boys, they also appeared to be more confident and more assertive. 'On the whole they are much better educated,' Javed said.

This was no ordinary gathering – I was in for a musical extravaganza. It was billed as 'Abrar-ul-Haq Night, with Omar Sharif'. Abrar-ul-Haq is one of the hottest stars of Pakistani music; he made his name with his debut album, *Billo Day Ghar* (*In the House of Billo*). Omar Sharif – not *that* Omar Sharif – is a comedian as well as an actor and film-maker, known for his sharp, caustic tongue.

The purpose of this function was more than mere entertainment. Abrar-ul-Haq was on a mission: this was a fund-raising event on behalf of his organization, SAHARA for Life, SAHARA being an abbreviation for Services Aimed at Health and Awakening in Rural Areas. The singer, in keeping with the fashionable trend among celebrities in Pakistan, had established a hospital in Narowal, a small town in a remote area of the country. Such projects are almost exclusively funded by donations from British Asians. The most famous institution to emerge with the help of British Pakistanis is undoubtedly Shaukat Khanum Memorial Hospital and Research Centre in Lahore, established by Imran Khan, the legendary Pakistani cricketer and politician. Tonight Abrar ul-Haq was seeking funds to equip his hospital with the latest medical technology.

We had taken our seats, in splendid isolation, at a round table. Gradually we were joined by guests Javed had invited. I sat next to Laiqa Khan, a senior lecturer at Bradford College, a boisterous woman in her forties, whose large features were framed by streaming black shoulder-length hair. Farzana Ahmad, sitting to my left, was an outgoing young professional in her late twenties. Born in Bradford to Mirpuri parents, she worked as finance manager at a Catholic school. 'My Nana joined the British Army,' she said, 'and all the family followed him to Bradford.' She knew nothing of Pakistan. 'Only been there once for a three-week holiday. But I've been brought up as a Pakistani. I am a pukka British Pakistani.' With her straight, classical nose, bright brown eyes, pencil sharp eyebrows and generous lips she reminded me of a young Greek beauty I once adored. But whereas that erstwhile belle had been short and podgy, Farzana was tall and gracefully slim. She wore a band round her neck, long dangling earrings, and her shiny black hair draped around her bosom. 'The perfect girl to fall in love with!' I couldn't help saying.

'No chance of that,' Farzana shot back. 'I'm going to have an arranged marriage; my husband can fall in love with me afterwards!'

'Don't you think arranged marriages are oppressive for women?' I asked.

Farzana gave me an incredulous look: surely, it said, someone like you should be able to differentiate between arranged and forced marriage. 'It is,' she replied, 'if you think marriage itself is a form of female bondage.'

Not to be disconcerted, I started again: 'Why does someone who learnt to speak English before she could speak a word of Urdu or Punjabi want to have an arranged marriage?'

'Because I don't want to humiliate myself by dancing to the tune of the dating game.' What kind of a liberation is it, Farzana enquired, if women are expected to parade themselves around a disco for the sole purpose of being propositioned by any man who fancies his chances? And it neither begins nor ends there. Because the cultural convention itself is oppressive. However much women are supposed to be free, everywhere they are in chains to the same underlying message: dress, dye your hair, make up your face, buy the right perfume, and most of all be shapely, diet yourself to misery or starve yourself to death in a land of abundance and plenty, and all because this is necessary to get a man. And without a man, implicitly, no woman is a real woman. It is a recipe for insecurity. It is inherently demeaning not just to the intelligence but to the self respect of any sensible woman. People talk as if arranged marriages put women at a disadvantage and make them commodities to be shunted around. 'On the contrary,' Farzana insisted, 'the commodification of women is to be found in the idealized commercial standards of acceptable womanhood, the ever-changing, money-spinning fashions, fads and fanciful nonsense that reduces them to objects in a system of barter – bartering for self-worth. This public, open auction for social respect is the dilemma facing Western women. All the talk of feminism, liberation and the like has done nothing to enhance or change the dynamic. In many ways, it's made things worse. Women are expected to be superwomen, with careers, disposable income to spend on all the lifestyle dos and don'ts – and all it amounts to is the imperative to catch a man. And the ideal woman, the woman all women are encouraged to aspire to be, is bright, intelligent, beautiful, groomed from head to toe and svelte – look at all the models in the magazines. And it's not just their impossible, unwomanly shapes women have to contend with; clothes are actually designed and made for such impossible shapes as well. But ultimately they have to be sufficiently dim-witted not to notice they are still being offered nothing more than the ethic of the cattle market. Those who refuse to conform are frumps, dowdies, unchic, unhip, not the kind of person anyone wants to spend time with. It should give any sensible, intelligent woman the shivers. It's degrading and bruising to self-esteem.' Farzana paused, broke a small piece of *roti*, spooned on some chicken curry, and gracefully placed it in her mouth. 'Besides, I am too busy to waste my time on that sort of thing.'

'But how can you allow your parents to choose who you should marry?' I asked.

'Well, they'll choose and they will not choose,' she responded smartly and thoughtfully.

'How come?'

'The final choice of who I'll marry is totally up to me. They'll suggest potential partners. There'll be some mutual negotiations. They'll hope I agree with their choice; I'll hope they agree with my choice.'

Javed, who was listening attentively, intervened. 'But your parents are not going to let you marry outside the *biradari*.'

'No, they won't,' Farzana replied.

'So, in addition to an arrangement, your marriage will also have certain restrictions,' I said.

'Well, my parents are from Mirpur, right? Mirpuris like to keep things within the *biradari*. But I'm not going to have a *mangi* marriage.'

'*Mangi*?' I was out of my depth here. I looked at Javed.

'The local lingo for imported brides and grooms,' Javed explained. In a *mangi* marriage the British party is sent back to Pakistan to marry someone the parents have chosen from their clan, he explained.

'I'm going to marry someone here, born and bred in Britain like me,' Farzana asserted.

'Provided he's a Mirpuri,' I added. Farzana, I thought, was clearly a very strong young woman who could stand up to her parents. But not all Asian women can.

'We must remember the boundary between arranged and forced marriage is rather diffuse,' Liaqa said. She had supervised countless projects on arranged marriages at her college, all undertaken by eager young British Pakistani women, keen to learn and enhance life-giving tradition and to break the bonds of oppressive customs. 'Gentle persuasion often turns into unbearable persistence and, in the end, into outright force. The force can be a direct order from parents, a threat that unless the parties comply they will be shunned by their families, or the family will lose its honour. It's always emotional blackmail but it can be far worse.' When marriage is seen as a good system for bringing nephews and nieces to Britain, force comes into play. The *biradari* system is particularly prone to the use of force. It's the elders who often decide, basing their decision on honour and caste and clan. 'The bulk of our community is deeply conservative and tribal. Parental pressure is often too great for our young people to cope with,' said Laiqa.

'But the elders are constantly and consistently being challenged by young people,' Javed intervened. He thought Farzana was not an exception; in fact, she represented an emerging norm. 'Surprisingly,' he said, 'it's the women who put up the most resistance; men, on the other hand, give in to the demands of *biradari* more easily.'

We paused for a while to listen to the music. I took the opportunity to take a quick poll: everyone at our table was strongly for arranged marriage. But why?

Farzana sat next to a graceful, beaming middle-aged woman in an elegant white *shalwar kameez* adorned with a polka dot *duppata* (the long, trailing scarf-cum-shawl, sometimes called the 'cloth of modesty'). She handed me her card. I read: 'Nadira Mirza, Deputy Dean, Head of Academic Programmes, School of Life-Long Education and Development, University of Bradford'. 'We have a different approach to the whole question of relationships,' Nadira Mirza pointed out.

I asked: did she have an arranged marriage? Yes and no, she replied. 'I met my husband at a Sufi gathering; then we got our families to arrange the marriage.' This has also become rather common among British Asians: you find your future spouse yourself and then get your parents to 'arrange' the marriage.

The whole notion of relationships in Western society, Nadira said, is angst-ridden. 'The *goras* are so obsessed with relationships.' I was surprised Nadira used the word '*gora*', for she was a little *gora* herself: her mother was white, she had told me, although she grew up in Pakistan.

'I mean they get indoctrinated with this obsession from an early age. Five- and six-year-olds going to school parties and dances already alive to the imperative of having a boyfriend or girlfriend. They get socialized to the idea that not just living but your human and social worth, your standing in the eyes of your peers, includes the necessity of having a date, a lover, a partner, a cohabitee, or whatever the current catchphrase is.'

'But people need relationships,' I said.

'Yes,' Nadira replied. 'But what is being perpetuated is the idea that relationships are hell – by definition.' She launched into a forensic dissection of contemporary culture drawing on the underlying themes of television programmes such as *Sex and the City*, *Will and Grace* and *Friends*. She paused to judge the reaction around the table before offering her analysis. If relationships are hell, she argued, and everything seems to reinforce this message, then all relationships become conditional. What they are conditioned by and on is not impinging on personal self-fulfilment. They must never constrain personal freedom and the ultimate objective and quest of modern life: pleasure. Relationships must generate as much pleasure as possible, without any concomitant, uncool drags such as compromise, ties, responsibilities or the most uncool thing of all: obligations. The perfect, ideal relationship is one that enables both parties to just go on being single, but in company. 'A relationship cannot be based on being held, especially not being held back, so perhaps it is also not about holding on.' Being clingy, Nadira argued, is somehow conceived to be anathema to good relationships. Cohabitation without marriage then turns out to be just as brittle as the marriage vows most people try to avoid making. And generally, exponentially, cosmically, relationship angst goes on and on getting worse.

'But that's the human condition,' said a young journalist who was sitting next to Farzana. Miran Rahman, a recent Cambridge graduate, was from Guernsey. His father was what subcontinentals term 'Anglo Bengali' (in other words, his grandmother was white) and his mother was from Bangladesh. He had just got a job as a reporter on the *Keighley News*.

'No,' replied Nadira. 'This angst-ridden condition is not generically human at all.' It is a specific product, manufactured, devised and distributed in Britain, North America, Australia and such places. It is a brand-name product dispensed as consumer choice. It is the consumer choice of Western society, and its brand name is being modern. 'Asians, on the whole, don't buy into this and don't think so.' A quick glance around the table revealed heads nodding in agreement.

'But all of us, whatever our origins, have to find a partner, a companion, a helpmate, someone who cares about us, someone we can spend our life with,' Miran offered plaintively.

'This is a universal problem,' Nadira allowed before picking up steam again. But there are different ways of solving this all too human problem. The Asian way is to put your trust in the concerned interest of family and friends. Letting them scour the candidates cuts through a great deal of the embarrassment. On your behalf they organize meetings with potential suitors. None of that solo trawling of singles bars Farzana had alluded to, in the hope lightning will strike, or the ordeal of anonymous parties attended mostly by people with whom one devoutly prays never to be trapped on a desert island. An arranged marriage skips the endless cases of mistaken identity: she thought he was a prince and he turned out to be a toad; he thought she was a nice girl and she turned out to be a shrew. In contrast, in an arrangement, concerned people ask: knowing him, knowing her, are they likely to get along? Will their temperaments be suited? Are they the right combination for the ambitions of both parties? Such questions are for the long term, posed by people who know you intimately, because they are your background. And these matchmakers will be part of your life as a couple for the rest of your lives; you won't suffer the consequences alone.

I was surprised to discover there were two distinct varieties of British Pakistanis in Bradford, offering negative and positive images of British Asian futures. There were those, such as the people I encountered in Keighley, who clung to tradition at all costs and recreated their tribal structure and attitudes in their new home, including suspicion of strangers. Such pernicious obligations have no place either here or back 'home' in Pakistan. Theirs is, of course, the mentality of 'little England'; Britain ought to recognize how its own history of suspicion of foreigners and difference has echoes in the attitudes of other people. But Bradford also contains the voices of those reinventing tradition to suit the circumstances of their lives in Britain, such as my dinner companions at the musical extravaganza. Just as Hakim Sahib argued, they too seemed to accept that it is never enough simply to invoke tradition; one always has to be open-minded and critical about the meaning and substance it contains.

Traditional, modern, British, Pakistani, young, not so young – everyone around our dinner table in Bradford was an amalgam of multiple identities. British Asians exist in different worlds, each with its own distinctive worldview. Not everyone can cope with multiple identities easily. But those who can often turn their multiple selves to advantage: each identity is brought to the fore when and where needed, and when necessary more than one identity is projected to accomplish certain goals, or simply to confound the world. While the gathering in Bradford played creatively with their traditional selves, everyone strictly subscribed to one traditional dogma, as I discovered. No sex before marriage.

This puritan attitude to sex is, of course, connected to the traditional idea of honour; and a woman's honour, as Javed pointed out, has to be guarded at all costs. But hasn't modernity made some inroads here too? I put this question to my friend Amitava Kumar, who teaches English at the University of Florida. Amitava personifies the new breed of globalized Asians who travel, effortlessly and often, between India, Pakistan, Britain and the US, and who try to synthesize tradition and modernity while enjoying breaking the boundaries of both. I first discovered him through his book *Passport Photos*, in which he uses the metaphor of the passport to analyse the condition of Asian immigrants in Britain and America. In *Bombay–London–New York*, he outlines how Asians have turned these three cities into one continuum and how this continuum has influenced some of the most celebrated writers of the subcontinent, as well as British Indian and British Pakistani novelists. But his most illuminating book is *Husband of a Fanatic*, a 'personal journey through India, Pakistan, Love and Hate', in which he describes how he, an Indian Hindu, a Bihari from Patna, came to marry his wife Mona Ahmad Ali, a Muslim born in Pakistan. He lives in and in-between the three-city continuum he so affectionately describes.

'Sex? Just what is *that*?' Amitava replied in playful mood. 'Asians don't do sex,' he said emphatically. When it comes to sex, tradition stands unchallenged. There is no tradition of sex education in Asian homes and it is also conspicuously absent from the curriculum of schools in the subcontinent. Until recently, Bollywood films were a kissing-free zone. Ordinary, respectful 'Diaspora Asians', Amitava explained, of all religions, traditions and classes, like their counterparts in South Asia, do not believe that sex exists, or should exist, before or outside marriage. 'It's as simple as that.' And, on the whole, Amitava said, 'We walk our talk, give or take a few renegades!' And the renegades are not treated kindly even by liberal parents.

A slim, graceful man, Amitava has a film-star quality to him. In particular, he reminded me of my favourite Bollywood actor, Dilip Kumar, the Laurence Olivier of Indian cinema, as someone once described him. Amitava walked into my attic, my reading and writing paradise, looking like Dilip Kumar in swashbuckling *Aan*, complete with earring, but mercifully without the sword. I looked and remarked: 'what's with the earring?'

'Sir,' he replied (actually, he said '*Janab*', a polite and respectful Urdu term for addressing elders), 'on the day I defended my dissertation, an American friend of mine, a Jewish woman, took me out for a drink. She said I should get a tattoo. At the very least, she said, I ought to get my ear pierced. I liked the idea. I wasn't used to anything like this back home. Indian males didn't adorn their bodies, at least not the ones I was around. In fact, people didn't meddle with their bodies, unless someone died; then, you were forced to shave your head. I liked the irresponsibility of getting my ear pierced. Actually, I'd already done something somewhat irresponsible. In Bihar, you'll find that young Hindu males wear moustaches. They shave their moustache only when their father passes away. I shaved my moustache while my father was still alive. I felt guilty but also liberated. Then came the day when I got my ear pierced. When I went back home afterwards, my parents were, I think, more shocked about my lost moustache than the earring.'

Amitava, it seemed to me, thrived on multiple identities. But was he at ease with them? 'There is a part of me that belongs to small-town India,' he said. But he has been living in Britain and the US for decades. 'In cities like London or New York, I might recall my other Indian self. I use it like a shield sometimes. The truth is that when I'm back in India, in places like Patna or Puna, I find life claustrophobic and stifling. I wouldn't be able to last there for any substantial period of time.' This was a sentiment I had heard expressed many times before. There is little cultural or literary life, even in some of the major cities of the subcontinent; it is difficult for urbanized, literate British Asians to cope with such absences. 'My nostalgia is for something that doesn't exist,' Amitava said. He harks back to a tradition that has all but ossified. 'My life in the West hasn't really made me any more suitable for anything here, either,' he lamented. 'I go to parties sometimes where most of the people are Indians or Pakistanis who were born here, and my accent and my clothes suggest I don't belong in these gatherings. The Indians I know are far more immersed in the culture here. The Pakistanis tend to be far more traditional. I think that's great – but I can't relate to that either.' A natural problem for a globalized Asian, I suggested: 'If you belong everywhere it's difficult to fit in somewhere.' He laughed and fiddled with his earring.

We talked about what it means to be 'Diaspora Asians'. 'The past and its terrors,' said Amitava, 'matters much more to diasporic communities than the chaotic present. It is in the nature of being a displaced people.'

I had a problem with being seen as part of a diasporic community. The word 'diaspora', from the Greek, means to disperse. Originally the term referred to the dispersion of the Jews, from the Babylonian exile of the sixth century BC onwards, and is applied to all Jewish communities scattered 'in exile' outside Israel. The academic use of the term changed its meaning to include dispersion of any people, voluntarily or by force, from their homeland. So now we speak of a Palestinian diaspora, an Armenian diaspora and diasporas of migrants, expatriates, refugees, guest workers and exiles. The fact of displacement and the possibility of returning home are central to the notion of diaspora. But I never felt displaced, even though I was a migrant; I am at home in Britain, even if my belonging is under question. 'The Asians in Britain do not think they are in exile,' I told Amitava.

'Granted,' Amitava replied. 'But certain aspects of diasporic communities do apply to them.' There is, Amitava pointed out, more contact between Indians and Pakistanis in Britain than back on the subcontinent. Young Asians, for example, do not subscribe to the geographical boundaries constructed in South Asia; they are not hidebound by its nationalisms but mix freely and develop all types of friendship. People from totally different backgrounds but the same region, indeed the same city, who would never meet in India, come together in Britain. An upper-class woman in Calcutta, educated in a convent school, who spent most of her time at the club, would seldom see, let alone meet, an uneducated, untouchable woman who had never eaten at a table or sat on a toilet. In Britain, such differences become irrelevant. If they ended up as neighbours, they would be in and out of each other's house every day. 'Social and national realities in South Asia can be papered over and subsumed by the conditions in the new country,' Amitava said.

In this landscape of new interactions and relationships, the idea of 'home' acquires a new meaning. 'When does a new location become home?' Amitava asked. There is a difference, he argued, in feeling at home in a place and staking a claim to that place as one's home. 'The Asians may feel at home in Britain, but social exclusion and racism undermines their claim that Britain is their home.' A Punjabi woman may feel more at home in London than in Lahore or Amritsar, but she may insist on defining herself as Pakistani or Indian to affirm her identity, particularly if she feels it is being denigrated and placed outside 'Britishness'. Under these circumstances, it is not the subcontinent that is seen as home, but its history and tradition become the focus of a desire for an abstract idea of home.

'It is my belief that for the *desis* the diasporic condition turns the soft emotion of nostalgia into the hard emotion of fundamentalism,' Amitava asserted. The term *desi* literally means a person from the countryside or rural area. It has been adopted as a self-description by South Asians in the West and is applied to all British or American South Asians, thus deliberately avoiding any reference to country of origin, ethnicity, or allusion to caste or *biradari*. It implies and confers a broader, common identity. *Desis* retreat into a fixed notion of history and identity – an imaginary construct of their lost abode – to confirm their identity in their new home. This is why, Amitava pointed out, all varieties of fundamentalism – Islamic, Hindu, traditional, ethnic – have become entrenched in Britain. Being a diaspora turns out to be a paradoxical condition: on one hand it provides opportunities for the Asian minorities to transcend their national, regional, ethnic and caste differences; on the other, it forces certain segments of these communities to entrench themselves in imagined certainties. Forced marriages, Amitava suggested, are a form of fundamentalism; their main function is to maintain the internal boundaries of family, caste and *biradari*.

'But tradition can also be used in its soft forms both to enhance identity and to lay claim to a new place as home,' I said.

'Granted,' Amitava replied. This is exactly what is happening among middle-class British Asians. The *desis* are reinventing arranged marriage in a new form to reconnect with their traditions and to define a new British Asian identity. Amitava's travels and research suggested that arranged marriage has made a strong comeback in the last years of the old millennium and the beginning of the twenty-first century. 'It is really fashionable now for *desis* living in the West to go in for arranged marriages again,' he said.

'Of course,' Amitava continued, 'we can't do anything whole-heartedly. *Yahan pe sab kuch adha-adha. Adha doodh, aadha paani.* [With us, everything is half-half; half milk, half water.] So, parents and other relatives fix your marriage, and then, in the weeks and months leading up to the wedding ceremony, you fall in love with your betrothed. It is being called "arranged-cum-love-marriage".' And the younger generations use all the modern means available, from speed-dating to internet sites, to arrange their marriages. The opportunities to meet and develop friendships across conventional national, regional and ethnic boundaries mean mixed marriages are becoming less unusual. Amitava himself had a cross-cultural marriage.

'How did you end up marrying a Muslim?' I asked.

His wife was born in Karachi, Amitava explained. They met in New York, where they were attending different universities. 'It would have been impossible for us to have met in our respective countries,' Amitava noted. Theirs was a relationship particular to the diaspora. They got married when India and Pakistan were at war high up in the Kashmiri mountains of Kargil. He was immediately put on the blacklist of an extremist Hindu organization. In the days after the wedding, which took place in 1999, he received calls from journalists who wanted to know whether he and his wife had battles over Kashmir. They didn't. 'But how do you tell a journalist my wife and I fought over many small, stupid things. We didn't know whether we should keep the futon in the living room or just throw it out. We had a fight. These battles escalated and threatened peace. But of course this had nothing to do with politics in the subcontinent, or even politics *per se*. It had to do with two people.' He paused to think. 'When I was courting Mona, I remember writing a poem for her . . .'

'No doubt – a bad one,' I interrupted. Amitava ignored me and continued.

'. . . in which I was trying to represent our identities in larger terms. I wrote (in Urdu):

> *I have lost India.*
> *You have lost Pakistan.*
> *We are now citizens of General Electric.*

'I think,' Amitav continued, not pausing for a critique, 'we need to take account of the fact that our nostalgia is for a past that no longer exists.' The politics of memory, which is to say how we remember, and how we act, and therefore how we live, as well as how we pass on tradition and therefore how we are going to live, is something we must understand better.

I concurred. 'But for that to happen *desis* have to recognize that what they left behind in India, Pakistan and Bangladesh has not remained static – it has changed and is constantly changing.'

'I couldn't agree more,' Amitava said emphatically. 'A great deal of churning and a great deal of change is taking place back in India and Pakistan.' And furthermore, there's no doubt *desi* culture is dynamic and has changed Britain a great deal, he said. But it is also simultaneously backward-looking. 'I think we need to establish feedback on changes taking place on the subcontinent and how things are changing among the Asians in Britain.' What is needed is to make a new synthesis, a dynamic fusion of our present for our future. Amitava declared himself as eager to see what will come out of provincial towns such as Aligarh and Mirpur as he was to see what comes out of Bradford and Birmingham. 'Nothing will be that pure, but surely something will be authentic. That which is freed from the anxiety of finding a place in Britain will speak in a voice that is its own and will therefore be somehow more universally appealing.'

The idea of authenticity is intrinsically connected to the notion of being true to oneself. British Asians return regularly to the subcontinent to discover their true selves, but they often simply reinforce the identities they have built in Britain. For in India, Pakistan and Bangladesh, as anywhere else, you find what you desire. If you are looking for ties to your *biradari*, or to nourish your spirituality or fundamentalism, or for a boost to your honour or charitable causes, or indeed a spouse, you will find them easily and readily. But what you can discover as easily in Karachi as Bradford, Mumbai and Birmingham, is that tradition can be suffocating as well as life-enhancing. 'Authentic tradition' is in contrast not something that is fixed or frozen in history. It is a form of becoming; it changes from epoch to epoch as our understanding of ourselves, our communities, our cultures and our multiple selves evolves.

Indeed, the sustenance that British Asians draw from their different worlds, as well as the flexibility and dexterity of tradition, never fails to surprise me. And in nothing has it surprised me more than in my own marriage.

Chapter 6

BHAWALNAGAR WEDDING

Marriage, arranged or otherwise: the entire subcontinent is obsessed with the subject. In the West people gabble on endlessly about 'relationships' and 'dating', while Asians talk of nothing but marriage. It is the all-consuming subject of the wonderful dramas on Pakistani television channels, the grand narrative of all Bollywood films, and the regular fodder of newspaper and magazine columns. *The Times of India* devotes most of its page 2 – ahead of important world and national news – to matrimonials: 'Well-educated girl looking for a Bengali Brahmin professional groom, PhD preferred.'

The subject was not uppermost in my mind when I first returned to Pakistan. It was the summer of 1975. By this time I had finished my degree in physics and an MSc in information science at the City University, London. I had become an ardent Muslim critic with a passion for reform, a subject about which I spoke earnestly and was active in various associations; it was also a subject on which I had resolved to write. My activities brought me the offer of a job in Saudi Arabia I simply could not refuse. Nevertheless, my mother instructed me to take three months off work and join the whole family on a trip 'to rediscover who we really are'.

Mumsey's agenda of reunification was radically different from mine, and rather more extensive than she openly acknowledged. It was deeply strategic, in support of a stealth campaign for the fulfilment of her long-nurtured objective. When my parents migrated from India to Pakistan, in the aftermath of the 1947 Partition, the family was spread all over the new country. Kinship ties were under pressure; there was extensive concern that the bonds of family might weaken. Faced with an incipient social crisis, my mother, with the able assistance of her younger sister, took counsel and they determined to be proactive heroines in a stand against the crumbling of the bedrock of civilization as they knew and lived it. They made a pact: if their eldest progenies turned out to be of opposite sex, then they would do everything in their not inconsiderable powers to get them married. And in the lottery of recombinant DNA, they won the jackpot. To my mother a son, to her sister a daughter were duly and safely delivered. I was married before ever I was born. I was nurtured in the cause of my marriage as I grew to maturity. I was groomed through the years of my innocence with Mumsey's scheme ever in her mind. I, a mere boy child, became aware of the pact only when I turned eighteen. And I did not like it a bit.

The stealth campaign notwithstanding, I too felt it was time to make our visit. I agreed to join the family for a three-month sojourn in Pakistan. My brother Jamal, shrewdly calculating that where one strategic imperative had been revealed a second-phase backup plan would not be far behind, was a bit more reticent. He required much more persuasion. Eventually, the entire Sardar household returned to Pakistan for the first time in the summer of 1975.

We started our visit in Karachi and stayed with Farid Mammu, the eldest brother of my mother. He was living in Model Colony, close to Karachi airport. When we arrived at his house we found Farid Mammu resting on his *charpai*. 'After all these years you are back!' He stood up to greet me. There was something in his embrace that said, 'You have never left. You were always here. Here right beside me.' No sooner had I left the embrace of Farid Mammu than I was grabbed by his younger brother. Waheed Mammu was a special man, considered by most of the family to be simply mad and beyond the pale. But he was a particular kind of mystic with the ability to disappear and reappear! He had appeared from nowhere to greet me. We hugged each other like long-lost brothers. One by one all the members of the family came out to hug us. In an instant I was reunited with the child I had been and accepted as the person I now am. I became complete. So complete that I could feel the natural reflexes of childhood rekindled. I wormed rather than wriggled to get away from the hugging onslaught and ran to my Nani, my mother's mother. She was old but not frail. She patted me on the head and kissed my forehead. The respite was momentary. I was grabbed by more family members and the hugging ritual continued, elders succeeded by children.

There were so many of them. I was suddenly conscious of my inattention to all those airmail letters. There were customs, etiquette to be observed, this I knew, though I knew not which and to whom. I was floundering. Before I could observe even the basic appropriate behaviour, I had to know who was who. Recognition was the first essential, but in fifteen years faces change. If one cannot negotiate the hurdle of recognition, the conventions of nomenclature intervene to assist: an uncle had to be addressed as *mammu* or *chacha*, depending on whether he was older or younger than your mother, an auntie is a *mumani* or *chachi*, a younger cousin with his or her first name or nickname, the wives of elder cousins as *bhabhis*, though after that came the countless children whose genealogy confounded me. My mother, ever alert to my lack of diplomatic capabilities, appointed my cousin Hameed Ahmad Khan, aka Gudu, the eldest son of Farid Mammu, as chaperon; he was given strict instructions to ensure I displayed due decorum at all times and showed both old and young, men and women, proper respect. 'My son,' said my mother, who has never knowingly oversold me, 'has few virtues and none of them relate to appropriate social behaviour.'

Gudu was the same age as me; I had played with him whenever we came to Karachi during my childhood. Reunited, we became instant friends; we shared a bed in the crowded house and went everywhere together. Almost every morning relatives would come to visit us. Gudu, sitting by my side, would whisper in my ear who they were, the nature of my relationship with them, how I should address them, indeed, what I should say. He also served another estimable function. Everyone who came to greet us would insist we have dinner with them. A polite refusal would offend. It was Gudu's job to find appropriate inoffensive, yet cogent and compelling, excuses to decline, of which he had a long list – visiting the graves of long-dead but exceptionally important relatives, impending arrival of relatives from far corners of Pakistan, imminent death of an elderly relative who had to be visited before he/she breathed his/her last breath. And if all else failed, he would revert to his favourite: 'We went to such and such a place last night, the food was exceptionally good, but now everyone is down with severe, life-threatening diarrhoea.' No one would ever question that assertion made on behalf of a returnee such as myself.

One day, an old man arrived in the late afternoon. I was sitting on the veranda with Gudu. The moment he saw me he burst into tears, they rolled down his cheeks like a waterfall and washed over his white, bushy beard. I thought he must be an exceptionally respected relative genuinely moved to tears of joy at seeing me. Without waiting for Gudu's instructions, I instinctively leapt up and hugged him. The old man kissed me on my forehead, covering my face with his salty tears, and held me in a very tight embrace. He was inconsolable. Eventually, Gudu freed me from his grip. 'My God,' I said to Gudu, 'he must be a very important relative.'

'He is not a relative,' Gudu replied, suppressing a smile. 'He is one of our neighbours.'

'So he's not crying because he's happy to see me?'

'No,' replied Gudu. 'He's crying because his wife died last week.' After a pause he added: 'Express your condolences to him. And ask him how his children are coping.' I did as instructed.

When the old man left, Gudu said: 'There is one group of people even more important than our relatives; and they require even more attention from you. Our neighbours.'

Soon another matter requiring diplomatic attention hove into view. Mumsey's younger sister Zubida arrived from Bhawalnagar to see us. Zubida Khala was slightly taller than my mother and cut an impressive figure. She was head teacher of a primary school in Bhawalnagar and used to giving orders. The two sisters were instantly inseparable. It was unmistakably evident that High Command had convened. They talked animatedly; this was clearly a decisive meeting reviewing strategy, checking the plans, perfecting the final details of their long prepared campaign. A few days later, the two sisters summoned my brother and me to their presence. There were no preliminaries; they had settled for a full-scale outright assault. Zubida Khala had brought a picture of her daughter. She placed the photograph in my hand. It showed a young girl sitting on some sort of wall in front of a huge mountain.

'What do you think?' Mumsey asked.

'It's a very impressive-looking mountain',' I replied.

'What do you think of the *girl* in the picture?'

'I can hardly see her.' I handed the picture back. 'Anyway, you know, Mumsey, that I am not interested.' The rebuff, cavalier and disdainful – surely that's how Asian men swat aside these womanly ploys?

The expressions on the faces of the two sisters changed dramatically. 'So you don't want me be to be happy?' said Mumsey as she shifted gear, launching the missile of filial guilt, speeding it on its way with high-octane pathos.

'You don't want to fulfil the promise and dreams of two sisters who have suffered so much.' Zubida Khala moved in, going straight for the jugular. I could feel monsoons of tears massing as I looked at them. Desperately, the man in me cast around for some face-saving ploy, anything to forestall the rains.

'Yes. Yes. Yes,' I replied, attempting reassurance. 'I want you to be happy. I want you to fulfil your dreams. But I don't want to marry this girl, someone I have never seen and hardly know.'

'*Teyk hay* [OK],' Mumsey replied, gritting her teeth. High Command would regroup and launch the rearguard action. 'You will go to Bhawalnagar to see her.'

The drama then shifted to focus on my brother. He was handed another picture. 'She is the daughter of Auntie . . .' Zubida Khala began, '. . . oh, what's her name? Anyway, she is a distant relative; you don't know her. But this girl is a pearl. She is studying for her medical degree.'

My brother Jamal looked at the picture, and then handed it to me. 'Bloody *Emergency Ward 10*,' he said.

The photo showed a girl standing on the steps of a building which was clearly a hospital. Someone on a stretcher was being borne into the building, and a parade of people were coming out or going into it.

I handed the picture back to my brother. 'If you use a magnifying glass you will be able to make out her features,' I said, suppressing a smile. 'That ought to be good enough for you to make a positive decision.'

'No rush, take your time,' Zaubida Khala said, as though Jamal was eating a plate of *biryani*, not being confronted with a life-changing decision. She took the picture back. 'If you don't like this girl, there are many others. We want you to be happy.'

It dawned on me, and not without a sense of inequity and

injustice, that while I was being presented with a *fait accompli*, my brother was being offered variety and options.

A few days later, Gudu took me and my brother on a guided tour of Karachi. It was as I remembered, much like any and all Pakistani cities I recalled from my days as a young boy. People everywhere, overcrowded buses, motor rickshaws weaving their way through alleys just six feet wide. But the perspective of childhood had been altered. The roads were a little wider than I remembered and there were many more concrete buildings. There were more cars on the road and the city's affluent area, the Defence Colony, looked out of place with the city as a whole. But huge camel carts were still to be seen carrying sacks of goods from the port to the city centre, from Kimari to Bunder Road, just like the ones I used to follow with so much delight. As a child, I would run behind them and sometimes climb over them. The 'local' train still went around the city; now it appeared much slower, older and more polluting, a sclerotic geriatric. Within a few minutes I saw a fatal accident involving the train – a sight familiar from childhood.

A few minutes later, we witnessed another serious accident, this time the tangled outcome of two buses racing each other: another characteristic Karachi sight. The potholes around Memon Masjid were still there, except now they looked bigger and more ancient; everyone seemed to know the location of each hole and negotiated a circuitous path around them. Saddar, the prime focus of the city, hadn't changed a bit: the same bazaars, the same stalls, the same narrow footpaths where individual entrepreneurs displayed their wares, leaving little space for the pedestrians to walk. Even the cinemas hadn't changed. Huge placards with gaudy paintings announced the current attractions. As usual, there seemed to be more people outside the cinema than inside.

After lunch in Saddar, Jamal announced he had something important to do and would not be proceeding to Clifton, where we had planned to spend our evening by the seaside. I was surprised, but not overly inquisitive or concerned. 'OK,' I said, 'if you've got something to do, you've got something to do. Go and do it. We'll see you in Model Colony.' Jamal left us and we continued with our journey.

There was so much going on, so many relatives were coming and going, so many dinners being attended, no one noticed the absence of Jamal. Next day, Mumsey casually asked, 'Where is Muna? I haven't seen him for a few days.' Now she mentioned it, neither had I. I recalled we had left him in Saddar with something important to do, but I had no memory of seeing him since that time. Now it was everyone's business to start looking for Muna, 'the little one' – Mumsey's nickname for my brother. He was nowhere to be found. 'What is wrong with this bloody family? Why do people keep disappearing?' Mumsey screamed. This was the first and only time I ever heard my mother swear. But she didn't actually use the word 'bloody'. She said *haram khour* – those who eat from illegitimate wealth. Family members telephoned around the *khandaan* – the extended family – and went out to look for Jamal but he could not be found.

The following morning I awoke to the sound of wailing. Mumsey and Zubida Khala were embracing each other and sobbing. Tears ebbed from the eyes of all the women in the household; a phalanx of men sat around looking despondent and gloomy.

'What happened?' I asked Gudu.

'A telegram has arrived,' Gudu said.

'So?'

'Someone has died.'

'Who?'

'Maybe it's bad news about Muna,' he offered tentatively.

'Well, what does the telegram say?' I demanded, gripped by sudden alarm.

'I don't know. No one's opened it yet.'

I jumped out of bed and made straight for Farid Mammu. He was sitting on his *charpai*, his head in his hands, tears rolling from his eyes. The telegram lay on his pillow. He picked it up and handed it to me. I opened the envelope; and read the telegram aloud:

GONE BACK TO LONDON. DO NOT WISH TO MARRY PAKISTANI PEARL WITH OR WITHOUT A MEDICAL DEGREE. VERY HAPPY. JAMAL.

After a month's stay in Karachi, High Command initiated Phase Two of Operation Marriage. Gudu and I flew to Lahore, the cultural centre of Pakistan, from where we took a bus to Bhawalnagar.

We arrived in time for breakfast. Everyone was there to greet us. We were ushered to the veranda and sat on a *charpai*. While we talked and said *salaams* to young and old alike, a young girl brought us tea. She was slim, but not tall. Her black hair, parted in the middle, was pulled back into a single, thick, elegant plait. Her face had a natural balance: large black eyes under neat, curving eyelashes; her nose, pleasing without being formal; her lips, neither too thick nor too thin, atop a flawlessly round chin. She was wearing a green, flowery *shalwar kameez* suit over which was draped a paper-thin black *duppata* (shawl). She seemed to glide rather than walk; there was an extraordinary air about her of integrity and innocence.

Gudu nudged me. 'It is she,' he said.

I took a sideways glance – and couldn't help feeling enchanted.

Enchanted or not, marriage was still not on my mind – and especially not an arranged one. I looked for grandfather, but Nana was not in the house. 'He is in his surgery,' I was told. Nana was a prodigious man. He had ten children, four sons and six daughters. 'I am one short of fielding a full cricket team,' he would say. His youngest son died in infancy. His eldest son, Abdul Basit, married Zubida Khala, and worked for the local district council; he was, therefore, the father of my predestined bride. The second son, Abdul Muqeet, deputy headmaster of a boys' secondary school, had married outside the family. The youngest son, Mujeeb, married a distant relative, Naima, and followed Hakim Sahib into traditional medicine.

I arrived at his surgery to discover Hakim Sahib sitting cross-legged on a cushion listening attentively to a patient. I took a seat near him, keeping a respectable distance from the private space between a *hakim* and his *mareez* (the patient). When he finished, Nana looked up: 'Even fifteen years hasn't changed you!' He got up and we hugged each other. 'I *knew* you were on your way,' he said.

'Oh?' I said. 'I tried to telephone to let you know but your telephone . . .'

Nana interrupted me: 'Still you have not learnt? There are other ways of communicating, other ways of knowing.'

The following day, I got up early to join Hakim Sahib in his surgery. It was his practice to wake up just before dawn, say his morning prayers, and spend the early part of his day making medicines. I found him at the back of the surgery he used as his laboratory, brewing up some concoction, using poison from a snake that had been killed recently. Once the task was finished, I joined him at his regular position in the front of the surgery.

'I suppose you are appalled at the way I make my medicine?' Hakim Sahib commented without looking at me.

'Not really,' I replied. 'But it is unconventional. Modern medicine is developed in sophisticated laboratories and manufactured at industrial plants.'

Hakim Sahib glanced upward, another of his repertoire of trademark grins playing around his physiognomy. 'You are saying that *hikmat* is unconventional and therefore inferior. But who defines what is conventional and what is unconventional?'

I said nothing. He asked me to come a little closer.

'Conventional, you would say, is clever and modern; and unconventional is traditional and obtuse.'

I kept quiet.

'No doubt,' Hakim Sahib continued, 'you think of yourself as clever and modern.'

I tried to suppress a smile.

'I hear,' Hakim Sahib went on, 'you are writing a book. A whole book! What's it about?'

'It's about science and technology in the Muslim world.'

'Oh! A clever and modern book.' Hakim Sahib waited for my reaction. But I knew full well I was being led, gently if unsubtly, along a particular path. It was wisest to keep quiet. There was a silence, not so much a pregnant pause, as the intake of breath before the imminent pangs of labour ensued.

'There is nothing wrong with being clever and modern,' Hakim Sahib dropped his words sweet and soft, like rosewater into a bowl. 'Provided you are not arrogant. I think arrogance is perhaps one of the most unforgivable of all sins. Do you know what the worst form of arrogance is?'

'No.' I shook my head to encourage the explanation.

'The belief that your way is the only way and there is no other way. If you define your way as the conventional way, then it becomes the dominant way, the right way, the only way. That's what the *farangis* believed: that their way of knowing is the only way of knowing. All else was superstitious ignorance. That's why they systematically destroyed *hikmat* and knowledge systems that integrate wisdom and values. Their modernity looks down on our tradition and tells us that everything we have learnt over the ages is unscientific (as though they invented science), superfluous and dangerous (as though we have no idea how to look after ourselves). It tells us our medicine is useless, our agriculture is useless, our cuisine is useless, our education is useless, our religion is useless, our culture is useless, our morality and ethics are useless, our reason and way of thinking are useless. So ultimately we are useless people. Is this the modernity you have embraced?'

I tried to say something, but I was a butterfly skewered on a pin; no sound came from my mouth.

Hakim Sahib continued: 'You will meet lots of modern writers. Good and bad, famous and not so famous. But most of them are peddling fake sentiments wrapped in arrogant notions of modernity and superiority. You don't have to be wise, indeed even very intelligent, to be a good writer.' Nana paused. We looked at each other. We held that gaze for what seemed an eternity. Eons passed and still we sat motionless.

'A writer,' said Nana eventually, breaking the silence as he still looked me straight in the eye, 'a real writer ought to be like a *hakim*. Someone who knows there is more than one way of knowing. Someone who understands there are numerous ways of being, and, hence, countless different ways of doing. Someone who understands what ails humanity, and is in tune with people's emotions and knows instinctively what's wrong with them. A writer may not be able to cure, but certainly ought to be able to give sensible counsel.'

I nodded sage agreement. What better prospect could there be?

'The central predicament of humanity,' Hakim Sahib said in a world-weary tone, 'the most common sicknesses in the world, stem from the diseases of the heart. Heartache is the outcome when relationships are not in harmony. Most of my patients suffer from malfunctioning relationships. Indeed, most of their physical troubles are a product of their relationship problems. Everything comes down to relationships; and relationships in the end determine whether we are happy or unhappy, fulfilled or sick.' Our conversation, I soon realized, was being gently steered in a particular direction, not unconnected with the purpose of High Command in dispatching me to Bhawalnagar.

Nana went on to elaborate traditional notions of contentment.

First, he said, we must appreciate life is one long struggle with desire. Let your desires control you, Hakim Sahib said, and you are doomed to an angst-ridden life. Keep your desires under control and you have found the prescription for happiness. Second, you can't be happy if those around you are unhappy. So, your own happiness is dependent on making other people happy; it's a function more of giving than taking. Third, humankind is made for relationships. 'One,' Hakim Sahib said, 'is not just the loneliest number of all, it is an impossible number, a unit outside the scope of nature.' One must always become two. Fourth, relationships are the foundation on which happiness is built. And here we complete the cycle. A relationship of two must be mutual, which means it requires control of certain desires on the part of both parties; it requires accommodation, commonality, giving and taking, and the old-fashioned, original compromise.

Compromise. I feared that word. I had done my bit to placate my mother and her long-laid strategic plan. I had embraced the child I had been, I had reconnected with tradition, the loadstone of Asian existence. Tradition was no dead letter, modernity no unquestionable champion over a vanquished irrelevance. The task was to be aware, critical, engaged with both. It was necessary to seek what wisdom tradition and modernity had to offer and reflect on both well springs, while rejecting their dross for the poisoned dregs they both could be. The question was, how could I embrace that aspect of tradition that undermined all my modernist tendencies?

Compromise was not merely in the air. It seemed to be required of me. Compromise my modern principles and accept an arranged marriage. It was a pretty large dose of compromise. 'But, Hakim Sahib, I have been asked to marry a woman I do not love. Worse, I don't even know her.'

This was the first time I had ever called Nana 'Hakim Sahib'. He was taken aback. He took off his glasses, cleaned them vigorously with his handkerchief, placed them on his nose, and adjusted them to bring me into sharper focus. 'One's grandchildren,' he said, 'are always one's grandchildren no matter how old they become. And even modern grandchildren are required to show respect to their grandfathers.'

'Sorry, Nana.' I hung my head in supplication. 'But I am being forced to compromise.'

'The first things you have to appreciate, young man,' said Nana with stern demeanour, 'is that arranged marriages are all about an *arrangement* through mutual cooperation leading to happiness. It involves *arrangement* between mutually consenting, concerned and caring people.'

Nana looked for some reaction. I kept quiet. 'Look,' Nana continued, 'all marriages, modern or traditional, come in two parts. The first – the *object* of obsession in Western society – involves finding a partner. Here, I think tradition offers a better option. You are not alone in the search. The second involves living with a partner – the *subject* of concern in traditional society. It is not good enough to get married; one has to have a successful, happy and lasting married life. What is arranged, the second part, is life-long commitment.'

'What if the marriage goes wrong?'

'Unlike modern pacts, where you worry about relationships because relationships themselves are a problem, in an arranged marriage you worry about problems and not the relationship. The woman feels secure in the relationship even if it has problems. The man, as an integral part of the extended family system, is not likely to walk off the moment her breasts begin to sag. At times of crisis, whether they are emotional, financial or purely pragmatic – someone to look after the kids or fill in while you are working – there will always be people who will see it as their responsibility to do the necessary. Thus the central problem of the human condition – a fulfilling relationship – acquires a more manageable shape.'

'But what about love?' I shot back, ever the British child of the times. 'If I put my relationship into the hands of others, even if those others are my parents, don't I foreclose on the option of love?'

'This is a monumental fallacy,' Nana replied. 'Arranged marriages are more romantic than what you modern people call "love marriages". Why? Because they embody and offer love and romance without recourse to the obvious first step: sex. In an arranged marriage, trust and romance come first and sex comes after the marriage. Which, if you think about it, is far more romantic. Isn't it?' Nana looked at me for a reaction. I smiled back as if to say: perhaps.

'*Teak hay,*' he said. 'Look at it this way. Love is like K2, a huge mountain you need to keep climbing. If you marry someone you think you love, with whom you have already had sex, you're already near the top. It is very difficult to climb further, particularly when you are not equipped with the right gear. Some people manage to climb a little higher, but most simply have only one way to go. With an arranged marriage, you start at the bottom and work your way to the top, knowing full well that both love and good sex require hard work. An individual is a fathomless entity; getting to know another human being is the work of a lifetime. Appreciating another person, as they deserve, requires openness, ease and sharing along with them in all the ups and downs of living. When you do that with commitment for any length of time, bonds of mutual respect, understanding and a deep love, far beyond simple attraction, mature and flourish. Marriage becomes the beginning of an awfully big adventure, not an end point. You are always in love. And continue to be more and more in love – you have the entire mountain to climb!'

'All right,' I said when Nana had finished. 'There is more to tradition than meets the eye.'

'But what do you really think?' Nana asked. 'Does the traditional arrangement offer a better option or the modern counterpart?'

'I don't suppose you will allow me to reserve judgement?'

'Well, that is an option too.'

'She is very beautiful,' I conceded. 'But even if I did agree to marry her, how would I know that she wants to marry me?'

'This is an enterprise between mutually consenting adults. If she does not want to marry you, we'll have to look elsewhere. But I think the omens are good. She has already agreed.'

'But, Nana,' I said, sensing I had found a patch of solid ground, 'you know how tradition works here. When a girl is asked by her parents and elders for consent, if she says "yes", that's fine. If she stays quiet, it's taken as consent. If she says "no", it's taken as her being too shy to say "yes"! So there's no way she can actually say "no".'

Nana laughed. 'You are getting the measure of things. Like modernity, tradition can be deadly too; particularly when it produces its own self-satisfied sense of superiority. This is why we must always take a critical stance, guard against its dangers and the horrors we can make of it. I shall make abundantly sure your intended bride has a full opportunity to say "no".'

I looked at him and grinned. He smiled back. 'That's enough play for today,' he said. 'Do we have an agreement?'

'I choose to remain silent,' I said, 'and allow you to interpret it any way you choose.'

Nana laughed. 'You can take the donkey to water . . .'

We left it at that. I returned to London; but I returned captivated. That's what I brought back from my first return visit to Pakistan. That and a respect for tradition, which I discovered to have life-enhancing possibilities. On one level, Pakistan was radically different from Britain: simple everyday things, such as commuting in London, or taking a train from London to Bradford, could not be more different in Pakistan, where they could be extremely dangerous. Pakistan was a world apart – a world full of people I admired, but whose daily lives I could barely comprehend. Yet,

Pakistan made me whole again. The love and passions of my relatives, the humanity of ordinary people I encountered, suggested that the parts of my being moulded in Pakistan were just as valuable as those shaped in Britain. I comprehended I was British and Asian and would ever remain both – simultaneously.

I had not totally rejected the idea of an arranged marriage; the conversations with Nana had had some effect. But I was anxious about the whole enterprise: the sweet or bitter water to which I had been led remained untested. I wanted to find out just how sweet or bitter was the refreshment my entire family thought best for me. With more subtle diplomacy and ambiguity than is usual for me, once the proposition was clearly defined I had not rejected it out of hand. I entertained the possibility, juggled with its potential, fidgeted and fretted with it, maintained an open-minded uncertainty. I had listened, observed and managed to keep my own counsel. It was, of course, a principled stand: concern for the freedom of choice of the woman, her right to genuine consultation beyond all pressures, family or social. I was, as a result of my time in Britain, the prototype of New Asian Man. And I was also full of my own fears. Marriage is an awesome decision, a life-long commitment. In addition to the usual trepidation of making such a decision, there was a host of personal insecurities that were a product of growing up in Britain, alongside all the traditional ones discussed with my Nana. One thing was certain: I couldn't get out of my mind the picture of a graceful, angelic girl handing me a cup of tea. But the real dilemma was simple: I wanted to be wanted for myself, as me. To the rumblings of discontent from my mother we left Bhawalnagar with nothing decided, but our return to Pakistan had proved distance was no real separation, merely a temporary and in many ways illusory disjunction.

Maybe I wanted to bring the whole affair to some sort of conclusion. Maybe I wanted another cup of tea from the angelic girl. Maybe I wanted another dialogue with Nana on arranged marriage. Or maybe I was simply tired of my mother's nagging. In December 1977, I decided once again to take leave from my job to accompany my mother and sister to Pakistan, beginning our visit in Karachi at Farid Mammu's home. After a few days, Mumsey decided everyone, the whole ensemble of our family in Karachi, should go to Bhawalnagar. Moreover, we should go as a *baraat* – a wedding party.

'Mumsey,' I said, 'you can only have a *baraat* if you are going to have a *shaadi* (wedding). There is no *shaadi*. The couple concerned have not even agreed to get married. So there cannot be a *baraat*.' My cogent, lucid protestations had no effect. Once Mumsey had made up her mind, nothing was going to change it. One by one, everyone conceded to the authoritative pronouncements and fell in line. Seats were booked on a train, a date for departure was set.

The entire Bhawalnagar clan gathered in Nana's house to greet us. I caught sight of the angel of the tea cup. She was carrying a *balti* of water. This was my chance to hear what she wanted from her own mouth. 'Oay,' I shouted to attract her attention. 'Do you think I would make a reasonable husband?'

'Probably,' she shouted back, 'but not for me.' Then she threw the water over me!

We were too many for all of us to stay at Nana's house. Some were found accommodation with the neighbours; others stayed with relatives in different parts of the town. Gudu and I commandeered a little corner on the veranda for our luggage and slept on the *charpais* outside the house. Various relatives came to console me. 'In matters of the heart no one can do anything,' they said. Hakim Sahib pointed out: 'Now you know traditional women know how to say "No".' Mumsey wandered around the house trying to compose herself and hide the distress clearly visible on her face.

One morning I woke up to the sound of a huge tent being

erected in front of our house. I asked one of the men putting up the pavilion what was going on.

'This is for a wedding,' he replied without looking at me.

'Oh really!' I exclaimed. 'Whose?'

'Yours,' he said, looking up and smiling.

Had she of the *balti* changed her mind? My knees became wobbly and I felt dizzy. I went inside the house and noticed most of the women were dressed in yellow. As soon as they saw me, they started singing and dancing. Remarkably, whole Himalayas of anxiety vanished instantaneously – only to be replaced by new mountain ranges of concern. I was accepted and accepting, that much was arranged. But I still had to confront stage two anxieties – anxieties about the life that comes after marriage.

A traditional, modest Pakistani wedding can last several days. Each day is devoted to a different ritual, the origins of which lie buried deep in myth and history. Mine was more modest than most because the bride and groom shared the same roof; there were no differences to settle between the two families – for it was one and the same family – or anything in particular to negotiate. The women of the house took over the whole project. I, the mere groom, was instructed to keep out of the way, to be present when I was required, and not under any circumstances to try to see the bride. My faithful assistant, Gudu, was always by my side advising me to do this or not to do that.

The following day there was a big celebration known as a '*Mehndi*'. *Mehndi* is best known by its Arabic name, henna. It's a large plant with white flowers common in South Asia, Southeast Asia and the Middle East. Its leaves have a cooling effect on the skin, and it has been used since ancient times as a cure for bruises and skin diseases. As a natural brown dye, *mehndi* is also used to colour cotton, wool and silk. During weddings, it is used to decorate virtually the whole body of the bride with elaborate patterns. Even though I was banned from entering the house,

I managed to take an occasional peek. I saw my intended sitting on a cushion, after being washed in rosewater, surrounded by a multitude of women. Some were mixing henna in a pot, adding mustard oil and a spoonful of juice to the henna powder, then giving the concoction a good stir. Others were applying the resulting *mehndi* to the bride's hands and feet. Some were applying it with their fingers; others used matchsticks. I was quite astonished at the skill on display: Mughal flowers, Paisley patterns, stars, vines, spirals, leaves, water drops, waves, pitchers, peacocks were all being created with consummate ease. It took hours; and when the design was completed, the bride had to remain stationary – to prevent the paste from cracking – for another five or six hours while the henna dried. It was the perfect occasion for inordinate words of wisdom and the fruits of womanly experience to be dropped into an innocent ear, along with gossip, songs and much more from the extensive repertoire of traditional ingredients. From time to time, lemon juice and sugar were sprinkled to keep the *mehndi* moist. When the paste turned dark red, the bride's skin was rubbed with mustard oil, the paste was scrubbed off, and she was washed. It seemed to me the small, delicate hands of my bride were being made to resemble intricate lace gloves. Outside, the men were stringing hundreds of coloured lights over and around the house, and all over the large tent that now covered most of the street.

The wedding ceremony was held the next day. I wore a white, with a hint of blue, traditional Pakistani *shalwar kurta* suit – the *kurta* so loose it could easily have fitted both Gudu and I together; the *shalwar* about as baggy as the tent in which I sat and almost impossible to walk in. A winter Afghan cap – not unlike a Russian fur cap – was placed on my head. I sat on a bench, feet dangling, a garland of roses around my neck, a round cushion behind my back. Hakim Sahib sat on my left, Gudu to my right, while Uncle Waheed hovered here, there and everywhere.

The bride was seated inside the house, decked out in the

traditional custom-built, ornate red wedding dress. She was drenched in jewellery: huge round earrings, a necklace that covered most of her chest, and a large pendant with dangling pearls on her forehead. One could hardly see her face – not that there was any evidence she wished her face to be seen: most of the time she sat there, eyes firmly fixed on the ground, looking rather sombre. Women would come to 'see her face': they would, ever so gently, raise her chin with their hand, take a good look and exclaim '*Ma sha Allah*!' – whatever Allah wills! Then they would leave some money in her hands. I, on the other hand, received no money: those few who liked my face simply placed a garland – mostly made out of cardboard and absurdly big – around my neck. Children ran wild, inside and outside the house, collecting dried dates, sugar crystals and mixed nuts, which were being dispensed generously by family elders.

The local mullah, a young man in his mid-twenties, arrived carrying a huge register. He sat next to me. 'Marriage,' he whispered in my ear, 'is a solemn and sacred contract in Islam. Both parties must mutually agree and enter into the contract. Do you accept Saliha Basit as your wife?'

I nodded to say 'yes'.

'Say "*Jee Haan*" [Yes sir].' He repeated the question again and again. Then he went inside the house and asked Saliha: 'Do you accept Ziauddin Sardar as your husband?'

I am told she paused and thought for a moment as though she was having second, or perhaps even third, thoughts. I like to think she was overwhelmed with emotion. She eventually managed to whisper, '*Jee Haan.*'

The mullah moved his ears close to her mouth: 'Can't hear you.'

'JEE HAAN! JEE HAAN! JEE HAAN!' Everyone heard.

The mullah, whose name was Muhammad Ismael, came back to me. 'The marriage gift – *mehr* – is a divine injunction; it is an essential part of the contract,' he whispered in my right ear. The gift, also termed a dowry, is money exclusively for the personal possession of the bride. 'I understand you have settled the terms of the *mehr* at a nominal sum of 20,000 rupees.'

'It is news to me,' I replied. 'I have not settled the term of the *mehr*; and I don't think it should be nominal.'

'Moderation is recommended,' replied Maulvi Ismael. 'Do you want to pay the *mehr* now or defer to a later time?'

'Half of everything I have to be sorted out later.'

Maulvi Ismael opened his register; either it was very new, or he had performed only one other wedding. In any case, the details of my wedding were to be entered on 'Form number 2'. He started to fill the form, and asked for two 'adult and sane witnesses'. Everyone pushed Waheed Mammu away. Hakim Sahib came forward and signed from the bride's side. One of his sons-in-law signed on my behalf. I noticed the Maulvi paid no attention to what I said and wrote 'Rs 20,000' in the *mehr* column. When the form was completed, he produced a large seal and proceeded to stamp the form. Then he tore it from the register – he did such a bad job that most of the right side of the form remained firmly attached to the register – and handed it to Hakim Sahib. He rose to give his sermon, in which he urged the bride and groom to a life of piety, mutual love, kindness and social responsibility.

The sermon was followed by a sumptuous feast. Hakim Sahib had hired professional cooks, who set up their kitchens in the street outside. They prepared food in pots so huge it required three or four people to carry each one of them. It was traditional fare – *biryani, korma* (mutton curry), grilled chicken and *raita* (yoghurt with cucumber), followed by *zarda* (yellow sweet rice). All this was washed down by *Rooh afza*, a drink associated with *hakims*. It was the first 'drug' to be produced, in 1907, by Hamdard, the laboratories that specialize in Islamic medicine. *Rooh* literally means 'soul', *afza* is 'elevation': this pink, delicious liquid is supposed to refresh and elevate your soul.

The celebrations continued well into the night. Saliha, my wife, was brought out to the wedding tent. She sat next to me, hands together, eyes rooted to the ground. During Pakistani weddings, it is not unusual for someone to write a special marriage poem, known as *saraa*. It's a traditional ritual. Every Pakistani family has an aspiring poet or two and it falls to one of them to write the special poem for the special occasion. The *saraa* follows well-established conventions: the names of the bride and groom, as well as most of the family, are interwoven in the verses, the virtues of the marrying couple are highlighted, and their joint destiny, with all their similarities and differences, is lovingly explored. Our *saraa* was written by Hakim Sahib and he recited it with great zest to the delight and pleasure of the gathering. Soon afterwards, a photographer arrived. Countless photographs were taken, with various members of the family taking turns to stand behind the bride and groom. I must admit I look pretty strange in these pictures, but, unlike Saliha, I do seem to be enjoying myself. Photography over, Saliha was taken back to the house and into the bridal chamber. I sat outside waiting for the visitors to go home. But no one wanted to leave. It seemed half of Bhawalnagar was there, and since everyone lived literally around the corner no one was in any hurry. So I waited and waited.

At around three in the morning, I was summoned inside. Hakim Sahib and Gudu accompanied me to the bridal chamber – one of the two rooms in the house – which was decorated with beads of jasmine flowers, the floor covered generously with rose petals, the bed dressed with red covers. Saliha sat at one corner of the bed, looking divine in her jewellery and voluptuous red wedding dress, eyes still downcast, her net *duppata*, enriched with handworked gold embroidery, covering her face as though it were a veil. I stood at the door for a few moments, taking in the sight from a distance, admiring her and my fate.

Slowly, the entrance to the door constricted, the space crowded. A group of young girls appeared and blocked my way. They

demanded money to let me through. 'Let's negotiate,' I mumbled.
'No negotiation,' they said in unison. 'Pay up or you will be
standing here till dawn.' I looked at Gudu and Hakim Sahib. It
seemed my Nana had come prepared. He took a wad of notes from
his pocket and started to count them. As one, the flock moved
towards Hakim Sahib. The door was unattended. Gudu quickly
pushed me through and closed it behind me. Once inside the room,
I could not move. I stood there in front of the door looking at
Saliha. I could hear Hakim Sahib counting the money and handing
it out, to screams of joy. Slowly, the noise and the buzz around the
house subsided. Someone had put a *ghazal* on a tape recorder;
clearly I could hear Munni Begum, the peerless diva of Pakistani
music, singing:

> *I am drinking with my eyes,*
> *Let not this atmosphere change.*
> *Do not lower your gaze*
> *For this night may fade away.*

I managed to walk a few steps; and sat beside Saliha.

> *There's still some night left*
> *Do not remove your veil.*
> *Your faltering and falling drunk*
> *May regain his balance.*

She removed her *duppata*, placed her arms around my waist and
embraced me.

> *Owner of my life*
> *Put your hands on my heart*
> *I fear that the joy of your arrival*
> *Would stop my heart from beating.*

Then, she leaned forward, grabbed a book that was lying under the cushion and handed it to me. I read the title: *Intermediate Biology*.

A week or so later, it was time to make our way to Islamabad and organize Saliha's visa for London. The British High Commission is located in the 'Diplomatic Enclave' in the Ramna area of the city – it was, and is now even more, heavily protected and almost impossible for ordinary mortals to enter. There was a huge crowd at the front gate. I had to fight and elbow others away to get close to the entrance. The guard was exceptionally rude; he would not even talk to me, let alone allow me inside the compound. I tried to reason with him and even showed him my British passport. He dismissed me and pushed me aside. This stirred my most offended 'Disgusted of Tunbridge Wells' outrage at all petty-fogging bureaucracy and hindrances on the natural freedoms due an Englishman. It was one of those rare occasions when I truly lost my temper. I started shouting at the guard. 'I want to get inside my own embassy. You get the hell out of my way.' The guard reciprocated in kind. A fracas developed.

Eventually a consul came out to investigate. 'What's the problem?' he asked politely.

'I want to lodge an application for my wife's visa,' I replied.

'OK, OK,' he said. 'Calm down and come with me.'

He led me to a fortified room in the compound. I waited for a while and was eventually seen by an officer, who examined my passport and marriage certificate. 'You have to admit,' he said, 'it doesn't look very convincing. For one thing, almost a quarter of it is torn away.' Inwardly, I cursed Maulvi Ismael for doing such a bad job of detaching my certificate from his register. The officer explained I would not be able to take Saliha with me to London. The marriage would have to be investigated to make sure it was genuine; my wife would have to be questioned. It would take at least six months before she could even be interviewed. He gave me a few forms to fill in. To my astonishment, I discovered one could not submit a visa application at the High Commission itself; it had to be sent from a special Federal Express office in the city.

It seemed highly offensive that, having gone through years of equivocation, mental preparation, endless concern, reflection, deep consideration and the final on–off rush of marriage, we had attained merely conditional matrimonial status. Did British bureaucracy have any idea how much emotional effort by how many people had gone into the making of this marriage? Could they conceive of how bonded, how entwined were the two lives they proposed to scrutinize with cold hauteur? I had a clear appreciation of the background and motivation at work. The various permutations of immigration law, specifically framed to discriminate against British Asians, were designed to staunch the flow of more people like me by all means possible, even when entirely legitimate. It was official policy which found its true reflection in the infinitely varied means by which as much harassment and humiliation as possible were handed out by junior civil servants at offices across the subcontinent. I knew all this, and yet to experience it personally, wrecking the most important days of our new married life, was quite another matter.

I was immensely sad Saliha would not be able to come with me to London. It might be a year before I would see her again. She held me tight. 'I don't want you to leave me behind,' she kept saying. Bureaucracy can appropriate the power to dislocate lives, but ultimately it is powerless to prevent what has been arranged: a commitment to a life-long bond.

Three months later, Saliha was given an interview date. Three months after that she went to Islamabad for an interview; she was asked to bring as much evidence as possible to 'prove' we were married: copies of my passport, birth certificates, a 'proper' marriage certificate, photographs of the wedding ceremony, even the wedding invitation card. My experience of British officialdom being more extensive, I was nervous. But Saliha reported that the interview was pretty straightforward. A few days later, she got her 'Settlement to Join Husband' visa. She arrived in London on a bright, sunny day. It was 11 June 1978.

I have always regretted the fact that we did not keep the *saraa* Nana wrote for our wedding. But I do remember it pointed out that Saliha – as her name itself, which means 'righteousness', indicated – would keep me on the path of virtue. She was, the poet suggested, the summation of all the women I had loved, the only woman who could encapsulate all the women I could possibly love in all my possible futures. This, despite the fact that we grew up in different environments in different countries. We were different, Saliha and I. Her outlook was traditional; mine was shaped by living in Britain. She was delicate, sensitive and sensual, patient and forgiving, and spoke softly; I was – am – loud, rowdy and speak my mind whatever the consequences, impatient in everything. Our differences turned out to be like superglue – they bonded us in seconds. We were different and we gave to each other what we most needed, what we dearly cherished, what we did not even know we lacked.

How, I often wonder, could our family have been so prescient, so sure that our differences would provide the enduring strength of our marriage? My anxieties had all been about the process of the arrangement. Those who arranged the matter looked further and saw more clearly, beyond the differences of our upbringing. They realized that an enduring marriage is about more than attraction and allure. Any true fusion grows from marrying the best of tradition with the best modernity can offer. It would be up to us to find those best qualities, it would be our challenge, but without the necessary ingredients, those derived from our differences, we would inevitably flounder and remain incomplete. Perhaps there was one other thing our family knew. Until our marriage, my life and Saliha's had been different, but these differences arose from the same history. Our lives were different because of a history shaped by Partition, migration and dislocation. To find a complete and comfortable identity with which to live and grow, we would have to find a way to live across and beyond the history from which we both emerged. To achieve that objective we needed each other. We needed to learn from each other and the differences we brought to our life together.

Chapter 7

CHILDREN OF BRITAIN

When the intrusive immigration laws had been placated, Saliha came to London. Another round of bureaucratic formalities had to be negotiated before she could join me in Saudi Arabia, where I worked. She took to London relatively easily. Six months later she joined me in Jeddah, where I assumed she would feel more at home. But she hated its austere, male-dominated environment. 'This place gives me the creeps,' she said. 'Can't go out, can't drive, must wear the *hijab*, must be accompanied by a man, can't do this, must do that! Get me out of here!' My work in Saudi Arabia studying the *hajj*, the annual pilgrimage to Mecca that is an essential requirement for all Muslims, aimed to rescue the best of tradition from obliteration by rampant modernization. Saliha's presence and her response to Jeddah added new dimensions to my thinking. She helped me to appreciate that aspects of tradition were perverted in ways which a man is simply able to ignore. I learnt that traditional practices too need to be more accommodating and humble. We stayed long enough for Saliha to accompany me on a pilgrimage. When she became pregnant, we said a permanent goodbye to Saudi Arabia. I was about to become a father. My child would be born in Britain, she would be British, and would raise further questions about the relationship between the subcontinent and Britain and what it means to be a British Asian.

In London, we lived with my parents. I had saved enough money in Saudi Arabia to buy a house, but we decided to move only after Saliha had given birth, following traditional Asian practice. Sometimes we live out tradition because it is practical, the most serviceable answer to our circumstances. I had started a new career as a freelance science journalist in furtherance of my ambition to become a writer, and needed to establish myself financially. Another reason for staying with my parents was the location of the council house my father had bought, just a short walk from St Mary's Hospital.

'When are you going to deliver?' I asked Saliha like clockwork every day.

'When I am good and ready,' she would reply. 'Be patient.'

I accompanied her regularly to the ante-natal clinic. The appointed date for delivery came – and passed. I became more and more concerned. Almost two weeks after the due date, I said to Saliha: 'Right, ready or not, we're going to the hospital.' It was eight in the evening. I picked up her hospital bag and we walked the few hundred yards to St Mary's. As we reached the main door of the hospital the contractions started. Saliha was rushed immediately to the labour ward. At 5.01 a.m., the next morning, my daughter was born and I went berserk with joy.

'What are we going to call her?' Saliha asked, when we had some quiet time together. 'We must take particular care in naming our child: it will shape and determine her future.' Saliha had a long list of possible names – Fatimah, Aisha, Sabiya – which we went through one by one, rejecting each as we went along. When my father first saw the baby, he exclaimed: 'She is so sparkling,' and suggested Afshan, 'sprinkled with gold dust', as one possibility. My mother thought the baby looked rather regal and suggested Sultana.

I wanted my daughter's name to capture something of the event of her birth, particularly the time, as well as her personality. We noticed she had distinctive brown eyes with a slight tinge of green from my mother. Once, staying with Bedouins on the outskirts of Jeddah, I had spotted a deer, just before a misty dawn; the only thing I could actually see was its distinctive green eyes. So I suggested Ghazal to capture both the beauty of the gazelle and the lyricism of Urdu and Persian love poetry, which in its most popular form is called *ghazal*. There was some dissent in the ranks. We consulted my brother-in-law, Khalid Siddiqi, who had just finished his doctorate in Islamic studies at the School of African and Oriental Studies. He thought for a day or two and then came up with Maha, the proper Arabic name for the green-eyed gazelle that can only be spotted just before dawn. So it was.

Maha brought out the Asian father in me. Conventionally, Asian fathers are supposed to be authoritative – indeed, authoritarian – and are more powerful figures in the household than mothers. The Asian father is protective, strict on issues of personal autonomy, and drives children to excel. I gave her a nickname, just as Nana did for all his children and grandchildren. I called her Duniya – 'world', *another* world, *her* world, as well as *my* world. And just as Nana took the children of the household with him, I took her everywhere. When she was a toddler, she would sit on my shoulders, with her arms around my head. Later, she would hang on my back, rather like a rucksack. I took her to work, to meetings, on the bus, on the underground, on the plane. But my Asian-ness had been tempered by liberal Britain, where I acquired the instincts of a New Muslim Man. I announced loudly and often to any-one who would listen that I would give my daughter her proper freedom to flourish. I wanted Maha to propel herself rather than be driven by her father. It soon became apparent I had no need to be so outspoken. Maha was aggressively independent from infancy; it was obvious any attempt at parental control, apart from the nominal, was not going to succeed. Thankfully I had opted for

Nana's school of parenting by conversation rather than dictat; I encouraged her to ask questions and talked to her about everything.

Four years later, in April 1983, Maha had a brother. He was born a couple of weeks early and had to be kept in an incubator for a few days. We had decided that all male members of the Sardar household would have names beginning with Z and he was called Zaid, pronounced just like his initial. Again I was inseparable from my son. Where Maha had been a rucksack, Zaid developed the technique of a baby koala bear; he would cling to my midriff for hours while I wrote at my electric typewriter.

We had bought and moved into a house in Colindale. By British standards, it was not big enough for two highly independent and active children, but we hated the idea of moving. Asians are usually not keen on moving house. The notion of climbing the housing ladder, buying larger and more expensive properties, with ever bigger mortgages, is mostly shunned by subcontinentals. We have already migrated. Once we find a satisfactory place to live, the desire is to stay and put down roots. So with the help of my brother, we turned the unused garage of our house into an extra room. When, four years later, we had a third child, another room had to be added.

I missed this birth. I had been organizing a conference in Mecca and was there for the opening session, which turned out to be the morning after the birth. We called him Zain. He was born with his feet pointing inwards and needed a series of corrective operations. He spent most of his first six years with both feet and legs up to the knees in plaster. He would sit, his plaster-encased legs crossed beneath him, in an impish lotus position. Then, like a frog on a lily pad, from this seated position he would leap vertically and simultaneously propel himself forward some distance at considerable pace. He had a particular penchant for breaking everything that stood in his path, with appropriate added sound effects, and damaging other things he simply wanted to kick. Wear and tear on the house was considerable. As time went on, or need arose, I extended the kitchen, built a conservatory and, to top it all – my pride and joy – I transformed the attic into my study. The building stopped only when we decided we did not want any more children – and the planning permissions ran out.

Having children made me aware of the difference between how kids grow up in the subcontinent and in Britain. In Pakistan, I spent most of my childhood roaming about – and occasionally getting lost. In Sahiwal, a lush, agricultural town where we lived for a few years, I played outside on streets and in fields. Almost every imaginable fruit tree grew there. Our own garden had an old guava tree, several mango trees and a whole bunch of banana trees. I would often climb them, plucking the fruits from our own and other people's gardens. Most of the farmers near our house grew sugar cane and oranges. When the gardens lost their lustre, I would run straight into the sugar-cane fields, with nothing on my body except my *chadi*. There I would be joined by other boys from the neighbourhood. We would find ourselves a comfortable spot deep inside the field and sit there for hours plucking sugar cane, peeling it with our teeth, chewing and sucking till the sweetness disappeared and it was time to spit the remains. Sometimes the farmers would detect signs of our presence by coming across a vandalized patch in the middle of an evenly grown harvest. They would creep in and try to grab us. But we were always too fast for them. I have never known that kind of freedom again. In Britain, where we are conscious of safety and security, children tend not to run around without the protective eye of adults. I feared my kids would not have the freedom I enjoyed.

There was another concern. In Britain, child-rearing is largely the responsibility of the parents. In the subcontinent, children are brought up by the whole extended family. I was brought up not just by my parents or my Nana. Our house was full of matriachs. There was my grandmother, Dadi, whose real name was Ahamedi

Begum. A strong, feisty woman, she was a polymath: a practising herbalist, a religious scholar, a renowned poet who wrote not just in Urdu but also in Farsi, and a fiery orator. Her favourite pastime was smothering me with kisses and reading to me – usually from bulky Urdu novels which held little interest for me. There were my two aunts: *bari puppu* and *choti puppu*. *Bari puppu*, Rabia Durrani, was a medical health officer. My younger aunt, *choti puppo*, Aisha Durrani, was a doctor. Both spent their free time chasing and playing with me. Then there was our neighbour: a woman called Kaki who was my mother's best friend. She was always in our house, and thought she had parental rights over me. All these women competed with my mother for my time and played a part in bringing me up. I wanted my own children to have the kind of love and attention I had. But in a society where nuclear family is the norm, this kind of childhood is impossible.

For British Asians, I would say, childhood does not exist as a distinct and different concept; it is always considered within and through the concept of family. Children exist as part of multi-generational families; they scamper about being kids, or perhaps just little people, as part of daily life in all its aspects. Grandparents, who often live in the same household, play an equal part, and children belong to the entire range of relatives in the extended family, as well as all the unofficial relatives created by circumstances within British Asian communities.

My father assumed the role of Hakim Sahib with ease. He loved telling stories to his grandchildren. My mother saw it as her duty to teach my children Islam, good manners and basic etiquette. But our extended family in Britain was not that extended. I still wished my kids had a string of aunts and uncles, and a few neighbours, to spoil and help rear them. Asians invest high hopes in their children; we expect great things from them. We see our children as extensions not only of ourselves but of our family in its widest sense.

Yet the generation gap, the impossible, contentious, inevitably acrimonious tension between young people and their elders, is present in the Asian community too. I think this is a product not just of the breakdown of the Asian extended family, and the consequent inability of parents who often work of giving due attention to the children's issues, but also of the fact that Asian parents and elders put intolerable pressures on their children to conform – to tradition, religious norms, family customs and educational aspirations. It also seems to me that the youth are somehow obligated to rebel against their upbringing. And this adolescent rebellion is nothing like the rebellion of my youth; it has less and less to do with concerns about the inequities of society, the world order or violations of common humanity. In our consumer-driven paradise, and this is as true of Britain as it is of the subcontinent, the rebellion's only focus is unrestrained indulgence of personal freedoms. It is defined as much as satirized in the Kevin the Teenager character created by comedian Harry Enfield, and consists in rejecting one's parents, finding them intolerable as human beings, social embarrassments before the hanging jury of one's adolescent peers, and generally seeking any way possible to affront and assault their parental sensibilities. Children and adolescents have become commodities of the culture of consumption, shaped by drives and influences devised beyond the scope of family. I often wondered, would my own offspring rebel against their parents simply because we were trying to inculcate them with our values? Did I live in fear of my own children?

I was musing on such thoughts one evening when my children were still young while I watched my friend Ashis Nandy and his wife, Umma, devote their attention to Maha and Zaid. With evident pleasure and enthusiasm Ashis and Umma got down on their knees and joined the kids in play. It was not just that Ashis treated my children as though they were his equals – adult thinkers – there was also something 'childlike' about him.

Eventually I intervened to pose a question. 'What is it,' I asked Ashis, 'that makes people fear childlike behaviour in an adult?' Ashis gave me one of his seraphic smiles, signalling he had an answer. This noted Indian thinker was ready for another game, an intellectual joust. I had known Ashis for about ten years and was aware that he had spent decades thinking about childhood. We met through our membership of the World Federation of Futures Studies. We made common cause in our search for a world shaped by the multiplicity and diversity of human culture, tradition and thought, and a future that transcended the legacy of colonialism. Our friendship bridged the senseless divide, the sibling rivalry becoming ever more destructively absurd, between India and Pakistan.

'We've been programmed to fear childhood,' replied the famous Indian intellectual who happens to be a qualified psychologist. 'Every adult dreads being childish; the norms of society knock out any remnant of childhood in adults.' He thought for a moment. 'And as a corollary, the child is best appreciated when he or she is least genuinely childlike. When he or she can perform incredible feats of gymnastics, sing like the best tenors, play out adult fantasies projected onto the suffering minor.'

Our conversation was interrupted by one of Maha and Zaid's special performances in homage to Bollywood films. 'Oh, jolly good,' Ashis commended the children in his most rounded Anglo-Indian tone. Zaid reminded his sister to join him in taking their bows. 'Thank you, please,' they said in a mocking Indian accent. Ashis and I repaired to the conservatory, where he settled himself on the cushions and began lighting his pipe. 'You know, there's something else at work in your question about childhood,' he eventually offered, 'something very particular in your case.'

'And what's that?' I was suitably intrigued.

'You're very conscious of not treating your children as colonial subjects,' Ashis replied.

'Colonial subjects? What's colonialism got to do with my relationship with my children?'

Ashis settled more comfortably on the cushions. 'How people in Britain treat and think about childhood mirrors how British imperialists conceived of the subject people of the colonies. You are subconsciously revolting against that notion of childhood,' he said.

'You mean that what their fathers did to colonial administrators in their childhood, on and off the playing fields of Harrow and Eton, they tried to do to the subject people they ruled?'

That was one way of putting it, Ashis allowed, but it went much deeper. Underpinning imperial policy in all its phases, he explained, was a set of ideas about Other, non-Western peoples. The widespread ideology was that people beyond the bounds of Europe were children. They could be children of nature, like the American Indians, or living relics of the childish phases of European development, like Indian Indians – but children they were. Towards these children Europe assumed a right to rule and a duty of care. In other words, colonizers stood *in loco parentis*; they took possession of distant lands because only they knew the real needs of the colonized: to be educated and transformed into proper human beings, to be made men in the mould of Europe. This is the true root of paternalism, a term as expressive as its meaning is exact. And never forget, Ashis noted, the idea of suffering is a central metaphor at the heart of the Christian vision. Subliminally, by association and extension, the exhortation to 'suffer little children to come unto me' becomes a sanctification of the entire concept of empire; it makes colonial rule a moral virtue in all its varied modes of operation.

'OK,' I interjected as Ashis paused for some determined puffing on his pipe. 'I take your point about the child metaphor, but surely there's a major contradiction here. The British were obsessed with uncovering the history of India. How did the antiquity of Indian civilization fit with the metaphor of Indians as children?'

'Quite true,' Ashis mumbled. 'But that's exactly how the metaphor worked best. It was possession of India's past, defining its history as both ancient and unchanged, that confirmed the inferiority of Indians and the superiority and right to rule of the British. What was old and unchanged became simultaneously young and childish in the scale of human civilization.'

'So India ends up looking like the world Alice encounters in Wonderland.'

'Well, I rather think that's exactly what colonialism was! And Lewis Carroll is a fascinating study in relations with childhood, you have to admit.'

Before Ashis could sidetrack himself into a detailed psychological analysis of Charles Dodson, I insisted we return to the contradiction between childlike Indians and their ancient civilization.

'The British made it their business to possess India's past. Most important of all, the British considered they understood India's past because they had progressed beyond it. India was living the past of Britain, therefore only the British knew what India's future should be, only they were capable of delivering India into a future beyond the constant reliving of its antiquity. And when you come to think of it, that's a fairly accurate definition of a parent. Parents are people who once were children but have grown up.'

'A pretty comprehensive justification for everything,' I had to agree.

'Especially when the metaphor morphed to become the basis of philosophy and science, the bedrock of academic disciplines.' Ashis added the cherry to top off the confection.

And I had to ask: 'How did they do that?'

By the time India became a genuine intellectual curiosity for Europe it was a potential threat to the biblical framework central to Western thought. The other Indies, the Americas and its peoples, not mentioned in the Bible or the works of ancient Greece and

Rome, raised questions about the nature of antiquity. Voltaire, driven by his anti-clericalism, tried hardest to raise perplexing questions about the antiquity of India. Initially, he championed the claims of Chinese civilization to be older than the accepted dating of biblical events. Then he came into possession of an ancient Indian text which he believed proved Indian civilization was even older than the biblical account of mankind's origins. Alas for the great luminary of the French Enlightenment, this text proved to be a forgery produced by his arch enemies, the Jesuits. But trying to prove Indian civilization to be younger than the biblical story occupied all the great minds of Europe. It was an obsession with Sir Isaac Newton. It was the first matter of business for Sir William Jones, who discovered the connection between what he called Indo-European languages, and was the first president and guiding light of the Bengal Asiatick Society. Established not long after the British assumed control of Bengal, the Asiatick Society was their principal institution for studying and eventually authoring India's past for the use of the British.

It was the Scotsman Adam Ferguson (1723–1816) who argued that the history of mankind was one long progression, a migration route along which various peoples had stalled; they became littered wreckage, living relics, of how the rise of civilization had happened. Civilization understood as one process was one linear history. Ferguson's *An Essay on Civil Society*, published in 1767, called the stages of human progress savagery, barbarism and civilization. Savages owned everything in common; private property defined the transition from savagery to barbarism. Barbarism included commercial society and the pursuit of individual self-interest and wealth. Civil society, however, was marked by overcoming barbaric individualism through the establishment of social bonds based on refined moral and ethical sentiments. In this schema, India remained at the barbarous stage.

Ferguson's ideas had considerable influence on how Britain

thought about governing India. Just ten years before he published them, the Battle of Plassey took place. After their victory the East India Company obtained the ruling from the Mughal Court that gave it authority to rule Bengal. Ferguson's ideas reassured Britain that it had the superior moral and ethical sentiments to organize, reorganize or otherwise revolutionize the conditions of India for profit, while advancing Indians in the path of civilization.

Ferguson had succeeded the philosopher David Hume as librarian to the faculty of advocates at Edinburgh University in 1757. Hume encouraged him to publish his great work, although he always considered it a thoroughly badly written book. Despite Hume's reservations, Ferguson's theories provided the intellectual and philosophical framework for investigation, thought, analysis, as well as political discussion, of imperial policy into the twentieth century – and perhaps beyond. At Edinburgh University, Ferguson taught Adam Smith; Dugald Stewart substituted for Ferguson while he attempted to find a peaceful settlement for the problems of the rebellious American colonies. After this Ferguson considered a career working for the East India Company before settling for becoming tutor to the family of John Stuart, Earl of Bute, Britain's first Scots prime minister (1762–3) and head of a family at the heart of British power and society. Bute had retired from politics and devoted himself to the role of patron of the sciences and arts. He patronized, among others, Samuel Johnson (1708–84) and William Robertson (1721–93). Robertson, along with Ferguson, had in 1754 been among the founding members of the Select Society, the intellectual circle that was the Scottish Enlightenment. In 1784 Robertson published a work on the ancient knowledge of India. Dugald Stewart, meanwhile, was nurturing the talents of the son of a Montrose cobbler, one James Mill (1773–1836). In 1818 James Mill produced his own monumental *History of India*, the canonical tome for the education of generations of East India Company employees and the Indian Civil Service. To speak of the

Scottish Enlightenment purely as an intellectual movement is to ignore the intimate relationship between ideas and political power; it is to be economical with the network of relationships that spun the web of history which constructed Empire as a work of knowledge as well as a system of rule.

James Mill's *History* openly acknowledged he had never set foot in India and had no knowledge of any Indian language. Nevertheless, he set out to ascertain India's true state in 'the scale of civilization'. He argued with the likes of Sir William Jones over India's place in that scale. Jones came out to India as Chief Judge for the newly acquired territory of Bengal. He was already famed as an antiquarian and student of languages and had established a link between Indo-European languages. Jones, like many Orientalists in the first flush of acquaintance with the subcontinent, had a high opinion of India's ancient achievements. As president of the Bengal Asiatick Society, he studied India's history, looking into its ancient customs and laws. Once he had cleared up the problem of chronology, uncovering the fascinations of this ancient civilization became his gentlemanly pursuit. But he had a low opinion of the living India that surrounded him. Ancient custom and law preserved as the secret knowledge of Brahmins had stultified. Modern India had become superstition. Even among those sympathetic to India's history, it was for ever immature, young in the arts of civilization and fit for rule by the progressive civilization epitomized by Britain.

For Mill, India was stalled in barbarism; its history Hindu and horrid. Indians were a 'rude' people who had made 'but a few of the earliest steps in the progress of civilization'. 'In beholding the Hindu of the present day we are beholding the Hindu of many ages past; and are carried back as it were into the deepest recesses of antiquity.' By the application of sound government, seeking the greatest happiness of the greatest number, Britain could engineer the lives of the hapless Indians. The publication of his *History* gave

Mill the opportunity to do just that; it secured him a job with the East India Company, where he remained for the rest of his days, eventually becoming the Examiner, the most senior position in its London office. There is no real mystery about his *History* becoming the standard text for Company employees.

The Mill prescription for India, indeed for the entire globe, was 'light taxes and good laws' as the basis for national and individual prosperity. In Mill's view, such necessary policy was beyond Indians themselves; but, so long as the business of government was 'well and cheaply performed' it was 'of little or no consequence who are the people that perform it'.

In 1834, Thomas Babington Macaulay (1800–58) took a ship to India to take up the post of legal adviser to the Supreme Council of India. During the voyage he read the works of classical Greek and Roman writers and Mill's *History of India*, the only text on the subcontinent he consulted. In India, Macaulay found nothing to disagree with Mill's assessment of the state of Indian civilization, concluding 'a single shelf of a good English library was worth the whole native literature of India and Arabia'. Macaulay proposed teaching Indians English so that they could assist the civilizing mission. The educational mission was second only to good laws. What do children do after all but go to school? Hinduism was 'identified with so many gross immoralities and physical absurdities that it gives way at once before the light of European science.' The objective of Macaulay's famous 'Minute on Education', written in 1835, went much further than creating a compliant class of English-educated Indians to help run the Raj. It would transform the subcontinent totally, making it an 'imperishable empire of our arts and our morals, our literature and our laws'. Macaulay was unsure whether Indians might progress so far as to demand European institutions and government of their own – but if they did, they would by that time have been remade as proper Englishmen, so it would matter little.

Education was a very personal concern for James Mill. He applied his rigorous concept of scientific parenting to the rearing of his own son, the philosopher John Stuart Mill (1806–73). Theirs was, perhaps, one of the most singular father–son relationships in history. It fascinated the psychologist in Ashis. Mill *pater* taught his son Greek at the age of three, Latin at eight, and felt there was no need for association with other children. By fifteen, John Stuart Mill became a devotee of the work of Bentham, and coined the term 'utilitarianism' for the theory that the rightness or wrongness of an action is determined by the amount of happiness its consequences produce in the greatest number of people. Two years later he began working for his father in the offices of the East India Company; he remained an employee until the Company ceased to exist in 1858. Mill the younger succeeded his father in the post of Examiner, the last there ever was. He developed into a 'grim' man who suffered a mental breakdown in mid-life. And yet he remained tellingly faithful to the main precepts of his father's vision of India. He elaborated on the hierarchical classification of societies: 'The state of different communities, in point of culture and development ranges downwards to a condition very little above the highest beasts.' The step on the ladder occupied by Indians was 'paternal despotism', a condition they attained in ancient times when they were 'brought to a permanent halt for want of mental liberty and individuality; requisites of improvement which the institutions that had carried them thus far entirely incapacitated them from acquiring'.

'The antagonism of influences,' Mill argued, 'is the only real security for continued progress.' Among Orientals, only the Jews, thanks to a line of prophets, had achieved this. And thus Mill, like so many nineteenth-century thinkers, historicized, philosophized and transmuted the Christian biblical model into the basis of scientific thought. Onwards and upwards went European society, though Mill the younger found much lacking in southern Europeans of his own day – even the French were too essentially southern for his tastes. The only people who had completed the entire trajectory of civilization were 'the self-helping and struggling Anglo-Saxons'. For those on the lower rungs of progress, improvement had to be 'superimposed from without' by a 'government of leading strings', which was 'only admissible as a means of gradually training the people to walk alone'. The liberal moral purpose of Empire was assured. 'The dominion of foreigners' could carry people 'through several stages of progress' and 'clear away obstacles to improvement'. In *On Representative Government*, Mill made clear this 'ideally best polity' was not suited to all people. Indeed, for most of humanity subjugation to 'foreign force' and a government 'in a considerable degree despotic' was appropriate and even necessary. India as a nation that could walk alone was definitely a long way off.

The liberal project of improving India provided a suitable context for missionaries. The East India Company had used its monopoly to prevent missionaries going to India, the better to avoid upsetting the natives on whom its trade and profits depended. But in the years after Plassey the temper of Britain changed. A Methodist revival swept the land. When the charter of the East India Company came up for renewal in 1813, William Wilberforce, the towering moral force behind the abolition of the slave trade, was enlisted to argue the entry of missionaries into India be made an essential condition of granting the new charter. The presence of missionaries was a utility for the colonial administration: at the time education in Britain was the particular province of the Church and religious groups. If India was to be educated, missionaries were the necessary agency.

Missions survived in India through the financial support of the British public. Regular reports, as well as pamphlets and books, were weapons in the armoury of their survival. Along with the literary efforts of evangelical colonial administrators, whether historical, antiquarian, linguistic, ethnographic, fictional or fact, stock images of the barbarous customs of India filtered into the British popular mind. Two of the most prominent images were *sati* – widow burning – and *thugee* – ritualized murder by bandits who were devotees of the goddess Kali. Ashis is something of an expert on the subject of *sati*, a practice represented endlessly in the art, literature and drama Europe produced about India. It became an almost obligatory episode in the career of the British official in India to rescue some poor woman from a funeral pyre. Ashis's investigations suggested the British ban actually led to its increase. Just as Christianity increasingly became the badge and marker of difference between the rulers and ruled, so dedication to tradition, even if it had but slender warrant in religion and previously had been a rare occurrence, increased among Indians the more it was opposed by the British. The melodrama of *thugee*, which had its latest recorded outing in the Hollywood blockbuster *Indiana Jones and the Temple of Doom*, was another conventional image of the barbarism of India. *Thugee* provided too good a morality tale of pacification and moral improvement, as well as constant work for colonial officers to do.

The barbarous image of Indians as naughty children sunk in wickedness took on a new dynamic at the end of the 1850s. The crisis of 1857, which the British call the 'Indian Mutiny', produced a permanent shift both in British and Indian psyches. Indians regard this uprising as the first war of independence. Britain imagined this trauma through the massacre of English women and children by Indian sepoys at Cawnpore and the privations and heroism endured by the English at the siege of Lucknow: the rulers saw themselves as victims of the brutality of barbarism. The following year Charles Darwin published *The Origin of the Species*. The British linear view of civilization had a new ally: the idea of biological fitness. The parent–child metaphor, itself obviously biological, naturally accommodated evolutionary implications and, in the popular mind, the biological explanation of evolution gave it the mantle of genuine science. It was the social philosopher Herbert Spenser who coined the phrase 'survival of the fittest', which everyone thinks was Darwin's explanation of his theory of descent with modification. Social philosophy had been Darwinian long before Darwin, and John Stuart Mill's works, also written at this time, seamlessly imply Darwinian theory.

The year 1857 marked the growing separation between the British and the Indians they ruled. British policy became increasingly racist and evolutionary. The older Orientalist and liberal ideas could still be accommodated within the new harsher tones; ambiguity and contradiction have never been a problem for colonialism. Missionaries were no longer in fashion. The sepoys' suspicion that their religions were being undermined to prepare the way for conversion to Christianity was implicated as a cause of mutiny. In the Proclamation of 1 November 1858 by which Britain wound up the East India Company and nationalized its rule of India, Queen Victoria stated: 'Firmly relying ourselves on the truth of Christianity' – a phrase inserted by Victoria herself – 'we disclaim alike the right and the desire to impose our convictions on any of our subjects.' Empire was itself the embodiment of Christian mission and moral duty, the proof of the fitness of British civilization.

But no one used the rhetoric of race or vaunted the claims and virtues of the Anglo-Saxon race more than the laureate of high Empire: Rudyard Kipling.

'Aha!' I exclaimed when Ashis mentioned his name, and quoted the line from Kipling I remember most: '"Half devil and half child"', the perfect post-Darwin epithet for Indians'.

'We'll come to that in a moment,' said Ashis. 'But first, let's consider perhaps the most telling character in all of Kipling. Do you remember where *Kim* begins?' he asked.

Who could forget the opening scene of Kipling's novel? We find the eponymous hero, the child Kim, Friend of all the World, before the House of Wonders, otherwise the Lahore Museum. The old lama befriended by Kim enters the museum to consult an ancient document essential to his spiritual quest. The lama has merely heard rumours of the existence of this antiquity; the museum founded by Englishmen possesses the actual document. At a crucial point the lama is offered a pair of spectacles by the Keeper of Wonders, the curator of the museum. To study his own religion and history, to fulfil himself as a man of tradition, the lama requires, depends upon and is assisted by the entire policy and rationale of Empire. And the description of the curator is based entirely on John Lockwood Kipling, Rudyard's own father, a noted artist, illustrator of his son's books, who for a time was indeed curator of the Lahore Museum. Kim, a mere child, knows India and all its peoples completely. But as the novel progresses we learn Kim is no ordinary street urchin; he is revealed to be a pukka *sahib*, a genuine Englishman, the son of a soldier. Rescued and educated as is appropriate to his birth, Kim uses his knowledge of India in the secret world of espionage essential to securing the safety of the Raj.

Children are best fitted to know children, argues Kipling, the child born in India, whose psyche was scarred by being sent back to England to be educated. He is fascinated by the difference of Indians, but there is one class of Indians for whom he never had a good word: English-educated Indians, especially the kind who joined nationalist movements for independence. In his short story 'The Enlightenment of Padget M.P.', he neatly reverses the educational lesson of Empire. It concerns a Member of the Mother of Parliaments visiting India to learn more about the nationalist cause with which he sympathizes. A clear message emerges: Indians are unfit for national independence. If granted independence, the divisions within and among its people would tear India apart. It is only the colonial administration that can deliver civilization. The colonial officer, in this and other Kipling stories, provides the archetypal portrayal of a Christ-like man imbued with honesty, probity and an unrelenting work ethic of duty and honour, sacrificing himself in the fetid climes of India to bring improvement to the benighted Indian.

Kipling was not alone in feeling that, however hard they tried, however much they were educated in British civilization, Indians remained unfit children. When General Reginald Dyer unrepentantly explained his ordering of the Amritsar Massacre, he used the rhetoric of the stern schoolmaster disciplining naughty children. Dyer's evidence to the committee of inquiry was shot through with paternalistic imagery: 'it would be doing a jolly lot of good and they would realise that they were not to be wicked', he said of the order he gave. His actions, though horrible, were 'merciful' and Indians 'ought to be thankful to me for doing it'. As children, Indians were not capable of governing themselves, and defiance of British authority was by definition rebellion against properly constituted moral order. Dyer was no aberration. He received widespread support across the colonial service in the Punjab where he was based – indeed throughout India – and was acclaimed in the House of Lords back in Britain, where a fund to support him raised £26,000.

'Let us look more carefully at those lines from Kipling, "half devil and half child",' Ashis said with a hint of devilish glee. 'They are not an exhortation to British Empire. In fact, they are an exhortation to America and demonstrate how the idea attained maturity.' The poem was written at the time of the Spanish-American War of 1890, when Kipling was living in America. The specific 'half devil, half child' referred to is the Filipino; America had just attacked the Spanish colonies in the Philippines. America was Britain's first genuine colony, a settler colony. It was the birthplace of imperialism, its civilizing mission to be worked out upon the American Indians. The settler colonists may have rebelled against British government, but they did not throw off the imperial mindset. They used it to justify and fulfil their manifest destiny in America. The logical thing to do once Americans had declared their internal frontier closed, in 1890, was to continue the process beyond their own boundaries by becoming a global imperialist. This is exactly what the great expositor of American Empire, Theodore Roosevelt, another devotee of the Anglo-Saxon and Teutonic races as well as the British Empire, urged.

'So the cycle of Indies came full circle!' I said.

'In political reality it was always a global vision,' Ashis offered. 'But the question that really fascinates me,' he continued, 'is how much of these old ideas persists? Do they, overtly or more likely covertly, influence how British Asians are thought about today? Does the debate about multiculturalism owe more to the old paternalism? How much recycling of old images and ideas is alive and well in Britain today?'

My head was swimming with too many connections and recurrences to tackle the innumerable answers to that question. It would have to wait for another day.

Children change us. Certainly, thinking of Indians as children changed the British psyche. The past from which I and my children sprang had been contested territory. The past and identity I recognize as my own contend with those prepared and ascribed by British imperialism. For British Asians our past was the enterprise of Empire, a work of knowledge overwritten on our identity. To be myself, to enable my children to author their own identity for the future, I needed to disentangle this disputed territory, and its legacy of old ideas that falsify our identity. We had to release ourselves from the complex web of history spun around our identity. We had to repossess our own heritage and ancestry.

Instead of being told who we were – and therefore are – we have to regain authority over our own belonging.

Questions of my own belonging, I felt, were tied up with the life and personality of my Dada, my grandfather. But the only person who knew him, my father, was not talking.

Chapter 8

EMPIRE AND ENTANGLEMENT

On the eve of the millennium my father died. I was having a small anti-festivity party at my house in Colindale, where 'milloonium' egg cups, suitably nonsensical mementos, were being passed around. My eldest son, Zaid, had dubbed the global hysteria 'milloonium' and the title had stuck. Our gathering was firmly of the 'not my milloonium, mate' fraternity. In the midst of our smart quips about the global firework displays chasing midnight ever westward on the television, the phone rang. My parents, along with my sister and some of her family, were in Pakistan. As I lifted the receiver, it occurred to me that some of the youngsters might phone as midnight approached in London. It was my sister, ringing to tell me of Bawaji's final heart attack. It didn't make sense. It didn't sink in. Matter of factly, I hung up and announced: 'My father is dead.' The hubbub was instantly stunned to silence before rising in a chorus of incomprehension that subsided into wails, 'whats?' and 'wherefores?' Saliha and Maha melted into tears, collapsing into the nearest available set of comforting arms; my boys stood dumbstruck. I watched them all through a thick fog.

Later, I found myself sitting with my head in my hands in my study in the attic. My face was damp. I became aware of time restarting. I felt exhausted, drained of everything except an overwhelming sadness. I don't do emotion very well. I become immobilized by a paralysing uncertainty of how to respond, surely the consequence of growing up among so many different cultural possibilities. How to act under any given circumstance, which etiquette to follow, becomes too complex a process of selection to perform under stress.

When I rejoined the gathering downstairs the aftershock had settled around an urgent question: the funeral. My God! The funeral. Something practical to focus upon. By custom the funeral would be held before sunset tomorrow. In Pakistan. Flights. Taxis. Milloonium! What? Visa! To get to Pakistan you have to have a visa. The whole of Britain may think you're a Paki, but the land of your birth begs to differ. It has become the delight of the Pakistan High Commission to respond, like for like, to the imperious, prejudiced practices of the British Immigration Service in Pakistan and at all entry points to Britain, especially Heathrow airport. To this end a cattle pen operates in the bowels of London's Pakistan High Commission, where eager applicants for visas mill aimlessly for hours at the behest of surly, indifferent bureaucrats. They can't stand me in Pakistan – too many critical articles over the years. They delight in making delays and difficulties. They know me, though. I can speak to someone suitably exalted in the hierarchy. Surely even I can grovel at a time like this? And under the circumstances someone must be able to overcome the red tape. Then it hit me with a palpable shock. Milloonium! The entire world was on holiday. There was no chance whatsoever that anyone would, even if they could, be on hand right now to wrestle with the intractabilities of issuing me a visa.

'I can't get there,' I muttered into the cross-currents of disjointed conversation. A pall of silence fell as we all acknowledged the inevitable truth. I was stranded, bereft, with nothing I could do.

I can never be sure why Bawaji decided to go to Pakistan in the dog days of 1999. He had never shown any interest in returning after our initial family excursion, whereas Mumsey could seldom be restrained. My mother is an adept world traveller. Single-handed, she peregrinates from London to Pakistan and returns only to depart again for California, where my sister, Huma Siddiqi, is settled among a vast network of Pakistani families who spend their days hosting social gatherings where Mumsey holds court. But on this occasion it was my father who was utterly single minded. He was going to Pakistan and that was that. Did he know? Did he plan the journey with a purpose? I devoutly pray that Bawaji peaceably closed the circle of his earthly journey, but I was left frustrated and shut out from any sense of closure. The sense of loss was compounded by distance and inactivity. I could not be involved, as an eldest son should be, in attending to the proper formalities of leave-taking. It was all disjointed, unfinished and incomplete. It was another partition in a life, my life, already complicated by serial partitions. A major link in my chain of being had been removed. With this partition went all the things I had meant to say, or should have said, all the things I wanted to know but never asked. Bawaji's death, though, in many ways led me to knowing the past better. It was because of his death that my curiosity about his family history – about my Dada – was reawakened. And through this I learnt much about how Empire had affected me and all British Asians.

A few of the obsequies were left to me. I wrote letters to multiple bureaucracies that had to be informed, took papers here and there so that records could be properly maintained. It required rummaging through drawers, pulling out the contents of cupboards. This disinterred details of Bawaji's life and interests I was aware of but had casually forgotten in the course of daily events. He liked to paint and he liked to write. He also kept photographs of our lives before and after we were together. So it was that the old faded photo of my Dada, his father, Hon Lt Subadar Ahmad Ullah Khan, Khan Bahadur, Sardar Bahadur, reappeared.

Throughout the 1980s, I nagged my father persistently to write about his father, to fill in the pages of *Record Our Family History*, the book I had given him as a present. But Bawaji had been stubborn. He would give one of his smiles, flash his eyes and say gnomically, 'We will see.' Eventually, he rewarded my unrelenting harassment by filling in the first two pages about Dada. In the 'Adult Life' section he wrote:

Medical education. Joined army, where he became extremely celebrated soldier. Doctor.

Titles: Khan *Bahadur*, Sardar *Bahadur*, O.B.I., I.O.M. Special (District) Magistrate (Hon). Awarded *jagirs* (land).

Wars.

(1) Kabul war (1878, 79, 80) Medal.

(2) Sikkim F.F. (1888, 89) Medal and Clasp.

(3) Black mountain (1891) Clasp India.

(4) Order of Merit (2nd class).

(5) Wazirestan (1894, 95) Clasp India.

(6) Actin of WANO. Special Service Order of British India (2nd class) and title of *Bahadur*.

(7) TOCHI F.F. Frontier. Medal and Clasp.

(8) China war 1900–1901. Medal and Clasp.

(9) Plague duty Lahore District.

(10) Special Services in Dharamsala Earthquake.

(11) Honour of Present Asm at his transfer from 20th Infantry of Dera Ismail Khan.

(12) Coronation Darbar at Delhi 1911. Medal specially presented by H.E. C-in-C of India. Sword of Honour and Khillat presented for exceptional services rendered to the Government of India.

(13) Public service, 1920, 1921.

(14) Assistance, Bekrid Festival, 1931.

(15) Assistance, Civil Disobedience, 1931.

(16) Governor of UP granted *jagir* in Bijnore District, 1907; *samad* (certificate) of meritorious services on three different occasions.

(17) *Jagirs* from Government of India, 1921.

Here had been feast after famine, and it had proved indigestible. Of course soldiers win medals. Yes, Dada had a number of medals; that much had always been evident from the photograph. But Sword of Honour? Had he really seen action in China and Kabul? My instinctive response was doubt. How could he, my father, a mere child when his father died, remember so exactly all those dates and specifics of events that long predated his birth? Indeed, how much of all this had simply been a product of Bawaji's ever fertile imagination?

I examined Bawaji's list with care. It was a litany of the North West Frontier wars. Bawaji had presented me with a family history in which the pages of Kipling came to life. I could hear the 'Boots – Boots – Boots, marching up and down' as the lusty soldiers cheered for 'Bobs, Bobs, Bobs', that 'plucky Khandaharder' 'Bobs Bahadur'. There it was in black and white. According to my father's list my Dada was one of those who marched behind Field Marshal Lord (Bobs) Roberts in the campaign that made him an icon of the Empire. I was devastated.

Dada's first military action, according to the list, was in the Second Afghan War (1878–80), one of those quintessentially colonial wars. The war was opposed by officials on the ground, who argued it was as unnecessary as it would be counter-productive. It had no purpose other than to impose the doctrine of imperial power on native peoples in reprisal, retaliation and revenge for their audacity in seeking to defend their independence. In this case, Afghan independence was fought over for geopolitical strategic reasons. In my time, such conflicts, the scourge of the Third World, were consequences of what was known, erroneously, as the Cold War. A century earlier it was more dismissively known by Kipling's epithet, the 'Great Game' – the subtext and subject of his novel *Kim*. Afghanistan lay between two imperiums: imperial Russian expansion across Central Asia and the British Empire in India. For most of the nineteenth century the delusional *idée fixe* of British foreign policy was Russian expansion, an ever-present threat to British interests in and tenure of India. So Afghanistan was trapped in a classic pincer between two imperial powers, like so many emergent nations in my time. Indeed, Afghanistan would relive this history as a recurring nightmare up to and including the present day.

Unfortunately for Britain the Afghans have never knowingly been compliant to any outside ruler. It did not help, in the First Afghan War (1839–42), that the commanders of Britain's Indian Army were appointed on seniority and not ability, according to the established practice of the East India Company. When it marched into Afghanistan, the army was led by incompetents who made every mistake possible. There was death in abundant, superfluous horror. The Afghans defeated the British forces in a major engagement at the southern city of Khandahar. They fell back on Kabul, where again military misfortune overtook them. A general withdrawal was ordered and on the long retreat the entire army was set upon. This included the enormous baggage train of camp followers, stretching for thirty miles behind the military column. Many, including English women and children, were taken captive. The Indian sepoys and camp followers were killed or stripped naked and abandoned to their fate in the freezing cold of an Afghan winter. Mile upon mile of the road out of Afghanistan was strewn with corpses. Just one man rode out to carry the dreadful news.

A punitive expedition to secure the release of the English captives was mounted. Many Afghans died before a tense stand-off was arranged. But Afghanistan remained lodged in the imperial mind as an enduring problem. For forty years the Raj camped on the edges of the famed North West Frontier, watching the Khyber Pass. It was only a matter of time before proud Britannia found reason to reassert her glory over these troublesome, turbulent tribesmen. And that's where my Dada began his military service? Meting out punishment on behalf of Victoria Imperatrix! And what is more, since I had always understood our family to have Pathan origins, Ahmad Ullah Khan was being employed to punish his own people.

Bobs Bahadur, ennobled as Lord Roberts for leading my grandfather on this imperial adventure, was the personification of high imperial values. As Kipling notes in his poem 'Bobs', he was a moralistic martinet, against drinking. But more importantly, he was a devoted advocate of the theory of martial races and believed that certain races were intrinsically militant. This classic piece of racist nonsense would have secured Dada's life-long association with the army. It was the basis of what Nicholas Dirks calls the 'cultural technology of rule', the manipulation of India's diversity, the divide-and-rule strategy that focused on difference, and operated in the interests of and for the benefit of the British. The peoples of India were pigeonholed in racial categories; each had a particular character, customs, dress and much else that marked their diversity. According to this lexicon, the Oriental races in general were effete, decadent and therefore cowardly and timid, which also made them treacherous. But the peoples of the Punjab, tall and classically Grecian in their manly bearing, were a race apart, distinct. They were by nature martial in more than physique. They were warriors with a code of honour bred through generations, from father to son, for the military life. Once enlisted in the armies of the Empire, fidelity to their unit and their humane commanders was their watchword. As martial races, they were exactly the cannon fodder needed to run a far-flung Empire on which the sun never set. They could be Sikh, Pathan, Hindu or Muslim, but once segregated into units on the basis of caste, religion and region, they became superb fighting units. These martial races underpinned the power of the Empire. They tended to serve on the North West Frontier, where Dada allegedly spent most of his career.

The theory of martial races turns out to be a nonsense fashioned after the great trauma of 1857 to promote the employment of soldiers from the Punjab. British rule and expansion across India had been made possible by its army. But this army relied on Indian soldiers: three quarters of its soldiers were Indian before 1857, and two thirds was considered prudent after. But it was not only the balance of Indian to British troops that changed. Before 1857 the East India Company recruited its Indian soldiers, predominantly Brahmins, from the region around Benares and the province of Oudh. They accounted for fifty to sixty per cent of the sepoys. The remainder were often soldiers enlisted from defeated native armies as British rule rolled out across the subcontinent. Service in the army was something of a family business. Entire villages would exist by sending their sons to serve, this continuous chain of enlistment guaranteeing the remittances that they sent home, which constituted a major part of the villages' wealth. Then suddenly, this army turned upon the British in deeds of barbarity and treachery. The proximal cause was the distribution of new greased cartridges, which the sepoys had to tear open with their mouths. The grease was rumoured to be beef – anathema to Hindus – and pork – anathema to Muslims. The reason for the Mutiny was rooted in the customs of Indians, a product of superstition and obscurantism.

The hardest and longest fighting during the uprising was in Oudh, technically an independent state and a prime recruiting ground for East India Company sepoys, until 1856 when John Company announced its annexation. The last vestige of independence of the homeland of most of the Company's army vanished. In retaliation for fighting against the moral order of Empire, the historian C. A. Bayly notes, tens of thousands of Indians were slaughtered by the British. At this time of rising population in India, he adds, only the regions of Benares and Oudh showed a decline in population, which accompanied their long descent into abject poverty. The martial spirit had departed those regions for good.

The units that remained loyal during the Mutiny were the newly recruited regiments from the recently acquired British territory in the Punjab. Suddenly, the Punjab regiments were discovered to be the martial races, and thereafter some three quarters of the Indian Army was recruited from this region, among them my grandfather.

By racial classification my Dada was in fact a Pathan, but on the North West Frontier he monitored and frequently engaged in clashes with the dreaded tribal Afghans, many of whom were also Pathans. All the negative stereotypes of Orientalist Islamophobic imaginings have been visited upon these Pathans and generically upon Afghans. The demonic tribal Afghans became familiar figures in the history of the Raj, and even more in the popular literary and cultural works that made India familiar to the British public. They are the Red Indians of the East, the lurking menace waiting their chance to sweep down and eradicate civilization as we know it. Like all savage enemies on the borders they were imagined as incarnations of malice, barbarism and evil, bereft of context or motivation except as bringers of death and destruction. Quite literally, they were embodiments of hate for everything the Empire represented. They populated the ripping yarns of *Boys Own* stories, the biographies of a long procession of retired English officers – indeed all forms of popular literature. And when cinema arrived, they were a natural subject for action-adventure pictures. The Indies were restored on celluloid. Nor has this tradition ended. The Taliban, awful as they were, merely confirmed centuries of preconditioning; they were exactly what we expected of Afghanistan. Old fears informed all thinking about the Taliban's Afghanistan as a training and breeding ground for modern terrorism. The armies of NATO today confront a landscape and people unchanged in our minds from those who menaced the army in which my Dada served.

The Indian Army was the backbone of Empire, not just in India but wherever the logic of military force was needed. Indian troops were entirely serviceable and fit for the purpose of Empire in East Africa, the Middle East, Southeast Asia and Hong Kong – indeed, anywhere imperial interests and prestige were at stake. Thus was Dada sent to China.

China had been the engine of global economic growth until the beginning of the nineteenth century. Gradually it was overtaken by the industrialization first of Britain, then of Europe and America. By the end of the century China's isolation and independence were no longer an option as far as the industrialized powers were concerned. Already it had been enfeebled by the Opium Wars. The East India Company had been advised by England's first ambassador to India, Sir Thomas Roe, to seek profit from 'quiet trade'. It found the perfect recipe in trading opium grown in India for tea and much else produced by China. The opium trade, in my mind, is the perfect analogy for colonialism. It created dependence by undermining and subverting the self-worth of people; a nation turned into junkies is enfeebled and loses its productive capacity, thus becoming submissive to the interests of Empire. Britain was joined by the newly imperialized United States of America in the opium trade. Their justification was the classic liberal policy of open access to trade. The 'Open Door' policy, as it was so superbly misnamed, was free only at the barrel of a gunboat. As China sank further into instability and chaos, various nationalist reform movements pushed the Manchu dynasty to resist the colonial powers. One such movement was the Boxers. In 1900 the Boxers laid siege to the foreign legations in Peking. An international coalition of forces was hastily gathered to confront this terrorism, Britain and the United States taking the lead. And my Dada was there as part of the Indian Army contingent.

How was it possible to be Ahmad Ullah Khan, servant of imperialism? When I surveyed Bawaji's list, instead of finding myself I found an enigma that defied my understanding. It made me feel like an abandoned orphan. The era of high imperialism shaped the myths I have spent my life trying to deconstruct. Mine has been a career of denunciation. And it turns out I have been denouncing the very enigmas my grandfather played a part in bringing into being. This was not what I meant by family history at all.

By definition, to be a Pakistani is to be a person whose identity was forged in the struggle for independence, someone whose consciousness is nurtured by the need for autonomy from colonial imposition. Where in that ancestry could I fit Dada? Not only had his honour and fidelity been given to the force that maintained colonialism in India and beyond, but, as the tail end of Bawaji's list suggests, he resolutely supported the Raj during the long campaign for Indian independence.

To read Bawaji's list of his father's career was like reading a charge sheet. Then I noticed my father had inserted a short note on another page. It read: 'He always felt extremely sorry to serve the British and without any reward. He once said, "If I had done only one tenth for my nation of what I had done for the British, my nation would have"' – the last words are in Urdu – '"*quam sar per bethati*"': 'my nation would have put me on their head.' One poignant grace note. It did not leap from the page, and for a long time it did not make a difference. I had wanted a complete family history to make things clear. What I found was a more tangled intractable mess than I was ready to deal with. I could think of no way in which learning about Dada helped to resolve the question of identity.

Now with my father's death the picture of Dada taunted me. I looked at the photograph again and again. There was my Dada with all his medals, standing proudly – but what was he proud of?

The British Empire? Did the British themselves recognize his contribution to Britain? If so, how could I be seen as a 'new' immigrant? True, India sought political independence, full autonomy to determine its own affairs. But so did Canada, Australia, New Zealand and South Africa. The modern Commonwealth was fashioned to recognize, sustain and maintain the long historic links with the subcontinent. The peoples of India were not 'new' to Britain once independence was declared, for not only had they been a constant presence in Britain over centuries but they also fought for and on behalf of Britain – as my Dada's photograph demonstrated – right through the twentieth century.

During the First World War Asian soldiers joined the British Army in droves. One and a half million were deployed on the Western Front. In the first battles of 1914 the British Expeditionary Force got a mauling from the Germans. Indian Army regiments sent to Egypt were hurriedly re-routed to Flanders. In the ghastly realities of rapidly developing trench warfare, Indian soldiers were brave cannon fodder disproportionately held in the frontline and returned to service more quickly after being wounded than their British comrades in arms. One of the first regiments on the frontline in Flanders was 126th Baluchis; actually there were no Baluchis among them – the men were Punjabi Muslims, Mahsuds and Pathans. The Indian regiments fought through the First and Second Battles of Ypres, at Festubert, Neuve Chapelle, Loos, the Somme, Passchendaele and Cambrai. Badly provisioned, badly kitted out and ill prepared for the conditions in France, they fought gallantly. 'It is like the destruction of the world,' one soldier wrote home. 'I cannot give you an account of this hurricane.'

In the First Battle of Ypres, Khodadad Khan, of the 129th Baluchis, became the first Indian ever to receive a Victoria Cross, bestowed 'For Valour' and the highest decoration granted by the British military. Before 1912 no Indian soldier, by virtue of being an Indian, had been eligible for such a medal. Press reports say

Khodadad was left manning a machine gun alone after all the rest of his unit had been killed. Despite being wounded, he kept firing until his position and gun were secured. King George V personally presented him with his VC at a military hospital in Hampshire. In the same war ten other Indian soldiers were awarded VCs. The Lion Gate Monument in New Delhi is a memorial to those who died. It bears 58,000 names. Indian soldiers served not only on the Western Front, but in Egypt and Palestine, Gallipoli, Salonika and East Africa, as well as in the doomed 'No-Man's Child' campaign in Mesopotamia, a litany of horrors worse even than Gallipoli. The campaign, which took place in what was to be turned into Iraq in consequence of these events, included what has been described as 'the most humiliating disaster to have befallen a British expeditionary force since 1842 [the retreat in the First Afghan War] . . . It was to remain the most humiliating disaster until Singapore fell in 1942, because of the decisions of a series of half witted military planners.' This judgement was written by the Australian author, Russell Braddon. The Mesopotamian excursion was an adventure for oil. It was ill-conceived, incompetently planned and murderous for the soldiers, more than 600,000 of them Indian. The worst disaster was the battle and siege of Kut al Amara, not far from Basra.

Thousands of Indians wounded on the Western Front were brought to England for medical treatment. So concerned were the authorities with public opinion back in India that they ensured, for once, that Indian troops got better treatment and care than was usually their lot. Brighton Pavilion, that superb architectural piece of Indian ornamentalist display, became a makeshift hospital – presumably to make the sepoys feel at home. But it was insufficient for the number of casualties and other buildings all around Brighton were also pressed into service. The greatest care was taken to segregate the wounded soldiers according to caste and religion, to feed them according to caste and religion and to ensure they were buried according to caste and religion. There are graves of Indian soldiers dotted around the south of England. Some are buried near Woking mosque, the first purpose-built mosque opened in Britain. Hindus were cremated at specially arranged burning *ghats* on the South Coast. Even greater care and concern went into ensuring wounded Indian soldiers had no opportunity to fraternize with English women. When a newspaper published a photograph of Khodadad Khan VC with an English female nurse in attendance, there was a terrible funk in the War Office and the India Office. Memos flew.

Many more British Asians, the sons of Indians resident in Britain, also served. After persistent questioning, Dadabhai Naoroji, the first Asian MP, forced the War Office to admit 'the intention of the military authorities is to exclude all candidates . . . who are not of pure European descent' from being commissioned officers as 'a British private soldier will never follow a half-caste or native officer'. Nevertheless, Naoroji's grandson, Kershap, a student at Cambridge, served in France in 1915 as a private in the Middlesex Regiment. He obtained a commission as a lieutenant only later when serving with the Hazara Pioneers in Mesopotamia/Iraq. Four of the grandsons of Mahomed Ebrahim Palowkar, the first Indian to open a tobacconist shop in Britain, all served in France, despite the fact that their family back in London were suffering abuse because neighbours thought their name was German. Some Indians who joined the fledgling air force did get temporary commissions as pilots: 2nd Lt H. S. Malik had been a student at Balliol College, Oxford, when the war began, and as a Sikh always wore his turban, not the regulation Biggles flying helmet; 2nd Lt S. C. Welinkar, a student at Jesus College, Cambridge, probably got his commission through some influential connections; and 2nd Lt Indra Lal Roy became a flying ace. Born in Calcutta, Roy had come to England at the age of ten to be educated. When the war broke out he was anxious to serve, applied for a temporary commission in the Royal Flying Corps and, possibly supported by a personal recommendation, was accepted. He distinguished himself in his service with 40 Squadron. In a dog-fight on 22 July 1918 his plane went down in flames. He was posthumously awarded the Distinguished Flying Cross. Roy was nineteen years old. Less than four months later the war ended.

Despite this intricate intertwined history, the Britain that greeted people like me was the eradication of memory, the obliteration of history and the defiance of sense and reason. Instead of building on the entanglement of Empire, the familiarity with India and its peoples that was widespread and commonplace in British society, British Asian migrants of the 1950s and later have been deliberately constructed as new people. And not only were we new, we were threatening. What was repatriated with the shrinking of Empire was not a history of mutual belonging but the prejudices and perceptions of difference that structured India for British rule. Race, and the racist prejudice all its connotations released, became the shorthand for revitalizing all the negative stereotypes of tradition and embodying them in British Asians, whether they applied or not.

With the picture of my Dada in my hand I was seized by an urgent impulse to discover the missing pieces in my ancestry. I displaced all my regrets at the loss of my father as I latched onto questions of how I could come to know about my grandfather and his perspective. It occurred to me that bureaucracy, the imperishable creation of the Raj, would provide a lifeline to reconnect with my own family history; that Dada's past would be found written down in documents and records. I had simply to uncover them.

What I had wanted from my father was stories, the memories and reminiscences that were his patrimony. Instead of delightful oral tradition, my father had entered precise details in the pages of *Record Your Family History* that seemed not so much improbable as impossible. How could Bawaji know all this? Had Bawaji's reticence been his way of telling me something he knew I would be reluctant to accept: that my grandfather had been a pillar of the social order of the Raj? Was Bawaji's perennial silence an indication that he too had reservations about the life choices of his own father? Who was my Dada? And what was his life? What I needed was a starting point for a documentary search.

The only living witness I could think of was my aunt – *bari puppu* – Rabia Durrani, the elder of my father's two sisters, who still lives in Pakistan. I have always been exceptionally close to her. She calls me *baitay* – my son – and is always very frank.

'Why is everyone so reluctant to talk about Dada?' I asked. 'Are you not proud of him?'

'*Baitay*,' *Puppu* began, 'your father was always very proud of your Dada. At least, till he went to Britain. I think his own experiences there made him re-evaluate your Dada's achievements. The rest of us were never too happy about his involvement with the British Army.'

'Do you see him as a traitor?'

'No,' she said with a sigh. 'He chose his path. But it was not the path of those devoted to the freedom of India. It doesn't do to glorify the achievements of someone who fought on behalf of the British, to preserve the Raj, nowadays. I think he too regretted his choice towards the end of his life.'

'How did he end up in the British Army?' I enquired.

'Well, the story I heard,' *Puppu* replied, 'is that he ran away from home when he was seventeen. One day his mother gave him some money and asked him to go to the market and buy some vegetables. He went to the market but never returned. Eventually some members of the family traced him to Agra, where he had enrolled at the medical college. But he refused to come back. Later, he joined the 6th Lancers. In the army he became very friendly with a man called Lord Birdwood, who was a major influence in his life.'

Of course, I knew the name: Birdwood! Bawaji's friend

Lady Birdwood, about whom he wrote so warmly in his letters from London, while I was running about in my *chaadi* in the fields of Sahiwal. Surely they had to be connected? Here was something definite to be investigated. I asked Mumsey for her explanation of how our families became interlinked. Her reply was that Dada had served in China during the Boxer Rebellion with Lady Birdwood's husband. Or at least Mumsey thought it was her husband. When we moved from our first ramshackle flat to the more spacious quarters of Hillsea Street in Hackney, the grande dame actually descended upon our little household. She complained of the smell. 'It's curry,' Bawaji had explained.

I tried to remember. Lady Birdwood was a tall woman with a great air about her who wore Edna Everage-style spectacles. She swept into our house with her dog, looked around imperiously at everything like a bird, and as if from an exalted perch, offered advice. She stayed only a short while, and left without eating the dinner my mother had spent half a day preparing in her honour. Before departing, she placed a couple of pamphlets in my hands and issued a stern order: 'You must learn to speak pukka English,' she said grinding her teeth, 'and do read these books.' The books were the *Protocols of the Elders of Zion* and *The Longest Hatred*; they came accompanied with various pamphlets outlining the 'Jewish conspiracy' and questioning the historicity of the Holocaust.

When I returned from my convalescence in Broadstairs, Lady Birdwood had become a regular visitor. Once or twice a month she and the dog would arrive to investigate and prognosticate on our 'progress'. I used to seethe with anger that my father tolerated this *lèse majesté* in calm silence. I, the child of Independence and Partition, found it incomprehensible and eventually intolerable. On each of her visits the demented Lady continued her programme of indoctrination by which, evidently, she hoped to groom me for membership of her group. It was the time of Enoch Powell and his 'rivers of blood' speech. Seemingly, what England needed was a lad such as me to provide the justification for wholesale repatriation of troublesome and inassimilable tinted folk of all stripes.

Just after my fourteenth birthday, Lady Birdwood made me an offer. 'We are about to start a new magazine,' she declared. 'It will be called *New Times*. We are looking for people to help us with it. You can write for it, and help us distribute it.' Lady Birdwood fidgeted. 'What do you say?' I looked at my father; there was a smile on his face. Not a grin but a suppressed smile of amusement. Bawaji evidently knew and was preparing to enjoy the denouement.

It was a seismic event. Pent-up frustration and straightforward rage poured forth in a reasoned, articulate, Pakistani-accented but pukka English denunciation of all the abominations for which she stood. Lady Birdwood was stunned. Her hopes demolished, she struggled to maintain her dignity undented. In silence, she patted the dog – the only one visibly distressed by the turn of events. She put on his leash, rose to her full height and made to leave. My sister ran to open the door. As Lady Birdwood exited my sister shouted: 'And I hate your dog too.' We never saw her again, though I remember reading, some years later, a newspaper article about her being arrested for National Front activities.

I hoped to discover something about my Dada through the Birdwoods. Dada was the first link in the chain, Lady Birdwood the terminal nut. I decided to begin with Lady Birdwood: a grande dame of the British Empire would be easier to track down than one native soldier. Once I started googling for Birdwoods they were not hard to find. It quickly transpired that the demented Lady Birdwood was not quite the grande dame of memory but a colonial immigrant. She was a Canadian, born Joan Pollack Graham in Winnipeg, Manitoba, and her grandeur derived from being the second wife of the second Baron Birdwood, Lt Col Sir Christopher Bromhead Birdwood.

Dismissing juicy details about Lady Birdwood – she was once voted spectacle-wearer of the year – I concentrated on her husband's entry in *Burke's Peerage*, conveniently available on the internet. It informed me that the second Baron Birdwood, Clifton College and Sandhurst, was commissioned in the splendidly named Probyn's Horse, otherwise King Edward VII's Own Lancers, of the Indian Army in 1917. He saw service in the First World War, curiously it seemed to me, as an aide-de-camp to the general officers commanding the Australian Corps. After the war he returned to India and fought in the Waziristan campaign of 1919–20. He was aide-de-camp to the Commander-in-Chief, India, in 1929–30. In 1937–8, by now a major, he was back on campaign in Waziristan. He served in the Second World War and rose to the rank of Lieutenant Colonel. I also learnt he was a literary man, having written books about Partition and a book on Nuri as Said, Britain's 'Mr Fix It' in Iraq until he met a sticky end at the hands of the Iraqis. Lady Birdwood's husband had died not long before I made her acquaintance. Clearly, he had been an India Army man at the heart of the Raj. But his dates and details just did not fit with the stories about Dada. This Birdwood would have been a child at the time of the Boxer Rebellion, far too young to have been the major influence in the life of my grandfather.

Burke's Peerage makes it ridiculously easy to connect people. Each individual is listed as son of, married to and progenitor of as prelude and postscript to the details of their career and achievements. A mere click on any of the highlighted names sets you wandering through history one life at a time. It is not only simplicity itself – it very quickly becomes compulsive, and highly educational. The second Baron Birdwood could not be the Lord Birdwood I wanted, so what about the first? My computer screen filled with considerable detail about the father, Field Marshal Lord William Riddell Birdwood. When I read the highlights of his life I found answers to my questions about the son. Lady Birdwood's husband, a newly commissioned officer in the Indian Army, became aide-de-camp to the Australian Corps because his father was the commanding officer. And this explained how the Birdwoods were ennobled with the improbable title of Barons of Totnes (in Devon) and Anzac (the Australian and New Zealand Army Corps). The Field Marshal was the officer commanding at the fateful Anzac Cove, scene of the futile, bloody landings of the Gallipoli campaign. The internet was awash with entries under his name.

Soon I discovered that this Birdwood had been born in India and, after Clifton College and Sandhurst, was commissioned into the Indian Army, first in the 12th and then the 11th Bengal Lancers. Various campaigns on the North West Frontier were mentioned; he served in the Boer War, was secretary to the government of India in the army department, and a member of the governor-general's legislative council. After his service with the Anzacs in the First World War he returned to India and rose to be Commander-in-Chief of the Indian Army – at which time his son again served as his aide-de-camp. On his retirement in 1930 he became Master of Peterhouse College at Cambridge University, and then Captain of Deal Castle. The Field Marshal died at Hampton Court Palace and had during his life amassed an immense list of initials signifying honours and awards aplenty.

Without doubt Field Marshal Lord Birdwood had a long career in India at a time when Dada would have been a soldier. I looked carefully at the details of the Field Marshal's early service. The campaigns listed seemed familiar: Hazara, Black Mountain, Isazai and Tirah. I looked at the list Bawaji had written in the family history book and there they all were. Now I had a match with the exploits of a Lord Birdwood, but there was still no mention of China, and the numbers of the Lancer regiments were wrong. A quick excursion through an elaborate internet site assured me that renumbering of regiments occurred at various times as part of army reorganizations. So perhaps that was sufficient explanation for any discrepancy.

Searching the internet is like hacking through a jungle: you have to chop away great quantities of exuberant undergrowth – dross of little purpose or relevance and possibly questionable validity – to discern a path, let alone an information highway. I knew I was still at the clearing-the-undergrowth stage. But somehow it fitted my mood: filling the spaces between work; preoccupying my attention at times when otherwise my mind might wander where I did not wish to be taken. I found myself looking forward to framing a useful question for the day to start a search engine trail that might take me nearer to my objective of uncovering the precise connection between Dada and Lord Birdwood. It would tell me, I thought, what my Dada actually did in the British Army and what the British meant to him. I discovered that the Birdwoods were a clan, a *biradiri*; there were so many of them, so many involved in the business of Empire building, in constructing an image of India as the domain of inferior people, that I lost count. The Birdwoods were sausages off an imperial production line: most of them were born in India, and followed each other through Clifton College, Peterhouse and Sandhurst, then into the Indian Army and thus back to the land of their birth. They even married mostly within their own *biradiri*! So nothing new there.

Then, two things happened which led me further on my search for Dada. Birdwood's entry in the *Peerage* informed me that the Field Marshal had written an autobiography. One day I got lucky and found myself on the website of a specialist bookshop offering a copy of this book, *Khaki and Gown*, for sale at a modest price. I arranged the purchase immediately. Then Mumsey brought me an official-looking envelope she had found among Bawaji's papers. Not knowing what it contained she passed it on to me. It was a registered letter from the Home Office addressed to 'Mr S. K. Sardar [my father], 222 Evering Road, London E5'. I tried to decipher the date; 63 was clearly visible, but the month and the day were difficult to read. Someone had written, in pencil, 'no answer':

the letter was delivered at the second attempt at 5.10 p.m. Inside were eight crumbling pieces of paper. They were difficult to hold in the hand, and their edges were discoloured and frayed. There was something printed on them in old hot-metal type, along slightly crooked lines, in a number of different typefaces. I laid them out on a table and manipulated them like some weird jigsaw. Eventually, order began to emerge.

It was a record of military service printed as a roll of honour on a 16 × 12 inch sheet. The heading read: 'Roll of Retired Indian Officer of the Indian Army. I.M.D.' In the column entitled 'Name, Father's Name and Caste', I read: 'Hony Lieutenant Ahmad Ullah Khan I.M.D. Khan Bahadur, Sardar Bahadur, O.B.I., I.O.M. Son of Hakim Mohammad Imam Khan. Pathan'. In the column headed 'Residence (with name of nearest Post & Telegraph Office)', it stated: 'Ahmad Manzil, Sherkot, Tahsil Dhampore, Bijnore District UP. Sub Post Office Sherkot. Telegraph Office, Sherkot (Bijnor)'. The third column was headed 'Length of Service, rank held in the Army, the date he attained the rank, & the date of retirement'. Here, I read: '36 years 7 months. Subadar (Commission granted 8th [the month is missing] 1889). Date of Rank of Lieutenant April 1900. Date of Retirement. 22nd May 1919'. There were two other sections: 'Peace and War Services' and 'Distinguished Services and rewards received for the same'. These columns matched, almost exactly, what Bawaji had written in *Record Your Own Family History*.

My father had copied the details of Dada's military service direct from the official records he must have requested from the bureaucratic archives. Where I had hoped to venture, my father had gone before. Now I had the documentary evidence in my hands in black and white: 'Sword of Honour and Khillat presented (as special award) for exceptional services rendered to Government of India'. Indeed, I found Bawaji had left out a few entries. Dada had received '2nd class Order of Merit for conspicuous gallantry' during action at 'Ghazikot on the Black Mountain (Hazara 1891)', on which occasion, I read: 'notwithstanding his being exposed to heavy fire, he performed his duties of attending to the wounded in a most energetic manner and also defended a wounded man against a fanatic who rushed up and endeavoured to kill him'. He was involved too 'in saving the lives of two British officers at Wano attack 1894'.

As I pored over the pieces of the document I presumed that when he first came to Britain my father had requested this information. Some obliging civil servant had scoured the records and put together the salient details of a life of service. I could not begin to know why Bawaji had done this, since when under duress to fill in the *Record Your Own Family History* he had never mentioned the existence of these aged pieces of paper. I could not get the answers I most wanted because my father was no longer there to reply. However much information I amassed, I would have that silence with me for ever. But armed with this new document I might be able to chip away at the enigma of Dada.

A few days later, the postman delivered my copy of *Khaki and Gown*. I had high hopes of the book. With eager enthusiasm I devoured its pages. Never have I been more disappointed. The Field Marshal was long on details of where he went in India, how he travelled, miles covered per day and weather conditions prevailing, but had virtually nothing to say about people encountered, let alone personal thoughts and feelings. A life lived at the very heart of Empire in times of enormous change provided little insight into hardly anything.

Lord Birdwood was an inveterate name-dropper, and possibly something of a snob. He never missed an opportunity to mention meeting important people. He became an intimate of Bobs – Field Marshal Lord Roberts – who was godfather to his son. Yet he describes Roberts no better, or at least no more intimately, than the famous Kipling poem. He mentions making a special effort to meet

Kipling's father, John Lockwood, curator of the Lahore Museum, but has nothing to say of the man. He dutifully mentions every encounter with royalty, underlining how intimately the institution is connected to the army. He waffles on about the 'Old Duke' – the Duke of Cambridge, elder cousin to Queen Victoria. The other great hero he acknowledges is General Kitchener, of 'Your Country Needs You' poster infamy, whom he served as aide-de-camp in the Boer War and again when Kitchener was Commander-in-Chief in India. Apart from this Lord Birdwood was at school with Douglas Haig ('Don't be vague, blame General Haig'); and was a contemporary of the entire litany of First World War commanders familiar to any fan of *Oh What a Lovely War*.

On the subject of his career in India, Birdwood is, as usual, infuriating. Everything I most wanted to know – did he meet my Dada, what did he think of him, did they fight together in the North West Frontier, in China? – was bubbling below the surface of the printed words, succinctly unexpressed. However, the book did give a clear picture of the routines in the life of an Indian Army officer. It was an ordered pattern of daily activity heavy on playing games and slaughtering, but which usually involved wildlife rather than human enemies, real or imagined. No country squire back home in England could compete with the zooicidal obsession of the British in India. Whether military or civilian, wherever they went the British insisted the locals rustle up wildlife for their sport. Aside from pig-sticking and tiger hunts, a daily kill was de rigueur. The fragile ecological state of India today owes much to this unabashed gun-and-sabre fetish which brought numerous species of the subcontinent's wildlife almost to the point of extinction . When not hunting, playing games and taking exercise were just the things Birdwood most relished. There was polo, of course. No military base anywhere in India was complete without its polo ground. Or there might be cricket, hockey, football or marksmanship, with contests and cups for almost everything.

Birdwood and his colleagues even found time to invent the game of snooker.

According to Lord Birdwood, life in the Indian Army was a permanent boy scout camping expedition. The army set huge numbers of people endlessly moving over the face of the subcontinent. But, Birdwood notes pointedly and with pride, in his day the *sillidar* system – the tradition by which sepoys provided their own horses and every two sepoys employed a groom to rustle up the daily rations necessary for man and horse – meant all this movement could be accomplished at no extra expense to the Exchequer. An Empire on the cheap which ensured maximized profit: the ideal solution for a system created by a trading company.

Such labour as army officers engaged in consisted of supervising the durbar. The original durbar in the Mughal court was for the hearing of petitions and accounts, reviewing administrative arrangements and so forth. This regular assembly involved the officers intimately in the lives and concerns of their soldiers. Petitions for leave for all manner of complex familial reasons and disciplinary matters of all kinds were raised and discussed before the assembled regiment. It is no exaggeration to say the ordinary sepoy soldiers belonged to their regiments. The regiment was a family business for the sepoys just as it was for the British officer caste. The *sillidar* system positively encouraged chain recruitment. After Partition many of these soldiers came to Britain, and villages continued the tradition of sending their sons to what now replaced the regiment – Britain itself. The migration from Mirpur to Bradford turns out not to be an anomaly but a continuation of a traditional practice.

Lord Birdwood's book led me on a journey into British and Indian history and their entanglement. Tradition played as important a role in the business of Empire as it does in the lives of British Asians today. It was in 1765 that Clive wrote to inform his employers, the Court of Directors of the East India Company, that they were now 'the Sovereigns of a rich and potent kingdom' by virtue of being granted the *dewani* of Bengal. They were not merely collectors but 'proprietors of the nawab's revenues'. For the British, the right to assess taxes, the function of proprietors of revenues, was a matter of law, since by British tradition the courts established and protected property rights. It was what the Magna Carta was for, and what made the ancient document the fountainhead of all the rights and liberties of an Englishman. The Court of Directors was concerned by their new powers, believing Englishmen 'unfit to conduct the collection of revenues and to follow the subtle native through all his arts, to conceal the real value of his country, to perplex and elude the payments'. Distrust of the natives, whose nature it was to deceive, was the quintessential British stance towards India. But Indians remember the British made such an appalling job of assessing the revenues that within five years they had caused a horrendous famine in which an estimated third of the population of Bengal died and large tracts of land were left uncultivated, leading to a breakdown of law and order with bands of dacoits roaming the countryside, preying upon the peasants and disrupting trade.

To secure the revenues meant resolving questions of land settlement, property ownership and rents. This would be the province of the law. When Warren Hastings became the first governor-general, he informed the Court of Directors in 1772 of a new policy to establish the Company's system of governance on a 'more equitable, solid and permanent footing', one based on the 'ancient uses and Institutions' of India. These would be found in the religious law of the Muslims and Hindus, who were in possession of 'laws which continued unchanged from remotest antiquity'. The first intimation of the religious tenets of the *gentoos*, or Hindus, had been published by John Zephaniah Howell in 1767, supposedly based on an unidentified '*gentoo shastah*' (shastra) he had been translating at the time of Siraj ad Daula's attack on

Calcutta in 1756. Howell lost his 'curious manuscripts', though he survived the Black Hole. Hastings, conscious of the need for knowledge of such ancient manuscripts, appointed a group of talented, bright young men to accomplish the task. Nathaniel Halhed was given the specific task of translating legal texts, and in 1776 published *A Code of Gentoo Laws or Ordinations of the Pandits*. As explained by Halhed, the process of its production was an Indian version of the game of whispers. The classical language of India was Sanskrit. Halhed had no knowledge of Sanskrit but sat with pandits – Brahmins who as a class were described as professors of law – who read out answers to specific questions. These answers were translated into and written down in Persian by Halhed's assistants and then finally translated into English by Halhed himself. It is an example of the subtle process by which translation becomes the invention of 'tradition', and it was typical of the quest to codify Indian law to serve the particular interests and requirements of the British administration. Sir William Jones, of Asiatick Society fame and appointed as a judge of the Supreme Court of Bengal in 1783, was dissatisfied with Halhed's translation. He set about learning Sanskrit in order to produce a proper codification of Hindu law, which is how he came to discover the linguistic links between Sanskrit, Greek and Latin, and to stimulate interest in what became known as the Indo-European language group and Aryan culture. Jones died with his legal task incomplete. The process was still underway when Macaulay came to India in the 1830s, and indeed it was finished only in the 1860s.

Two thirds of India had been brought under direct British rule by the time of the 'Indian Mutiny'. The remaining third was technically independent, yet utterly dependent on the panoply and payroll of Empire. It comprised more than 500 states, such as Baroda. By the time William Spiller commanded Baroda's army, between 1909 and 1917, Britain's attitude to traditional rulers of India had transformed. It had been reconstructed on the model of British

aristocracy. Britain began to see the conservative possibilities of
these indigenous rulers after the trauma of the great uprising of
1857. The Proclamation of 1858, which nationalized the East India
Company, confirmed the rights of these independent states and
their rulers. How Britain understood these rights was crucial to the
next phase of development. Britain brought to India its own vision
of feudal kingship, to spread hierarchy, deference and order across
the subcontinent. Indigenous ideas of lordship got lost in the
translation. It was a pattern that was authored in India and rolled out
across the Empire as a whole. There are various forms of religious,
ritual, social, political and economic lordship and innumerable
titles to be found among the world's peoples. The British Empire
was a process of homogenization that read all variety as a direct
translation of the model reconstructed from British history. The
process was reciprocal: along the way the British monarchy
was reconstituted as much as any native form of lordship. Titles,
precedence and ceremony became the ornamentalism of Empire,
the means of binding the diversity of rulers of far-flung lands to the
interests of Britain by granting them social status and precedence
within the increasing gradations of the British system of honours.
To keep pace with this development, the viceroys, the British
Crown's representatives in India, were elevated and exalted. In 1871
Disraeli made Victoria Kaisr-i-Hind, Empress of India. This entirely
new status was the engine of enormous change accomplished
in the name of tradition. The cult of monarchy was made
central to Britain's vision of itself and its role in the world, the
pinnacle of a global Empire. The conventional idea that the British
do ceremonial wonderfully was a deliberately created tradition invented
and perfected with a purpose in the high Victorian era. As the
British monarchy became increasingly constitutional, and thereby
politically limited, its ceremonial and symbolic functions became
more and more important. The monarchy was the centre of symbolic
power around which the whole of the hierarchy and ordered class

structure of British society revolved. It was the lamp to which the moth of colonial subjugation was drawn by design, and offered in the 'traditional' symbolism of durbars, jubilees, funerals, coronations and other state occasions.

The more I read of Lord Birdwood's autobiography the more I realized how entangled Britain and India actually were, and how deeply they shaped each other's traditions. But I could not find any physical point of contact between Birdwood and my own grandfather. My Dada was the son of a *hakim*, just as my Nana was a *hakim*. The tradition has been maintained down the generations among my extended family. Family history reports that Dada ran off to study medicine. Significantly, he ran off to study modern Western medicine – to become a traditional *hakim* he had only to remain at home. My Dada took the option of modernity, to cross the great divide the British created in India. Then he joined the IMD – Indian Medical Department – as a surgical assistant. If Ahmad Ullah Khan became modern he soon found, according to the systematic practice of the British in India, that he was only second-class modern. The inflexible rule of British governance created the unbridgeable divide between them and the natives. The Indian Army was, for all its familial metaphors, two parallel universes with different structures and naming of ranks: one for the natives and the real one for the British. No matter what their medical training and competence, Indian medics treated only native Indian troops. When it came to the sahibs they worked as assistants under the supervision of real, pukka English doctors. It was only after Kitchener's great reorganization of the Indian Army, a process that began in 1903 and continued till independence, that any hint of parity between these worlds was permitted. Dada became an Hon Lt – clearly the emphasis is on the Honorary – only after more than thirty years of service. It is similar to the apartheid that operated in the award of medals for gallantry.

My grandfather had saved the lives of British soldiers. Among the listings of his exploits on those crumbling pieces of paper was a reference to a book entitled *Deeds of Valour*. An e-mail to the British Library produced a photocopy of the requisite page of this book. It was the source of details I already knew from the Roll of Honour, but it identified the dates and places more precisely. With this in hand I then looked up what Lord Birdwood had to say of the Black Mountain campaign. He was indeed there; it was his very first experience of action under fire. According to the Field Marshal, the whole affair was an 'ineffectual campaign'. 'The only hard fighting of that expedition occurred when a detachment of what were called the "Hindustani Fanatics" made a desperate attack one night on a company of Sikhs at Ghazikot, on the river.' He explains that the so-called fanatics were Hindu descendants of the mutineers of 1857. On the night in question they came in nearly naked, their bodies oiled, and succeeded in killing a number of Sikhs 'before being driven off by my future father-in-law, Sir Benjamin Bromhead'. He notes one last memory of particular relevance to my search:

A press correspondent, writing home details of an action, ended his despatch by saying, 'Dhoolies took off the wounded' – a dhoolie being an Indian equivalent of a stretcher. Our joy may be imagined when a home newspaper elaborated this into: 'The ferocious Dhoolies swept down from the hills and carried off the wounded.'

According to *Deeds of Valour*, Senior Hospital Assistant Ahmad Ullah Khan, Subordinate Medical Department, Bengal, on 19 March 1891 at Ghazikot, 'notwithstanding being exposed to a heavy fire performed his duty of attending the wounded in a most energetic manner, and also defended a wounded man against a fanatic who rushed up and endeavoured to kill him'. I was not sure how I felt about the press report, which made Dada's valour as a *dhoolie* man a perverse parody to confirm all the worst imaginings about natives, nor about Birdwood's repetition of this anecdote. But when I looked again at the facsimile of the title page of *Deeds of Valour – Performed by Indian Officers and Soldiers, During the Period from 1860 to 1925*, another thought struck me. It was published in Simla, the summer headquarters of the Raj, in 1927 and prepared by P. P. Hypher of or for the army department. In 1927 the commander-in-Chief of the Indian Army was none other than Lord Birdwood, so perhaps he would have been influential in bringing into being a record of genuine reports of Indian valour, including that of my grandfather.

There was another occasion when their paths would have crossed. I suspect it is the moment recorded in the photograph that began my long excursion into family history. Dada stands before the camera displaying the Sword of Honour. At the Coronation Durbar of 1911, Dada was presented to the King Emperor, George V, by the Commander-in-Chief of the Indian Army, Lord Kitchener. Kitchener's aide-de-camp, the man who organized the ceremony was – you guessed it – Lord Birdwood. Yet, all his autobiography reveals is that the presentation of Indian soldiers turned into a debacle when one of the great durbar tents caught fire. Lord Birdwood had hastily to rearrange the ceremony and notes it eventually passed off well enough.

After forty-nine years of service, Lord Birdwood retired as Commander-in-Chief of the Indian Army. He writes: 'Notwithstanding our natural sorrow at the severance of our long association with India, it was good to be in England again. We landed at Plymouth on the 24th December, 1930.' What a neat tying of ends. He returned to Britain at the very place where the Birdwood family's involvement with India began. What struck me most forcibly was the amazing incongruity of his statement. Birdwood had just left the land of his birth and his entire adult career, India, to return to a country, England, which he notes elsewhere he had not visited at all for a period of twenty-five years. Over the course of his travels, recorded in detail in the autobiography, he mentions visiting England only on about three occasions. Yet, on Christmas Eve 1930, he was 'home'. Once in England he was whisked to Sandringham, where the King apologized for not being able to appoint him governor-general of Australia. The Australians had insisted it was time one of their own filled the post. Instead, Birdwood became Master of Peterhouse College, Cambridge. It was after all the family college, where his father, brothers and cousins – though not the Field Marshal – had studied. Like generations before him, Lord Birdwood seamlessly moved from India to mix with imperial British circles. For him – a man born and bred in India, where he spent almost all his life – there was no 'new' era, merely a continuation of a long entanglement that was the history of India and Britain, an entanglement over generations that was personal and familial, as well as political and public. Why should things be different for me and other British Asians?

In his retirement Lord Birdwood writes of his delight in receiving Christmas cards and letters from his old regiment in India, his only hint of nostalgia for the land of his birth and its people. Was this small, absent-minded comment an explanation of how Lady Birdwood ended up on our doorstep in Hackney? Was that strange visitation a tradition of the regiment, a tradition of Empire, offering one last fleeting acknowledgement before all connection evaporated in the newness of 'settled coloured communities'? Did Bawaji somehow renew and draw on the connection? Was it duty or desperation that might have prompted him to contact Lord Birdwood? Did he write off in hope and pride to secure a copy of Dada's military record so that he might have proof of his familial belonging to Britain readily to hand?

I started out seeking a personal point of contact with Dada. What I uncovered was something so much deeper, more dense and profound than I had expected. I and all British Asians like me are products of an entanglement that remade both India and Britain. There is no India, Pakistan or Bangladesh, nor their collective, conjoined history, without Britain, any more than there is Britain, its history, culture and self-image, without the subcontinent. The question that emerged was not how it was possible to be Ahmad Ullah Khan, servant of the Raj. The real enigma was how could I, Ziauddin Sardar, ever have been considered 'new' to Britain? It is not the life and times of my Dada but my own which are the anomaly, the truly incomprehensible misrepresentation.

The mystery of my grandfather revealed to me I am where I belong. Indeed, I have always been British. Now that I know more of who I am, I feel offended. I am offended at being described as an 'immigrant'. I am offended at how British Asian history, my history of belonging, has been expunged. I am offended by those who question my loyalty. I am also offended by all those who want to glorify colonialism or see it as a positive endeavour, particularly when its legacy still shapes the lives of people everywhere in Britain and in the subcontinent. The long extraction of wealth from the subcontinent to support colonial rule and transfer profits to Britain deliberately underdeveloped those lands and skewed their chances of attaining sustainability after independence. Most of all I am offended by the way the long history of entanglement between Britain and India has been ejected with colonial rule. The instantaneous volte face that made me 'new' staggers me, as much as it dishonours those in the know who permitted it to happen, had every reason to be aware of how perverse it was and the means to prevent it happening. It is a betrayal of history worked on the people of Britain as much as a denial of my history of belonging in Britain. Britain has deliberately created the problem of 'race', when the means to enjoy a very different way of living together were readily available at every turn.

How and why has Britain expunged the memory of the

entanglement of Britain and India? Like the construction of Empire, it has most significantly been a work of knowledge. It was constructed by thinking of India as 'over there', separate and distinct from 'here' in Britain; and furthermore, by thinking that India, Pakistan and then Bangladesh were different, made real and historically distinct in the very moment of their invention. And like the history of entanglement, the erasure of memory has been a mutual process. The consequences are pernicious and sour the condition of real lives in Britain today, as forcibly brought home by *The New East End* by Geoff Dench, Kate Gavron and Michael Young. It is a study of the multicultural transformation of the East End, an area that has always been the most multicultural part of Britain, the reception area for migrants down the centuries, the place where serial waves of people sweated at making better lives for their offspring. It is a follow-up to the classic post-war sociological study by Peter Wilmott and Michael Young, read by every student of sociology, *Family and Kinship in East London* (1957). In the old study, networks of family mattered and were preserved, mothers were central figures in maintaining the integrity and success of the family, and from these patterns of individual lives emerged a strong sense of identity, community and class consciousness. If one could look across cultural variation one would find remarkably similar expectations and attitudes among the Asians who came to live in the area. But that discovery of commonalities has not happened. Instead, the follow-up study identified a seething sense of displacement, betrayal, and losing out among the white families that found expression in the communal history of the Blitz, which distinguished and separated them from the 'new' people, the British Asians they saw as privileged at their expense. The white community increasingly feels that its members are penalized by the advantages being disproportionately awarded, on bureaucratic principles, to new incomers. This spiralling syndrome of frustration has less to do with race than the atrophy of memory, the history of the contribution of the Asian community to Britain as well as the Blitz, while the safety net of social provision has been withdrawn from those people who need it most. The white working class of *The New East End* feel that their identity – the collective history of their community – is not being accommodated. All I can see in this are legitimate, familiar concerns shared by British Asians. The disappearance of social housing, the rising costs of housing, changes in the labour market, pressure on all forms of social provision, such as health and education, impact most noticeably on the most vulnerable, but the pernicious focus on race, on difference and separation, creates the conditions for communities to turn against each other, to select the wrong targets for their anxieties and animus, instead of laying a solid foundation for common action across communities.

Would it have made a difference if the real history of India and Britain's entanglement had been remembered and memorialized, the long history which made Asians familiar figures on the streets of the East End? Indian seamen have frequented the docks of London for 400 years. Families of such seamen have lived, worked and struggled in the East End during that time. The service of Indian seamen in the merchant navy provided a lifeline for the plucky East End in wartime. The network of family, kinship and community origin ties today's British Asians to that shared wartime effort. The failure to remember the contribution of millions of Indians during two world wars betrays the sense of belonging British Asians have every right to claim. The simple commonplace fact that most British Asians are by family, kinship and community drawn from the very families and places where the Indian Army was recruited should subvert the slide into ignorant racism. India played a part in supporting Britain through its darkest days, but those who became British Asians played a disproportionately large role. If only we remembered.

Chapter 9

A HISTORY OF BELONGING

For two decades I lived in Britain oblivious to antecedents. I existed in a carefully constructed bubble in which British Asian history basically began in the 1950s, with the arrival of my father in Britain. I became 'genuinely British' by Act of Parliament, convinced people of my kind were an entirely new phenomenon, with no history of belonging in Britain. The general consensus during my adolescence was of Britain being 'flooded by immigrants'. It was deeply etched on my mind, permanently imprinted on my physiognomy courtesy of my broken nose. We had come, it seemed from nowhere, in such vast numbers that we created pandemonium. Enoch Powell MP predicted 'rivers of blood and tears' would soon be flowing on the streets. Mine did, and so did that of many like me. As new people, we were washed of history, shorn of connections, confronted only with new ground to break, devoid of expectations, but expected to be grateful for our place in Britain and compliant with what Britain condescended or grudgingly made available.

   Much of what I read confirmed this perception. As an undergraduate I spent the vast sum of twenty-two shillings on a copy of *Immigration and Integration* by Clifford Hill, subtitled

'A Study of the Settlement of Coloured Minorities in Britain', and 'written primarily as a source book for students and all interested in the field of race relations in Britain'. It told me that Asians began to arrive from the 'New Commonwealth' in the 1950s, a few years after the arrival of *Empire Windrush*, the ship that brought West Indians from Kingston, Jamaica. Immigration history was presented as if Britain acquired 'coloured minorities' in the way it acquired an Empire: 'in a fit of absence of mind', as the historian Sir John Seeley had so memorably put it in his 1883 lecture, 'The Expansion of England'. Hill's book left me with two clear impressions. First, leading the flood of immigrants were Afro-Caribbeans; and second, the central issue of immigration was race relations. With the focus on 'race', precedence was given to the Afro-Caribbean nature of the 'problem'; Asians were a secondary category not mentioned in and of ourselves. There the matter rested till I became a reporter on *Eastern Eye*.

On 2 November 1982 Britain acquired a new terrestrial television station. Channel 4 was created by an Act of Parliament to supply programmes 'calculated to appeal to tastes and interests not generally catered for'. It would provide for minority and special interests. Channel 4 would be a kind of publishing house of broadcasting; many of its programmes would be commissioned from other television companies, with a particular remit to support the work of independent producers as part of its public service. The commissioning editor for minorities was an enlightened black woman called Sue Watford. From London Weekend Television (LWT), she commissioned two programmes aimed at blacks and Asians: *Black on Black* and *Eastern Eye*. They would alternate in the schedules late on Tuesday nights. I noticed LWT's advertisement in the *Guardian*: they were looking for reporters to work on a programme for Asians by Asians. The best people to report on Asian affairs in Britain, it stated, were Asians themselves. I bought into that philosophy, and applied. A month or so later, I was working for LWT.

Britain already had a history of Asian broadcasting. The BBC had been making Asian programmes for decades. They flooded the schedules early on Sunday mornings, before the broadcast of church services. Made in Hindi and Urdu, they targeted mainly women, encouraging them to learn English. They were produced by a special Asian unit based in Birmingham, hermetically sealed from the rest of the BBC's operations. The programmes were no longer relevant to the community they supposedly served.

We were a motley crew at *Eastern Eye*. Our producer, Samir Shah, spoke only English and had recently worked on a series about race relations. There was an Oxbridge-style Indian who spoke Hindi, Karan Taper; he was well connected and mixed easily in elite British circles. Then there was a recently arrived East African Asian, Narendhra Morar, who spoke Gujerati and had to learn much about journalism. The fourth member of the team, Dippy Chaudry, was a young woman born and bred in Southall who spoke Punjabi. I was the kid from Hackney who spoke Urdu and could serve as the Muslim representative. Our collective experience in journalism and broadcasting was varied, patchy or in some cases entirely absent. Our experiences as Asians living in Britain were just as various, as was the diversity of our ancestry and backgrounds. We each knew something of a different Asian community, but the whole of the British Asian experience was something of an enigma, and much of its profound variation – only partially reflected in our small band – beyond our immediate knowledge.

We were expected to provide context – to know the background to Asians in Britain, to know the culture and politics of India, Pakistan and Bangladesh. Or, as our producer put it, to 'make connections'. To prepare myself, I went back to the books. The literature on 'settled coloured communities' had expanded considerably since my college days; there were shelves full of the stuff and journals aplenty. Race relations had become a growth industry. It was now a standard academic discipline, awash with its own jargon of refined sociologese. Among the books I picked up was Dilip Hiro's *Black British, White British*, published in 1971. It dealt largely with racism and Asian culture, providing only a few interpretative points on the history of British Asians. Hiro briefly referred to the origins of indentured labour recruitment in India and suggested that Asian settlement in Britain was a direct result of actions taken by British entrepreneurs to further their economic interests. He argued that Asians, unlike West Indians, did not see their migration in social or cultural terms; for them, economic consideration was the sole motive for coming to Britain. Moreover, Indians and Pakistanis did not discard their culture and skilfully recreated the environment that they left behind. Encouraged by this opening, I searched harder and found other books and journal articles offering fragmentary evidence of historic antecedents. But the history of Asians in Britain never went beyond the 1950s. And then, by chance, I met a man who knew more about that history.

On my way home from work one day, I literally bumped into him. We were both waiting for the Tube at Tottenham Court Road station. We looked at each other, smiled, and started talking in Urdu as though we had known each other for decades. In one respect we did. We recognized each other as people who could trace their lineage to the Utter Pradesh (UP) province in India and who spoke Urdu. He was heavily built, with short hair and a moustache, elegant and – given his background – by definition cultured, as UP is a place renowned for art and poetry. His name was Hamayun Ansari. He was studying for a doctorate in history at Royal Holloway College. He had been brought up and educated in England but returned to Pakistan to join the postal service at the end of 1970. Pakistan, however, did not suit him, so he came back to pursue further study.

We started talking about our parents. 'My parents never permanently settled in Britain,' he said. His father originally came to Britain in 1938 to read engineering. During the Blitz, he was evacuated to Swansea, where he joined the Home Guard. But he also became interested in the Pakistan movement, participating excitedly in the discussions taking place among Muslim students based in London at the time. 'Not once,' Ansari said, 'did I hear my father suggest he experienced racial discrimination.' He thought for a moment. 'Perhaps because he accepted British superiority; their dominance in interaction with him seemed natural.' His father returned to his home town, Saharanpur, on a 'convoy' ship via Durban in 1942, armed with an honours degree in electrical engineering. 'My father,' Ansari continued, 'by his own admission was an Anglophile.' He was hugely impressed by English culture, standards and authority, and especially, like many of his generation of modernizing professional Muslim elite, by the British educational system of which he was a product. For him, a career in the Pakistan Civil Service was the height of professional respectability and influence. This he had imbibed from what he had seen of the British officials in India. Naturally he was keen for his offspring to take advantage of a system that had served him so well, so he decided to send his sons, one by one, to study in Britain. Ansari attended a secondary modern school in the quaint Surrey village of Hamsey Green. His mother, herself a well-educated woman, looked after the children while they were young, but returned to Pakistan as they progressed to university.

Ansari told me he was researching the history of Asians in Britain. His plan was to spend the next decade writing a definitive account. I asked him the question uppermost in my mind: 'Did the Asians first arrive in Britain in the 1950s?' Ansari laughed. More like the 1650s, he replied. Suddenly, decades of history became four centuries. The first Asian arrivals were followed by different waves of migrants; each wave had its own characteristics. Ansari already had a four-phase schema for his history: the first arrivals were between 1600 and the 1830s; the second period from the 1830s to the First World War; the third was the interwar years; and this was followed by the post-Second World War influx, which finally led to the immigration of the 1950s and 60s.

The moment I was aware such a history existed it seemed so obvious, so self-evident. It was like one of those landscape drawings where a secret hidden face lurks in a tree or among the foliage. 'Can you see the face?' people ask. You look and look and all you see is the landscape. But once the hidden features have been pointed out you never see anything else, and that changes the landscape entirely. The possibilities of faces embedded in the landscape began to stir memories. Vague images in black and white swam to mind; images gleaned from watching the patriotic war films made in the 1940s and 50s that were endlessly replayed on television. Surely I had not invented the distant memories of smiling air crew, among them turbaned Sikhs, sitting around on grassy banks awaiting the signal to scramble for action during the Battle of Britain?

Throughout the 1980s, I kept bumping into Ansari – usually at Underground stations. I considered each chance meeting to be an opportunity. Ansari had unwittingly become my mentor, passing on what he had discovered through his extensive research. I learnt from him that some 2.5 million Indians served in the British armed forces during the Second World War, saw action in every theatre of the war and earned thirty-one VCs, the highest commendation 'For Valour'. In the Forgotten War, as the Burma campaign fought after victory in Europe is known, twenty-seven VCs were awarded, twenty of them to Indian soldiers. This Indian Army was the largest volunteer army ever assembled. When Britain declared war on Germany in 1939, the Viceroy simply informed India, without any consultation, that it too was at war. But there was no conscription in India and so volunteers came forward. Besides that, 8 million Indians were employed in auxiliary work for the armed forces and a further 5 million in industries producing munitions, as well as eighteen different centres assembling and maintaining aircraft. And then there was the matter of the merchant navy, Britain's lifeline in its darkest hours, which formed the shipping convoys that kept the nation fed and supplied so it could continue the fight for its survival. In 1938, 26 per cent of the labour force in British merchant shipping was Indian; this rose dramatically during the war. There are no accurate figures, but estimates of their numbers vary from 33,000 to 59,000. Nor was there any memorial in Britain to those Indians who perished on the sea, on land or in the air until 6 November 2002 when the Queen inaugurated the Memorial Gates on Constitution Hill, by the side of Buckingham Place, 'to honour the 5 million men and women from the Indian Subcontinent' and the Commonwealth 'who volunteered to serve with the Armed Forces during the First and Second World Wars'.

When, I asked Ansari, did the first Indian come to Britain? '"The first fruits of India" is how it's recorded,' he replied. On 22 December 1616, it is documented, the Lord Mayor and Aldermen, members of the Privy Council along with Governors of the East India Company, attended a baptism at St Dionis Backchurch in the City of London. A boy born in Masulipatnam, on the Coromandel Coast of India, and brought to London two years previously by the Rev. Patrick Copland was baptized. King James I selected the baptismal name: Peter. This grand occasion, just sixteen years after the formation of the East India Company, marks the beginning of Empire. The christianizing mission would eventually be secularized as the civilizing mission. The project of Empire was justified and validated by the education and conversion of this boy ('it bore fruit'). And the year 1616 had a bumper fruit crop. At the time Peter was being baptized, an Indian of another race had come to London. Mrs Rebecca Rolfe had sailed from Virginia with her husband, John Rolfe, the man about to launch the Virginia tobacco industry. Rebecca is much better known to history and popular culture by her native name: Pocahontas. It is probable that some of those who attended Peter's baptism had a financial interest in the Virginia Company, founded just six years after the

East India Company. There was considerable overlap in personnel between the two ventures. Pocahontas was the other sensation of the season in London, seated near the King at an entertainment staged for his benefit. Both Peter and Rebecca received stipends from their respective companies while in England. In 1617 Pocahontas returned to her native land, America, but once aboard ship she took sick and died. In 1617 Peter was sent back to India to take up work as a missionary to his own people. Little is known of his fate.

Empire was always subliminally present in Britain from its earliest beginning. The presence of the subservient dependents, the subject peoples, represented the exercise of power and control over expanding territories around the globe. Empire, the historian David Cannadine has argued, was a kind of performance art; 'ornamentalism' is his term. How could the performance continue without the essential set dressing and bit players: the presence of Asians, people like me? The surprising thing is that their presence on the streets of Britain was largely unrecorded for hundreds of years, despite Asians being in Britain since the seventeenth century. They were simply eradicated from memory and rendered invisible. The visible invisibility of Asians was a work of deliberation. It is not the recovery of their presence that is difficult – or at least it is no more difficult than uncovering the lives of any of the mass of the British working classes. The difficulty is explaining how this presence was reconstructed as the 'problem' of a 'new era' created by the arrival of 'new people' and defined by 'race relations'. The treatment of British Asians today has its roots in this construction. The Asians are fine as long as they remain invisible – their involvement in the corner shops and other trades notwithstanding. But the moment they make their presence felt by, for example, demanding decent housing or standing up to racism, they become a 'problem'.

★

Merchant ships brought Indians to Britain. Indian seamen, known as lascars, arrived in English ports. From the outset they were pawns in Britain's search for economic power. The Navigation Acts of the 1650s and 60s defined the monopoly of shipping, export and import between Britain and India granted to John Company, as well as to the other companies operating in the Americas, West Indies and elsewhere. The Acts restricted the make-up of crews: only a quarter of seamen on British ships could be Indian. Colonialism always protected British interests. The lascars were not merely poor wretches jumping ship, stranded in British ports begging till they could secure a return passage; they were a continuing object of the legislation regulating British control of trade. The Navigation Acts provided the basic framework for their employment, and did not entirely disappear until 1963. War, though, affected the number of Indian merchants sailing to Britain. In war the Royal Navy recruited more merchant sailors, leaving shipowners to flout the regulations and hire more lascars. At the end of the Napoleonic War, jack tars released from the Navy sought employment in British ports, creating tensions. The renewal of the charter of the East India Company in 1813 included the declaration: 'No Asiatic sailors, lascars or natives of any territories . . . shall at any time be deemed or taken to be British sailors.' As British control extended over India, and more and more Indians became British subjects, a clear distinction existed aboard British shipping. The point was reiterated in the 1823 Merchant Shipping Act (Lascar Act). Such legislation had various functions: to restrict the settlement of Indian sailors in British ports; to ban their recruitment; and to make lascars a charge on the East India Company or shipowners if they failed to find return passage for their Indian sailors. The attraction of lascar sailors was obvious: they were paid a fraction of British articled wages, and the regulations specified that less was to be spent on their food and they were to be allocated less physical space aboard ship.

The coming of the age of steam made lascar sailors even more important. Stoking the insatiable engines of steam ships in tropical waters was not white man's work. Firemen and stokers were predominantly lascars. As the economic and technological dynamics of shipping changed, so legislation was amended. In 1849 a new Merchant Shipping Act redefined lascars as British for the purpose of shipping, just as easily as martial races were soon to be redefined in India itself. In the heyday of steam navigation, after the opening of the Suez Canal, half of all seamen employed in the engine room were lascars.

However, lascars did find ways and means to stay around British ports. The Strangers Home for Asiatics, Africans and South Sea Islanders was opened in Limehouse, London, in 1857. It was the base for the Lascars Shipping Officer, an official appointed by the Board of Trade to operate an employment agency for Indian sailors. Not all lascars in British ports were viewed as a pauper problem. There were Indian sailors employed under British articles. There were those who married and whose children merged into the general population of the seaports. Some established themselves in small businesses, running lodging houses for Indian seamen, running restaurants (the origin of the genuine British Indian restaurant), becoming street hawkers and door-to-door peddlers. Not much is written about how these Indians fared, individual cases suggesting alternatively how easily lascars merged into the population and how problematic they were thought to be. They are visible not as a class of people but as oddities. We have no definitive evidence to assess the relations between lascars and British workers, only the opportunity to read our own prejudices and expectations into what little is known.

Lascars were not the only Asians brought from India as a consequence of Empire. British merchants in Calcutta during the eighteenth century were infamous for the enormous households of servants they employed; more than 100 Indians serving one merchant was not unusual. And in this community of men, white women were a distinct rarity. Merchants took local wives and raised their mixed-race offspring. If they survived India long enough to make their fortune, these graduates of the East India Company retired to Britain to invest their profits and live the life of country gentlemen or city swells. Returning English nabobs were accompanied by Indian servants, and in some cases their Indian wives and children. The nabobs lived a life of luxury at the heart of British power. They bought rotten boroughs and thus became Members of Parliament, where they had a large voting bloc dedicated to the Indian interest. They founded landed estates across the length and breadth of the United Kingdom. They sent their sons, mixed race or not, to public schools and then often into the army and thence back to India. Colonel James Skinner, founder of Skinner's Horse, one of the most famous and conspicuous regiments of the Indian Army thanks to its canary yellow uniform was the mixed-race son of a Company man and a Rajput girl. Skinner's descendants, such as Lt Col M. A. R. Skinner, were still serving in the Indian Army generations later. Just eighty years after he created his magnificent regiment, the original Skinner would have been ineligible to become a subaltern. By that time first-generation Anglo-Indians need not apply. Skinner was by no means the only offspring of mixed-race marriage to serve in the Indian Army. None other than Field Marshal Lord Roberts, the son of a general and born at Cawnpore in 1832, Commander-in-Chief of the Indian Army during 1885–93, was the grandson of such a union.

The men who went to India in the eighteenth century and returned to Britain changed the tastes, habits and face of Britain. They brought Indians as well as India to the notice of Britain. The debates refining the purpose and responsibilities of governing India took their cue from the profound effect the nabobs had on public opinion. The age of philosophizing and scientific explanation of Empire was also to be the age of re-moralizing it in secular garb.

Many became patrons of the arts and science, in which India was an essential connection. Sake Dean Mohamet, author of the first book in English written by an Indian, was the recipient of such patronage. In the conventions of his time he published his book by subscription. Some 320 people, the cream of Anglo-Ireland, subscribed two shillings and sixpence each to make the publication possible. Subscribers included seventeen noblemen, ten military officers, seventeen clergy (among them three bishops), one Vicountess, five Ladies and several Honourables, the daughters of titled personages. Was Dean Mohamet merely a superior kind of flunky in the household of his patron, Godfrey Evan Baker? He does appear to have been part of the ornamentalism of growing British power in India.

Many Indian servants remained in Britain for decades, some for the rest of their lives. Until the twentieth century domestic service was one of the top five employment categories in Britain. We catch glimpses of these Indian servants from advertisements for employment, a clear indication such domestics were versed in Britain's mores. I like the one placed in 1750 by an East Indian, fluent in six languages including Portuguese and German, who announces himself as converted according to the rites of the Church of England and 'seeks employment as footman'. Other advertisers refer to being in the country for twelve or fifteen years and seek employment with 'any genteel family' or 'any person of quality on reasonable terms'.

In the nineteenth century ever more *ayahs* or other servants were employed to ferry children back and forth, or attend wives and children returning to Britain. Many were engaged only for the journey and found themselves without a return passage, stranded in London. My home turf of Hackney had seen plenty of people of my kind long before the cold, foggy winter of my arrival. Around 1855 concerns were raised about the plight of *ayahs* destitute in London, with some fifty or sixty staying in one lodging house of dubious repute. In 1900 a hostel run by the London Missionary Society was opened at 26 King Edward Road, Mare Street, Hackney. Victorian paternalism always found plenty of work to do among the deserving poor, Asian or British. It is hard to reach beyond the episodic interludes of visibility to grasp who these *ayahs* were, how they coped and how they fitted into the life of Britain.

Ansari's second era of Asian presence in Britain, from 1830 to the First World War, covers the heyday of imperial policy in India. It was an era of administrative reform: Lord William Bentinck, governor-general from 1833–5, theoretically opened all posts in the government of India to Indians, a change effected at snail's pace. The English language education policy, commended by Macaulay in 1835, produced more and more Indians capable of taking up administrative jobs and searching for further education and qualifications in Britain. Ruling the Raj necessitated the presence of Indians in Britain in numbers and in ways that expanded over time. They were the fruits of deliberate policy, not accidental peculiarities.

Ornamentalism demonstrated the subservience of India to British rule. *The Times* provided exemplary proof in its daily Court Circular. It recorded formal audiences granted by Queen Victoria to an increasing number of Indian maharajahs, ranis, nizams and a whole litany of other fulsomely titled personages, most of whom had been relieved of the burden of rule and survived off generous pensions from the British, who encouraged them to live like proper aristocrats. The conspicuous gifts laid at the royal feet by this band of exotics, paid for by their government pensions, lushly caparisoned and richly jewelled, were symbolic testimony to the riches of India flowing to swell Britain's power. Over time the nobility of India became fixtures of the London season, regularly photographed and reported in the press. They were part of the celebrity culture of Victorian times. They ornamented ceremonial functions, an increasingly important part of the pomp of Empire.

Durbars, jubilees, funerals and coronations: none was complete without the Indian parade. And, where better for visible proof of the efficacy of the civilizing mission than on the cricket pitch? Ranjitsinhji, Maharajah the Jam Saheb of Nawanagar (1872–1933), played for Sussex and England, representing the country in the all-important Ashes Tests against Australia. In 1899, placards declared: 'Ranji saves England.' He was succeeded on the cricket pitch by a gaggle of nephews and the likes of the Nawab of Pataudi. Others of this class took part in gymkhanas, played polo and had strings of racehorses.

The Victorian passion for exhibitions, educative and improving displays open to the public, was another aspect of India's continual presence in Britain. First in the field, the Great Exhibition of 1851 had its India hall. A significant function of such exhibitions, popular all over Europe, was to present and thereby construct an ethnographic view of non-Western peoples and cultures which underpinned the moral of imperial rule. London and other cities enjoyed the impressive Colonial and Indian Exhibition of 1886, for which whole bazaars of Indian artisans were imported to display their timeless crafts for the amazement of the British public. Indeed, there had long been a consistent demand for Indian craftsmen to ornament public buildings and grand private residences. Queen Victoria was not slow to appreciate the point. Kipling's father, John Lockwood Kipling, is credited with designing the Durbar Room Queen Victoria had installed in her favourite residence, Osbourne House on the Isle of Wight. The principal work was done by master craftsman Ram Singh, whose skills other nobility also engaged. The British Empire Exhibition of 1924 was another grand display of the timeless exotica of India, even though the British working classes had by then given enthusiastic welcome to Gandhi, who brought the living reality of India to the consciousness of the working classes and the labour movement in Britain.

The cult of the Queen-Empress Victoria was encouraged among the British public. Postcards of the Royal Family, complete with Indian attendants, were extremely popular: the royal children with their Indian *ayah*, the Queen with wonderfully uniformed and turbaned escorts. Indians were essential visible ornaments in the British royal ceremony. But the process was not without its frisson of scandal. For the occasion of Victoria's Golden Jubilee in 1887, a new band of royal servants was imported from India. Among them was Abdul Karim, a 24-year-old clerk from Agra and Muhammad Bux, who was to be footman to the Queen. Within two years Abdul Karim had made it known to his employer he was not destined for the life of a serving man. Victoria promoted him to Munshi, or secretary, and began taking lessons in Hindustani from him. Rumours started to circulate suggesting that the Munshi had supplanted John Brown in the Queen's affections – or worse. In 1890, *jagirs* – grants of land in India – were awarded to Abdul Karim for his benefit, and cottages on the royal estates in Britain were provided for his use. In 1894 he was again promoted, becoming the Queen's Indian secretary with the title of Hafiz. The rumours in court circles went into overdrive: Abdul Karim was nothing but an upstart; his father an apothecary at the Agra jail, not a hospital assistant; the son was a nefarious influence on the Queen-Empress who could not be trusted to read sensitive state papers since he supported seditious elements in India. Despite the rumours, the Hafiz remained by Victoria's side till her death in 1901, but with her demise Abdul Karim was sent packing to India, as soon as all his personal papers in the cottages had been burnt. When he died, back in his home town of Agra in 1909, there was another *sati* of his personal papers. Soon after his mother's death, Edward VII decreed no Indian servants would be appointed, but during the London season, when the Royal Family was seen by everyone worth seeing, four Indian Army orderly officers would attend the King at court, levees and ceremonial occasions. The emphasis may have changed, but the photo opportunities never missed a beat – they were, after all, the essential point in emphasizing the dominance of Empire.

Imperial policy brought Indian students to study at British universities. Entry to the Indian Civil Service (ICS), the official embodiment of the Raj, was by examination. Although the jobs were open to Indians, the exams were held only in London. The Bar in Calcutta and Bombay was confined to barristers trained in England. And chances of senior appointments in other branches of public service in India were enhanced by British qualifications. It was not Anglophilia that brought increasing numbers of Indians to Britain, but straight economic realism, the prospect of better pay and upward mobility. Not all returned to India. The first Indian to pass through the Inns of Court, Ganendra Mohun Tagore, of the family that later produced the Nobel laureate Rabindranath, was called to the Bar in 1862 and then settled in Britain with his Bengali wife and accepted a teaching position at University College London, where my daughter did her law degree. Another of the Tagores, Satyendranath, was the first to succeed in the ICS examination, in 1864. Indian teachers at British universities instructed the men who would rule India in its languages and Hindu law. Oxford and Cambridge received their share of Indian students, male and female. Indeed, it is argued that the colleges of Oxbridge were concerned none should get a reputation as the Indian college, so they ran a quota policy of no more than two Indians in each intake. All who passed through Oxbridge – including many who went on to powerful positions – had mingled with fellow Indian students. All of the generation that secured Indian independence studied in Britain: Gandhi and Jinnah were law students; Nehru was educated at Harrow, Cambridge and Inner Temple; his daughter Indira went to Sommerville, Oxford. These are the most notable names, but the more one searches for Indian faces in the landscape of Britain, the more appear.

The Indians who came to Britain attained a kind of visible invisibility, but they certainly did not exist sealed off from the society in which they lived. In Britain Indian women took advantage of British culture and discovered more freedom. The sisters Toru and Aru Dutt were probably the first female students to attend lectures at Cambridge in 1869. Womash Chandra Bonnerjee, founding President of the Indian National Congress, trained in law in Britain, and sent his wife and daughters to Britain to live the life of English ladies. His daughters went to Cambridge – Nolini to Girton, Susie to Newnham – where both read medicine. Nolini made a reputation for herself as a doctor and welfare worker in Liverpool. Cornelia Sorabji became the first woman to read law at a British university – at Somerville, Oxford – only to find she could not read for the Bar along with the men. She took her case to court, appropriately enough. She won and thus pioneered the way for my daughter to become a barrister.

The fight for Indian independence also took root in the UK. The Indians formed organizations and associations to advance the cause of Indian independence. Anglo-Indians, those Britons who had spent years in the subcontinent, as well as those politically interested in the fate and future of Empire – for or against – were also members. Indians who came to Britain understood that change in India required changing hearts and minds in Britain. Recruiting the powerful and influential to join their associations kept Indian independence on the agenda of the British elite. Indians and Britons, then, were closely entrenched right up to the first half of the twentieth century.

Dadabhai Naoroji best exemplified the truism that, to change the life of India, Indians had to be active and present in Britain. An academic, businessman, politician, and Grand Old Man of Indian independence, he was the first Indian elected to the House of Commons, in 1892 as a Liberal MP. Among the earliest graduates of Elphinstone College, first fruit of Macaulay's Education Minute, he became the college's professor of mathematics. Also a linguist, he was founder editor of *Rast Gofar* and was actively involved in a variety of political campaigns through the Bombay Association he founded in 1852. In 1855 he came to Britain as a business partner of Cama and Company, and three years later he established his own cotton company. By that time he was already professor of Gujerati at University College London. In the college's University Hall in Gordon Square he helped found the London Indian Society in 1865, quickly superseded by the East Indian Association founded in 1866, for 'independent and disinterested advocacy of the interests of India and promotion by all legitimate means' of its welfare. The association collaborated with the Anglo-Indian fraternity, publishing a journal, lobbying MPs, holding meetings where Indian grievances were aired and reforms proposed. In 1868 Naoroji toured Indian cities to set up branches of the association and raise funds for its activities in Britain. In 1888 Naoroji, with the support of Womash Chandra Bonnerjee, set up the Congress Political Agency, which developed into the British Committee of the Indian National Congress and published its own journal, *India*. Through this committee, the Indian National Congress spent more on propaganda work in Britain than in India.

In 1901, Naoroji published *Poverty and Un-British Rule in India*, and another lecturer at University College London, Romesh Chunder Dutt, published *The Economic History of India*, presenting a detailed and critical analysis of the entire colonial period. Naoroji criticized colonialism and argued that excessive tax and the siphoning off of Indian trade surpluses were sinking India into poverty, famine and misery. Some £30–40 million a year of India's wealth was exported to Britain. India, he made clear, paid heavily for the privilege of being ruled by Britain. The Indian Army, funded by Indian taxpayers, was crucial for British power east of Suez, and Indians paid the high salaries and pensions of all those civil servants and administrators who governed their lives.

To further the cause of Indian independence, it was crucial for an Indian to be elected to Parliament. The first attempt was made by Lal Mohan Ghose, a barrister, who stood for the Deptford constituency as a Liberal in 1885. He seemed a good prospect in a working-class constituency with a large Irish population ready to be animated by the Liberal policy of Home Rule for Ireland. But Ghose found himself vilified as an 'Indian Baboo', 'a political adventurer' and an 'Asiatic foreigner' who was a 'stranger to English civilization and Christianity'. He lost by 367 votes, then he lost again the following year. Naoroji also stood in the 1886 election, for the Holborn constituency. He too failed to get elected, but did better than expected. His next chance came in 1892, when he stood for Finsbury Central, where he had been establishing himself as a prospective candidate for four years. He won by just five votes. The next Indian elected to Parliament, Mancherjee Bhownagree, was an opponent of Home Rule who stood for the Conservatives. Bhownagree was MP for Bethnal Green from 1895 to 1906. The swing to the Conservatives that carried him to Westminster ended the parliamentary career of Naoroji. The political tides of the early twentieth century became radical over the next two decades and the next Indian parliamentarian, Shapurji Saklatvala, stood as a Communist supported by the Labour Party and won Battersea in the 1922 election, holding his seat until 1929. It would be another fifty-eight years before an Asian again became an MP. Then it would be hailed as a ground-breaking development for the 'new era' of 'settled coloured communities'. But Keith Vaz, elected to represent Leicester East in 1987, was merely following in the footsteps of those no one remembered. The history of my belonging had not only been eradicated; it was also being controlled in the way it was being re-written.

Forgetting is no accident. History is a process of deliberate construction of remembrance and forgetting. As George Orwell reminds us: 'Who controls the future controls the past. Who controls the present controls the past.' In the year 1984, the ominous words of my favourite author had been invoked in an ad campaign across Britain. The words resonated as I uncovered the history of my belonging in Britain. A great many luminaries that year debated whether or not we had escaped the awful fate Orwell had envisaged. For every assertive 'yes', there was many an equivocal 'no'. The debate focused on the totalitarian vision of the Big Brother state, ascribed to Orwell's disaffection for Stalinist Leninism, which in the triumphalism of early Thatcherism everyone congratulated us for having escaped. In the West, Stalinism was a lost cause. More subtle readers of Orwell, however, argued that the techniques for manipulating opinion he had laid bare had taken root in our lives.

The consensus suggested that Orwell based the career of the central character in *1984*, Winston Smith, who was employed by the Ministry of Truth to rewrite history, on his own experiences working for the BBC during the Second World War. What I never heard mentioned was that Orwell was in fact in charge of the Empire Department, broadcasting to India and Southeast Asia between 1941 and 1943. His fictional slogans made perfect sense not only in the context of Stalinism, but also in the context of Empire. Born Eric Blair in 1903 at Motihari in Bengal, India, he was third-generation Anglo-Indian. His father, Richard Walmsley Blair, was in the Indian Civil Service and worked in the Opium Department. Orwell's mother, née Limouzin, was the daughter of a French tea merchant based in Burma. His paternal grandfather had served in the Indian Army. A scholarship boy at Eton, Orwell failed to get a scholarship to university so took the ICS exam and entered the imperial police service. He was an assistant superintendent of police in Burma from 1922–7. *1984* can be read as an accurate depiction of the Cold War world as it shaped the lives of peoples across the Third World. Orwell's views on Empire are of a piece with his denunciation of Stalinist totalitarianism and his socialist championing of the working class. He wished to 'escape from . . . every form of man's dominion over man', as he wrote in *The Road to Wigan Pier* (1937). However much I agree with these propositions in his novels, Orwell is someone who always occasions in me a lurking equivocation.

He described himself as 'lower-upper-middle-class', because his family were not the landed kind and had no extensive investments. They were dependent upon the generous lifestyle derived from careers spent in India. Orwell's background and the contacts it provided gave him opportunities of which none of the working classes could even aspire to dream. He dedicated himself to experiencing poverty, but I always have questions about people who take excursions among the underclass. The essence of working-class life and true poverty is the incapacity bred by real deprivation which permits no escape. It infects people with the virus of under-achievement, lack of ambition based on the belief that opportunities in the great wide world are not for you.

Orwell and Empire were bound together. It made sense that, alongside celebrating the writer's great novel, in 1984 Empire was writ large in the popular mind. The televising of *The Jewel in the Crown* in that year was closely succeeded on the airwaves by the lush bodice-ripper vision of old India in the dramatization of M. M. Kaye's *The Far Pavilions*, and the cinematic version of what is always described as the definitive novel of late Empire, David Lean's production of E. M. Forster's *A Passage to India*. These representations brought a great nostalgia for the Raj, validating the British perspective of India. They privileged British readings of Indian history, culture and civilization.

So far as I could tell, Indian history was firmly under British control, in the hands of white male British writers often with limited acquaintance with India. Paul Scott, author of *The Jewel in the Crown*, was in India for a few years while serving in the RAF during the Second World War. E. M. Forster spent some months touring

India in 1912–3 and was there again in 1921–2, working as personal secretary to the maharajah of one of the native states. And Indian history was in the control, as it had long been, of white British female writers whose literary fiction had done so much to fix the view of Indian character in the popular imagination.

M. M. Kaye had a longer connection to India. Born in Simla, the summer headquarters of the Raj, in either 1908, 1909 or 1911 (depending on which source one consults), she was the daughter of Sir John Kaye, who wrote the classic histories of the 'Sepoy Mutiny' and the First Afghan War. She married Geoffrey Hamilton, an officer in the Guides, the most romantic of all Indian Army regiments, which was raised to serve on the North West Frontier. The Guides appear in innumerable books about India, including M. M.'s own worldwide bestseller *The Far Pavilions*, published in 1978. Memsahib romantic fiction has a great deal to answer for. It reaches further and endures longer in the popular imagination than many acknowledged literary classics. It authored a vision of all things Indian which in insidious ways controls contemporary attitudes to the settled communities of British Asians.

When *The Far Pavilions* was adapted for television in 1984, *Eastern Eye* raised some of these questions, but it only served to emphasize how much of an enclave we were. We made no dent on the mainstream. It seemed to me that we should not merely be content with our status as special cases for special treatment. Whatever talking among ourselves could or would do for our entertainment, information or self-image, it had little effect elsewhere. And too often it failed to address the issues that shaped our lives as citizens living in Britain. British Asian problems were about employment, housing, education and health care, as well as questions of British foreign policy. Our concerns for the bread-and-butter issues of daily life were not so different in order and kind from those of our non-Asian neighbours. These were common human problems, not racial problems. The more ghettoized we were, the less interested people were in questioning the boundaries and conventions applied to such groups. For British Asians race trumped all, and our history in Britain – from our perspective – remained an unexamined, overgrown byway no one needed to explore.

At *Eastern Eye* we were big on racism. Racism was constantly in the news and incidents occurred regularly in London, Manchester and Birmingham, particularly the suburb of Handsworth, where a major riot occurred in the summer of 1981. Racist attitudes towards black and Asian residents, evident in heavy-handed policing, were the principal cause of the trouble. I travelled extensively in the Midlands looking for stories. What I discovered was a much more complex situation. Listening to people, I found the West Indian community felt aggrieved and further excluded by the phenomenal rise of prospering Asian-owned businesses. In turn Asians seemed to imbibe and regurgitate all the common stereotypes of the black community. I was shocked by the blatant racism I discovered within my own community.

I was equally shocked to witness for the first time on the streets of Birmingham, Manchester, Bradford and Glasgow the emergence of Asian gangs. Up to the end of the 1980s, Asians were seen as the most law-abiding citizens in Britain. But by the beginning of the 1990s hard drugs had arrived in Asian communities and created the social problems of increasing numbers of addicts and spiralling crime rates. The Asian drug gangs seemed willing to use violence to carve out territories and defend the enormous profits the trade can bring. Many of these gangs, I discovered, revolved around family and *biradari* stretching from urban areas such as Keighley, on the northern outskirts of Bradford, to the poppy fields of Afghanistan, where the Afghan *mujahideen* were fighting a war of liberation against the Soviet Union. In places such as the South Side of Glasgow and Moss Side in Manchester, one could pick out 'runners' – young teenagers on mountain bikes, making deliveries. Street dealers could be seen hanging around grocery shops and newsagents. The top of the chain was occupied by gang warlords who used family ties with Pakistan to arrange the courier routes that brought the drugs, nearly always heroin, back to Britain.

Eastern Eye gave me the opportunity to travel around Britain and take a close look at British Asians. The 1980s were characterized by three significant developments, reflected in the stories we covered. It was the decade when the first generation of British-born Asians came of age. Unlike their parents, they could speak English and did not see themselves as immigrants. They were more confident than their parents and saw their own neighbourhoods as home. For them, being Asian was much more than having a subcontinental ancestry; they were trying to discover a new model for being British *and* Asian. It amounted to a fundamental generational shift. The new generation included young women who were acquiring college educations and ideas other than preparing for married life – they were moving out of the house and developing their own kind of British Asian lifestyle. They had high expectations of Britain and their future.

Many young Asians joined labour, feminist and anti-racist groups and were actively involved in fighting deportation cases. Deportation was a simmering concern in the 1970s and went on to become a major issue in the 1980s. Asians saw these deportations as another sign of racism and an indication that Britain was still not a welcoming place. A number of controversial cases provided impetus for the emergence of a broad-based alliance to defend those threatened with deportation. One of the first cases was that of Nasira Begum, served with a deportation order after she divorced her abusing husband, who was a British citizen. She was denied her application to settle in Britain on the grounds that hers was a marriage of convenience and therefore it had been illegitimate in the first place. The case lasted over ten years. The Nasira Begum campaign finally succeeded in 1981 and she was granted the right to stay in Britain.

An equally important campaign was fought on behalf of Anwar Ditta, a British-born woman of Pakistani origin. In 1977 she was refused permission to bring her three children from Pakistan to live with her in Britain. The Home Office argued that her children belonged to another woman with the same name and that Ditta had in fact never been to Pakistan. She was trying to pass the children of one of her relations off as her own, it was alleged, with the purpose of gaining them illegal entry into Britain. The campaign attracted much attention from the media. Eventually, Granada Television investigated the claims in Pakistan and used the technique of DNA fingerprinting to establish that the children indeed belonged to Ditta and her spouse, successfully refuting the Home Office's claims. In March 1981 Ditta's children were given permission to join her.

The campaign to stop the violent deportation of Viraj Mendis was as prominent. Mendis was a Sri Lankan refugee who had lived in Manchester since 1973. Because he was a Communist, he claimed, he would be jailed or even killed if deported back to Sri Lanka. The Home Office branded him a 'bogus asylum seeker' and ordered his deportation. Mendis took refuge in the Anglican Church of the Ascension and invoked the right of sanctuary. As the police tried to enter the church their path was blocked by an army of supporters, who also provided Mendis with the basic necessities to live in the church without ever having to leave the building. The stand-off lasted 760 days. Finally, the police battered down the doors with sledgehammers and removed him. Still in his pyjamas, he was wrapped in a blanket and deported in January 1989. The deportation caused uproar in the House of Commons, where Clare Short, MP for Birmingham Ladywood, accused the Home Secretary, Douglas Hurd, of being economical with the truth. 'We are talking about a man,' Short declared, 'who might be going to his death. It is a serious matter. In the past year, 700 people have been killed in Sri Lanka, and the Government of Sri Lanka cannot give assurances because a political movement is behind it. The Home

Secretary gave us the assurance that there would be enough time to consider Viraj Mendis going to a third country. He is now moving so fast that that assurance is worthless. The Home Secretary has misled the House. He has given us a false assurance.' These campaigns played a major part in changing our attitudes to immigration. Deportations became exceptionally rare and the human rights of refugees and asylum seekers rose to the fore and became more important.

The 1980s also saw the emergence of a British Asian middle class. Asian businesses until then were largely the corner newspaper shop, halal butchers and grocery stores. But Asians began moving into electronics and computers, fashion and niche markets for ready-cooked Asian food. An Asian petty bourgeoisie class was evolving. I remember shopping at the Ambala Sweet Centre in Euston, London in the 1960s and 70s. It was one of the few places in the capital which sold quality Indian sweetmeats. It began as a dark, cramped, rather down-at-heel premises. But Ambala *barfi* was renowned, and people from all over Britain visited the shop. By the mid 1980s, there was a network of Ambala Sweet Centres throughout London. The Euston shop had been extended and displayed a sophisticated elaborate array of sumptuous delicacies to rival the finest French patisserie. By the end of the decade, Indian pickles were sold at the local Sainsbury or Asda. The foundation had been laid for the emergence of future British Asian millionaires.

I enjoyed covering these issues for *Eastern Eye* but I began to feel that *Eastern Eye* was a category mistake. The questions that interested me about British Asians and our history of belonging in Britain simply did not fit into the box marked ethnic journalism. Much to the surprise of my colleagues, I handed in my resignation.

British Asians, however, were in the process of discovering their own voice. It came largely in the form of music, and a new form of Asian music in particular: bhangra.

I first discovered bhangra in Southall. This London suburb is one of the best-known Asian districts in Britain. Over ninety per cent of Southall's population – around 70,000 – is from India and Pakistan, but Southall is distinctively Punjabi; the Indians are mostly Sikhs from the Indian Punjab, and the Pakistanis are from the other half of the divided Punjab. It also has the distinction of having the highest number of mosques *and* Sikh *gurdwaras* in one locality. During the 1980s, its main street, the Broadway, was the largest Asian shopping centre in Britain, and the local pub, Glassy Junction, was the only place to serve Indian draught beers and accept payment in Indian rupees. It was a tradition amongst Asian Londoners of all backgrounds to take full-day excursions to Southall for shopping, eating and total immersion in things Punjabi.

One day during the summer of 1987, I found myself, in the company of my entire family and the neighbours – Surita, her husband, Kumar, and their three children – strolling down the Broadway. Surita was much more than a neighbour. A devout Hindu, she was my mother's bosom pal. She was much younger than Mumsey and called her 'Auntiji', but the two women behaved as though they were sisters. Constantly in and out of each other's houses, they spent most of their time cooking for each other's families and watching videos (Bollywood films and Pakistani television dramas). Surita was a gregarious woman who liked to party and frequently organized all-women singing and dancing extravaganzas at weekends. During both Muslim and Hindu festivals, our households would become one extended family going wild on food and fireworks. All this jollity was limited to the women; the men were kept at a distance: we were there simply to eat, compliment and intermittently look bemused. Occasionally we were allowed to go out with the women, provided we followed rather than led. Our excursion to Southall was just such an occasion. Every now and then the entire entourage would stop at a shop – to examine the latest fashions in saris, or marvel at the recent imports of jewellery or look for Indian utensils. I remember that my mother was looking for a *lota* – an implement not easy to describe, or find in Britain. But every British Asian household has one. A *lota* looks like a teapot and is usually made of stainless steel, aluminium or plastic, but never ceramic. Its main function is to hold water used for cleaning after defecation. Asians, of course, use water rather than paper for this purpose. And unlike paper, using a *lota* is an acquired and accomplished art. We were in a shop examining just such a utensil when Surita stopped all of us in our tracks. 'Listen,' she said. 'What is this sound?' All I could hear was Indian film music being blasted out of this and every other shop on the Broadway. 'Listen carefully,' said Surita, who spoke Hindi and liked to dance. Then, she added in her best Punjabi accent: '*Koye bhangra pa rayya.*' Someone is throwing the bhangra. But the music perplexed her, it was not correct: it was bhangra and it was not bhangra.

Bhangra is both the name of a folk dance and the music that accompanies it. It is a fusion of music, singing and dancing to the beat of *dhol*, accompanied by traditional Indian stringed instruments such as *tombi* and *iktar*. The songs are simple, small couplets called *bolis* (short sayings) and usually celebrate harvest, love and patriotism. In the Punjab, bhangra is danced at harvest, weddings and social gatherings commemorating historic events. The movements of the dance depict rural scenes of ploughing, crop-cutting and sowing seeds, involving lots of throwing actions – hence the bhangra is 'thrown' rather than danced. We thought it was probably a wedding procession and went out to see. Following our ears for some distance we came to a hall, just off the Broadway. A large crowd of Asian youths, mainly Sikhs with turbans, was standing in front of the door. A group of elderly men, both Sikhs and Muslims, was standing some distance away, watching the young people. Some elderly men carried cameras and were photographing those who were going in and out of the hall in protest – particularly the young girls. I figured there had been heated meetings at the local *gurdwaras* and mosques about what the young men and women were up to at this hall. Surita and I fought our way inside. It was jam-packed with mostly young men, dancing. A Sikh band was playing – I could tell as they all wore turbans – but I wasn't quite sure what they were playing. It was bhangra – but with synthesizers and disco beats. Surita was appalled. Largely at the dancing. She knew how to 'throw' a pukka bhangra – the way they do it in the villages of Punjab. This jumping up and down, she said, wasn't dancing. 'Ram, Ram,' she exclaimed, 'the world will never be the same again'.

Before the arrival of bhangra, the Asian music scene in Britain was dominated by Indian film music. Music was an essential part of Hindu and Sikh weddings (Pakistani Muslim weddings in Britain tended to be rather boring affairs), where Asian bands played and men and women danced freely. These bands had names like Mussafir (Traveller) Pardasi (Foreigner), and Alaap; the latter, named after an Indian musical term, was regarded as the most popular Asian band. Mussafir tried their best to look like the Beatles; Pardasi played film tunes and emulated the Shadows. All that changed when bhangra became a craze throughout the Asian community during the early 1990s. All of a sudden Asians began clubbing. It was not uncommon for schoolchildren to play truant and sneak into daytime discos. Soon bhangra was fused with reggae, techno and house, gigs were being organized day and night, and bhangra stars such as Apache Indian, Harbhajan Mann and Jasbir Jassi were everywhere. When Punjabi MC collaborated with hip hop rapper Jay-Z, bhangra went mainstream. British Asians, or 'BrAsians' as they came to be known, were suddenly 'cool'.

The 1990s was the decade of 'Asian Cool'. BrAsian bhangra was so successful it was exported back to the subcontinent. Initially it faced stiff resistance: India and Pakistan were horrified at bhangra's journey from a folksy, sacred tradition to the profane enclosure of a Western dancehall. They saw it as vulgar and promiscuous, and objected particularly to the visual content of bhangra videos. Traditionally, bhangra is danced and sung in full Punjabi costume: the men wear colourful, flowing *shalwar khameez* with a turban, the women are draped from head to toe. In the BrAsian version, the men retained this tradition but the women were largely scantily-clad. To a traditional, conservative eye, it is visually shocking, blasphemous even – and even more so if the video invites you to inspect the female body at close quarters, with the camera lingering lasciviously. The images were totally out of sync with the Punjabi lyrics. But in the 1990s, the subcontinent was going through a disco revolution. The Punjabi lyrics of bhangra songs were no problem for disco-crazy Indians: few in South Asia could understand the words, and, in any case, they were totally drowned by the beat and the rhythm. When Bollywood rallied behind BrAsian bhangra, its ascent in the subcontinent was guaranteed.

The 1990s bhangra boom in the subcontinent was a significant watershed: it established a trend for British Asian culture to be repackaged – as ground-breaking, boundary-dissolving, cross-cutting modern and traditional practices – and 'returned back home'. Where bhangra led, other British Asian cultural products soon followed. The connections across the divide of migration were sustained not only by family; they lived in the cultural exchange that linked Britain and the subcontinent.

In Britain, bhangra came to signify an authentic British Asian ethnicity. Its attraction was its rustic, folk antecedents, its defiant play on the contrast between the modern and the traditional, the pristine and the mixed, the rural and the urban. 'Asian cool' was all about the fashionable projection of marginality and the allure of ethnic difference. Consumption of Asian ethnicity was the new fad; or rather, a new variation of the old familiar attraction of the exotic Other. Only, in this case, both the exoticism and the Other-ness were within Britain and, because they were 'hybrid', contained enough familiar elements to which the average Briton could relate. When I actually went to a mainstream bhangra club, on a rainy winter night in February 1997 ten years after my discovery of the phenomenon, I found most of the clubbers to be white and black. The Blue Note club in Hoxton, east London, was famed for its '*Anokha*' (Unusual) nights. *Anokha* DJ Talvin Singh had acquired a stellar reputation for his mixing of Asian underground music. The night was presided over by Sweety, who was described as the style queen of the new generation of locally born British Asians. She wore a striking sari, funky trainers and a black T-shirt. Many white women were also in saris or *shalwar kameez*. A group from a style magazine was busy on a fashion shoot, photographing white models in Asian dresses. The Asians on the dance floor were all ultra chic – to show their difference they had now acquired *atchkans* (men's Nehru-collared tunics) and *cholis* (the blouse worn under the sari). It was all far removed from the rough and edgy Asian-ness of Southall's daytime gigs.

I suspect that the 1990s, as exemplified by bhangra, the success of films such as *Bhaji on the Beach* (1993) and *East is East* (1999), and the Asian comedy show *Goodness Gracious Me*, were less about defining an Asian identity and more about making British Asian culture appetizing for British tastes. It was the curry and Indian restaurant syndrome moving into another domain. Despite all the praise heaped on *East is East*, for example, it is a deeply racist film full of grotesque (Pakistani) stereotypes. The highly successful *Goodness Gracious Me* played on many of these stereotypes – dominating fathers, clinging mothers, daughters treated as second-class citizens – and its mainstream popularity was based not so much on its being Asian as on the fact that it lampooned recognizable British traits. Most of its successful sketches simply reversed conventional British racism. In one of them, for example, a bunch of drunk Indians at an English restaurant in Bombay abuse the waiter and behave just like so many white yobs do in Indian restaurants in Britain ('Give me something really bland, right'). The recurring sketch in which an Indian film crew is making a documentary about London plays on the patronizing attitudes of British travel documentaries towards India. The British audience took to the show not because they saw anything Asian, but because they saw and recognized themselves.

The trouble with 1990s British Asian cultural products, the things that made Asians cool, fashionable and sexy, was that they were not generically Asian. To be a British Asian is to exist within the tension between a generic group label and the real diversity of the lives, backgrounds and experience of the people the label describes. The label makes it possible to praise the energy and success of British Asians and miss the reality of how many remain excluded and are left behind. 'BrAsian cool' was not generic, generalized success but the advance of a particular kind of Indian. Like the reccurring character in *Goodness Gracious Me* who insisted everything in Britain was Indian ('The Royal Family? Indian! Have arranged marriages, live in the same house and all work for the family business. Indian!'), this culture was rooted in and promoted middle-class India. For example, everyone who worked on *Goodness Gracious Me*, from the producers to the performers, came from middle-class Indian backgrounds; and the show's content echoed this.

The bhangra scene was so Indian that British Bengali groups went out of their way to distance themselves from it. British Asian reality was caught in the conundrums created by history. For many it seemed the old reflexes of the ethnographic state that was British India had made the migration with them and still affected their lives. The ethnographic state of the Raj manipulated ethnicity according to taste. Now, in Britain, it produced a pecking order within and among Indians according to the interests and prejudices of the British. The widespread belief during the 1980s and early

1990s that Asians were generically successful was based on the assumption that all British Asians were equal and enjoyed equal opportunity to thrive. Experience, however, suggested there was an acceptable face to the kind of British Asian Britain was content to promote, and certain unacceptable faces. More Asians were being recruited in professions and the media and making their presence felt in British society. But they came disproportionately from only certain segments of the community as a whole. There was a complaint, a lived disquiet, that Muslim Pakistani and Bangladeshi ethnicities, which comprised the majority of British Asians, were under-represented, under-recruited and failing to flourish within what was seen as a general advance. The concern existed long before statistics were gathered to show it was no delusion. It was too glib to assume that the presence of certain South Asians on our big and small screens, in dancehalls and fashion magazines, was an indication of success and 'integration'. The failure to recognize, engage with or debate the meaning of diversity meant that behind the facade of 'Asian cool' something rather unpleasant was brewing.

The questions we should have been concerned with were not only matters of where British Asians came from, and what ethnic and religious backgrounds they bore. The questions were compounded by where they settled in Britain and how they fitted into the cross-cutting patterns of British society. The British Asian community had a sizeable working-class component concentrated in those parts of Britain that fared poorly during the Thatcher years. The unemployed and underemployed among the Pakistanis and Bangladeshis had become an underclass that was invisible to the rest of multi-racial Britain as it focused on celebrating multi-culturalism. Walking the streets of Dudley in 1993, I was astonished to learn the majority of Pakistanis here were uneducated or poorly educated and unemployed. They had little or no prospect of getting a job. A sense of frustration and alienation was developing among young men, who were increasingly turning to crime and drugs. A few years later, I discovered virtually all the petty drug dealers in one area of Leicester were British-born Pakistanis. This was at the height of 'Asian cool', and Leicester was seen as the model multicultural city: one third of its inhabitants were said to be of 'Asian descent' and community relations were described by the local council as excellent. But the young Asians I met in Leicester told a different story: they were mostly unemployed, semi-educated and angry. It was the same story throughout the Midlands.

No one paid any attention to this growing underclass which, within a decade, had lost all hope in Britain. On the contrary, Britain was feeling rather optimistic about its Asian population – the achievements of British Asian music, film and fashion were being touted as the success of our multiculturalism and exported to the world. Indeed, after the election of New Labour in 1997, there was even a short period of euphoria about the prospects of Asians in general, and Muslims in particular. A number of Pakistanis entered Parliament, both the Commons and the Lords, and at the behest of the government, Muslims organized themselves into a political body: the Muslim Council of Britain. State funding was provided for Muslim schools, provisions were made for banking according to Islamic law. Sharia-compliant banking has grown into a £125 billion Islamic finance industry based in London. And generous grants were made available to Asian organizations across the length and breadth of Britain. Yet behind the genuine flourishing of a British Muslim community, with its faith schools and colleges, professional bodies and lobby groups, newspapers, magazines and digital television channels, the underclass was seething with resentment. The statistics made the extent of the problem clear: Asian Muslims were among the most disadvantaged in Britain, with one third living in the most deprived areas, around half in sub-standard housing, one third with no qualifications, and their unemployment rate was three times higher than the national average. In 1999, only thirty per cent of Pakistani students gained five GCSEs, compared to the national average of fifty per cent. Many in the Pakistani and Bangladeshi communities saw this in terms of racism. Something had to give and the underclass was about to make its presence felt.

Chapter 10

RIOTS, RACISM AND RESPECT

Racism was a constant, malevolent presence during my youth, and I wanted to protect my children from going through the same experience. They were schooled in the era of Thatcherism, when the Welfare State, long under pressure, was deliberately left to atrophy by malign neglect. The ladder of opportunity was removed from so many young Asians in the poorest parts of the country, the areas devastated by the destruction of Britain's manufacturing base. Everything became a matter of competition, including education, identity and culture. Getting the best for your children required careful deliberation, with the emphasis on competitive advantage. Everyone scrambled, and inequalities and inequities came to the fore. Difference was abroad in the land, and with it came threats to people who were deemed, and seemed to demand to be, different.

A good education in a good British school will equip children with – one hopes – a solid understanding of Britain, its culture and history. But then come concerns: my children are British born and bred but they are much more than simply British. How can they explore the full range of their potential if their schooling recognizes only one part of their identity and heritage of ideas? I constantly worried that my children would come face to face with the likes of

Mr Brilliant, my old history teacher. The fear materialized in a new manifestation.

My daughter came home from school one day in 1989 in a state of agitation. 'Dad, Islam isn't about killing people, is it?' Her question was mostly rhetorical, full of the defiance of critical outrage, yet with a hint of trepidation. Peer pressure can do that: create the frisson of self-doubt amid confident knowledge, even with the most strong minded. It was the height of the Rushdie affair and the prejudicial ignorance that was commonplace comment in newspapers and on television inevitably made its way to the school playground. I was amazed and gratified to see that my children responded robustly and with commendable critical acumen, as they resisted the onslaught. But the onslaughts kept coming.

Sometime later, my youngest, Zain, began to have doubts about being British. At the tender age of thirteen, he embraced the theology of cricket. He would spend most of the summer playing cricket and practise for hours during winter – in the garden, and even in his room, using the wall for catching practice. He started reading cricket books with some passion – C. L. R. James's *Beyond a Boundary* being his favourite. Somewhere he read about the 'Tebbit cricket test'. Norman Tebbit, a Tory cabinet minister at the time he issued his dictum, had watched British Asians cheering teams from their parents' home countries. This, he argued, demonstrated the loyalties of young British Asians were not with Britain. It was an assertion issued with as much glib self-assurance as Tebbit's infamous advice to unemployed youth across the devastated industrial landscape of Britain to 'get on their bike', as if that were a real option, an actual choice of practical possibility. The Tebbit tests, both cricketing and biking, were about identity and belonging. They suggested that to be properly British young people across the country had to forgo their communities and conform to a single dictate: market-driven competition and identities shaped and judged solely in free-floating, ever transient and amorphous consumer terms, not rooted in community, family and specific history. The trouble with competition is it breeds animosity. And when the terms of the competition are not fair, the animosity generated increases, frustration proliferates and trouble inevitably bubbles to the surface. The cricket test, by questioning the loyalty to Britain of young Asians, made it respectable to consider them conditional Britons. If they also happened to be unemployed, they were doubly dubious as worthy citizens. At this time the issue of immigration and asylum rose inexorably in the public mind, although immigration has nothing to do with second- and third-generation British Asians born and bred in Britain.

Naturally, Zain was upset by the cricketing aspersion. 'What if,' he asked one day, 'I were to support Pakistan? Would it make me less British?'

'The question of identity cannot be reduced to one dimension such as the cricket test,' I replied.

'Is my identity defined by the place of my birth or the homeland of my parents?'

'By both,' I responded. 'You are just as British as you are Pakistani. Just because you were born here doesn't mean you should deny or ditch your Asian heritage.'

'So what does patriotism mean, then?'

'Patriotism is much more than simply supporting a team. You were born here and are growing up here and that fact has instilled a love for Britain in you. You will always be concerned and involved with Britain. But patriotism is also ideas about history, a certain kind of community and a particular kind of people. The question is not which team you should support but whether Britain reciprocates – whether she sees other histories of which you are part as British history, whether she embraces the difference you represent – including the cricket team you support – as a necessary and good thing.'

'Well, does she? Does Britain respond?'

This was a difficult question. I replied that Britain responds in some measure. The situation is not as bleak as in my own youth. 'After all, isn't Nasser Hussain, who was born in Madras and migrated to Britain with his parents while still young, the captain of England?' I observed.

'So it's OK for me to support Pakistan?' Zain asked.

'Yes,' I replied. 'You are balancing your patriotism with the weight of history. Cricket was the creation of the age of Empire. It was exported to the colonies as a way of civilizing the natives. So, the call of Pakistan tugs at more than your emotional heartstrings. It reminds you of history differently experienced, unequally shared.'

'What if I choose to support both England and Pakistan?'

'That,' I suggested, 'would be a wise choice. But does that mean you'll always be hooting for a draw?'

'It means,' Zain replied, looking rather thoughtful for his age, 'it doesn't really matter who wins. What matters is how the game is played.'

For some Asians, the game was not being played fairly, and they were ready to show their resentment. On the morning of 24 May 2001 I received an anonymous call. 'If you want to witness a riot,' the caller said, 'come to Oldham. Soon.' I knew little about Oldham, apart from having a general impression of a dour place on a downward spiral of degradation. It was one of the northern towns where British Asians had settled, but a world away from Hackney. Yet the phone call was hardly out of the blue. Oldham had been in the news ever since the *Mail on Sunday* newspaper published a photograph of 76-year-old Walter Chamberlain under the headline 'Beaten for Being White'. The *Manchester Evening News* had been more strident: 'Whites Beware' was its version. War veteran Mr Chamberlain had been mugged and badly beaten, and his attacker was Asian. At the time and subsequently, Mr Chamberlain and his family denied any racial motive in the attack; to them it was just a mugging. But according to the media, this was proof of the existence of no-go areas in British towns and cities – areas closed to whites because they would be subject to racist violence from marauding Asian youths. The hysteria prompted the British National Party to establish itself in the area. In April the BNP had sought permission for a demonstration in Oldham to coincide with the forthcoming general election. Permission was denied and a three-month ban on public processions was imposed to preserve the peace. Nick Griffin, leader of the BNP, then declared he would stand for Parliament in the Oldham West constituency. A succession of skirmishes occurred in the town. When Stoke City played a football fixture against Oldham Athletic, fans initiated racist attacks and young Asians responded with petrol bombs. On the weekend of 5 May again there was trouble between racist and anti-racist groups in the town.

Mr Chamberlain had the misfortune to dramatize the temper of the times: growing racial tensions in areas with a concentrated Asian population; the theory that British identity was under threat from British Asians; the fear that Britain was experiencing a tidal wave of immigration and asylum seekers were putting unbearable strains on its infrastructure and civilization as we know it. To British Asians, this rang of blaming the victims. Across the country racist attacks directed at Asians were commonplace, had been going on for years and in perhaps a majority of cases were never reported, in the tacit expectation that nothing would be done even if a police report were filed.

One thing was clear to me as I prepared to depart for Oldham: 'riot' is neither new nor exceptional in British history. Britain has a long history made by riots. Riots have been politics by other means, the means employed by people who feel they have no other outlet except to take their grievances to the streets. Such were the means by which the mass of the British population acquired the right to vote, to organize in trade unions to defend their rights and interests as workers, and for the rights of women to be recognized. Similarly in India, where the Indian populace lacked any legitimate forum for their voices to be heard or their grievances addressed, change was effected by mass protest and political mobilization on the streets. Draconian Riot Acts were invoked and the authorities responded violently. The connection between riot and race has never been direct in British history. However, the connection between political and social grievances and riot has been invariant. The question in recent decades, however, is whether the course of history has changed. Are we in a 'new' era, where riots occur only in the context of race relations?

History would suggest otherwise. Immigration to Britain long precedes the coming of 'settled coloured communities'. I was reminded of this when reading the fascinating book *Bloody Foreigners*, written by Robert Winder. He provides evidence of how, down the centuries, Britain has embraced and been repelled by, often simultaneously, the arrival of waves of immigrants. A trickle has always been interpreted as a flood; Britain has always stood on the brink of being swamped and the language of disparagement and reaction against immigrants has been consistent. The epithets hurled at Huguenots, Flemings, Germans, East European Jews and the Irish are not dissimilar in kind to the daily chorus that attended my progress to and from school. The experience of previous immigrants followed similar, familiar patterns: they struggled to find their niche, make a living and put down roots that would provide greater opportunity and upward mobility for subsequent generations. All previous immigrants also faced complex questions of identity as they sought to retain cherished traditions of their religion and culture.

Disturbances and riots rocked British ports at the end of the First World War. The targets were so-called 'immigrants' and the substantive cause was the struggle for employment, as British seamen sought to reassert their claim on the diminishing stock of available jobs. The settled coloured communities resident in British ports at the time responded by resisting violence and defending their right to be British. Part of the context of these riots was the introduction of Alien Seamen Orders by the Home Office, designed to restrict the possibility of seamen settling in Britain and then gaining employment under British articles that entitled them to higher pay and better conditions. The effect of the orders was that Indian seamen, who were British subjects, were classed as aliens and thereby ripe for 'repatriation'. The legislation applied not only to Indian seamen, but to all seamen from all of Britain's colonies and led to joint protests by the various organizations representing 'settled coloured communities' and seamen's organizations. In such places as Glasgow and Liverpool, the legislation was over-zealously applied by police officers who wilfully struck out sections of the seamen's documents recording their place of birth, effectively making them stateless persons unable to travel or find employment. Among those affected were Indian seamen long resident in Britain, married to local women and fathers of families. Some of those victimized were men who had served in the merchant navy throughout the First World War and who had been torpedoed for their trouble.

The history of riots in Britain goes back centuries: the Peasants' Revolt of 1381 was an early riot, and London is by no means the only place in Britain where riots took place. Riots always have a political context, and signify a whole range of social grievances and injustices, but they are usually remembered in simplistic terms with simplistic labels. The authorities have almost always been at the heart of the matter, resented by demonstrators for responding, or over-reacting, solely in terms of a narrow view of law and order when what was at stake were more general issues of real and natural justice.

Recent history also demonstrates that rioting is as British as fish and chips. There were riots in Notting Hill, as well as Bristol,

Nottingham, Leeds and Luton in 1958, and again in St Pauls, Bristol in 1980, and in Brixton, Toxteth, Tottenham and Handsworth in 1981. There was the Broadwater Farm riot in 1985. But these events have been understood solely through the prism of race relations. I would be the last person to suggest race played no part, or that anyone should discount the pernicious and wide-ranging consequences of racial prejudice and discrimination. But I do maintain that to see these disturbances as belonging to a different category, as wholly unrelated to the long history of riot and uprising in Britain, constitutes a significant mistake. Old-fashioned social and political grievances are perhaps experienced more harshly because compounded by race, but they are not created by race alone.

If we see riots purely in terms of race, we miss the underlying causes of legitimate grievances – social injustice and economic inequality. Race becomes not just the focus of attention but also the vehicle through which solutions to social and economic problems are sought. Good community relations do not remove economic hardship or eradicate social problems. But investment in inner cities and degenerating areas not only improves economic and social well being; it also leads to good race relations. In Oldham, I was about to discover that race problems were a direct outcome of economic blight, unemployment and lack of opportunities. Moreover, racism in Oldham was an irony: the city's manufacturing history was closely entwined with India and the Asian community. Without them, Oldham would not have experienced the wealth that it enjoyed.

I arrived in Oldham on a Friday morning, and I was the only Asian in the town centre. Regulars began to gather in small groups waiting for the Wetherspoon pub to open. Old men in shirtsleeves mingled with heavily tattooed younger men and skinheads. Within half an hour, the pub was full. I sat quietly in a corner playing a mental game of spot the Asians – notable by their absence. I could feel many eyes on me, clocking my presence, noting me as an outsider.

There was a sense of menace on the streets. The general election was imminent, but I could detect not the merest hint of campaigning. There were no billboards, no posters, no one out electioneering. The shoppers seemed mute and listless. According to *Newsnight*, this was an area of high Asian immigration. Where were they? I found them when I ventured to Westwood and Glodwick: enclaves that seemed, in many senses, like Hispanic *barrios* in East Los Angeles. There was no smell of curry or spices in the air, no sound of Bollywood hits in the background. The stench was the universal stink of abject poverty. It was, I assumed, what gave the Asian faces of Oldham their stark look of helplessness and alienation.

I soon discovered that the town is divided into three segments, forming a triangle. The Bangladeshi community is confined to Westwood. The Pakistani community lives exclusively in the Glodwick area. And the white community exists in isolation on Limeside. It was as if the pattern of colonial settlement in India had finally made it back to the mother country. Lives were lived in separate parallel universes.

In Glodwick Road, I spotted three young men outside a take-away. Ghazanfar Ali had a business studies background but no job. Imran Mohammad was a fitness instructor with no one to instruct. Majid Khan worked as a shop assistant, but the shop had closed. They had given up on the idea of ever working again.

'We are the undergrowth, the weeds,' said Ali. 'When the politicians talk about opportunity for all, we're not included in the all,' he said.

'But at least they left us alone,' Mohammad joined in, 'now they want to pour pesticide on us.'

The three began to get excited, which attracted attention from others with nothing to do. Soon I found myself surrounded by a small crowd. They started to shout at me simultaneously. 'If there's an election on, why aren't they coming here to kiss our babies?' 'Why can't the police do something about the National Front thugs?' 'Tell them we're not foreigners. We was born here.'

This England, this Asian Oldham, had no time for politicians, police or people of the press. Everyone had a story to tell about the police. How they failed to turn up after repeated and desperate calls. How they always arrested the Asians and did nothing about the skinheads. I wondered whether Pakistani youths turned large segments of the town into no-go areas for white people as the media had claimed. 'Is this area off-limits to whites?' I asked the gathered crowd.

At that very moment, a heavily pregnant white woman pulled up right beside us in a car. Majid Khan called out to her: 'OK, love? Do you feel threatened?'

She laughed. 'Should I be?'

'Other people can come here,' said Khan, 'but we can't go to other areas.'

Mohammad Latif, an unemployed IT worker, intervened. 'We're being painted as racists,' he said. 'But who are the real racists? The white youths who abuse our children? The police who do nothing about it? The politicians who go on about asylum seekers and floods of immigrants?'

Iqbal 'Zebra', a taxi driver, suggested I go with him to the Breeze Hill High School on Roxbury Avenue. For the past few weeks, he told me, National Front members and sympathizers had been causing trouble at the school. 'The police know what's happening but they've done nothing.' I arrived in the middle of a stand-off. A mob of white youths was standing in front of the school and shouting racist abuse as the Asian children emerged. How it took me back to my school days. Where has all the time gone? I asked myself what we had we been doing in the meantime. Two Asian pupils told me they had just taken their exams. Their story was rudely interrupted as white thugs began to throw bricks and stones at them. Squads of police arrived and I saw them arrest four Asian youths. No white youths were arrested. I met two young Pakistanis who refused to give their names. They were members of 'Combat 786' (numerical value for 'In the name of God'), they explained. 'We're ready,' they said, 'to fight the white racists of Combat 18.'

On the morning of Saturday 26 May 2001, I encountered a mob of fascists in the town centre. They had been drinking in the Wetherspoon and other pubs. They seemed organized. I noticed they were being led by a heavily built middle-aged man I overheard people refer to as 'the General'. They were, I discovered, members of the neo-Nazi group Combat 18 and a gang of football hooligans known as Fine Young Casuals. I watched them from a safe distance as they sang 'Keep me English', 'No surrender to the IRA' and 'If you all hate Pakis clap your hands'. Iqbal 'Zebra' was also watching them. He spotted me and came over. 'Something's happening in Glodwick,' he said gritting his teeth. 'Come with me.' I jumped in his taxi.

A fight had broken out on Waterloo Street. A white youth had thrown a brick at an Asian youth, hitting him on the leg. I arrived in time to see a local resident, whose name, I later discovered, was Sharon Hoy shouting racial abuse. Evidently, she was drunk; she moved from words to deeds, throwing punches at the Asian youths. She then called someone on her mobile. 'A Paki has kicked the door in,' she shouted. About twenty minutes later three taxis arrived on Waterloo Road. A group of white men emerged wielding sticks and iron bars and rampaged through the street. 'Zebra' grabbed me by the arm and we ran inside an Asian shop. The shopkeeper locked the door but could not save his windows from being smashed. I could see the mob attacking anyone Asian. They were banging on doors, throwing bricks through windows, and urging the 'Paki bastards' to come out. Some Asians came out to defend themselves. Soon the mob was outnumbered. The police arrived, arrested a few and forced others to disperse. But with the officers' presence the violence escalated. Gangs of Asian youths arrived and started to attack the police. Within an hour, cars were burning, policemen were being pelted with stones, and Glodwick was engulfed in mayhem. Some 500 Asian youths battled ferociously with riot police. 'Zebra' managed to get us out of Glodwick to a place of safety.

The following morning, I went to Westwood, the Bangladeshi part of Oldham. It had escaped the ferocity of Saturday night's violence, and was shrouded in a deathly silence. The Bengal Food Store, beside the Jamia Mosque (a converted house) and the office of the British Bengali Community Council, was open. The store's owner, Mr Younus, offered me a rough-and-ready *paan*.

'The police say they were taken by surprise by last night's riots,' I said to open the conversation.

'When you are invisible,' Mr Younus replied, 'nothing you do can be seen. Oldham was on the verge of eruption for weeks. The only surprise is no one saw it.' He thought for a moment. 'A dying body attracts vultures. But someone with even a little life would try to fight them off.'

Mr Younus's words stayed with me, but the body in question was not the Asian community – it was the town as a whole. Oldham was dying; left to decay and degenerate. All its former glories had waned, leaving only a few civic buildings of Victorian exuberance.

The riot had as much to do with the overall state of Oldham as with race. Oldham was a town invented for and by the Industrial Revolution. It sprang up almost overnight on an improbable hilltop location to house newfangled steam engines, spinning jennies and spinning mules. Its factories processed raw cotton in the age when cotton was king. By the 1890s the town was responsible for thirteen per cent of the entire world production of cotton yarn. A century later all of Oldham's population, white and Asian, was stranded on a deserted outcrop of what was to be called globalization. Platt Brothers of Oldham – once the world's leading manufacturers of textile machinery – closed in 1982. All across the north of England textile machinery was going silent, and then sold off second-hand to Third World countries. Textiles had always been a labour-intensive industry, and cheaper labour in other countries made cheaper clothes to satisfy the demands of the rising consumer culture. What industrialization had given, it was as rapidly taking away. For the people of Oldham its decline had harsh physical and social consequences – whether they were white or Asian.

But the tension between white and Asian communities was also a cruel irony. Britain acquired its taste for cotton goods from India. When the Honourable Company of London Merchants Trading to the East Indies failed to secure the spice islands, they sought the best profits they could by joining in the local trade of the Indian Ocean. India was the leading producer of cotton goods; indeed, probably the original home of cotton weaving, evidence of which goes back to 3000 BC. Thanks to India the British learnt it was possible to live in the comfort of cotton drawers. Previously, scratchy linen had to suffice for those who could afford underwear. Once they discovered cotton the possibilities were endless: there were calicos and muslins, tablecloths and napkins, and soft sheets to sleep on.

Oldham's prosperity was engineered at the expense of India. The fledgling Lancashire textile industry was founded by immigrants, Flemings from the Low Countries, who brought with them weaving skills. To support this new industry legislation was passed in 1700 prohibiting the wearing of Indian silk and calico, and import duties were imposed on Indian finished goods. By 1760 these duties ranged from fifty to seventy per cent, and by 1813 they reached eighty-five per cent. Britain had a dual advantage. The Industrial Revolution was stirring into life as British rule spread across India. Therefore, it was possible to influence both ends of the economic equation. Technology to mechanize the processing and finishing of cotton enabled Lancashire to compete with fine Indian cottons. The machinery was developed in the 1780s and in the early decades of the nineteenth century steam-powered factory production – the typical northern mill – put an end to handloom production in Britain. Oldham became a boom town. Britain also governed the heartland of the Indian textile industry, Bengal, and was in a position to staunch Indian exports at source. Within five years of assuming the *dewani* of Bengal, and thanks to rapacious tax assessments, John Company had devastated the region. It now promoted the primary production of raw cotton for export over India's cotton manufacturing industry. Indian industry atrophied, starved of the investment it needed to compete with the new techniques of production. By the time Oldham was in its prime, India had become a captive market for and net importer of British cotton goods. By the 1890s, forty per cent of all exported British cotton goods went to India. In consequence the mass of the Indian population were tied to unremitting agricultural poverty. Village India, beloved of colonial administrators who considered this supposed timeless idyll their duty of care, was in large part constructed by deliberate design. Globalization, like consumer culture, had been around the block a time or two before the label was newly minted in our time, as if to describe something never before seen or experienced.

When India was struggling to gain its independence from Britain, Gandhi adopted the spinning wheel, the traditional Indian means of making cotton yarn, as a symbol of self-sufficiency. He was not the first to argue that India needed to repossess its history by regaining not just its autonomy but also self-sufficiency in its industry. From 1907 the Indian National Congress had been promoting the policy of *swadeshi*, home production. This called for a re-substitution of imports, a return to the original status quo before colonial intervention. Congress advocated boycotts of British cotton goods. When Gandhi returned to India in 1915 he transformed the policy into a moral argument for going beyond industrialism to a post-consumer culture ethos founded on homespun cotton, the *khaddar* cloth he always wore.

When Gandhi asked for a boycott of British goods in the 1920s, bonfires of Lancashire cotton were organized. As calls for self-rule in India grew more insistent, Winston Churchill, once MP for Oldham, saw it not only as meaning the inevitable capitulation of Britain to a third-rate power but the strangulation of Lancashire. By this time Britain's government of India, responding to the global depression, was acting as if India were already an independent economic entity. In 1921 it introduced an eleven per cent duty on goods entering India. The Lancashire textile industry began to squeal. For lack of orders from India, mills were closed as the depression bit across the cotton towns. In 1931 Gandhi arrived in Britain to attend the second roundtable conference discussing constitutional reform for India. He made a point of accepting an invitation to visit Lancashire. There were fears he might get a rough reception, but in fact Gandhi was warmly received by cotton-mill workers, people who seemed to appreciate their reciprocal entanglement, their mutual share in 'dominion over others' and their common political aspirations. At the end of the Second World War genuine political change arrived when Attlee's Labour government was swept to power. A new social compact to transform British life, the Welfare State, was created. And Labour's long-held support of independence for India also became a reality.

Britain's cotton industry was now producing less under harsher conditions and needed new supplies of workers prepared to take on night-shift work no one else wanted, but which was necessary to maximize the productivity of new machinery. Underemployed workers from the newly independent subcontinental countries – those whose jobs were stolen by Britain in the first place – were encouraged to come to Britain to do what they had always done on the subcontinent. Like all immigrants before them, they came to live in the poorest parts of town, the places already blighted by decline and abandoned by the locals who managed to get out. Their segregation was intensified by the pattern of their employment: Asians worked on the night shift; white women worked on the day shift. They might work at the same mill – but never the twain need meet.

When immigration legislation was debated in the 1960s to staunch the flow of migrants from the new Commonwealth, the myth of return transformed into a desperate rush to stay put and bring over wives and families before the door was closed permanently. Asian families in Oldham were housed in the poorest parts. The catchment areas of primary and secondary schools reflected and then redoubled the ethnic identity of each area. Most of Oldham's primary schools became single race and many secondary schools became ninety-nine per cent white or ninety-nine per cent Asian. Opportunities for parallel lives to engage and get to know each other better were never constructed, never considered a necessary part of civic responsibility. The chasm expanded with pernicious consequences. And all the time the effects of industrial downturn were spreading the poison of stunted hope and ruined dreams across white and Asian populations.

By the 1980s, textile workers across the north of England complained bitterly that their jobs were being exported to places such as India, Bangladesh and Sri Lanka. The British textile industry was dying because of global competition. Its real competitors were other developed nations, and the emergence of cotton industries in Eastern Europe. But cheap labour in Asian countries was more obvious and easier to blame. And this animus did nothing to build bridges with the British Asians in their midst, who were easy scapegoats, guilty by association – tacit proof that the problems were not only abroad but over here as well. But of what were these British Asian textile workers guilty, except again of being in the wrong place at the wrong time?

Everyone in Oldham shared the same deprivation and was now competing for what small advantages could be secured from the limited resources for regeneration available. The trouble was that virtually no regeneration was happening. In Oldham today the largest employer is the local council. British Asians make up eleven per cent of Oldham's population, but a mere two per cent of the council workforce. And in this hotbed of social grievance, outside elements found fertile ground for their poisonous activities. The BNP spread rumours about council spending disproportionately favouring minority areas and reaped eleven council seats at the election in the aftermath of the disturbances. But other culprits too have played their part in what happened in Oldham: governments, both Conservative and Labour, with their policies that neglected the plight of the region; the local council, which made no attempt to bridge the divide between different communities; and the police, tainted by accusations of racism. They have all participated in the long death of Oldham.

Racism is a complex phenomenon. It cannot be understood in a purely reductive way. One evening, I was watching a news report about sentences handed down in court for the neo-Nazi involvement in the Oldham riot. Nine white men and one woman received nine months each for affray. In contrast, twenty-two Asian youths were jailed for, on average, three and a half years for their part in the civil unrest. Similar disproportionality was evident in the cases arising from disturbances in Burnley and Bradford in the summer of 2001. I was watching the broadcast with my daughter, Maha. She was incensed. 'This is blatant racism,' she burst out. 'Dad,' she said, 'the courts in Britain are institutionally racist.' Her passionate intensity I understood and shared. But the idea of institutional racism caused me concern. For me, racist behaviour can only be ascribed to individuals – not institutions.

Maha read law at University College London, and then spent a year at Lincoln's Inn before being called to the Bar. She hoped to specialize in human rights law to help improve human rights in the Muslim world – but getting the right pupillage was proving difficult.

'I think the judge in this case may have been biased but I don't think that means the court system as a whole is racist,' I said.

Maha was taken aback. She sat up and looked me straight in the eye. 'Well, Dad,' she began, 'do you know what happened at my last interview? I was interviewed by eight lawyers, all white, with an average age of sixty. Do you know the first question they asked me?'

'Tell me,' I said, half expecting the answer.

'They asked: "Why does an Asian woman want to join the Bar and train as a human rights lawyer?" I told them what I thought of them.'

'I am sure you did,' I replied.

'The judiciary in Britain is institutionally racist,' she said in a matter-of-fact way.

I hugged her. 'I am sure it is dominated by ageing, white, conservative men who still live in 1066. But does that make it institutionally racist?'

'Yes, it does, Dad,' she retorted. 'It's just like the police. Do you think the discrepancy in the sentences for Asian youths and these white thugs is some kind of benign mistake? The Lawrence Report described the police as a racist institution. Institutional racism is rife not only in the Met but also in the judiciary and other institutions like the City.'

The Lawrence Report was published in 1999, following the Macpherson Inquiry into how the Metropolitan Police conducted their investigation into the 1993 murder of the black teenager Stephen Lawrence. He was stabbed to death by a gang of white youths as he walked innocently in the street. No charges were brought in spite of a long police investigation. In a search for justice Stephen Lawrence's family resorted to a private prosecution, which failed, not least because of the flaws in the police investigation. The Macpherson Inquiry into the affair concluded that the Met was a racist institution, and defined institutional racism as the collective failure of an organization to provide an appropriate and professional service to people because of their colour, culture or ethnic origin. Such institutional racism, it argued, could be detected in processes, attitudes and behaviour that amounted to discrimination through unwitting prejudice, ignorance, thoughtlessness and racist stereotyping, which disadvantaged members of minority ethnic groups.

The concept of institutional racism was not new. It was first defined in the United States to describe the endemic disadvantage experienced by black Americans. Nor was it new to Britain. It was considered carefully in the report Lord Scarman produced on the Brixton riots of 1981. The Scarman Report left no doubt that the operation of the hated 'Sus' law – the police powers to stop and search ordinary citizens on mere suspicion – was used disproportionately and in a discriminatory way by members of the Metropolitan Police to target young black men. The use of these powers was a significant factor in the disturbances in Brixton. But Lord Scarman preferred to see the implementation of this law as a problem of 'rotten apples', the misuse of authority by individual police officers. When he presented his report to Parliament, Lord Scarman was asked if Britain was an institutionally racist society. He responded: 'If, by [institutionally racist] it is meant that it [Britain] is a society which knowingly, as a matter of policy, discriminates against black people, I reject the allegation. If, however, the suggestion being made is that practices may be adopted by public bodies as well as private individuals which are unwittingly discriminatory against black people, then this is an allegation which deserves serious consideration, and, where proved, swift remedy.' Scarman was of the opinion that 'institutional racism does not exist in Britain: but racial disadvantage and its nasty associate racial discrimination have not yet been eliminated.'

What I wanted Maha to consider was the world of difference I believe exists between the 'rotten apple' thesis and the outright, wholesale acceptance of 'institutional racism'. 'We mustn't tar whole institutions with a single brush,' I said. 'I am sure there are enlightened policemen in the Met and progressive judges and lawyers in the judiciary. If we paint everyone with the same tarnished brush, the good gentlefolk as well as the racists, we'll end up depicting the whole lot of them as social psychopaths.'

Maha looked at me in disbelief. 'Are you, Dad, denying the findings of the Lawrence Report?'

I was simply suggesting that using the label is the shortest route to demonization. The step from demonizing an institution such as the Met to branding every policeman as racist, indeed demonizing whole cultures and peoples, is a short and logical one. This sort of labelling particularly appeals to those who shun complexity and diversity and see the world purely in terms of black and white. It is the same tactics Britain used with such devastating effect to demonize Asian cultures and institutions as savage and barbaric. I explained how this mechanism worked in the case of Islam. It started with the personality of the Prophet Muhammad and Islamic law, which were first described by Western scholars and writers respectively as 'vile' and 'barbaric' institutions. This was extended to include 'Caliphs' and 'Saracens'. Eventually, the whole of Islam – religion, civilization, history, culture, people, past, present and future – came to be classified as 'inferior', 'violent' and 'licentious'.

In more recent times, development theory dismissed 'traditional' institutions such as the extended family, peasant agricultural practices and indigenous medicine as inferior and an impediment to 'modernization'. Later, tradition *per se*, as well as traditional people, came to be seen as anti-progress and fit only to be eradicated by the complete reordering of their lives, whether they agreed or not. Family structures were deliberately destroyed, traditional agricultural practices replaced and indigenous medicine outlawed. And, it should be remembered, this mechanism was used not only abroad, not only in respect of Other people. Hierarchy, order and deference – the watchwords of imperial restructuring –

were also at work supporting the class structure in Britain, which ended up demonizing the poor, the working classes and marginalized elements at home. At times of economic change and distress Poor Laws were panic reactions used to ship the indigent anywhere but here or confine them to workhouses often termed – tellingly – 'infirmaries'. The poor were demonized as a 'problem', a threat to good order, then to law and order. In the process the poor became a perennial underclass demonized as inferior, innately deficient in the aptitude for upward mobility – what Bernard Shaw satirized in *Pygmalion* as 'the un-deserving poor'. Then the theories of Malthus and Darwin so easily provided rationales for this demonized underclass, and reasons to ignore their legitimate grievances. To this day politicians continue to argue, after Malthus and Darwin, that 'hand-outs' make the poor comfortable and encourage them to become single mothers! Was that not exactly the thinking behind Tebbit's other test – the 'get on your bike' ethos of leaving whole communities to wither and want at the dictate of market forces? Adapt or die was a social theory with a history of its own that worked on the entity Thatcherism did not believe in: society.

Now, the Lawrence Report was right in that it found the people, the processes, the decision structures within the Met to be racist. But this is not the same thing as describing it as institutionally racist – that is, everything that comes within the boundaries of this institution is intrinsically racist. That, I thought, made the demonization of the police respectable, I told Maha. Every policeman will automatically be seen by Asians as a racist. The institution we have to keep in mind is society. A racist society has many individuals who are racist. The Met reflects this social reality. The police will tend to respect those elements in society that society itself respects. And society can only respect that which it does not fear. And what does society fear? What it does not understand. And what it does not understand, it tries to control by labelling and defining. Maha seemed to understand. I went on to make my second point. The approach that reduces racism to a single cause or blames a single institution is very reductive. It sees racism purely in terms of black and white. But there is more to racism than simply the skin of one's colour.

'You mean there are different kinds of racism?' Maha asked.

'Indeed,' I replied. 'To the racism based on skin colour, we can add racism based on religion and culture. Pakistanis and Bangladeshis, for example, are not just victims of colour-based racism; their very religion and culture are also sources of discrimination. Colour-based racism – the biologically based theories of inferior races – is a rather late arrival historically. Before Darwin, scales of civilization were constructed out of social and cultural differences that were familiar long before race and skin colour became easy ready-reckoning shorthand. In constructing its imperial worldview Britain made much of the superiority of its Anglo-Saxon ancestry and its way of life. It is these attitudes which are now being put to such malicious use on Britain's streets against British citizens of Asian and Afro-Caribbean descent. Race is the glib label for the fear haunting British society of threats to its superiority and integrity: the triumphalism of "our way of life". In addition, we have racism based on perceptions of patriotism. Bring in the metaphors of "nation" and the "national way of life", based as they are on common descent, kinship ties, language and custom, and every Asian automatically becomes an alien Other. When patriotism is contrasted with the charged language of "immigrants" and "bogus asylum seekers", minorities become easy targets as representatives of unpatriotic outsiders. A variation of this form of racism afflicts liberal secularism. Cultures and religions demonized as "traditional" do not conform to the dictates of liberalism. When such traditional ways, such as rural customs and the marriage traditions of Asians in Britain, do not adapt themselves into extinction, they are demonized by liberal secularists who regard them as intrinsically inimical and hostile to their ideals and the British liberal consensus – that is, they are alien *par excellence*. So I would say arrogant liberals can be and are as racist as the easily identifiable, right-wing type,' I concluded.

'This does not mean that we should become colour blind, ignore racism based on colour, and not bother to legislate against it?' Maha enquired.

'No,' I replied. 'What it does mean is that racism based only on colour coding can only produce partial answers in a racist society. There have been real gains from anti-racist legislation in Britain for all minorities, including Asians. But these gains only take us a few steps forward, only treat the visible tip of the iceberg. Other forms of active racisms remain the *modus operandi* of power. Racism can be universally condemned and still remain. This is why the Lawrence Report has had so little effect on society.'

I referred Maha to an article in the *Sunday Times* (published in the summer of 2002), written by Sir David Calvert-Smith QC, the Director of Public Prosecutions at the Criminal Prosecution Service (CPS). He stated: 'it is my firm belief that British society is institutionally racist within the Macpherson definition from the Lawrence inquiry. A great deal has got to be done across the whole spectrum of British society . . . the whole of society has a problem.' Sir David defended his opinion on a BBC Radio 4 programme, which he did rather splendidly in my opinion. 'It has been painful for us and the police to be the only organizations in public life that have actually had the courage to admit we have a problem. It has been very convenient for everyone else to say, "Oh, yes, the CPS are a racist organization, the police are all racists, but nobody else is" – which I'm afraid is far from the truth,' he said. As succinct a statement of the real problem as one could hope to find.

'So what is the solution?' Maha asked, throwing her hands in the air.

'We need to tackle the ultimate racism of thought, beliefs and ideas, and not just emotional and irrational response to colour,' I replied. 'The antidote is a true exploration of the meaning of plurality. And that has to be achieved by society as a whole, not confronted solely by institutions such as the police or the judiciary.'

'But that's huge, Dad.'

'Indeed it is! It's the whole enchilada, chillies included,' I replied.

'I mean, where would you begin?' my daughter asked.

The deep problems underlying racial tensions have been examined in numerous reports during the last fifty years. Lord Scarman's lucid and wide-ranging analysis of the background to the Brixton riots pointed out, 'the police do not create social deprivation . . . while good policing . . . cannot remove the causes of social stress'. And concluded: 'we should not be surprised that the adjustment necessary to meet the problem of policing a multiracial community is not yet as satisfactory as it should be . . . British society as a whole is no better: we have yet to come to terms with ethnic diversity.' Coming to terms with diversity includes developing a more inclusive notion of citizenship. The young Asians who rioted in Oldham and elsewhere during 2001 had a very strong notion of belonging to Britain. Indeed, the second and third generations of Asians, born and brought up in Britain, see themselves as British citizens with the natural rights of a British-born citizen. For them, citizenship is a universal idea within which they seek to express their own, more parochial, identities. The problem arises when the universal features of the nation's subjects are seen primarily as white and English. Social exclusion, unemployment and lack of opportunities further strengthen the perception that citizenship is constructed in exclusive terms. Citizenship is not simply about the institutions that define and deliver rights to citizens; it is also about how the Asians, who are an integral part of the nation, think and feel as citizens of Britain. Citizenship is both a component of identity and includes the right to multiple identities. In one sense, the rioters in Oldham were seeking respect – respect for their difference and their communal space – a respect they perceived to be their natural right as citizens.

Lord Scarman, I found, had considered what might be necessary to give ethnic diversity the space and scope to express itself. Maha gave me an essay she had written on the history of Britain's blasphemy law to read. Her review of the law included the 1979 trial for blasphemous libel brought by Mary Whitehouse against *Gay News* Ltd. What struck me was the quote she included from the judgement handed down by Lord Scarman. He was of the view that, far from being redundant in modern law, blasphemous libel should be extended to protect the religious beliefs and feelings of non-Christians: 'The offence belongs to a group of criminal offences designed to safeguard the internal tranquillity of the kingdom. In an increasingly plural society such as that of modern Britain it is necessary not only to respect the differing religious beliefs, feelings, and practices of all but also to protect them from scurrility, vilification, ridicule, and contempt.' He concluded, however, this was not a matter for the courts but one for the legislature to deal with. I would say it is something for society as a whole in multiple ways to come to terms with.

At base it is a problem of education. Everything which the young British Asians I met in Oldham have been taught in school fits them with a sense of Britishness. Their sense of self, of belonging and entitlement, as well as their responsibilities and aspirations, are constructed in the mould of British attitudes, ideas and history. But this education has not fitted them for the reality of life where only their difference is recognized. What they and British society have failed to learn is the history of belonging by which British Asians are and have been made genuinely British. What we have all been taught are reflections, continual recurrences of old familiar attitudes to difference that encourage social distance and make it impossible for young Asians to be genuinely British. Into this vacuum have stepped not only thuggish racism but also pernicious perversions of traditional fundamentalisms.

When Gandhi was in Britain in 1931, just after his visit to Lancashire, he was stopped on the street by a young man, who asked, 'If a young man was about to go to India, and asked for your advice, what guidance would you offer him?' The Mahatma replied: 'Go out not just to teach, but to learn.' In Britain we neglected to learn how we have all been shaped by a long history of mutual entanglement and belonging. Without such learning we cannot give young British Asians the respect they deserve or appreciate the comfort so many have in living their compound identity, in being simultaneously British and Asians – let alone face the terrors ushered in by the new century.

Chapter 11

TERRORISTS AMONGST US

The new 'milloonium' and the years of the noughties have defied
the puckish wit of their naming. They have been lunatic and
maliciously evil. They have seen terrorism at home and abroad,
wars in Afghanistan and Iraq, and raise a string of justified and
unjustified questions about the nature of the British Muslim
community. For me they began with Bawaji's death, with loss that
gave way to new experience. Then came a summons from Hakim
Sahib. One of his numerous grandchildren was to be married.
April, the month Hakim Sahib had chosen for the wedding, was
inappropriate. Most people would be working, it would be difficult
for them to attend; the notice was too short for people to change
their plans and come to Bhawalnagar. But Hakim Sahib simply
would not change his mind. He insisted. There was nothing to be
done. One by one everyone gave in to the eldest and most
respected patriarch of the family.

I received numerous letters and calls insisting on my and Saliha's
presence at the wedding. Unfortunately, I just could not get away,
but Saliha attended. The wedding was as colourful as a wedding
should be. By all accounts, Hakim Sahib made his presence felt. He
moved slowly, with the aid of his walking stick, greeting, talking and

joking with everyone. Every time he got up from his *charpai*, a horde of young men would run to assist him. But Hakim Sahib refused their assistance. 'Thank you,' he would say politely, 'I am quite capable of moving about myself.'

The day after the wedding, Hakim Sahib gathered the entire extended family around him. He asked for various people by name. He mentioned those who were not present, and regretted their absence. Then, very quietly and calmly, he announced that he would die within the next seven days. A stunned silence dissolved as women began crying. At least a dozen doctors, traditional and modern, were present, all of whom rushed to examine him and reassure him. He looked quite healthy for his age; apart from being frail, there wasn't anything wrong with him. But Hakim Sahib brushed them all aside. 'Death,' he said, 'is not a disease. It's the natural outcome of life.' He began to console the women of the house. 'What will you say when I am gone?' he asked. And then, in the familiar style in which he interspersed Urdu with his broken English, he answered his own question: 'He went, or *aisay went, ka bus* went *he* went.' ('He went, and went in such a way that he totally went.') Everyone laughed. 'Whatever you do,' Hakim Sahib instructed the doctors of his family, 'do not take me to a hospital.'

Four days later, Nana went into a coma. There was heated discussion amongst the doctors in the family. The consensus was that he would get more care and attention in the hospital. So, despite his instructions, he was transferred to a hospital. Designated members of the family stood vigil day and night by his bedside. Three days later, he regained consciousness. 'What time is it?' were his first words. He was told the time. 'And what day?' He was told the day. 'Why am I late? Why am I late?' he kept repeating. 'I am late, very late!' Then he realized he was in a hospital. He asked to be taken back to his house immediately. The doctors and the male members of the family were reluctant. But the women insisted his wish be respected. He returned home to his *charpai*.

There he stayed for two more days, going in and out of consciousness. When he spoke he uttered the same words: 'Why am I late? Why am I still here?' Then, with deep contentment on his face, he articulated his final words, 'With Allah, the Beneficent, the Merciful.'

By all accounts, the whole of Bhawalnagar attended his funeral; the procession was several miles long. People jostled and jockeyed for the honour of carrying his coffin. Estimates of the number of those attending his funeral prayer ranged from 100,000 to 150,000. Not one of them had a bad word to say against him. And everyone had one question: 'Just how old was he?' Estimates varied widely. The general consensus was around 100 years, plus or minus five per cent. Whatever the magnitude of error, he left a diminished world behind, and a profound legacy of which I, and my children, are heirs and beneficiaries.

Just how diminished a world Nana had left behind soon became apparent. A few months after his death, while I was still trying to come to terms with his loss, I watched the horror of 11 September 2001 unfold on television. A plane emerged out of the clear blue sky of New York, described an elegant parabola, and swooped like a bird into the Twin Towers – in an instant all that seemed so solid melted in fire and death. Again and again we watched as the pictures were replayed on television in an endless loop, like a recurring nightmare. It seemed to me that the world was literally being blasted into the twenty-first century.

As well as the horror of the event there was personal panic in the Sardar household. The day before I had received a postcard from my nephew Atif, a colourful image of the World Trade Center in New York defaced by an X and an arrow pointing to one of its higher storeys; the message on the reverse read 'my office'. And to add to the alarm I had persuaded my sister to allow Atif's sister, my niece Hana, to do a graduate course at a New York university located downtown, just blocks away from the Twin Towers. We spent hours that day trying to contact my sister, or anyone we could think of for news. Atif had fortunately transferred to an office in San Francisco in the time it had taken the postcard to arrive and Hana was safely evacuated amid the smoke and debris.

Four years later, on Thursday 7 July 2005, a series of bomb blasts hit London's public transport system. Four explosions in quick succession began at 8.50 a.m. Zaid, my elder son, had set off for work just after eight. His younger brother, Zain, left around the same time on his way to Cambridge to attend a lecture on philosophy. Both were travelling to King's Cross, where one of the bombs exploded. Saliha was relaxing over breakfast, fitfully watching the television when the 'Breaking News' strapline appeared. As the first confused reports of something awful happening on the Underground fed onto the screen and King's Cross was mentioned, she ran to wake me in a state of alarm. We sat glued to the television in a state of shock as the scale of what was happening began to unfold. We feared the worst. It took us a panic-ridden hour to establish contact with both our sons. I wondered: what is it about my family, what exactly requires that they place themselves in the horror of the moment? Don't they know I'm a writer? I may work in non-fiction but that doesn't mean I can't imagine. I know what artistic licence is! In the next instant I was ashamed of myself for the half-laugh that followed the thought. But these close encounters of the fearful kind merely underline the indiscriminate character of the pernicious doctrine of terror. We are all proximate to its horror and that fixes the mark that remains. Our sons were safe, but still we were glued to the television. The news cycle repetitively replayed the initial horror, adding by increments sights and sounds no one should have to endure, captured and broadcast by the cameras of mobile phones. Vicariously we stumbled through the claustrophobic interior of disaster. The horror of the day reverberated endlessly, and yet we sat there fixated. This time the bombs killed fifty-two people and injured 700.

We feared the explanations of these horrific pictures. We had been here before. I left the stream of reportage on the television to think and prepare myself. I needed to be ready for the deluge waiting to engulf me. I needed time to wrestle with my own incomprehension before the telephone started to ring and people began to ask for explanations for this day's events. This has been a constant requirement of British Muslim existence since 9/11, in particular for any Muslim with a media profile. In the days immediately after 9/11, I responded with defiance: 'What makes you think I can or, worse, should understand such abominations?' But as time has gone on, though my defiance remains valid, my confidence in its sufficiency as a response has eroded. I have been haunted by a quotation I came across in those post 9/11 days, written by an Iraqi poet in the 1920s: 'The disease that is in us is of us and within us.'

It struck me as pertinent. Like most British Asian Muslims, I still could not believe what we saw and heard on this July day. But now, it seemed to me, it was necessary to try as best I could to find some answers. Why would young Muslims, born and bred in Britain, commit mass murder? What insane logic convinced them their actions were not only warranted but certain to be rewarded by an all merciful God who made all life sacred? It is the recurring nightmare of the British Muslim community and instances abound in the twenty-first century. There was Ahmed Omar Saeed Sheikh, who organized the kidnap and murder of the American journalist Daniel Pearl in Pakistan in February 2002. There were the first British suicide bombers, Omar Khan Sharif and Asif Muhammad Hanif, who in April 2003 targeted a Tel Aviv café, killing three in the explosion. Then, a year after the 7 July 2005 London bombings, twenty-four men, 'suspected of plotting to blow up transatlantic airliners', as The Times of 12 August 2006 put it, were arrested. This was followed by attempted suicide car-bombings in Haymarket in London and at Glasgow airport on 30 June 2007. In each instance, one thing became clear: most of the alleged terrorists were not only Muslims but of Pakistani origins. The overwhelming majority of British Pakistanis were stunned by these revelations and found it much too much to accept, let alone understand. The real and alleged terrorists were as invisible to the Muslim community as they were to everyone else.

Eight of the suspects allegedly involved in the 'transatlantic airliners' plot attended a single mosque in London: Masjid-e-Umar on Queen's Road, Walthamstow. The mosque, according to the *Sunday Times*, emerged 'as the hub where a number of the terror suspects may have met each other and become friends' (13 August 2006). I saw the imam of the mosque make a statement on television; his picture was in every newspaper. It was evident he was as astonished and horrified by the revelations as everyone else. I resolved to take my still jumbled thoughts about the disease 'of us and within us' to Walthamstow to see if anything became clearer. I did not doubt the astonishment of the imam. How could I? I prided myself in knowing the Muslim community intimately, yet the events of 7 July 2005 and the incidents that followed had taken me totally by surprise. By definition terrorism seeks to plot in secret, without raising suspicion or publicizing itself. What I wanted to examine was the existence of preconditions, the latent circumstances that might contribute to the explosion of a full-blown pathology.

A week after the arrests, I went to Friday prayers at Masjid-e-Umar. As I was leaving Walthamstow railway station, the station supervisor recognized me. He came out of his office to talk. Maqsood Hussain was pushing forty; he looked serious in his official uniform, complete with a blue tie. 'Who are these people? Where do they get these ideas from?' he asked without bothering with the pleasantries.

'I don't know,' I replied, 'you tell me. They're from your neighbourhood. You should know them.'

'I can tell you,' Hussain replied emphatically, 'these individuals and their activities have nothing to do with Islam.' The Qur'an, the Prophet and various schools of Islamic law all forbid killing innocent civilians, he said. It poured from him like water from a burst dam. I could see the perplexed frustration in Hussain's face as he repeated the general reaction amongst Muslims: Islam means peace, terrorism has nothing to do with us.

'It's all true,' I replied, 'but it does not change the fact the alleged terrorists are all young Muslims of Pakistani origins.'

Hussain thought for a moment. He now shifted his ground to the most frequently cited reasons for the emergence of British-born terrorists. 'Our young people are seething with anger,' he said. 'They have a strong sense of grievance at Muslim suffering; they are incensed at what America and Britain are doing to Muslim countries.' Wherever we look, Hussain said, we see Muslims being killed. In Palestine. In Iraq. In Afghanistan. Just as it was in Chechnya, Bosnia and Lebanon. 'How long can it go on? Why don't they see that their foreign policy is fuelling this thing?'

I had no answer to Hussain's question. There was no doubt in my mind either that British foreign policy, as a string of national and international reports confirmed, played a vital role in the emergence of terrorism in Britain. The cause, supposedly, was to bring the values of democracy and freedom to benighted parts of the Muslim world. The democratic voices of a, for once, unified British Muslim community argued this was wrongheaded and could not work. It was a heady moment. In the mass protests that preceded the war in Iraq, British Muslims discovered they could argue their case and stand and march shoulder to shoulder with an amazing cross-section of their fellow citizens, all of them, this time, together sharing what it is to experience being invisible. Despite all the protests and warnings, the entire Iraq strategy was mishandled, cravenly misjudged for private profit at public expense and atrociously executed. 'I told you so' is no consolation for the daily parade of death, dearth, destruction and destabilization the policy has produced. I was reminded of the pithy, anti-colonial slogan British socialists used in my youth: 'If you drop bombs on the heads of natives in their cities, the natives will drop bombs on you in yours.' It was a fact universally acknowledged – but obstinately denied by our government. As David Clark, a former adviser to the government, put it in the *Guardian* on 25 August 2006:

> We know it. They know it. We know that they know it. So why do they continue to deny it? I am, of course, talking about the very obvious connection between British foreign policy and the rising terrorist threat, and the government's refusal to come to terms with it. Politicians rarely admit to their mistakes, but this mental block is more than just routine political obduracy; it is a serious issue of national security.

When British Muslims said the same thing in an open letter to the Prime Minister, they were sanctimoniously told that they could have no veto over British foreign policy. They were also informed that Britain could not make policy cowed by potential threats – rejecting out of hand the informed opinion of British Muslims, who are closer emotionally to the 'Muslim street' whose hearts and minds are the supposed target of government strategy. It was the most effective way of telling the entire British Muslim community they were not British enough for their opinions to count.

I nodded agreement to Hussain's conventional wisdom. 'To be young and Muslim and Pakistani in Britain,' I said, 'is to be angry, frustrated and alienated.'

'If you live in inner-city areas,' Hussain added, 'it also means you are probably unemployed or underemployed. The young feel unrepresented by our organizations and mosques run by an older generation with little awareness of the problems they face. The more they seek to forge a genuine British Muslim identity the more pressure they seem to face.'

'Still,' I said, 'this does not explain why they have resorted to terrorism.' Hussain shook his head to indicate his bewilderment. There are many angry young Asian men and women in Britain, people of all faiths and none, I went on. They march, they demonstrate, they set up new organizations and institutions. Occasionally they may even riot. Yet the few, the exceptional ones who have been involved or implicated in terrorism in Britain do not come from Hindu or Sikh, but from Muslim families. 'Do you suppose part of the answer may lie in Islam itself?' I asked Hussain.

He was clearly disturbed by my question. I decided not to pursue it further.

Islam is a complex religion. It is faith, culture and outlook all rolled into one. Muslims from different backgrounds bring their own cultural and social perspective to their faith and see it and practise it in a number of different ways. This diversity makes it rather difficult to identify who would, and who would not, take the mantle of terrorism upon their shoulders. I wanted to explore this diversity, and to see if I could get to the heart of the problem.

I left the station and walked down Hoe Street. Walthamstow seemed to have changed little since the days I used to bring my mother to the local Cameo Cinema. Row upon row of terraced houses in streets that branched off from Hoe Street spelt out a working-class, low-income, immigrant area. But the shops on Queen Street suggested higher aspirations. In addition to the usual Asian food stores, now there was an array of fashion shops (Zobia's Collection, Moghal Fabrics) selling the latest models of *shalwar khameez* and *kurta pajama*, freshly imported from the subcontinent. A number of jewellers (Samina Jewellers, Chowhan Jewellers) displayed elaborate 24-carat gold necklaces in their windows. You couldn't buy these on income support or if you were unemployed. A wedding emporium, Dulhan Gift Centre, seemed to contain everything any Asian bride and groom could possibly want. The red-brick facade of Masjid-e-Umar fitted the neighbourhood. But the imposing stature of its green dome and minaret had an awkward presence. At street level, it looked like the gated house of a wealthy Asian, the kind ubiquitous on the subcontinent and increasingly common in Britain. It was midday, but the mosque was closed. So I crossed the road, and went into R. N. B. Enterprises to pass the time.

It was a bookshop, typical of the Islamic bookshops one finds in Muslim neighbourhoods. A woman in full *jilbab*, a kind of billowing coat that covered her from head to toe, minded the shop, which sold, apart from books, clocks, *attars* (Asian alcohol-free oil-based perfume), *ihrams* (the two unstitched garments worn by pilgrims going to Mecca), *hijabs* (in every colour as long as it was black), prayer mats and *miswak* (the natural brush that is a small twig, usually from an olive or walnut or arak tree, sold in small neat bundles and used by Muslims to clean their teeth). A sermon was playing on the CD. I asked who it was: 'Anwar al-Awlaqi, a Yemeni Imam, who is very popular in the US,' the woman told me. Imam al-Awlaqi was going through a list of Muslim sects that, he announced, 'would go straight to hell'. I started browsing through the books. In between translations of the Qur'an and books on traditions of the Prophet, dictionaries and Urdu language courses, there was some pretty nefarious stuff. The title of one Urdu book announced *Democracy is Forbidden*. The message was straightforward: Muslims had to stand up and fight all those who advocated democracy. Another, entitled *Purdah According to Shariah*, declared: 'when a woman steps outside her house she is accompanied by the Devil.' It advocated women should keep themselves totally covered, including their feet, at all times, even from the family of her husband, even when taking a bath. Any woman who looks at any man other than her husband is cursed, it announced. Another pamphlet declared the Jews were the enemy of Islam since the time of the Prophet Muhammad and will continue their treachery till the Day of Resurrection. Peace with them is not allowed, and they must be fought at every opportunity. Others openly advocated *jihad* against all unbelievers, glorified violence and advocated the establishment of a global Islamic state where *shariah* would be supreme. This certainly wasn't the Islam of peace which Hussain, the station supervisor, had talked about.

Leaving the bookshop, I went into New Style Hair Dresser opposite the Masjid-e-Umar. The barber was busy with a teenager. I started a conversation in Urdu with two young men waiting their turn. Did they know any of the men who were arrested? They were reluctant to talk, but opened up eventually. The suspects were well known in the community, I was told by a tall, slim boy, barely out of his teens. 'They were just like me,' he said. Ordinary young men who liked football and cricket, music and books, who wanted nothing more than to succeed. One of them studied biomedical sciences at London Metropolitan University. One of them ran a pizza parlour and was a member of a street gang. One of them was recently married. One of them worked as a security guard and helped with his father's dry-cleaning business. Another was into rap music and reading and was looking for a wife. The second customer, in his early twenties, with shoulder-length hair that he wanted cut short, thought the alleged terrorists were not even all that religious. 'A couple of them went to the mosque,' he said, 'but that's all. They were into dating and clubbing,' he added disapprovingly. But they were well liked and got on with everyone, both concurred.

It was very puzzling. The Walthamstow suspects, and those involved in terrorism before them, came from diverse backgrounds, defying stereotypes of class and education. They came from inner cities as well as middle-class and gentrified towns. Some were dropouts, others highly educated. Some had criminal records. A few were educated at British public schools. There was no bond of 'social exclusion'.

When the Masjid-e-Umar opened, I went inside. The mosque had the air of clinical efficiency, designed with functionality rather than grace in mind. The main door led straight to an area designated for storing shoes. Having taken mine off, I walked into the main prayer hall and sat on the green carpet. It had a low ceiling and felt claustrophobic even though the sun was shining brightly outside. I was early and there were only a few other worshippers, so I started to chat with the man sitting next to me. He told me that Masjid-e-Umar followed a strict Deobandi line. 'But there are Deobandis and Deobandis,' he said. 'We are a more open-minded bunch, not to be confused with the close-minded aggressive Muslims who also describe themselves as Deobandis.' The Deobandis are undoubtedly the most vocal and visible community of British Asian Muslims, although they are in fact an overall minority in Britain. They are at the forefront of most Muslim organizations, take an active part in protests and demonstrations, and frequently speak on behalf of the community to the media. They go out of their way to tell other Muslims that if they do not do this or that, their faith will be diluted and they could be labelled unbelievers. They are a majority in Blackburn, Rochdale, Manchester and Glasgow and have a strong presence in Bradford and Birmingham.

The Deobandis follow the teachings of the religious scholars of Daral Uloom, Deoband, a small city ninety miles north of Delhi. The seminary (literally, House of Knowledge of Deoband) was established in 1867 as a response to British rule in India. The Deobandis believed that the best way to fight the colonizers was to reform Islam by purifying it of un-Islamic accretions and re-emphasizing the practices and example of the Prophet Muhammad. The Deobandi reformists adhered to strict application of prescribed Islamic law in all matters. Their thought focused on five main principles: strict monotheism, following the Prophet in every detail big or small, unquestioning love and admiration of his companions, giving preference to the opinions of the earliest jurists of Islam, and engaging in *jihad* against all evil.

For much of the twentieth century, the Deobandi revivalist movement was limited to the Indian subcontinent. But it acquired global dimensions during the 1970s when it received ideological and financial support from Saudi Arabia. The Deobandi scholars were deeply influenced by Wahabism, the dominant ideology of Saudi Arabia, so the alliance between the two ideologies was natural. During the 1980s, Deobandis also received encouragement from Pakistan's military ruler, General Zia ul-Haq, himself a devout Deobandi. He eased the way for Deobandis to be recruited to the army and government services, and helped set up a string of Deobandi *madrassas* – religious schools – in northern Pakistan. Students from these *madrassas* played an active part in the 'Afghan *Jihad*', the resistance movement that drove the Soviet Union out of Afghanistan. Later, they became the backbone of the ultra-puritan Taliban, who ruled Afghanistan for a short period.

Naturally, the developments in Pakistan had both direct and indirect impact on the British Deobandis. A whole generation of young British Pakistanis has grown up on Deobandi literature, widely available from Islamic bookshops, such as R. N. B. Enterprises, located near most mosques and community centres. But young Muslims first come across Deobandi thought in *madrassas*, which many Muslim children attend after school, and where the old syllabus is strictly followed. Many imams in British mosques were themselves trained in Deobandi *madrassas*. Those imported from the subcontinent went to institutions such as Daral Uloom, Karachi; those who qualified in Britain attended local *madrassas*, also often called Daral Uloom. Not surprisingly, by the end of the 1990s, Deobandi thought had acquired a strong hold on the minds of some young Asian Muslims.

The imam of Masjid-e-Umar, Mawlana Mohammad Shoaib Nurgat, I was told, was himself an accomplished Deobandi scholar. Born in Dewsbury, he acquired his religious credentials at the Daral Uloom in Karachi. My attention was directed to the front of the hall where Imam Shoaib was beginning his sermon. He started by telling the congregation in fluent, cogent English that Islam condemns terrorism, suicide bombing, murder and all kinds of aggression. He moved on to talk about lies. 'Muslims,' he said, 'should be very careful when using their tongues. Do not open your mouth to say something when you are not sure of what you are saying. All our calamities are due to lies: we speak out of ignorance and spread ignorance in our communities.' I looked around the congregation. The mosque was now full; I estimated there were around 500 worshippers. The overwhelming majority were under thirty; teenagers, who constituted at least a quarter of the congregation, fidgeted and sat gawkily on the floor. There were two rows of chairs on the left side of the prayer room, reserved for the elderly – but not all of them were taken.

Imam Shoaib moved on to the 'double standards of the West'. 'Lies,' he said, 'are not a monopoly of Muslims. Lies have become our worldview. We tell the world we want peace in the Middle East but sell weapons to everyone; we condemn the rockets falling on Israel but encourage Israel to bomb Lebanon. We want others to stop building nuclear weapons while we continue to stockpile them.' The congregation was mesmerized. Imam Shoaib, sitting on a large white chair inside the *mihrab* (the niche that indicates the direction of Mecca, and is occupied by the person leading the prayer), had a rather saintly aura around him. He was a short man with a well-kept short beard, dressed in a long, brilliant white shirt that went right down to his knees, and a white skull cap. Green light emerged from a small chandelier that hung from the ceiling of the *mihrab*; it combined with the rays of sunshine entering through three small windows, and bounced off the white chair and dress of the imam, to produce a strange, surreal effect. Above his head, red fluorescent digital clocks flashed to announce the Islamic date and prayer times. It was clear that Imam Shoaib was an accomplished orator. 'We have saturated the world with lies,' he declared. 'Advertising tells us lies all the time. The media spreads nothing but lies. World powers wallow in lies.' He had criticized everyone without mentioning any names. Later, I learnt his listeners were not limited to the congregation; his sermon was broadcast on citizen band radio. All Muslim households in a two-mile radius of the mosque had been supplied with receivers, duly tuned in to the right frequency (4547875 FM), so they could listen in comfort at home.

When the congregation stood up for prayer, I noticed that a number of men, all sporting full, boisterous beards, were wearing what could only be described as a uniform. They were dressed in the standard *shalwar khameez* but the garments fitted their bodies according to a particular formula: the shirts (*khameez*) were the size of elder brothers, while the trousers (*shalwar*) would have fitted younger brothers. Just before the prayers started, they all dutifully turned the bottom of their trousers up to reveal even more of their ankles and legs. They belonged to a particular evangelical group known as Tablighi Jamaat, and wore the required attire. It also suggested that Imam Shoaib was an ecumenical man, tolerant enough to allow a different sect in his mosque.

After the prayer, I caught up with Imam Shoaib. He had to rush off to the police station and apologized profusely. He refused to say anything about the terror allegations ('the police don't want me to give any interviews') and insisted on filling me in on the history of the mosque. 'We have been serving the community for over twenty-five years,' he said. Like most mosques in Britain the Masjid-e-Umar started in a small house where a few people gathered to pray. When the community grew, they were able to collect enough money to buy an old synagogue. Many alterations were made to the synagogue, bought in 1981, to convert it into a mosque. In 1987, extensions were added to the side and front to accommodate larger areas for ablution and toilet facilities. But this mosque proved inadequate for the needs of the Muslim population of Walthamstow – which stood at over 40,000 in 2006. So the old synagogue was demolished in 2002 and a brand-new mosque built in its place at the cost of 2 million pounds. Imam Shoaib was exceptionally proud of his mosque and insisted I go on a guided tour.

He left me in the hands of two trustees. Musaji Hariff, a retired factory worker, was the chair of the mosque's trust. A slim, tall man in his seventies, he reminded me of my father. Saleem Qazi, an accounts manager in his early fifties, was gracefully dressed in a *kurta pajama*. Both had been involved with the mosque from its inception. Musaji led the way and took me to the first floor, which had a prayer hall slightly smaller than the main one downstairs, several classrooms and a small library. Downstairs I visited the women's prayer area, ultra-modern ablution facilities, a mortuary and the generator. 'The mosque has underfloor heating,' Musaji said proudly.

After the tour, we sat in a corner of the main prayer hall to chat. I asked Musaji who he thought was radicalizing young British Pakistanis.

'The three deranged mullahs,' he replied without hesitation.

Saleem Qazi added by way of explanation, 'The Muslims were considered amongst the most law-abiding citizens in Britain before they arrived.' They changed everything.

Musaji was referring to Omar Bakri Mohammad, Abu Hamza and Abu Qatada, who established themselves as spokes-people for radical Islam in Britain during the 1990s. Omar Bakri, a Syrian who came to Britain seeking political asylum, was believed to be involved with various violent organizations. In Britain, he established a branch of Hizb ut Tahrir, a fundamentalist organization based in the Middle East and Central Asia that has been implicated in violent activities. He broke from Hizb ut Tahrir to set up a radical off-shoot called al-Muhajiroun (the Strangers). By 2001, members of al-Muhajiroun had become a common sight outside mosques, where they recruited young, disenchanted Muslims to their cause. But in 2004, under pressure from the authorities, Omar Bakri disbanded the organization, which simply reformed itself with a new name: al-Ghurabaa (the Poor). Like al-Muhajiroun, al-Ghurabaa aimed at 'creating a worldwide Islamic state and encouraging Muslims to support the *mujahideen* who undertake violent *jihad*'. Omar Bakri himself left Britain in 2005 to establish himself in Lebanon.

Omar Bakri was closely associated with Abu Hamza al-Masri, a former nightclub bouncer. Born in Alexandria, Egypt, his real name was Mustafa Kamel Mustafa. He came to Britain in 1979 to study engineering, married an English woman and became a naturalized British citizen. He claimed to have fought with the *mujahideen* in Afghanistan, where he lost an eye and a hand (apparently while clearing landmines). His hooked hand and slightly unhinged persona gave him the air of a James Bond villain. He and his followers took over the mosque in Finsbury Park, physically ejecting the imam and trustees, and established the headquarters of their organization, Supporters of Shariah, dedicated to the rule of Islamic law. Abu Hamza's nefarious teachings attracted the attention of the security services and he was questioned a number of times by officers of Scotland Yard on terrorist-related matters. His son, Mohammed Mustafa Kamel, was involved, with other British Muslims, in a terrorist bombing incident in Yemen. In February 2006, Abu Hamza was jailed for seven years after being found guilty of inciting murder and racial hatred.

Abu Qatada became one of Britain's most wanted men in December 2001, when he went on the run on the eve of government moves to introduce new anti-terror laws. A Jordanian over six feet in height and weighing more than twenty stone

(127 kg), the father of five arrived in the UK in September 1993 on a forged passport. He was granted refugee status in June 1994 after claiming asylum for himself and his family and was given leave to remain for four years. Variously described as a 'truly dangerous individual' and a 'key UK figure' in al-Qaeda related terror activity, he was convicted of terrorism offences in Jordan. He was also alleged to have connections with the 'Hamburg Cell', the group of terrorists living in Germany who were involved in the 9/11 attacks. Richard Reid, the British 'Shoe Bomber', and Frenchman Zacarias Moussaoui, both jailed for involvement in terrorism, were said to have sought religious advice from him. From October 2002, he was confined without trial, firstly in Belmarsh prison and then in his own home.

All three 'deranged mullahs' openly preached a perverted, violent form of Islam that justified terrorism; all three glorified Bin Laden and al-Qaeda. The tapes of their speeches and sermons were widely distributed by their supporters, and their videos and literature were openly on sale in Islamic bookshops. They fascinated the British media, which lavishly provided them with the 'oxygen of publicity', to the despairing frustration of the majority of British Muslims. Omar Bakri and Abu Hamza quite literally fulfilled every Orientalist and Islamophobic stereotype. I long ago came to believe that much of the media harboured the thought that these fanatics were the 'authentic', 'real' Islam. Their prominence made every debate between Muslims and the mainstream in Britain more convoluted, difficult and inherently defensive. 'For over a decade,' Saleem said, 'these three systematically laid the foundation of radicalizing our youth.' Musaji added: 'The followers of these people are fanatics. They are against all that we stand for. I don't blame the non-Muslims, I blame my own Muslim community.' What the 'deranged mullahs' were doing was no secret. The contents of their message and practices were known to everyone, from the Muslim community to the police to the intelligence services. Yet despite repeated, insistent complaints from the Muslim community, no action was taken against them. Only after 9/11 did the police and intelligence services give them the attention they deserved.

I could only agree. But, I asked Saleem Qazi, what about Tablighi Jamaat? The Tablighi Jamaat, undoubtedly the largest grassroots Muslim organization in the world, had emerged as a common link between several of the men arrested for the transatlantic airliners conspiracy. Almost all the suspects who prayed at Masjid-e-Umar were involved with the Tablighi Jamaat. The 7/7 London bombers Mohammad Siddique Khan and Shehzad Tanweer were also known to have attended Tablighi Jamaat meetings. And I had already detected the heavy presence of the Tablighis (as they are called) during Friday prayers in Walthamstow: they were the long-shirt and short-trouser brigade. Saleem and Musaji laughed. They looked at me as if to say: we don't have to tell you! The Tablighis are nothing more than a benign, apolitical lot. They don't have anything to do with this.

Saleem and Musaji's reaction was typical of British Muslims. It is a common enough response across the breadth of the Muslim community in Britain. The Tablighi Jamaat is known for its piety and devotion and its declared abhorrence for politics. The vast majority of Muslims see Tablighis as simple people devoted to teaching Muslims how to be better people. The Tablighi Jamaat is not so much an organization in the conventional sense but more of a network, with a fluid, changing membership. It was established in India in 1926 by Mawlana Muhammad Ilyas (1885–1944), a religious scholar who combined Deobandi purity with Sufi mysticism. Mawlana Ilyas was motivated by what he saw as the contamination of Muslim beliefs with Hindu ideas amongst the rural poor of northern India. He wanted to reassert the authority of orthodox Islam and aimed at nothing less than reawakening the faith and religious identity of Muslims of the subcontinent. But he was also influenced by the teachings and practices of great eighteenth- and nineteenth-century Sufi masters of India, such as Shaykh Ahmad Sirhindi and Shah Wali Ullah. So his teachings placed as much emphasis on orthodox belief as on spiritual practices.

The Tablighis are devoted to *tabligh* or *dawa*: preaching Islam. They believe nothing should interfere with this, and see politics as a social evil that spreads dissention amongst Muslims and prevents them from proper performance of their duties. The teachings of the organization are based on 'six points': every Muslim must be able to make a correct declaration of faith, know how to perform ritual prayers correctly, inculcate a habit of remembering God, respect other Muslims, behave honestly and decently, and spend some time in passing on this message to other Muslims. These points form the core of Jamaat's textbook, *Tablighi Nisab* (*Tablighi Curriculum*), the only book the Tablighis ever read. Members are discouraged from asking questions, arguing, or making political comments. They are organized into mobile units and sent out to target Muslims lacking in faith. The object of the exercise is to lure the weak ones into the mosque, where they can be subjected to the 'six points' programme. The Tablighis come to remind Muslims of the simple, unarguable verities of a shared religion, making it impolite in the extreme and nigh on impossible to just shut the door in their face. Just as I discovered so many years ago: I ended up accompanying them because of my sheer inability to find a decorous way of getting them to leave on their own. I found them to be naïve, disorganized and unworldly, not to my taste and definitely not to my reasoned understanding of Islam in the contemporary world.

The organization has millions upon millions of followers throughout the world. Often people join the Jamaat for a few weeks, attend their meetings, live with other members, go out knocking on doors, and then return to their normal lives. Some, of course, become life-long Tablighis – these rise through the ranks to become leaders of groups and then district and regional organizers. The Jamaat's annual conventions in Raiwind, Pakistan, and Tongi, Bangladesh, attract over a million members from all over the world. During the meeting, everyone dresses in the same simple Pakistani dress, lives as austerely as possible, and joins in regular prayers to purify themselves. In Britain, one of the biggest Tablighi mosques and the headquarters of the organization is in Dewsbury, where an annual convention has been held for decades. Most British Muslims have at one time or another become Tablighis, and attended the convention. It is difficult not to. The Tablighis are ubiquitous, do not give up easily, and their simple message resonates with nascent minds. The secret of their success lies in direct, personal appeals and the emphasis on rituals. That is why they are most successful amongst the young.

But there are other reasons for the striking success of the Tablighis in Britain. The network works invisibly, hidden from prying eyes; the members move like darkly clad ninja in the night. You will not see them at public meetings, demonstrations or rallies. They shun all publicity. They are dedicated, highly motivated and spend their own money working for the Jamaat. Their network has been encouraged by governments both on the subcontinent and in Britain, to counterbalance more politically overt Muslim organizations. Members of the Jamaat travelling from Pakistan to Britain seem to have no problems in getting visas, and often arrive in their thousands every year to do their *tabligh* amongst British Muslims.

Given this history, any suggestion that the Tablighi Jamaat is associated with terrorism generates universal disbelief in the Asian community. But changes in Pakistan during the last two decades of the twentieth century had an impact on the Tablighi Jamaat. By the end of the century, Tablighi Jamaat had ceased to consist exclusively of people devoted to religious pieties and ritualistic observances.

The changes began in early 1990s, when Pakistan was going through a rare period of democracy. The prime minister, Miah Nawaz Sharif, was an active Tablighi, and he invited the Jamaat to preach to the army. Members of the armed forces were permitted to participate in Tablighi meetings, and the Tablighi Jamaat was regularly invited to address the army. Not surprisingly, many army officers, from low to high ranking, became devout Tablighis. Even the director general of Pakistan's Inter-Services Intelligence (ISI), the main internal intelligence and security body, joined the Tablighi Jamaat as a full-time member. A group of Tablighi soldiers broke away from the main organization and added a seventh point to the Jamaat's conventional 'six points' programme: *jihad* in Pakistan and abroad. In October 1995, this group was involved in plotting to overthrow Benazir Bhutto, the then prime minister. The plot was discovered, and Bhutto purged the army, sending a string of Tablighi officers into early retirement. But the new faction, to all intents and purposes indistinguishable from the old one, went on to establish its headquarters in the northern Punjab town of Taxila, from where it advocated active involvement in politics and *jihad*. When the Bhutto government was replaced by Nawaz Sharif for his second term as prime minister, the Jamaat's influence increased once again. Now even the president of Pakistan, Mohammad Rafique Tarar, was an active member of the Tablighi Jamaat. Many Tablighi went on to occupy important political and administrative posts.

So, the Tablighi Jamaat, despite its history, had ceased to be wholly apolitical by the millennium. The mainstream of the Tablighi Jamaat certainly has not deviated from its original mandate and programme, but it has become a recruiting ground for violent, *jihadi* movements such as Lashkar-e-Toiba, the banned organization blamed for many atrocities in India and responsible for sectarian violence in Pakistan, Chechnya and Dagestan. Most of the members of Harkat-ul-Mujahideen, the leading organization of the Chechen fighters, are members of the Tablighi Jamaat. It would hardly be surprising if a few adherents of the Tablighi Jamaat in Britain also subscribed to the goals and methods of extremists and violent Pakistani organizations such as Harkat-ul-Ansar and Lashkar-e-Toiba. An unquestioning mind, which is what the Tablighi tends to produce, can easily be redirected towards violent ends. But of course a mosque has no way of telling who does, and who does not, subscribe to the original mandate of the Tablighi Jamaat. For those who manage and run mosques throughout Britain, a Tablighi is just a Tablighi.

Musaji and Saleem offered to drive me back to Walthamstow station. As I had planned a tour of mosques in the area, I decided to walk. What I remembered from my youth was just how difficult it was to find a mosque in Walthamstow. The couple that existed in the mid-1960s were nothing more than front rooms in devout households. During religious festivals such as Eid al-fitr, which marks the end of the fasting month of Ramadan, we had to pray in parks hired for the occasion. But British Muslims, particularly the Asians, have been prolific mosque builders. By 2006, there were more than 1,600 mosques in Britain; one could pray all the five daily prayers in a purpose-built mosque while driving from St Ives to John O'Groats. In Walthamstow itself I noticed some thirteen – a few, such as Masjid Abu Bakr in Mansfield Road and Qadria Jilani Mosque in East Avenue, were within walking distance from Masjid-e-Umar.

A great deal about a mosque is signified by its name. For example, Masjid Abu Bakr, named after the first Caliph of Islam, is a Deobandi mosque, just like Masjid-e-Umar, which is named after the second Caliph of Islam. The Deobandis highly venerate the Companions of the Prophet, especially the first four caliphs, and have a particular dislike for saints and Sufis. But the Qadria Jilani Mosque is named after the famous eleventh-century Sufi saint Abdul Qadir Jilani. He was born in Jilan, in Iran, south of the

Caspian Sea, and studied in Baghdad. This mosque represents an opposite view: it's a Barelvi institution devoted to upholding the customs of saintly spirituality. The largest mosque in Walthamstow is on Lea Bridge Road. It looks like a big, rectangular red-brick office block with two minarets stuck on the top. Managed by the Walthamstow Islamic Association, its full name gives the game away: Jamia Masjid Ghousia. 'Jamia' means it's a central neighbourhood mosque where the entire community gathers for Friday prayers. 'Ghousia' is a technical term used in Indian mysticism to indicate an exceptionally high spiritual status. In subcontinental religious tradition this station belongs to only one Sufi saint, Abdul Qadir Jilani, who is also sometimes referred to as 'Ghousal Azam', the supreme holder of the exalted state of Ghousia.

The majority of British Asian Muslims are not Deobandis but Barelvis. British Barelvis were largely invisible to public gaze right up to the end of the twentieth century. They venerate mystics and spiritual mentors, and have a strong tradition of visiting the graves of saints; they also devote considerable energies to community service, attending to the poor and the needy whenever they can. Most Barelvis on the subcontinent belong to the urban poor or middle class who cannot afford to go on pilgrimage to Mecca, so make do with visits to local shrines on important anniversaries and festivals. In Britain too, Barelvis, who are also known as Ahle Sunnah wa Jamaat ('The Community of Those Who Follow the Tradition of the Prophet'), tend to come from poor, working-class backgrounds. In cities such as Birmingham, Manchester and Bradford, they constitute the majority of British Asian Muslims. In Bradford over half the mosques are Barelvi. There are also a number of Barelvi pirs (gurus or teachers), who belong to various Sufi orders and wield tremendous influence on imams, mosques and their communities.

Although the Barelvis trace their lineage to eleventh-century mysticism, they emerged at about the same time as Deobandis – that is, soon after the Great Uprising of 1857, the 'Mutiny'. The founder of the movement, Mawlana Ahmed Riza, was born in the small town of Bareilli, a centre of Muslim power in UP, India, during the Raj. But Mawlana Riza kept himself away from politics, and his movement was devoted largely to the needs of the poor and to organizing and promoting festivals around the lives of saints and mystics. Most of his followers were descendants of converts from Hinduism, and Barelvi thought has an eclectic mix of Islam, Hinduism, Sufism and rural folklore. The Deobandis utterly despise this amalgam; hence the eternal tension between the two groups. The Deobandis consider themselves to be purer and more authentic representatives of Islam, uncontaminated by Hindu influences, and describe themselves as the *Ashraf*, or high-born. They consider the Barelvis to be *Alaf*, low-born and impure. The Barelvis describe the Deobandis as heretics who have perverted the true tradition of the Prophet Muhammad.

Both in Britain and Pakistan the Barelvis remained largely invisible and apolitical for much of the second half of the twentieth century, despite their prominence in the community. In Britain, they made their presence felt during the Rushdie affair when they played a leading part in organizing demonstrations against *The Satanic Verses*. The only thing guaranteed to stir the Barelvis was an attack on those they venerate, and the Prophet Muhammad naturally occupies pride of place. In Pakistan, where political power has conventionally been in the hands of Deobandis, the Barelvis remained apolitical. But all that changed with the arrival of the new century.

During the last two decades of the twentieth century, the Barelvis became increasingly concerned at the militancy of certain Deobandi groups who dominated politics in Pakistan. The initial Deobandi objective of cleansing Islam of the corrupting influence of Hinduism had now expanded to include Christianity, secularism and the Shia faith. During the 1990s, Pakistan witnessed violent sectarian strife between Deobandis and Shias, with massacres in mosques and assassinations of notable clerics on both sides. The Barelvis, who like the Shias venerate saints and lean towards mysticism, feared they would be the next target of Deobandi wrath. There was also an ethnic dynamic at play. Most Barelvis are *mohajirs* (migrants) who came to Pakistan after Partition, a large proportion settling in Karachi, the biggest city and the only port in Pakistan. The *mohajirs* claim they suffer discrimination and neglect from the bureaucrats in Islamabad. The perception of prejudice and fear of Deobandi attacks galvanized the Barelvis into organizing themselves.

The turning point was a demonstration in Islamabad on 14 April 1999. It was organized by Barelvis to protest against the alleged demolition of the mausoleum of Amina, Prophet Muhammed's mother, in Saudi Arabia. But the demonstration turned into something much more – a political statement by the Barelvis. As the *News* of 25 April reported, 'the armed forces of Pakistan were publicly accused of supporting militant parties which profess to wage *jihad* in Kashmir'. In other words, the Barelvis openly accused the Pakistani Army of sectarian violence and terrorism. Barelvi leaders stated their intent to combat militant Deobandi groups, such as the violent Lashkar-e-Toiba, which, they claimed, had 300,000 armed terrorists and was hell-bent on leading Pakistan towards civil war. Although in reality the Barelvis, as the *News* also reported, were in no 'position to combat what they perceive as Deobandi threats because they lack trained militant cadres, organizational structure and finance'. Nevertheless, the Barelvis had shed their apolitical stance and were now deeply involved in politics.

The Barelvis of Britain followed suit. When the Muslim Council of Britain (MCB) was formed in 1997, as an umbrella organization for all British Muslims, 'dedicated to common good, to the betterment of the community and the country', the Barelvis kept themselves aloof. Although the MCB boasted a few prominent Barelvi scholars, a large number preferred to keep themselves out of community politics and refused to join. They also believed – rightly so – that the MCB was heavily influenced by Jamaat-e-Islami and the Muslim Brotherhood, two organizations with a worldview not too far removed from that of the Deobandis. But the increasing politicization of the Barelvis in Pakistan led their British counterparts to set up an alternative umbrella organization. The British Muslim Forum, which links over 300 Barelvi mosques in Britain, was set up in March 2005. It was quickly joined by Shia organizations. The Shia, a minority within a minority, constitute less than five per cent of the British Muslim population of 2 million. A few months later, the 7 July London bombing brought the Forum into the forefront. Leaders of the Forum have been particularly vocal in condemning terrorism, suicide bombings and extremism.

Conventionally, the Barelvis only make their presence felt through *jaloos* – religious parades – which are held to commemorate the birthday of Prophet Muhammad (Milad-un-Nabi) or the anniversary of Abdul Qadir Jilani. I attended a Milad *jaloos* in May 2001 at the Lea Bridge Mosque. The parade started at the mosque just after the midday prayer, went around Walthamstow, and returned to the mosque two hours later in time for the afternoon prayer. It was a lively procession: the participants sang religious songs, shouted '*Allah O Akbar*' ('God is Great') and '*Ya Rasool Allah*' ('O Messenger of Allah!'). The procession seemed to grow exponentially as it moved forward, gathering more and more people, who joined to listen to the devotional songs. In post 9/11 and 7/7 Britain, Muslims have become rather more self-conscious, so these parades, which would be viewed with considerable alarm, have disappeared. Indeed, the majority of Muslims now try to carry out their religious duties as quietly as possible. After Friday prayers, worshippers tend to disperse quickly rather than congregate outside the mosque for a chat and gossip. But some have taken the opposite stand: they want to make their difference all too visible. A small but determined group of young men not only have full-flowing beards but also dress in Arab garb. Some women have replaced the conventional head scarf with a full veil (*burqa*), while a tiny minority have even started to wear the *niqab*, which leaves only the eyes visible.

A country with a plethora of Christian denominations should have little difficulty in appreciating the multiplicity of the British Muslim community; it is just as complex as the diversity of British Asians. But somehow the point is seldom appreciated. And a great deal of responsibility for that oversight rests with Muslims themselves. We perennially claim Islam is one, our law is one and all Muslims are together. It is the triumph of aspiration over reality, fidelity to the conceptual ideal of *tawhid*, or unity, over the experience of diversity, even though Islam as a religion accepts the validity of unity in diversity. Even for Muslims themselves it is sometimes difficult to distinguish between the different sects, affiliations and styles of observance practised in Britain. It would not be difficult for an invisible community of militants to move from mosque to mosque, organization to organization, to persuade and recruit young impressionable minds to travel a different route. My sojourn in Walthamstow convinced me of one thing: the confirmed or alleged would-be bombers are radicalized with such speed that not even the mosques they attend, the organizations they join, not even the friends they meet in the neighbourhood or their own families detect the change happening before their eyes. And what radicalizes them is not one thing – but many.

This does not mean we cannot say anything about what transforms young Muslim men into terrorists or the influences that motivate them. There are two prerequisites for a potential terrorist. The first is a strong inclination towards narrow, doctrinal rigidity, which may not always manifest itself outwardly but serves as a template into which certain ideas can be planted. The second is a total and unconditional acceptance of the contemporary philosophy of *jihad*. The term '*jihad*' literally means 'to struggle', and traditionally any earnest struggle for the sake of God, involving personal, economic, intellectual or physical effort, for good and against oppression and wrongdoing, was seen as *jihad*. But in its modernist reincarnation *jihad* has been reduced to armed struggle. It acquired a romantic dimension in the last two decades of the twentieth century when a global network of Muslims emerged, almost spontaneously, to engage in *jihad* in Afghanistan, Bosnia and Chechnya. Needless to say, not all puritans are violent. The vast majority of puritans in Britain, such as the Deobandis I met in Walthamstow, and on the subcontinent, may be doctrinally rigid and nostalgic about the purity of an Islamic society shaped by the first generations of Muslims, but they are also overtly peaceful. But when puritan inflexibility is combined with idealistic notions of *jihad*, based on the belief that cleansing violence is the only route to the salvation of Muslim societies, an unstable and explosive mixture is created. In Britain, would-be terrorists are most likely to be highly devoted, idealistic young men, not necessarily rootless or alienated, with totally fixed ideas about Islam and *jihad*, and a burning desire to put things right.

To explore the roots of radicalization is not to provide justifications for extremism and terrorism; it is an attempt to answer the persistent demands for explanation thrust upon Muslims everywhere. For mass slaughter and indiscriminate murder there are no justifications. For every individual radicalized to brutality there are hundreds of thousands, even millions, who share the same conditioning and yet are not pathological. The acceptance of *jihadi* ideas by a few owes a great deal to the litany of ills of the Muslim *ummah*, the worldwide community of believers in all their diversity. The sheer evidence of the extent and continuity of suffering and injustice must be added to the preconditioning of violent despair. Every circumstance plays its part. The vast swathes of the Muslim world contain many of the world's poorest nations living in countries where national independence has been another chapter in dependency and impoverishment. Yet there are also flourishing and growing economies along with the super-rich enclaves surfeiting on oil wealth. There is economic injustice on a global scale and within Muslim nations. Most of all there is the oppressive restraint of civil society and democracy almost everywhere across the Muslim world. Routine oppression by regimes supported by the West has been tolerated for decades. It has bred the impotence that is the enduring political condition of Muslims everywhere, in majority Muslim nations as much as among minority communities in the West.

Impotence is a terrible inheritance when set against the historic achievements of Islamic civilization. But it is also true that all attempts at revival have stalled due to the general disorganization and inherent inabilities of the Islamic movements. Islamic organizations and political parties have repeatedly disappointed the faithful by notorious underachievement. The last thing the majority of Muslims anywhere expected to emerge from Islamic activism was fanatics who would resort to terrorism. That fanatics could cause mayhem within Muslim countries was never in doubt, and not much noticed by anyone else. But no one, least of all British Muslims, expected them to perform terrorist acts in the greatest, most sophisticated cities of the world. Responding to this sense of impotence, small bands of fanatics have preached the subtle seduction of the gun and the bomb. The cathartic ending of the suicide bomb is surely the ultimate solution to impotence: absolved of living with the condition or the consequences of action against it. But everyone these days wants a quick fix, a simple, simplistic, one-stop solution – otherwise why would everyone turn to the British Muslim community demanding straightforward answers that don't exist or theorize about Islam as the one-stop source of all explanation?

And so we come to it at last. Are these terrorists the real face of Islam or is Islam the religion of peace Maqsood Hussain described at Walthamstow station, a view shared by the vast majority of Muslims in Britain and around the world? There is no want of slipshod thinking among politicians, the media, strategic experts, academics, students of all stripes, polemicists (in particular fundamentalist Christian rabble-rousers) and opinion-formers who survey the globe and see the presence of Islam and its rhetoric employed to radicalize and motivate political violence. Ergo, *quod erat demonstrandum*: Islam is the reason, the cause and motive force for terrorism. I tell you, their nightmare visions frighten even me. The trouble with such alarums is their want of sense and reason, but it often requires strenuous effort to appreciate this lack of sense. The only way the nightmare theories work is by denying any diversity of history and current conditions to people and places that are markedly different, for all that Muslims are present in each. It can work only when people have the most limited and purblind ignorance of Islam as religion, civilization and history. It can work only when the diversity among Muslims and their interpretations of Islam now and in history are eradicated. It can work only when the rhetoric of Islamic preaching and discourse is read out of context and devoid of the complexity and diversity of Muslim interpretation. It is like saying the rhetoric of 'Onward Christian Soldiers' and the 'Battle Cry' of the Salvation Army are literal and literally the sum and only meaning of Christianity. The rhetorical trope of unending war against evil is part of all religions, and all have succumbed in their history to the construction of such invisible communities of combatants – and it has never been the totality of any religion. The hold such theoretical explanations have on public discourse disenfranchises the vast majority of Muslims. We are thrown out of authentic possession of our own beliefs by this rising tide of fear and confusion.

Let there be no doubt. Terrorism has no place in Islam. The teachings of Islam are unequivocal. The Qur'an says: 'Even if you stretch out your hand against me to kill me, I shall not stretch out my hand against you to kill you. I fear Allah, the Lord of the World' (5:28). And the Prophet Muhammad adds: the murder of one innocent person is akin to the murder of the whole of humanity. Islam forbids the killing of civilians, women and children, the old and infirm, the wanton destruction of property, the burning of crops and the slaughter of animals, even at the height of a full-scale war. Hussain was correct, as are most Muslims who point to these teachings.

Can the suicide bombers justify their actions in term of martyrdom? Is there something in the Islamic idea of martyrdom that could motivate young British Muslim men to become terrorists and buy a ticket straight to heaven? Islamic theology is not a business transaction. One of the fundamental precepts of Islam is that no one knows whether they will go to paradise or not. Even the Prophet was not sure of the outcome and wept with fear that he might not be forgiven. The Islamic doctrine of martyrdom was crystallized in the action of Imam Hussain, the grandson of Prophet Muhammad, on the battlefield of Kerbala in October AD 680. He stood with his seventy-odd followers against an army of 4,000 well-equipped soldiers, to uphold justice against injustice in the full knowledge that it would cost him his life. His sacrifice was the inevitable consequence of holding firm to what is morally right, not a sought-after, self-chosen, wilful self-sacrifice of one acting beyond any moral or ethical restraint. At the very least, martyrdom in Islam requires following a just cause with a just means. To sacrifice one's property, security, ease and comfort and, if it can be no other way, one's life, for the cause of good, what is right and just, is martyrdom for all faiths. But faith also teaches the limits of human understanding, that we will all be judged and the meaning of our actions made clear by the Most Compassionate, the All Knowing. Martyrdom, like life, is the gift and judgement of God and not of men. Only within the bounds of belief, within attachment to the moral responsibilities and duties of faith, can any believer hope to walk the path to paradise, if God so judges. From an Islamic viewpoint, the claim of young terrorists that they are seeking martyrdom and paradise is totally ridiculous.

But the teachings of Islam do not absolve the British Muslim community, indeed all Muslims everywhere, from their responsibility. Islam teaches that Muslims are an *ummah*, an international brotherhood and sisterhood bound by faith. The *ummah*, the Prophet said, is like a human body: if one part of it suffers, the whole body feels the pain. I believe that terrorism is a cancer that can spread and destroy the whole body of the *ummah*. The British Muslim community cannot be complacent about terrorism, in Britain or elsewhere, even if terrorists are an infinitesimal minority. It is a religious duty of every Muslim, every community, to stand up and fight this affliction.

One precondition for terrorist violence is the feeling of victimhood in the Muslim community. The idea that the West is out to get us has a deep hold on the Muslim subconscious. If you believe that the world is divided into 'the abode of Islam' and 'the abode of infidels', as many puritans do, then the assumption that the rest of the world is against you comes naturally, and little room is left for argument. The complexity of the political and economic situation, and its ethics and morality, become irrelevant. Disgruntled Muslim youth, strong on emotion and gut reaction, and eager to 'serve Islam', are handed a ready-made cause on a plate. So it is not too surprising that these young fanatics see the campaign against terrorism as a war against Islam.

British Muslims are in the best position to stand up to this notion of victimhood and lead the fight against terrorism. I believe it requires confronting the rhetoric of puritanism that dominates the British Muslim community. The majority of puritans, such as

Deobandis and followers of ideological parties such as the Jamaat-e-Islami and the Muslim Brotherhood, may be peaceful, but their one-dimensional interpretation of Islam is obsolete and dangerous for all concerned. To define Islam in total opposition to all others – not just Christians, Jews, Hindus, secularists and the West, but all other interpretations of Islam as well – is to place Islam in an enclave. If you insist that your interpretation must be seen as *the* 'authentic', 'pure' and 'undiluted' version of Islam, then you should not be surprised if some young hot-heads see it as the final solution. The slogan on the T-shirt of Yasir Khan, the young man from Crawley killed in Kabul in October 2001 while fighting for the Taliban, summed up the reductive logic of this message: 'Al-Islam' is 'the final revelation', 'the final message', 'the final system' and 'the final conquest', it read. This is the kind of Islam that some young Muslims imbibe in the religious schools and mosques run by all varieties of puritan sects – an Islam condensed to pious bare bones, stripped of its ethical and cultural elegance, reduced to a strident, militant call to remake the whole world in simple faith and total opposition to all who stand against this impossible vision. It is the rumbling crescendo of the impotent fury of Muslim rhetoric that speeds these lads on their way to the front.

An essential part of fighting terrorism involves developing new and more humane interpretations of Islam. The British Muslim community, with its increasing base of critical scholars, intellectuals, thinkers and young activists, is probably the best-equipped community in the Western world to lead on this front. But to evolve new interpretations, to demonstrate the perversion of puritanism, one must be able to discuss openly the humane message of Islam without being overshadowed, misunderstood, misrepresented or doubted. This is why it is important not to paint the entire Muslim community, with all its diversity and complexity, with the same brush. Muslims must have the public space to articulate their ideas, their values, their ethical and moral conscience. Muslims in Britain have to be able to engage in society on the basis of their faith as constructive, conscientious people dedicated to tolerance and cooperation for good. Such possibilities are neither easy nor always open. The fault is shared, a failure of Britain as much as British Muslims.

There is another disease that is 'of us and within us'. It is the British foreign policy that has played a major part in promoting terrorism. British foreign policy, particularly in the twenty-first century, has created a toxic environment in which terrorism could mushroom. In a globalized world, where everything is interconnected and the local and global are intimately related, we cannot be complacent about what we do in foreign lands. What happens in Pakistan, Bangladesh and India, as I suggested in Chapter 5, has direct implications for British Asians. And British Muslims are equally affected by Britain's involvement in Iraq and Afghanistan. The notion of Muslim victimhood did not emerge out of thin air – it has some basis in history and political reality. Without a radical transformation in British foreign policy, a shift from military intervention to the politics of engagement, young Muslim puritans will always have a cause to kill and die for. The siren voices that urge them to self-destruction come from all sides, from those who advocate imperialistic jingoism and those who fall back on the comfort of puritanical, self-righteous rhetoric.

We all share responsibility for the rise of terrorism, and we are all part of the solution. The dissatisfaction of young men who would rather kill and die than live with the difficult conundrums of building a better world with all its moral doubts and uncertainties, all its intractable constraints, has multiple causes. It is fuelled by narrow and bigoted interpretations of Islam as well as British foreign policy, by racism as well as injustice and marginalization, by the little Englander jingoism that fulminates against immigrants and politicians who manipulate these sentiments. Together we succumb to the tactics of fear and confusion marshalled by all sides.

The resulting phobias have led many to argue that multiculturalism has failed. But the overall experience of British Asians suggests otherwise. A significant part of the solution to terrorism lies in how we see and shape a multicultural society. From the Asian perspective, we need multiculturalism more than ever before.

Chapter 12

FORWARD TO A NEW MULTICULTURALISM

'Britain is the most multicultural society in the West – bar none.' Indu Kalraiya was emphatic. 'While we may not have succeeded in every respect, we have produced a highly integrated society where all citizens, no matter where they originally come from, are equal before the law. Our minority communities have equal and non-discriminatory access to the health service, education and social security. We are fairly represented in the corridors of power and the media.'

Both British Asians and Britain as a whole have benefited tremendously from multiculturalism, Indu said. The proof is all around us. Twenty-first-century Britain is far less racist than it used to be, the black community has made significant strides, and an educated, participatory Asian middle class has emerged that has transformed the economy and cultural landscape of the country. British Asian films such as *Bend It Like Beckham, East is East* and *Bhaji on the Beach,* and television shows such as *Goodness Gracious Me* and *The Kumars at No. 42* have transformed our image at home and abroad. 'All this,' Indu said, 'is due to multiculturalism.' Like Indu and many Asians, I too think multiculturalism is a great idea.

Indu, a slim, feisty, elegant woman, with short black hair and distinguished good looks, is one of our oldest friends. I first met her husband, Ayrun, when I worked for *Eastern Eye*. He was a film editor and worked on a number of my reports. It turned out he lived nearby, and we started meeting socially at weekends. Our wives liked each other instantly; indeed, they became quite inseparable. Indu was a regular presence both in our home and in our lives. She always arrived as a category two tornado, at whirlwind speed, either bearing presents or a *thali* (a large circular metal plate within which are placed small metal bowls, each carrying an accompaniment to a meal such as dry and wet curry, curds and desserts) and other food (*samosas*, *pakoras* or *gulab jaman*, and quite often her special *daal*, a particular favourite of my children), greeted everyone warmly and took time to sit with and talk to everyone individually. Moving at such speed has its consequences, and Indu and her family are accident prone. There is always a broken arm or a wounded knee to attend to – and she faces every calamity that befalls her or her family with equal bravado. She is always smiling, laughing and cracking jokes – mostly at the expense of her husband or me. 'Asian men,' she has frequently opined, 'still live in the Stone Age. They need a jolly good kick up their bums to bring them to modern times.'

Indu's father came to Britain in the 1950s. He had a textile business and settled in Birmingham, with the intention of returning soon to India. His eldest son was epileptic, so he brought him over for treatment. But then her father was hospitalized, so Indu's mother had to come to look after them both. It seems the accident-prone gene is hereditary. Soon the entire family joined them and the idea of returning was abandoned. They are Jains. Jainism, as Indu insists, is not Hinduism, but an even older Indian religion. The cardinal principle of Jainism is symbiosis, the interdependence of things and people. 'Life,' Indu once explained, 'is a gift of togetherness, accommodation and assistance in a universe teeming with interdependence.' Jains are surprisingly free of dogma, the only one being a strict rejection of all kinds of violence. 'When my uncle was asked to join the British Army before the Second World War,' Indu once told me, 'he declined politely saying that it was against his religious principles to fight.'

To visit Indu is to see the Jain principle of symbiosis and interdependence in action. Her house is like a railway station with a constant stream of people arriving and departing. No one leaves without eating something, everyone is greeted as though they have just returned from a long journey, all speak simultaneously, the rumpus synthesizing with wafts of aromas from the kitchen to produce an enchanting, almost magical, atmosphere. Most of the visitors are actually her close relatives. I have never kept count – but Indu's family is large, very large. The immediate family of just her brothers and sisters consists of over twenty, young and old. Next, there are the families of her uncles, aunts and their children, some twenty-five people. Then, there are the families from her husband's side. At a rough count, I would say there are over sixty members of her immediate family, all of whom believe they must visit each other at least once a week.

The women, who tend to arrive with large dishes of food, go straight to the kitchen and compete with each other to cook, heat what they have brought or serve out whatever has already been prepared. The kitchen, I have noticed, does not belong to Indu. The boss of her kitchen is the slim, tall, elegant Didi. In all these years, I have never discovered Didi's real name; she is just Didi, literally 'the elder sister', and she is not just Indu's elder sister, but everyone's elder sister. When she arrives, all the women step back and let her take charge. Didi then issues polite instructions to the others and begins cooking. She starts with the *puris*, made from small, rolled-out circles of wheat dough, which are deep-fried till they are swollen, while other women prepare the dry vegetable dishes such as potato *bhaji* or *bhindi*, with which the *puris* are eaten. Everything will be served piping hot, and everyone present is obliged to eat from *thalis* that arrive in an endless stream.

Jains are strict vegetarians. Like most Jains, Indu does not eat garlic or onions; some Jains do not even eat plants that grow in the dark such as mushrooms. 'I don't eat mushrooms,' Indu admitted, 'simply because I don't like them.' You might think there would be limits to the diversity of the output of Indu's kitchen. You would be wrong. What Indu can do with vegetables, the sheer number of ways she can fry, boil, steam, bake, grill, stuff and otherwise make them enticingly palatable is truly astonishing. 'What we can eat may be limited,' she once commented with a large grin on her face, 'but our imagination is not.'

There is one way Jains do tend to be limited. Traditionally, they marry strictly within the community. 'I was given no choice,' Indu said. 'Ayrun was presented to me gift-wrapped and I had to accept him. Though I was delighted when I unwrapped him!' She laughed uproariously. 'It's a diet marriage,' she continued. 'Who else but another Jain would accept a diet like ours?' Surprisingly, she also regards her marriage to Ayrun as a multicultural marriage, a product of their lives in Britain.

'How so?' I asked. 'You're both from the same religion and from the same community.'

'Ah,' Indu replied, trying to suppress her laugh. 'We are not from the same community. I am a Punjabi. Ayrun is from Madhya Pradesh. We speak different languages and have different cultures. I would not have married him if I lived in India.'

This was a revelation. I had always thought Jains were largely from the Gujerat province of India and spoke Gujerati. Indeed, a Punjabi Jain is a rare species. But it turned out Ayrun too was anything but Gujerati. He spoke a dialect of Hindi called Khichari, also the name of a simple dish consisting of a mixture of boiled rice and lentils. Commonly, the word *khichari* is used to describe any kind of mixture. Whenever we were together, we spoke *khichari* too: a mixture of English, Urdu, Hindi and Punjabi. 'What could be more multicultural than *that*?' Indu pointed out.

Indu teaches at the London Academy in Edgware, a short distance from where we live. It's about as *multi*cultural as a comprehensive school can get, with English, Indian, Pakistani, Chinese, West Indian, African and Christian, Jewish, Muslim, Hindu and Buddhist pupils. She teaches A-Level mathematics to working- and middle-class students. 'In my experience it is not the cultural background of my students that determines how they do but which social class they belong to,' Indu said. 'Middle-class children from all cultural backgrounds do rather well. But working-class students struggle, largely because for one reason or another they cannot get proper backup from their parents.'

'So are you saying that cultural differences do not count in educational attainment?' I asked.

'Culture and tradition require us to treat people differently according to their own criteria,' Indu replied. 'In Britain, we are learning to do just that. We have learnt, for example, that sometimes you have to treat people differently, according to their cultural norms, to treat them equally. But we haven't paid enough attention to class differences, particularly how the daily struggle in working-class lives makes getting out of the poverty trap or educational problems that much more difficult.'

'What do you think,' I asked Indu, 'about the suggestion that the emphasis on diversity has fragmented Britain, the idea that multiculturalism has failed because it has gone too far?'

'Rubbish!' Indu is no equivocator. 'The emphasis on diversity has made a positive difference to people's lives. It has helped the most economically deprived communities. It has brought forward a vast array of literature, art, music, dance, comedy and films that binds us together.' She paused for a thought. 'It is not that multiculturalism has gone too far. Rather it has not gone far enough. It is not inclusive enough.'

'How can we make it more inclusive?'

'Well . . .' Indu gathered herself to expound on a subject she had clearly thought deeply about. 'We talk about tolerance. But tolerance is such a patronizing concept. To be tolerant of someone is to accept them grudgingly. We need to accept diversity as an intrinsic good.' She took a deep breath. 'And we must think of the *goras* as part of this diversity. The *gora* community, despite being as diverse and multilayered as any ethnic community, stands apart from multiculturalism. We should celebrate the diversity and plurality of the *goras* as well!'

On her next visit Indu brought me a copy of *Key Stage Four Citizenship: The Study Guide*. Together we examined the material sixteen-year-olds now have to study for GCSE to become good citizens. Indu excitedly pointed out the section on 'Being British'. 'Everyone has a social identity,' it said. 'Being British means different things to different people.' Under 'Multiculturalism in Britain', the study guide argued that the cultural diversity of Britain makes it unique. 'Imagine life,' it said, 'without Indian curries, Turkish kebabs, Japanese karaoke, Jamaican reggae . . .' There was an acknowledgement of 'racial issues' and 'racial inequalities' in Britain, and even an indirect mention of institutionalized racism. Indu gave all this her full support. 'It's brilliant!' she said. But there was a glaring absence. Nowhere in the course did one learn that whites too are part of this cultural diversity. There was a conspicuous silence about the distinctive cultures of Wales, Scotland, Northern Ireland and England and other subcultures within them.

The Home Office's 2004 report *Life in the United Kingdom*, subtitled 'A Journey to Citizenship', recommends what new immigrants should know about Britain to become fully fledged citizens. It contained useful guides on law, governance, employment and 'everyday needs' such as housing, health and education. But Indu was horrified by its take on British history. It has virtually nothing to say about British Asians. 'It's what has come to be known as Henry and Hitler with nothing in between,' she said. 'This is a very exclusivist take on our past; it does not give our students a sense of belonging.'

For Indu secondary education is all about inculcating a sense of belonging. She believes the alienation of some Asian youth, particularly the Muslims, is largely because they cannot relate Britain's past to their own heritage. Was she, I wondered, shocked by home-grown terrorism; that some young Muslims from immigrant families, born, educated and reared in Britain, could kill their fellow citizens?

'Shocked but not too surprised,' Indu said. 'If you are going to tell them they are strangers in this land, that they have no history of involvement and entanglement with Britain, you should not be surprised they end up feeling like strangers. What we think of our past shapes how we view the future. We cannot throw away all that multiculturalism has achieved because of terrorism.' She thought for a moment. 'We need to teach a yogic interpretation of British history.'

That caught me by surprise. In Jain thought, the world consists of two kinds of energy: *Jada* and *Chetana*, matter and life. *Jada* is the energy that keeps the materialistic world moving; it sustains the universe. The more subtle forces of *Chetana*, silence and solitude, have to be harnessed with love and sympathy. Indeed, the very definition of intelligence in Jainism is the loving use of peace and quiet to harness the forces of *Chetana*. That's what, for example, yoga does.

'What would be a yogic interpretation of history?' I asked, leaning forward.

'Well, it would focus on the symbiosis of Britain's relationship with its colonies. It would highlight all those things, such as the role of Britain in India, Pakistan and Afghanistan, the Asian presence in Britain since the Middle Ages and . . .'

'The role Islam played in shaping European civilization,' I added.

'All those things,' Indu continued, 'on which conventional history is so mind-numbingly silent.'

I took the opportunity to tell Indu I was involved in developing a GCSE syllabus in the history of science designed to enthuse and involve children of diverse backgrounds. It explored the Indian and Islamic origins of algebra and mathematics, and showcased Muslim, Hindu and Chinese contributions to physics, biology and medicine. It is designed to reflect a more robust interactive past than can be found in the usual school curriculum of multi-ethnic Britain.

'That's what we need,' Indu said enthusiastically. 'Contexts and connections.' It is possible, she went on to argue, to deliver lessons on subjects as apparently exclusive to Britain as the Middle Ages or Elizabeth I in a way that draws parallels with Muslim and Indian historical experiences. For instance, we can draw parallels between the Middle Ages in Britain and the Muslim presence in Andalusia, and between Elizabeth I and the first interactions between the British and the Mughals in India.

'The history taught at school,' she said, 'could easily provide a context for current crises. A more balanced perspective of the Palestinian issue. Or how Iran's contemporary woes are related to how Britain and the US interfered to overthrow popular, representative leaders.'

'When teaching the First World War we could also point out how Britain tried to undermine the Ottoman caliphate,' I added.

'There,' said Indu, 'you're flying like a yogi already!'

Indu is the self-confident face of British Asian existence, someone making a significant contribution to the life of British society. Like her, most educated Asians are aware of the deficiencies in education that produce conventional British attitudes – it is the *goras* who need to be convinced about the benefits of multiculturalism. There is a lack of equity, openness and honesty about the cultural diversity of British culture. What minorities embrace in multicultural education strikes many of their white British neighbours as undermining history as they have known it. For a large segment of white Britain, giving minorities a sense of belonging and pride in their ancestry and heritage requires subverting, undermining or the wholesale dismantlement of British identity. Multiculturalism is something done for and to minorities; what it achieves for the mainstream, apart from giving them a guilt complex, is nebulous – something that does not feel like a positive identity. Before conventional British attitudes can accept the content of multiculturalism, they have to be convinced of its truth, convinced it is not merely special pleading to make minorities feel better. But far from multiculturalism being seen as intrinsically good, it is now projected as a divisive notion that leads to entrenched ghettos, undermines 'our way of life', promotes terrorism, and is generally destroying Britain in all ways possible.

The backlash against multiculturalism began with the millennium. The riots in Oldham, as well as Burnley and Bradford, in the summer of 2001, led to widespread questioning of the benefits of cultural diversity. The British right has always looked at cultural diversity with suspicion. It tolerated the presence of British Asians on the strict condition that they will assimilate and disappear into a national culture and a monolithic British identity. But the riots, and the 11 September 2001 atrocity in New York and terrorist attacks in London on 7 July 2005, also galvanized the left-leaning liberals against multiculturalism. As the late Hugo Young, one of the most respected liberal commentators, wrote in the *Guardian* on 6 November 2001, multiculturalism 'can now be seen as a useful bible for any Muslim who insists that his religio-cultural priorities, including the defence of *jihad* against America, override his civic duties of loyalty, tolerance, justice and respect for democracy'. In a highly discussed article in the February 2004 issue of *Prospect*, editor David Goodhart talked about 'stranger citizens' and argued that multiculturalism was eroding our 'common culture'. Numerous other voices, from the left as well as the right, have denounced multiculturalism and gleefully announced its demise.

Most of this diatribe against multiculturalism is little more than thinly disguised anti-Muslim racism. As Arun Kundnani of the Institute of Race Relations shows so convincingly in his *The End of Tolerance* (Pluto, 2007), Muslims have been routinely singled out as the culprit: it is their cultural difference that needs to be limited, it is they who need to demonstrate their loyalty to Britain and British values, and it is their cultural heritage and history that must be subsumed within Britishness. The obvious suggestion was not just that Muslims are totally alien to Britain, but that they could never be British; they preferred to be segregated and could only become decent citizens if forced to integrate. The New Labour government enhanced these anti-Muslim sentiments with its 2002 White Paper *Secure Borders, Safe Haven: Integration with Diversity in Modern Britain*. It suggested that multiculturalism had led to over-emphasis on cultural diversity and moral relativism. Rioting young Muslims in northern English towns had to be assimilated into British values, and tolerance of cultural diversity was to be replaced with community cohesion. Integration became the watchword in twenty-first century Britain. Young British Pakistanis I met in Oldham, born and bred in England and who spoke English with broad Yorkshire and Lancashire accents, were now classed as aliens in need of integration.

The riots in Oldham, as I discovered, had little to do with race and even less with Islam. They were not a product of multicultural policies or liberal over-emphasis on diversity, but an outcome of industrial decline and economic deprivation. Yet multiculturalism and Muslims were now being blamed for self-segregation. The underlying assumption in all this was that Muslims like to live in ghettos and thrive on economic deprivation, social injustice and marginalization. Multiculturalism had allowed them to give vent to their worst aspirations and in the process turned Britain into a haven for terrorists and loathsome cultural practices.

As a British Muslim, I am quite appalled at the emergence of this anti-Muslim political culture. But it is not a new phenomenon. It was first identified in 1997 by the Runnymede Trust's report on Islamophobia. The report noted that hostility and hatred towards British Muslims was becoming 'more explicit, more extreme and more dangerous'. It recognized the period after *The Satanic Verses* as the first decade of Islamophobia, and expressed concern that 'organisations and individuals known for their liberalism and anti-racism' were quite happy to 'turn a blind eye to the fact that this society offers only unequal opportunities to Muslims'. Worse: some liberal secularists did not hesitate to express openly their prejudice against Islam and Muslims. The situation has deteriorated enormously since the publication of the report. It seems to me that the left, with New Labour's blessing, has made anti-Muslim diatribes quite respectable.

The representation of British Muslim Asians as a segregation-seeking community hostile to British values (however they are defined) has little to do with the reality of how most Muslims actually live their lives and practise their faith. I discovered this in Tower Hamlets, an area of London most strongly associated with the Bangladeshi community. One in three of all Bangladeshis in Britain lives here. This is not just the highest concentration of Bangladeshis in the UK (71,389 according to the 2001 census), but also the highest number of Muslims in a single locality. The stereotypes of the Bangladeshi community suggest that it is the least integrated, least educated, most economically deprived, most religiously introverted and most passive community, and generally at the bottom of all social scales.

I knew the area well from my adolescence. When we lived in Hackney, I used to take the 253 bus every Saturday to Whitechapel. In those days, London was rather short of halal meat and Asian shops, and Whitechapel was one of the few places we could get our groceries. What I remember of my weekly trips to the area is the eruption of council estates, where all kinds of deprivation were congealed and left to fester. The great social experiment of the 1960s and 70s provided less of a blank canvas for a new beginning than a bland expanse of disorienting breezeblock and pebbledash. The masses were huddled in a new space and left to wrestle with the same old question: 'Where do we go from here?'

In many ways not much has changed in Tower Hamlets. The old Whitechapel Road market is still there, still badly served by the council, still selling shoddy goods to the perpetually poor. Unemployed men in duffle coats kill time on the streets. There is dirt and debris, rotting vegetables and abandoned junk food everywhere. If you look back towards the City, you can see the 'Gherkin' and other shining new steel and glass monuments to the world of finance. But turn into Sidney Way and you discover the other world, the world of the underclass passed over and forgotten by the vision of 'we're all middle class now' Britain. You enter a world of rapidly degenerating housing estates long past their best days, if they ever had any. The rough, tough world of deprivation, where drugs and crime are all too evident, which was so vividly captured by Monica Ali in *Brick Lane*. Still there; still very much alive.

But just when you think this is a familiar story of alienation, of a hopeless underclass writhing in its modernized squalor, there are surprises. There have been changes after all. Like me, it's older, more worn down by use. It's lived in and had been knocked around more by life. And, like me, it has changed from the inside. Rather as if the old cockney sparrows who mudlarked hereabouts had simply been transformed from within, infused with the DNA of the Bangladeshi spirit.

Take football. Almost every estate in Tower Hamlets now supports its own football team. But football in Tower Hamlets is not about the beautiful game. It is a focus around which pride can be marshalled and motivated. It is a way of tackling a universal problem to be found everywhere across the estates of Britain. In Tower Hamlets, the problems are being confronted, given the Vinnie Jones tackle, by a distinct sense of identity kitted out in the particular resources that belong to the local Bangladeshi community alone. The school and the mosque are where that drive is most in evidence.

I visited Stepney Green School in Ben Johnson Road in May 2005. Its pupils, predominantly Bangladeshi, come from disadvantaged backgrounds. There was no playground. Classrooms were dilapidated and in bad shape. But the ramshackle building belied the atmosphere inside. I tried to engage with a group of shy and rather reserved boys. Their faces lit up the moment I mentioned GCSEs. 'I did very well in my mock GCSEs,' said one boy as he proudly told me his grades. Another said he wanted to go to the City and become a stockbroker. Another wanted to study law. I was rather surprised. In May 2000 the school had been labelled a failure by the Office of Standards in Education (Ofsted) and marked for closure. There was a dispute between the headmaster and the governors, which eventually led to his sacking. Stepney Green was declared by the *Sun* newspaper to be the 'worst school in Britain'. So, what had happened since?

'The whole community rallied behind us,' the new headmaster, Sean McGrath, a jolly, self-confident man told me. The parents, who are desperate for their children to do well and go to university, dropped one of their key demands: that Bengali should be taught as a compulsory second language. A collective effort was made to identify the special needs of the children, and a team consisting of teachers and learning mentors was established. Within a couple of years, the school was achieving GCSE results higher than the national average. 'Now most of our pupils go into further education,' said McGrath. The school excelled in mathematics and computer studies and was seeking the status of special college. The spirit of the school was displayed for all to see on its outer wall. It was covered with a brilliantly coloured mural, consisting of 900 tiles, each crafted individually by students and staff, sandwiched between stylized paintings of local monuments and environmental themes. 'It's astonishing,' reflected McGrath. 'It hasn't been disfigured or damaged once!' He thought for a moment. 'We could not have turned the school around so rapidly without the wide support and participation of parents and the mosque.'

The mosque has now become the prime focus of community spirit. Tower Hamlets has over twenty-seven mosques spread throughout the borough. The most important one is the East London Mosque, which has a history going back to 1938. Like most mosques in Britain, it began as a single building. In 1940, three houses were purchased in Commercial Street and knocked together to serve as a rough-and-ready prayer place. The buildings were acquired by the Greater London Council under a compulsory purchase order in 1975; in return the GLC provided land and a temporary building in Whitechapel Road, a short walk from Aldgate East Tube station. Ten years later, a fully fledged mosque had been built. And, like the community itself, it has continued to evolve; in 2005, it was described as the 'largest Muslim complex in Western Europe'. It will not win any prizes for design, but it houses a secondary school, a Job and Career Advice Centre, an Enterprise and Business Development Centre particularly for women, and a Youth Centre; no doubt, anything else the community thinks it needs will be added.

Matching the building's undistinguished facade, the interior is functional rather than ostentatious. The obligatory green carpet and shoe racks lead to a large circular prayer hall that overflows with worshippers at prayer times. Women climb the short staircase to the balcony. Infants and juniors go down to the large room that serves as a primary school. There is always a bevy of bare-footed, bearded young men, arguing as though the very survival of the world depended on what they have to say; and women, mostly with scarves around their head, purposefully ushering children or other women in one direction or another. There are community liaison officers, community cohesion programmes that aim to bridge the young–old divide, and a Rapid Response Force that works with the police on drug issues. I walked into a meeting of the Young Muslim Organization, a nationwide predominantly Bangladeshi group that has its head office in the mosque. The executive were advising their members to be proactive, and 'speak out gently but firmly for peace and justice'. Elsewhere in the mosque, a protest against the campaign to clean up Whitechapel Road market was being planned. In one room, I discovered a group of elders discussing the 'Agenda for London', which was being spearheaded by the East London Communities Organization (TELCO).

It was never like this during my youth! What cosmic force has generated such enormous changes? The answer is multiculturalism. Multicultural policies provided subsidies for community development and targeted grants at specific projects. During the 1990s, the community received just enough financial support to galvanize and transform itself. The last decade has seen 'a seismic shift in the attitude of our community', explained Dilawar Hussein Khan, the director of the mosque. The sole aim of the earlier generation of Bangladeshis, mostly seamen and cooks, was to earn enough money to support their families back home, to become self-sufficient and return. This idea of returning to Bangladesh has been unceremoniously ditched. 'The elders of the community finally realized,' says Dilawar, 'they were not going back. They are here to stay! Their children are British and proud of their identity. They belong to Britain and Britain belongs to them.' This mental transformation had a corollary: the focus shifted from what is happening 'back home' to what is happening in the local community. The desire to reproduce the culture they had left behind in every detail was abandoned as counterproductive. Instead, a great deal of effort was put into generating a new fusion that is as much Bangladeshi as British, and thanks to the multicultural policies of the borough, the community had access to some funds to achieve their goal. Once things had been kick-started, the community became proactive, eager to help itself.

Dilawar is a self-effacing, bearded man. He oozes ease and confidence in equal measure. He not only represented the emerging leadership in the Asian community, but also personified its changing attitudes. He came to London from Sylhet at the age of nine. 'During those days,' he said, 'we were not encouraged to go into higher education. As soon as we finished school, we were put into the rag trade or catering.' He left school to start a small garment business. 'But I realized that to change things within the community, I had to start with changing myself.' He went back into education and obtained a degree in accounting and finance from South London University.

There is a world of difference between the elder generation and their young counterparts. The elders shunned not only education; they also rejected politics and all the social activities associated with youth. Mosques were little more than prayer places. The '1971 generation', as they are known locally, who fought in the anti-racist movement of the 1970s and led the mosques, have moved out to be replaced by younger, politically conscious, educated professionals, who not only believe in multiculturalism but live a multicultural life. The new generation has transformed the mosque into an educational, social and political institution. It is leaping over a particular kind of traditionalism to encourage authentic communal power. It is thinking and responding to tradition in new ways and, thereby, giving it a distinctive British identity. In consequence the community is being changed out of all recognition.

Ostensibly, what has turned the area around is regeneration. The borough's regeneration scheme focused on housing, business, neighbourhood projects and community development, providing young Bangladeshis with an opportunity to develop and empower their community. The regeneration schemes may have been a product of the multicultural policies of council bureaucrats and planners, but their success was largely due to the people themselves. Perhaps that's what needs to be remembered everywhere. Regeneration schemes are not guaranteed to succeed, but are susceptible to a whole series of pitfalls. Only vibrancy and self-confidence within the community can ensure success.

This self-confidence is all too evident at the mosques in Tower Hamlets. What surprised me most was the sheer speed with which Bangladeshi mosques move to tackle community problems. When truancy in the borough's primary schools became a big problem a few years ago, the mosques took the matter into their own hands. Representatives of the mosques started visiting the parents of the offending pupils. The initiative was such a success that the government began to recommend it as a general policy for Asian communities. The drugs problem was being tackled with equal efficacy. Hard drugs began to appear in the borough towards the end of the 1990s. The East London Mosque responded by setting up drugs awareness classes and establishing a drugs rehabilitation programme, Nafas, which uses an Islamic approach – natural therapies, in-house sauna, group work and helping addicts find a sense of purpose in life – to cure drug addiction. But it also took an unusual step. On Friday nights the keys of the mosque were handed over to young people for the whole weekend. Volunteers, some as young as fourteen and fifteen, went out into the community and ushered street kids, addicts and pushers, as well as members of local gangs, into the mosque. An intense debate ensued with young Bangladeshis lecturing other young Bangladeshis on the importance of education and community development.

The new generation has also brought a new attitude to Islam, most evident amongst the women. Their approach to Islam is radically different from that of their mothers. 'The older generation of women were the product of a tradition that denied them education and confined them to the four walls of their homes,' said Rosy Awwal, director of Graduate Forum, a careers advice and guidance centre in Greatorex Street. Awwal looked small and delicate, her round face, circled by a scarf, shining like a full moon, but she talked tough. 'We reject the "we demand" mentality of our parents. We are the "we do" generation.' They were married young, usually by arrangement, and often lived in overcrowded houses, burdened with caring responsibilities. 'The new generation use their knowledge to show that many traditional restrictions have no basis in Islamic law,' Awwal said. They are educationally motivated and tend to marry late. They still have arranged marriages but choose their own partners and go out freely. 'They take it for granted they will go to college and university and work.' And they are not afraid to tackle sensitive issues such as domestic violence and sexual abuse.

Nowhere is the new mood more evident than in Brick Lane. The whole Brick Lane area, where street names are given in Bengali as well as English, has changed as drastically as the Bangladeshi community itself. During the 1970s, when Brick Lane was one of the few places where one could buy halal meat, I was a regular visitor. The best-known restaurant in Brick Lane was the Clifton. It was as famous for its food as its decor. Pride of place on the menu was given to brain *masala*, *nihari* (an incredibly rich and fatty broth slowly cooked all night) and *payah* (sheep's feet): testimonies to the art of conjuring food from the ingredients of poverty. The walls were covered with huge paintings reminiscent of Indian film posters. The paintings, mostly of semi-clad, generously proportioned women, reminded the regular local patrons, men living on their own, of their wives and loved ones back home to whom they expected to return one day: a woman inside an oyster lying on a bed of pearls; a woman playing sitar longing for her lover; a lonely woman catching a fish; two lovers with the man's head gently laid on the shoulder of the woman. A juke box incessantly intoned the latest romantic hits from Bollywood. Patrons were often greeted by the owner, Musa Patel, a man as generous with his smile as his facial hair. To walk into the Clifton was like walking into a street-side café in Sylhet.

Old Musa Patel died in the early 1990s; the Clifton has changed hands a number of times since. Now called Prithi, it is twice the size of the old restaurant. The flock wallpaper and gaudy red carpet have given way to wooden floors and Georgian windows. The menu has a strong bias towards seafood, with an accent on Bangladeshi freshwater fish. The restaurant's clients tend to be City types out for a 'Bangla evening'. But the trademark paintings have been kept, after being lovingly restored by a Japanese painter.

Even the new names of the restaurants reflect the transformation and confidence of the community. In the 1960s and 70s, Brick Lane restaurants had names such as Nawab of Bengal and Curry House – names designed to rekindle images of the Raj and remind the community of its history. In the 1980s, we had names such as Taj Mahal and The Red Fort, which invoked images of rich history and tradition that had been left behind and masked British pretensions to possession of an Empire while reclaiming their own history. In the 1990s, the names shed their colonial connections: Karahi and Balti became the most common terms in their names. The new century took the naming thing to a new quantum level. Now they have names such as Dawaat (literally, invitation), Alishan (Palatial) and Saffron. The new names indicate not only a certain authenticity of expression, but also the self-confidence of having arrived. The first restaurant, a fast-food joint, you meet as you turn from Whitechapel Road into Osborne Street, which leads into Brick Lane, is called Khushbu – fragrance. The name is apt as the entire area is suffused with a strong waft of fragrant aromas. It is an announcement that you are entering a different area, an area where conventional stereotypes do not hold. Here a 'chop' is not a lamb chop – but a round or oval potato cake with a fish or meat stuffing which is dipped in egg and breadcrumbs, then crisply fried. A 'cutlet' may be lamb, chicken or even prawn, but it is long and flat, coated and fried, with a little bit of bone or a prawn tail hanging out. A 'pickle' is in fact an oily fish paste. Enter, say the aromas of Khushbu, and leave your preconceptions behind.

Preconceptions were all in evidence when a film crew arrived in the famous street, in July 2006, to film *Brick Lane*. The local community, and in particular the restaurateurs, did not look on the 2003 novel of the same name with favour. They saw its author, Monica Ali, as an 'outsider', with little knowledge of Bangladeshis in Tower Hamlets, who 'insulted' the community by portraying too many stereotypes. As one local resident told me, 'She is not one of us, she has not lived with us, she knows nothing about us, and she has insulted us.' An impromptu community action group was established, under the guidance of the Brick Lane Traders' Association, to halt the 'despicable insult'. *Brick Lane* does contain a few stereotypes – not least the protagonist, Nasreen, the archetypical bride who comes to Britain via an arranged marriage. But the novel portrays the Bangladeshis of Tower Hamlets as they were in the closing decades of the twentieth century. The local traders had changed and just did not see themselves in these terms any more. With Asians, pride is an all-important and all-consuming emotion. The Brick Lane community is not only proud of its achievements; it also has the confidence to stand up for itself and demand that it should be represented the way it sees itself. The campaign involved the community at every level: men and women, old and young, and the local gangs. Women were organizing petitions, the young were leading protests, and the gangs were ready to barricade the streets. In the end the community had its way, and Ruby Films, the production company making *Brick Lane*, withdrew.

It is when minorities stand up for their rights, which sometimes leads to questioning liberal values, that multiculturalism runs into problems. But liberal values do not exist in isolation. They make sense only when combined with other principles, such as social justice and fair representation – only when these values are firmly embedded in society can other fundamentals of liberalism come into play. In any case, I think such tensions are important and necessary if we are going to negotiate a viable notion of citizenship and nationhood. Integration and cultural learning are a two-way process – while it is important for the minorities to have some understanding of liberal values, it is equally important for liberal secularists to understand the concerns and issues of minorities.

Multiculturalism, as Tower Hamlets demonstrated, has played an important part in achieving greater social equality in Britain. It has been highly successful as a state policy designed to accommodate and empower those defined by reference to race, ethnicity and religion. It was consciously constructed in opposition to policies of assimilation and ideals of pure liberal individualism. In Britain, it was always about the inclusion of marginalized identities. As such, we should not be surprised when it sometimes clashes with cherished liberal principles.

Where multiculturalism is even more problematic, I think, is in its emphasis on ethnicity. The word has its roots in America, where all except European immigrants are classified as 'ethnic'. Ethnicity connotes, more than anything else, primordially constituted Otherness in relation to non-ethnics, the Europeans, who are the true Americans. It is the polite term for a racial hierarchy within American society. The European whites are never ethnic: they are Italian-Americans, Irish-Americans or German-Americans. The non-Europeans (Chinese, Asians, blacks) are always ethnic. Hyphenated Americans amble through the corridors of power;

ethnics occupy lowlier positions. The term is inherently racist. In the British context, overemphasis on ethnicity has led to divisions within society and lack of – to use a term that has become popular in government and policy circles – community cohesion. If each individual has an immutable right of attachment to a distinct ethnicity, then problems of difference become insurmountable. Worse still, those who are not members of distinct ethnic groups are forced to manufacture new identities in order to assert their distinction. Ethnicity fuels an insatiable desire for difference; it leads to dissatisfaction, frustration and animosity. Instead of focusing on common values, society gets embroiled in issues of cultural difference.

The problems with multiculturalism, as we understand it at present, have to be acknowledged. But these problems would neither lead to its death nor make it go away. Standing against multiculturalism is like defying gravity. Multiculturalism has existed for millennia, in the sense that there have been many societies that are heterodox, multi-ethnic and multiracial in composition. In the contemporary world it is a reality that cannot be avoided. It is not only a dominant trend, but a global custom on a planet where media, travel and business accelerate the process of cultural mixing. Cultural boundaries have become fluid, shift constantly, mix and remix to produce new hybrids and synthesis. Cultural diversity, multiple identities and a fusion of everything from music to arts, food to literature, dress and fashion, religion and worldviews, is now the norm in every society. And Britain is not and cannot be an exception.

This new form of heightened multiculturalism is quite daunting and presents us with radically new and different challenges. The sheer diversity of British society, the connections of British citizens to other countries, the impact of global news channels, immigration and emigration, wars and terrorism – all this places hitherto unimagined demands on both minority and majority communities. The simple reaction in the face of this complexity is to retreat into one's ideological cocoon, denounce multiculturalism and force everyone to fall in line in the pursuit of some monolithic notion of nation or national identity. This is a prescription for disaster.

What we need to appreciate is that we lack the right framework, tools and skills to deal with the level of complexity we are confronted with in the new heightened, globalized multiculturalism. Conventional political theories, institutions, vocabulary and strategies we have developed over recent centuries in a homogeneous British state, dominated by a particular class, are not only inadequate but sometimes a positive hindrance in dealing with the rapidly changing and complex diversity we find in contemporary Britain. We need new ways to resolve the demands of unity and diversity, of developing a consensually based political community, and cultivating a sense of belonging and togetherness amongst British citizens. And Britain has been fortunate in having a towering thinker who has spent decades developing a new definition and a new way of looking at multiculturalism. So I went to the Mother of All Parliaments to talk to the Lord of Multiculturalism.

We met in the tea room of the House of Lords. I walked past bored policemen and was directed to the 'peers' entrance'. Lord Bhikhu Parekh greeted me enthusiastically. 'It is time,' he said, 'we had a proper chat.' We were first introduced by our mutual friend Ashis Nandy. In those days, Bhikhu was professor of political theory at the University of Hull. He went on to teach at the universities of British Columbia, Concordia, McGill, Harvard, Pompeau Febra and Pennsylvania, ending up as Centennial Professor in the Centre for the Study of Global Governance at the London School of Economics. In between, he found time to write his seminal work, *Rethinking Multiculturalism* (Palgrave Macmillan, 2000), and to chair the commission on the Future of Multi-Ethnic

Britain, 'The Parekh Report' (2000), which has become the basis for almost all discussion on multiculturalism in Britain. A warm, congenial man of medium height, Bhikhu has a penchant for smiling generously. His white beard and feathery white hair remind me of Hakim Sahib, my grandfather.

Bhikhu ordered a cream tea, and we sat in a semi-secluded area to talk. 'Let's start by looking at the terms that constitute multiculturalism,' he began. The tea arrived and I poured some Darjeeling for us both. Multi, he said, suggests plurality; contemporary society is characterized by a plurality of cultures. Its members subscribe to different systems of meaning, and structure their lives differently. Although some of their values invariably overlap, others do not. And even if they do overlap, different cultures sometimes define and prioritize them differently. Unlike a culturally homogeneous society, members of a multicultural society do not share a common substantive vision of the good life, and disagree about the value to be assigned to different human activities and relationships.

'So how are we to understand multiculturalism? Is it a *de facto* acceptance of reality since we can no longer lead isolated, self-contained lives? Is it a political doctrine based on the idea of cultural diversity, or a central moral and political fact of modern life? Or a new philosophical school with a distinct theory of social relations?' I asked, while spreading jam on my scone.

'Multiculturalism is best understood as a perspective on and way of viewing human life,' Bhikhu replied. He explained that in his opinion it has three central insights. First, human beings are culturally embedded in the sense that they grow up and live within a culturally structured world and organize their lives and social relations in terms of a culturally derived system of meaning and significance. Second, different cultures represent different systems of meaning and visions of the good life. Since each realizes a limited range of human capacities and emotions and grasps only a part of the totality of human existence, it needs other cultures to understand itself better, expand its intellectual and moral horizons, stretch its imagination, save it from narcissism and guard it against the obvious temptation to see itself in absolute terms. Third, every culture is internally plural and reflects a continuing conversation between its various traditions and strands of thought. This does not mean it is devoid of coherence and identity, but that its identity is plural, fluid and open. Cultures grow out of conscious and unconscious interaction with each other, define their identity in terms of what they take to be their significant other, and are at least partially multicultural in their origins and constitution.

'So how would you actually *define* multiculturalism?' I asked, smearing my scone with Devonshire cream.

'I would define it as a belief that no culture is perfect or represents the best life, and that it can therefore benefit from a critical dialogue with other cultures.'

I had not heard such a radically different definition of multiculturalism before. It placed considerable onus on those cultures which regard themselves as perfect, immutable and above question. I wasn't just thinking of Islam but also of the culture of the Enlightenment and the values that the liberal orthodoxy in Britain gets so worked up about. A string of questions also sprang to mind. Does this notion of multiculturalism automatically lead to a dialogue between cultures? Does it force us to respect all cultures equally? What do we do about cultures that insist on remaining in splendid isolation?

'Before we go any further,' Bhikhu said, leaning forward, 'let's agree on what multiculturalism does not mean and cannot imply.' I thought this was an excellent idea; to understand something it is often necessary to separate it from what it is not. 'First,' Bhikhu commenced, 'multiculturalism does not mean we are determined by or prisoners of our culture. To stress the value and formative influence of culture does not mean we cannot criticize or rise above it. Second, it does not imply every society is or should remain divided into neatly self-contained cultures, each morally self-sufficient.'

'That would be both absurd and impossible,' I added.

Bhikhu nodded and carried on. 'Third, it does not imply all cultural beliefs and practices deserve respect. We are obliged to understand and view other cultures sympathetically, but we cannot abdicate our responsibility to evaluate them.'

That I thought was very important. The prevailing idea that multiculturalism requires you to keep quiet and not criticize obnoxious cultural practices had done a great deal of damage.

'But how do we actually evaluate them?' I asked.

'Don't be impatient,' Bhikhu replied. 'We will get to that later.' He sipped his tea, and gave me a look which suggested I had broken his chain of thought. He continued: 'Fourth, multiculturalism is not committed to maintaining the existing form of cultural diversity. Cultures are not museum pieces but living, changing, thriving systems, and cultural diversity is a moving feast – interaction of cultures will always throw up new forms of cultural diversity.'

I was going to interrupt but decided it was wise to stay quiet. It began to dawn on me that Bhikhu thought in precise, clear, logical steps. His inclination towards the philosophy of Gandhi required him to state his arguments in simple, digestible lists. I was being presented with a *thali* of ideas, each signifying an absence – 'what is not' – by its very presence. Fifth, Bhikhu explained, multiculturalism does not imply cultures are totally distinct and closed worlds with nothing in common. If that was so they would have no resources with which to understand, interact and engage in a dialogue with each other. Sixth, multiculturalism does not imply relativism. Moral judgements within cultures are not closed to criticism. While acknowledging different visions of the good life, multiculturalism maintains that these visions are limited and can benefit from critical dialogue with others. Seventh, multiculturalism is not committed to the view that all cultures are equal and equally good. Such a view implies we have a transcultural standard by which all cultures can be judged equally. While acknowledging that certain values are universal, multiculturalism insists these values can be interpreted and combined differently and that there are other values that are specific to each culture. Eighth, multiculturalism does not imply the state cannot intervene in the internal life of a cultural community and ban some of its unacceptable practices. No cultural community can claim absolute right to non-intervention.

The list of what multiculturalism does not imply, it seemed to me, implicitly connected it with our ideas of human rights. Simple-minded critics and commentators often represent multiculturalism and human rights as either/or options. If you are for multiculturalism, then you are automatically against human rights, and vice versa. This is disingenuous. Multiculturalism cannot be invoked to justify such practices as forced marriage, female circumcision, honour killings or other violations of the basic rights of women. Neither can age old prejudices, such as those against homosexuals, be allowed to go unchallenged because of multiculturalism. Moreover, multiculturalism does not dictate that we see minority cultures as homogeneous, defined by the most reactionary men, who are then allowed to do whatever they wish because of custom or cultural practice or what the Qur'an supposedly says. To make such an assumption is the height of folly.

When Bhikhu had finished, he took a big gulp of tea, and looked at me as if to say: 'Now, what were you asking?'

'What about cultures that do not want to interact?'

'If some groups wish to lead self-contained lives and avoid interaction with others, multiculturalism respects their choice as long as they meet the consensually derived basic conditions of good life. A multicultural society accommodates those who do not share its dominant cultural ethos precisely because it cherishes cultural plurality,' Bhikhu replied.

'But aren't you arguing that cultural diversity itself leads to dialogue?'

'No,' Bhikhu demurred precisely. Multiculturalism, he explained, values intercultural dialogue not as a way of coping with the *fact* of cultural diversity, but rather to exploit the *value* of cultural diversity and to reap its benefits. Cultural diversity is a necessary, but not a sufficient, condition for dialogue. 'No dominant culture likes to take the risk of dialogue,' he continued, 'because the outcome of dialogue cannot be predicted.' Moreover, the dialogue requires it to justify assumptions it has taken for granted and whose validity it cannot always be sure of establishing.

Two conditions have to be met before dialogue can be established. First, the dominant culture should face criticism or at least serious questioning from within and create space for internal debate; and second, non-dominant cultures should have the confidence and the courage to challenge the hegemony of the dominant culture and to demand respect for their values and visions of a good life.

This brought us neatly to what I consider to be the two immovable objects: liberalism and feminism, both of which see themselves as grand, universal truths.

'From a multicultural perspective, no political doctrine or ideology can represent the full truth of human life,' Bhikhu explained. Liberalism is embedded in a particular culture, represents a particular vision of a good life, and is necessarily narrow and partial. It is an inspiring political doctrine stressing such great values as human dignity, autonomy, liberty, critical thought and equality. However, these can be defined in several different ways, of which the liberal formulation is only one and not always the most coherent. Liberalism also ignores or marginalizes other such great values as human solidarity, community, a sense of rootedness, selflessness, deep and self-effacing humility and contentment. Since it grasps only some aspects of the immense complexity of human existence and misses out too much of what gives value to life, it cannot provide the sole basis of a good society. The assumed universality of liberalism is nothing more than an extrapolation of the particularities of Western identity. It is not surprising that the fathers of liberalism, John Locke and John Stuart Mill, articulated liberalism in terms of Western supremacy.

'What about feminism?' I asked. Feminist writers have been the fiercest critics of multiculturalism. They think multiculturalism requires respect for or at least tolerance of all kinds of cultural practices, including the unequal treatment of women in certain cultures.

'Multiculturalism implies no such thing,' was Bhikhu's reply. What multiculturalism does require is that we first understand other cultures from within before passing judgements and that the criteria we apply for judging others should be shown to be universally valid. The feminist critique also makes the mistake of abstracting gender relations from other social relations and judging them in isolation. A culture might treat women unequally in civil and political matters but give them a superior social and religious status, or treat them as inferior when young or unmarried but revere them when they are old or are grandmothers. Since women in different stages of life or different relationships are perceived differently and are endowed with different rights in different societies, 'women' is too simplistic an abstraction to allow cross-cultural comparisons of gender equality. There is also the further question of how women themselves perceive their position. If some of them do not share the feminist view, it would be wrong to say they are victims of culturally generated false consciousness and in need of liberation by well-meaning outsiders. That is patronizing, even impertinent, and denies them the very equality we wish to extend to them.

'But some may be brainwashed,' I said.

'They may well be,' Bhikhu replied. 'But we have to avoid the mistaken conclusion that those who do not share our beliefs about their well-being are *all* misguided victims of indoctrination.'

I agreed with much of what Bhikhu had to say. It was exactly the kind of new formulation of multiculturalism we needed, I thought, to move forward. But there was still the vexed question of getting all the various cultures in Britain to develop common goals and commit to a common political community. At the end of the day, multiculturalism has to bring us all together.

To my surprise, Bhikhu suggested that commitment to Britain, our political community, does not involve commitment to common goals. 'Members of a community may well deeply disagree about common goals,' he said. Nor does commitment to Britain imply a common view of its history, which may be read very differently by different sections of society. Nor does it mean commitment to its form of government, about which citizens might entertain very different views, nor to its dominant cultural ethos, of which some might strongly disapprove. There was only one commitment that Bhikhu was concerned about. 'The commitment to the political community involves commitment to its continuing existence and well-being, and implies one cares enough for it not to harm its interests and undermine its integrity,' he said. It is a matter of degree, and could take such forms as a quiet concern for its well-being, deep attachment, affection or even intense love. Multiculturalism allows for all options.

'Would such a commitment lead to a feeling of belonging?' I asked.

'Commitment and belonging are reciprocal in nature,' Bhikhu replied. A citizen, he explained, cannot be committed to her political community unless it is also committed to her; and she cannot belong to it unless it accepts her as one of its own. The political community therefore cannot expect its members to develop a sense of belonging unless it in turn belongs to them. It must, therefore, value and cherish them all equally and reflect this in its structure, polities, conduct of public affairs, self-understanding and self-definition. This involves granting them equal rights of citizenship, a decent standard of living, and an opportunity to develop themselves and participate in and make their respective contributions to its collective life. In a multicultural society, different communities, Bhikhu said, have different needs; some might be structurally disadvantaged or lack the skill and the confidence to participate in the mainstream of society and avail themselves of its opportunities. Both justice and a need to foster a common sense of belonging then require such measures as group-differentiated rights, culturally differentiated applications of laws and policies, state support for minority institutions, and a judicious programme of affirmative action.

This, it seems to me, is the crux of the problem of belonging in Britain. The alienation of British Muslims, born and brought up in Britain, comes from the fact that they do not feel that Britain is committed to them. Where the state shows commitment, as in Tower Hamlets, the Muslim community reciprocates. Where the state shows neglect, as in Oldham, the Muslim community feels estranged. But the state's commitment is not limited to issues at local level. The British Muslim community does not exist in isolation from the rest of the *ummah* – the international brotherhood and sisterhood of Islam. Its sense of belonging is also affected by how the state behaves towards the *ummah* as a whole and whether British Muslims feel that their voice is being heard on issues of foreign policy and international relations. The global dimension of both Islam and multiculturalism cannot be overlooked.

Bhikhu's thinking, I couldn't help reflecting, would be anathema to liberals and modernists, who see the values of the Enlightenment as supreme; to people who see rights only in terms of the individual; who see the modernist project in terms of instrumental reason; and all those Islamophobes for whom the idea of the *ummah* is an anathema. His *thali* had transformed into manna for deep thought.

I wanted to pursue the question of the alienation of Muslim youth further. In Britain, I said, we do provide state support for minorities, we do have culturally differentiated policies which have, for example, led to the extension of racial equality to religious minorities, and we do have programmes that focus on the needs of minorities that have enabled the economic upward mobility of some of them. We have a vibrant culture of hybridity in food, fashions and popular entertainment. 'So why have we still failed,' I asked, 'to create a sense of belonging amongst Muslim youth?'

'While equal citizenship is essential for fostering a common sense of belonging, it is not enough,' Bhikhu replied. Citizenship is about status and rights. Belonging is about acceptance, feeling welcome, a sense of identification. The two do not necessarily coincide. One may enjoy all the rights of citizenship, he explained, but feel one does not quite belong to the community and is a relative outsider.

The feeling of being a citizen but an outsider is caused by a number of factors: how the wider society defines itself; the demeaning ways the rest of its members talk about these groups; and the dismissive or patronizing ways in which they treat them. Although members of these groups are in principle free to participate in public life, they often stay away for fear of rejection and ridicule or out of a deep sense of alienation.

'When the dominant culture defines minorities in a demeaning way and systematically reinforces this by institutional means, such as the media and other means at its disposal, they consciously or unconsciously internalize the negative self-image, lack self-esteem, and feel alienated from mainstream society,' Bhikhu said.

'And sometimes that alienation can express itself in extreme ways,' I added.

We finished our tea. Bhikhu looked at me as if to ask: 'How was it?' I thought for a moment. 'Even after ruling India, directly and indirectly, for several centuries, the Brits have not learned to make tea properly. Tea bags in the House of Lords! We have some way to go in discovering how to make a proper brew!'

It seemed to me, as I left the House of Lords, that the new multiculturalism requires us to ditch numerous antiquated notions we have taken for granted. In the contemporary globalized world, the idea that any person does, or could possibly, belong to a single, unchanging culture is untenable. All cultures change, and multiculturalism has itself changed and is changing. It has become the driving force of our cities, the engine of our economic growth, the motive power of our cultural products. But it has also been globalized – what happens on the streets of Karachi and Bombay often has a direct bearing on the streets of Birmingham and Bradford. We cannot understand the emerging forms of multiculturalism through old categories and vocabulary. The complex realities of tomorrow's Britain demand we ditch categories such as 'black and white', 'Asian and Muslim', 'ethnicity' and 'difference'. It makes no sense to ascribe ethnicity to a group, when traditional similarities and differences are dissolving. The language of belonging, exile and diaspora becomes irrelevant in the face of this new pluralism, where 'home' is both here and there. Even the term 'immigrant', when equated with 'blacks', 'Asians' and 'refugees', has become meaningless. Most 'immigrants' to Britain between 1991 and 2001, according to official statistics, were 'white': from Canada, the USA, Australia, South Africa and the former Soviet Union. Moreover, to suggest that an area with Asian concentration is a 'ghetto' or an indicator of segregation has now become absurd. Some of the most thriving areas in Britain, such as Brick Lane, Southall and Manchester's curry mile, have heavy concentrations of Asian populations, while some of the most deprived areas, in inner-city Glasgow or towns in Wales, are totally white. Far from being a barrier to integration, clustering has allowed Asians to develop niche businesses and organize transformative political power. It is high time that we moved away from using place and space to frame difference – to demonize them with terms such as 'segregation', 'invasion' and 'no-go areas'. Instead, we need to focus on how place becomes a source of pride and self-confidence, which shapes local identity and leads to a sense of belonging. Neighbourhoods succeed or fail not because of the colour or culture of the people who live there, but because of the presence or absence of ordinary provisions such as jobs, housing and community facilities. Those who think that integration is a one-way process, that Asians must assimilate according to some fixed and romantic notion of Britain and Britishness, betray a colonial mentality. We all need to integrate with each other – whites as well as Asians. Britain is not a static place; it has changed radically over my lifetime and continues to change rapidly. As a nation we are in a process of becoming.

The trouble with pluralistic, multicultural societies is that they are just too complex and multi-layered. The ongoing process of change and becoming also makes them somewhat chaotic. And handling chaos creatively and humanely, so that we move from the edge of chaos to a new order of being, is both challenging and exhausting. My sojourn in the House of Lords left me gasping for a dose of fresh air.

Conclusion

AFTER THE DRESS REHEARSAL

On the afternoon of Thursday 10 August 2006, I went for a walk.

I am a Londoner, not a mere townie. There is a big distinction, especially when a Londoner goes for a walk. Londoners walk further than people in any other British town or city to accomplish the simplest activity. Changing platforms on the Tube, for example, is in non-London terms, a major hike – for a Londoner it's mere routine. And there is a London way of travelling. Londoners venture determinedly, concentrating on their individual objective, seemingly oblivious to all else. In London no one is ever looking where they are going, yet everyone knows exactly where they are and how to get there. And all this happens at a pace. Loitering and leisurely ambling are not London ways; it's how one spots the tourists, the better to avoid them. Have you ever noticed how travellers on the London Underground jostle for precise positions on the platform as they wait for the next Tube train? Each one is directed by an internal positioning device to seek out a precise carriage – the one that will debouche them nearest the 'way out' sign at their destination. To be a Londoner is to seek the shortest, quickest route between two points.

Like all Londoners I am an habitué of subterranean travel, but by choice I like to walk. And by natural disposition I walk fast. When I say I walk fast, I mean fast by London standards. This is a perennial source of annoyance for Saliha, or any other companion, who straggles in my wake complaining bitterly. Because I prefer to walk whenever the opportunity presents itself I feel I know London, a city more than any other full of byways, side alleys and half-hidden lanes that, in the right locale, allow the adept pedestrian to arrive even more promptly than via the famed London black cabs.

But this walk was different. My escort, Nick Robins, was an equal match, pace for pace. An energetic, youthful chap, Nick works in the City where he manages socially responsible investment funds. History, which he studied at Cambridge, remained his passion, however, and he devoted several years to excavating the history of the East India Company. In the last few years, he has hosted walks around London, tracing the remains of John Company. What better way of concluding my exploration of identity, of unwinding the long history of entanglement, than walking around its physical remnants?

We arranged to meet at Aldgate Tube station. As I emerged from the Underground it struck me that it was one of the locations of the 7/7 bombings. But I had not come to make trite connections between old and present horrors. There had to be other endings. Outside the station the city was bathed in late-afternoon sunshine, the kind of glorious summer evening that comes after rain. I bowed my head in silent *dua* (prayer) for the victims, then I marched into the sunlight to join Nick, a hopeful explorer in search of new horizons. I was desperate to be gone from this memorial to multiple failures, encouraged that Nick kept pace with me.

We crossed to Fenchurch Street and in no time were standing before our first port of call, the East India Arms. It was an undistinguished pub, but Nick pointed to the coat of arms of the Honourable Company proudly displayed on the pub sign. Two rampant lions support a shield displaying a blue ground on which three ships gallantly sail. Nick turned my attention to the building next to the pub.

'You wouldn't know it,' he said, 'but these smart-looking City flats were once East India warehouses.' He produced a copy of an eighteenth-century map to prove the point. It was a 'Tallis street view'. John Tallis, a London publisher and cartographer, printed a series of street guides, a precursor of the modern *A to Z*, but much more sophisticated since each building was labelled and drawn to scale. There was little doubt that, during the Company's heyday, the warehouses were the dominant attraction on Fenchurch Street.

We walked down to Leadenhall Place. When Elizabeth I granted the charter to create 'The Honourable Company of London Merchants Trading to the East Indies', this was where its business was done. Nick pointed to a house situated near the narrow Philpot Lane, the City mansion of the Company's first governor, Sir Thomas Smythe. Little remained of the stately home but the site echoed its past in the appropriately named Spice Trader restaurant, with Balti dishes on the menu. We moved on to Lime Street and the main site of East India House. To my surprise, its place is now occupied by the headquarters of Lloyds of London, housed in a hideously ugly glass and steel tower, designed by Richard Rogers. It competes for attention with the erotic 'Gherkin', designed by Norman Foster.

'It was from here that the Company's directors guided its global operations and where its famous quarterly auctions were held,' Nick said. I looked for the 'blue plaque', the traditional way London memorializes historic connections. Eventually, I found one below the stairs of one of the entrances: 'Near this place,' it read, 'WILLIAM DUCKWRA founded the LONDON PENNY POST in 1680.'

'But where's the plaque that tells us this was the site of East India House?' I asked.

'There isn't one,' Nick replied. 'There's nothing that marks the tumultuous impact of this once mighty colonial corporation. That's the whole point of this tour. To show we suffer from serious amnesia, and deliberately hide our colonial history.'

It took a while for this nugget of information to sink in. Meanwhile, I kept glancing round, expecting some significant aspect to materialize from glass, concrete, steel or stone to reveal an elaborate practical joke. Nothing did. I turned to look Nick straight in the eye. 'You mean to tell me you dedicate your spare time to escorting people on tours of things that aren't there?' He nodded slowly, affecting a sage and knowing smile. 'Invisible tours!' I expostulated. 'Don't you ever worry about the trade descriptions act?'

'More like tours of invisibility,' Nick gamely replied. 'It's just the point. We've retreated from Empire but there's never been an accounting of what Empire in general, and the East India Company in particular, did to India – no reckoning of the impact of colonialism either on India or on Britain itself.'

'Not even a blue plaque,' I added bitterly. The blue plaques, dotted on buildings all around London, mean its inhabitants routinely travel through a history of connections and associations. Moving through places where history happened is an innate part of being a Londoner. I had come across blue plaques recording the residence of writers, artists, scientists – all sorts of luminaries. An entire museum occupies the house where Sigmund Freud lived out the last two years of his life – but the East India Company, the corporation that gave us the quality of life and shaped the history of modern Britain occasions only tours of invisibility!

Nick elaborated on his theme. East India House, he explained, was first occupied in 1648, and went through numerous incarnations during its life. In the 1690s it was known as 'the house belonging to East India Company which are a corporation of men with long heads and deep purposes'. By the beginning of the eighteenth century, it had become a major landmark in the City of London. Along with the South Sea Company and the Bank of England it formed the corporate trinity of the age.

We moved on to Cutlers Garden in Devonshire Square. Here, in rectangular buildings that retain some of their old facades, the Company stored its goods. The whole area has been gentrified. Where once the wealth of the world was housed now live the City types who manipulate the wealth of the world: these are luxury flats designed to cater especially to the denizens of globalized stock markets. Nick pointed out that some of the old signs had been preserved; they serve as decorative devices over a number of entrances. I examined one closely. What looked like two sea serpents with lion heads buttressed a merchant ship; a circle above listed the goods the Company stored in these warehouses: ivory, carpets, spices, feathers, cotton, silks, skins, tea – the stuff of global trade of an earlier era. Today's inhabitants of these buildings probably spend most of their time shifting money around the globe as green blips on computer screens. But they have the same worries about the British economy as the merchants who preceded them. We travel according to the rules they established.

We circled the square to get a feeling of the scale of the warehouses. Nick took out a copy of his book, *The Corporation That Changed the World: How the East India Company Shaped the Modern Multinational*, a meticulously researched work, and read aloud a poem. It was by John Masefield, who toured the complex at the beginning of the twentieth century, and set his impressions in verse:

> *You showed me nutmegs and nutmeg husks*
> *Ostrich feathers and elephant tusks*
> *Hundred of tons of costly tea*
> *Packed in wood by the Cingalee*
> *And a myriad drugs which disagree*
> *Cinnamon, myrrh, and mace you showed*

Golden paradise birds that glowed
And a billion cloves in an odorous mount
And choice port wine from a bright glass fount
You showed, for a most delightful hour
The wealth of the world, and London's power.

'There are always two sides to an equation,' I said. 'What was added to these warehouses was subtracted from India.'

We went through the Royal Exchange and came out of the other side – in front of a statue of the Duke of Wellington. Mounted on his charger, he looked down imperiously on passers-by. Here was another luminary who rose to greatness via India. The Iron Duke, victor of Waterloo, always maintained his greatest military achievement was Assaye, the central battle of the Second Maratha War (1803–4), which his brother, Richard Wellesley, then Governor General of India (1798–1805), claimed would lay 'the foundations of our Empire in Asia'. The Wellesleys were involved in one of the Company's most aggressive expansionary phases. Nick surveyed the statue. 'This man,' he said, succinctly, 'believed in terrorism.' As commander of the Company's troops on the Malabar coast he was utterly ruthless. Nick rummaged for his book and read aloud a quotation: 'the more deserted villages you burn and the more cattle and other property that are carried off the better. The people of Malabar are not to be coaxed into submission: terror, however, will induce them to give up their arms.' We contemplated the words silently. Wellington was unperturbed as ever by his opinions. 'War on terror, anyone?' we said simultaneously.

The final stop on our tour of invisibility required a ten-minute trip on the Underground to Westminster. Leaving the station, we walked down Parliament Street, turned into King Charles Street, home of the Foreign and Commonwealth Office, and there before us was a larger-than-life statue of Robert Clive. 'Here,' Nick announced, 'stands the "great nabob-maker", Britain's "heaven-born general", the man who personified what the East India Company was all about.' I looked up at the statue. Its pedestal depicts scenes from his life on three of its four sides. One showed the saintly figure of Clive standing in deep contemplation, surrounded by woodland trees. The inscription informed me it was 'On the eve of Plassey, June 22 1757'. Memories of Hakim Sahib's lessons on Plassey, during my days in Bhawalnagar, came flooding into my mind. The men who subdued and ruled India are richly memorialized around London. But how they achieved their eminence, and the consequences of their entanglements with India, remain invisible, without monument or remembrance.

Today, one might think, Clive stands haughty and proud before the Foreign and Commonwealth Office, symbolizing something about Britain's history of relations with the world, a proof of its ancestral claims as a world power. But that was never the way it was. India was never a foreign land, never the preserve of the FO. When the East India Company was nationalized in 1858, India became a Crown Colony. The Governor-General of India became the Viceroy, the Queen's representative in the subcontinent. The Viceroy reported to the Secretary of State for India, a member of the Cabinet who presided over what Lord George Hamilton, Secretary of State for India 1895–1903, described as 'a miniature Government in itself'. And this government in miniature was unique among British departments of state in being funded not by the British taxpayer but from Indian revenues – like everything else about British administration in India. The India Office too is now rendered invisible, having become part of the precincts of the Foreign and Commonwealth Office. If you take a virtual tour inside the FCO, its website will give you a glimpse of the magnificence India provided for its rulers. The old India Office building is vast, lush, ornate, colourful, resplendent and, like all the rest of the history we toured, a physical space whose significance is invisible to the ordinary citizen.

Our encounter with invisibility concluded, we turned to walk down 'Clive's steps' towards St James's Park. 'Look at the wealth of Britain from the City of London to Westminster: it was all accumulated at the expense of India,' Nick commented. 'Whenever people talk about Empire and imperialism their last defence is "at least we built them railways", to argue we did this or that worthwhile thing that "gave" them the infrastructure of modernity. All we ever did was to manipulate India's wealth for our own purposes, we never paid, gave or donated a thing. And for good measure we invented the multinational corporation, which continues the inequities of the global economic system pioneered by the East India Company.'

Nick ends his tours at St Matthias Old Church in Poplar, just off the East India Dock Road. The East India Company established itself in Poplar in about 1612, using the area to build and fit out its ships. The original church was built in the 1650s, but replaced with the present building in 1776; the ceiling of its nave is carved with the coat of arms of the East India Company. Almost from the inception of the Company, Poplar and the surrounding area of the East End of London has been entwined with India. Poplar, Bow, Limehouse, Bethnal Green – these were the portals through which the people of the subcontinent first arrived in Britain. It was in this part of London that the heterodox, polyglot, diverse working classes became radicalized. It is where Annie Besant organized the protests of the match girls before going off to India to support Indian independence. Meanwhile, this part of London voted for Indian politicians, enabling the first, forgotten Asian parliamentarians to make their invisible mark. Once there was common cause and collaboration in the old East End. Why should I need a tour of Poplar? It is part of my London, the London where I arrived as a child and grew into the citizenship of my identity.

India is as plain as plain can be in British history, as evident as it is ignored. From bedlinen and cotton knickers to a nice cuppa tea, long before the days of chicken *tikka masala*, India has been intrinsic to the daily life of Britain. Visual signs and symbols of India became commonplace motifs. The black American Nobel laureate Toni Morrison argues that the whole of American history, narrative and visual culture is structured around an elephant in the room, the African elephant of Negro chattel slavery. What Morrison notes of the Negro experience in American art and letters is as true of India in British art and letters – albeit slavery isn't involved. India is archetypal and ubiquitous; it is overt and subliminal. An entire repertoire exists with accompanying stereotypes that invoke, interweave, refer to and infer India. Generations were raised on *Boys' Own* stories in which the Raj, and especially the North West Frontier, provided a formulaic narrative structure and stereotypes, the Eastern Westerns of British fiction. And for ladies the same locales provided exotic, romantic fiction. In nineteenth-century novels any unwanted character could be sidelined by being sent to India. Think *Vanity Fair* (but not the latest cinematic incarnation by Indian-born director Mira Nair). In English fiction any storyline could be transformed by a return from India with jewels, or curses, or mysteries or fortunes.

Paintings and monuments referenced India in the great age of civic construction, the Victorian formation of the British urban landscape. But this is merely the effulgence of something much deeper and more profound. India is central to forming Britain's worldview: ideas about time, humanity and national character, science and philosophy, by which all thought is structured and the entire world is known. From statistics to anthropology, from liberalism to barbarism, from ecology to economics, without India Britain would neither think nor do anything as we know it. It was the seedbed, laboratory and proving ground of just about everything; the essential prop, the inevitable factor, the unavoidable rationale in shaping British history.

There is another thread, not fictional: the personal entanglement that runs through the lives of generations of the most influential and powerful Britons. Once I became conscious of this thread I found it everywhere, not just among the statesmen and governors, the soldiers and administrators. Thackeray, author of *Vanity Fair*, was born in India; his father was a judge in the employ of the East India Company. Dickens collaborated with Wilkie Collins to rush out a story based on the massacre at Cawnpore, a now forgotten part of his oeuvre, but essential reading in the aftermath of the 'Indian Mutiny'. Two of Dickens's sons set off for India and are buried in Calcutta. A central figure in dear Aunt Jane Austen's life was her relative Eliza, born in India and the goddaughter of Warren Hastings, unacknowledged by the most prolific biography industry in British letters until Claire Tomalin and David Nokes simultaneously set the record straight, in 1997. Men with ambition, such as Macaulay, author of the 1835 'Minute of Indian Education', went to India as a stepping stone to illustrious careers and honours in England. Just as illustrious figures in Britain, such as the Mills – father but especially son – shaped and manipulated India for Britain's benefit without ever setting foot there. The landed estates and family fortunes of the movers and shakers, the thinkers and writers, are all entwined with India, just as India was an enduring and inescapable motif in the popular imagination. William Beveridge, author of the Beveridge Report on which the Welfare State was founded, was born in India. He wrote a biography of his parents (his father was a judge in the Indian Civil Service), entitled *India Called Them*. Clement Attlee learnt the reality of the need for Indian independence two decades before he became the prime minister who made it so. Where is India in this construction of Britishness? This is Britain's invisible community, and its only legacy is to be banished. The results of this eradication of memory have been visited on the British Asian community.

How was it possible for such mutuality to simply vanish? For 400 years, Britain was made in and with India. In reciprocal ways

India, in its history and opinions and all their twists and turns, was made by and with Britain. How could this history end with immediate disassociation? How could its culmination be the arrival of 'new', 'immigrant' people? Why was their arrival accompanied only by the repatriation of the very worst ideas, aspects and practices of the colonialism Britain had just abandoned? The British consistently considered themselves strangers in the land of India, the better to preserve their identity. But to describe the erstwhile Indians who came to Britain as strangers was not mere symmetry; it was an unconscionable category mistake whose consequences we have yet to transcend.

What Bawaji, my father, discovered by living in Britain was that the solid Britain–India relationship he understood existed from his father had melted into air, vanished with wilful forgetting, become invisible. Alienation was constructed at the very moment of arrival of the British Asian community – as well as the Afro-Caribbean communities. If you look carefully at the grainy images most often displayed to record the arrival of the *Empire Windrush* from Jamaica, you will see young men in civilian clothes, some in large incongruous overcoats and big hats. Less familiar film footage of this same arrival shows young men in RAF uniforms smiling as they lean over the ship's rails. The selectivity of disassociation and dissembling was at work from the outset. Alienation begins with this history of forgetting; all the actual and potential threads of connection, mutual understanding and nation-building it eradicated and so profligately ignored.

Exploring the forgotten narratives of my own life and communities, the story of my Dada and the arrival of Asians in Britain, has opened cityscapes, histories and whole worldviews founded on the same principles. It has made me genuinely post-colonial. But what does this frequently fashionable term actually mean? To be truly post-colonial is not a stance for or against imperialism. It is the understanding that our histories are entwined, our identities commingled, that we are inseparable because for centuries we have not been discrete, bounded, separate communities. Britain and India partook of each other but generally ignored their interpenetration. Against the weight of fact, against the human truth of personal, social, intellectual, economic and political history, Britain and India continue to be seen, understood and contemplated in separate compartments. In the process India has been further dismembered with the categories of Pakistan, Bangladesh and Sri Lanka, countries precariously uprooted in time. Given new venerabilities all parties then search for and insist on an authentic, discrete identity defined by their differences. The search aims to realize them in perfect isolation from outside influence. Reality is, and always has been, otherwise. How can we make sense of anything when the object we conjure with is misconceived? This is exactly the mistake the British authored in India about India. Thus they never came to know the India whose history was constantly changing, adapting and transforming in protean diversity as much after and because of the arrival of Britain as before. What we miss by retaining this misguided conception of reality is the bridge across and between boundaries. British Asians are not Indian, Pakistani or Bangladeshi but British people who have a special relationship to India, Pakistan and Bangladesh. These countries represent their ancestry as much as their religious affiliations: Islam, Hinduism, Sikhism, Jainism and Buddhism. If they too sometimes feel the need to exercise the reflex desire to be pure and authentic it is, dare one say, a proof of how genuinely British they are.

Our Britishness has been doubted since the dark clouds gathered on 11 September 2001 and spread devastation in the dark intestines of London on 7 July 2005. The urgency of the questions of identity posed to British Asians, and especially British Muslims, has intensified in the aftermath. But the form of the questions, the issues and assumptions they raise are neither new nor convincing.

By what you ask you define how little you know, how unwilling you have been to listen and engage with people who have been flourishing as a part of British society for half a century and whose history of belonging reaches back centuries.

Hakim Sahib used to say, '*There is more than one way to know.*' I have made this book a tour of my way of knowing my identity. This book is an artefact of my cultural identity: the Pakistani portion with its tradition, history lessons and characters; the Hackney era and the struggle against racism; the ever-present issues of marriage, the concern of Asian parents with passing their tradition on to the children, the children's constant struggle to understand their multiple identities, the bonds of extended family that hold the Asian household together; the problems of being a minority in a multicultural society; the Muslim references, Islamic influences and religious experiences. They are not separate strands but are lived together. I live in the places where these fragments meet. I am the product of their mutual influence. Apart they make no sense to me. It is this way of knowing I have attempted to make visible.

Britons have founded multiculturalism on the ethos of the Raj: leaving people alone to get on with being different. We indulge multiculturalism with non-interference, just as the Raj did – staying away from difficult topics that might stir up trouble, until trouble occurs. The effect of the kind of multiculturalism we have patronized has been to create mutual ignorance. The consequence has been to render invisible what is really happening in lives like mine: diverse cultural influences authoring the citizenship of compound identity. We have assumed cultural identities are authentic only when static. We have empowered all those who neither think nor reason with the meaning, intent and purpose of their values, the core of their identity. Therefore, multiculturalism embraces and encourages all that clings to antique form, exotic difference, the strange and peculiar without ever questioning its why and what for. We have created no space, found no common course for the majority who live their compound identities – all those who are as British as they are Asian, because that potentiality is already contained in their personal histories and their critical awareness of being Muslim, Hindu, Jain or Buddhist.

I travel with multiple selves. I cannot cease to be Muslim, any more than I can cease to be British, an 'Asian', an 'Indian' or a 'Pakistani'. Islam is the enduring source of the most profound and significant values that make me human; it instructs my humanity and humane ideas. My life has been shaped by Partition and migration. I have lived a life peregrine, buffeted by dislocation and led far and wide by the opportunities it created. But I have carried the influence of Hakim Sahib within me on all my travels – cornerstones of the person I have become. And now I incorporate the spirit of my Dada. They and my extended family are the connective tissue of my history, they resonate in my being, ineradicably part of who I am. To imagine me, you have also to imagine their lives and then the lives of all those who belonged to them, because in diverse ways they too are part of me. When I came to rest as a child in a cold, dark and forbidding London, I was accompanied by this invisible community. It was the presence of our invisible companions that made us a British Asian community. When British Asians meet they always end up speaking of family, invoking this presence, the links of our chain of being. This is the meaning of ancestry; it is the driving force of our culture. To understand the British Asian experience it is vital to acknowledge this shared possession. We are people of different ethnic, geographical, linguistic and religious origins but we all live with the influence of our invisible travelling companions, and that helps us to understand each other better. We comprehend each other whole, people replete with invisible communities, with our history and ancestry attached; people, by virtue of who and where we are, who live amid the jumbled wreckage of tradition and change.

Invisible communities are not merely our inheritance, beyond our control; they can also be fashioned by conscious choice. We can prune the branches of our personal history, chose between our ancestry to derive an invisible community whose inspiration and ideas become the sole tradition and worldview we honour. Surely this was what my own family did in their silence about the career of my grandfather, Ahmad Ullah Khan. History is the charter we manipulate to make the present work. In the era of independence, my family selected the threads of ancestry that bound them most effectively to the present they valued. My two grandfathers, Hakim Sahib and Ahmad Ullah Khan, represent distinct trajectories of history: Hakim Sahib stood firm on traditional ground the better to resist the encroachments of colonialism, though it never inhibited his critical faculties; the Sardar Bahadur chose modernity, which in his time and place meant learning Western medicine and enlisting in Britain's Indian Army. As for their descendant, my grandfathers, in their different ways, bequeathed me the means of synthesis: the humane, enriching possibilities of tradition and modernity and the roots of belonging in my new home.

All cultures and civilizations are a kaleidoscope of diversity, they are a work of humanity in history, constantly worrying, working and reworking at their enduring ideas and sources of inspiration. They are never a monolith, never inflexible. Cultures and civilizations may parade idealized visions of themselves but they are ever beset by perplexities, conundrums, perennial questions, juxtapositions and the invidious choices of real circumstance. None of us is the textbook definition of what we ought to be, or that it is thought we should be, either by our own assessment or other peoples'. All identities, societies, cultures and civilizations continually negotiate with change.

To rail against change is insanity. It is to nail your colours to anti-immigration policies that threaten identities and make them insecure and fragile. It is to think that there are some intrinsic 'British values' – usually said to be associated with class and Middle

England – that are exclusive, and which all those described as 'new' must subscribe to. Diversity assumes that values are shared by all cultures, while allowing different cultures space to be themselves. Britishness is something that we define mutually together in a Britain whose future we shape collectively.

Our future must be founded on the continuity of cultural identity. It will be a plural way of being, sharing plural pasts with other communities to shape our collective future. Those who think – or, indeed demand – that we can be British only in one single and static way are, in effect, asking Asians to abandon all that makes them so rich, diverse and dynamic. Of course, no one actually believes this is the choice being forced upon certain segments of the Asian community. Yet this is how the recurrent clamour of problematic immigrants and the persistent noise of ignorance about Islam presents itself to British Muslim Asians. British Muslims are required to apologize so often for their existence – for the way they look, dress, wish to educate their children – it is no surprise that many see themselves as victims and cling to ossified tradition. Both defensive forms of apologia distract their energies from critical debate and awareness of potential futures, just as the defensive embrace of Little Englander emotions pulls up the drawbridge across which we must meet to create a better future. It is not enough to listen to ourselves speak; we have to listen to how we are heard – it's the only way to gauge how well we understand and can understand each other.

The pluralistic future would not mean the impairment of British identity. It would not require Britons to vote for their disestablishment, devolution or dissolution. Plurality is intrinsic in your identity as well as mine. Asians too have to understand the identities of white Britons as a relational attribute. A plural future of assured diversity means we will all continue with our identities, cultures and histories, and through this continuity determine what change is beneficial. Our task is to make the plural relationships of living together creative; to find what we share, what we hold in common and how best we can make a better future. The sources of acrimony and dissension are most often practical difficulties that have no racial, ethnic or religious implications, though they may have much to do with class and economic inequality. We must disentangle the identity question from the fictions spun around social problems.

In the course of this exploration I have learnt the nature of something I have never had cause to question: who I am. I have found myself in a host of new ways as British. The possibilities of a more harmonious future put me in mind of a concert I attended a few years ago given by the legendary Indian sitar master, Ravi Shankar. He came on the stage of London's South Bank Centre with his entourage, bowed to the audience, sat crossed-legged, and started to play. He was joined by the late Ustad Allahrakha Khan, the renowned tabla player. It looked as though the old maestros were competing with each other – whatever the sitar said, the tabla responded in kind. This went on for about fifteen minutes. When it finished, the audience burst into rapturous applause. Ravi Shankar and Allahrakha bowed gracefully. 'If you enjoyed us tuning our instruments,' Ravi Shankar said, 'you will love the real concert.'

The South Asians in Britain too have been merely tuning their instruments, in preparation for the real thing. Things change. And communities change things. My parents' generation was learning how to adjust to their migrant status, how to come to terms with yet another displacement after the partition of India. My generation was part of a full-blown dress rehearsal. We were British – but there was always this unease, a slight uncertainty, some hesitation in seeing ourselves as truly, fully British. We needed to learn that we are where we truly belong – our history is as British as the history of monarchy. The new generation of Asians are the real thing. They are as naturally British as eating Balti. They have changed, and are changing, their own communities, constantly reinventing themselves while remaining the same. In the process they will transform the asymmetry and symmetry of Britain itself.

The best is yet to be.

Acknowledgements

'Why do you have to travel on modes of transport you can hardly spell?' Merryl asked in exasperation. Going through various drafts of this book, she had discovered that I spelt rickshaw in three different ways: rackshew, reckshow, and rickshaw. 'And I do wish that when you intend to "wonder" about something you would not "wander",' she added for good measure. But it wasn't just my spelling that Merryl corrected – she helped with research, suggested ideas and drove me on when I was down. Merryl Wyn Davies has been a true friend: always there, always supportive, always ringing to encourage, always loving, always arguing, always fighting – she demonstrates what total commitment to a friendship actually means. How does one thank such a friend? 'Riches? . . . There's always *objet*, of the *d'art* kind – even you might learn how to carry things when on your travels!' she suggested. Thanks a lot, Merryl; and dream on!

Urdu poetry has been a source of many of my dreams. It is written largely to be sung, and there is an established tradition in Pakistan and India of famous singers singing poems by famous and not so famous poets. Josh Malihabadi is well known and most of his poems, including 'the prison is under attack' that I have quoted, are on the lips of lovers of Urdu poetry. Anwar Mirzapuri, on the other hand, is not very well known. But his poem, 'I am drinking with my eyes', has been sung by every classical singer of recent times both in Pakistan and India, including Farida Khamnum, Mahdi Hassan, Ghulam Ali, Talat Aziz, Iqbal Bano and Talat Mahmood. My favourite, however, is the Munni Begum version. During the 1970s, when I first visited Pakistan, Munni Begum had suddenly become very popular and everyone was listening to her. I have stayed loyal to Munni Begum, who is like an aunty next door, ever since.

John Masefield's poem, quoted from Nick Robins's *The Corporation that Changed the World: How the East India Trading Company Shaped the Modern Multinational* (Pluto, 2006), is also cited in Penelope Hunting's *Cutler's Gardens*, which was commissioned and published by The Standard Life Assurance Company in 1984. On page 68, Hunting writes: 'The sight of vast quantities of exotic goods attracted visitors, among them Queen Alexandra and Princess Victoria in July 1913, King George V and Queen Mary in February 1914. The Poet John Masefield was another visitor who was fascinated by what he saw, thanking his hosts with the gift of a book and these lines'. Hunting doesn't exactly state that his poem was written in 1914, but her reference is as follows: 'Visitor's Book, Cutler Street warehouse, (1871–1967), Port of London Authority Library. Preliminary report on Cutler Street warehouses by GLC Department of Architecture and Design AR HB/N (1970).'

My thanks also to Khalid Sayyed for his invaluable help in translating Urdu, a language that I can read, write and speak very well but cannot think in and therefore cannot adequately translate. I should also thank my old friend Samir Shah who, after finishing a documentary on Asian immigration to Britain, biked over numerous hefty files of picture and film research. They were not of much use – this is evidently a book, not a film – but my gratitude to you anyway, Samir. And I must not forget my editors at Granta, Sara Holloway and Bella Shand, who have been so encouraging and good natured.

Thanks.

Index